TROUT FISHING IN CALIFORNIA

Fifth Edition

Secrets of the Top Western Anglers

Ron Kovach

featuring these Top Western Anglers...

- "Crappie John" Beale
- Bob Bringhurst
- Alan Cole
- Jim Emmett
- Leonard Hashimoto
- Michael Jones
- Dennis Lee

- Art Liebscher
- Jon Minami
- Dave Nollar
- Glen Oshima
- Danny Stearman
- John Wyatt

ISBN 0-934061-32-7

90000>

9 780934 061322

MARKETSCOPE
BOOKS

119 Richard Ct.
Aptos, CA 95003
(408) 688-7535

*"The leading publisher of
fishing books for California Anglers"*

About This Expanded and Updated Edition

The first editions of this book were a big surprise. We had no idea that so many thousands of Californians would buy a book about trout angling. Outdoor writers praised it and anglers obviously found it useful. It's still selling at a fast pace, but now we've decided to make it even bigger and better. More strategies. More tactics. More tips and tricks, and more illustrations. Quite simply, this new edition has more of everything for the California trout angler. We hope you like it.

The Editor

ISBN 0-934061-32-7

Cover Design: Electric Art Studios
Mountain View, CA

Technical
Illustrations by: Linda Kovach

Layout and
Typesetting by: Laura Spray

Dedication

This second book of the California fishing trilogy is dedicated to Professor Robert Emerson. Under his guidance I developed my skills as a writer. To my friend and academic mentor, thank you, Bob.

Ron Kovach

Acknowledgments

Many thanks go to the following fishermen for their kind contributions and insights in making Trout Fishing in California a reality: "Crappie John" Beale, Bob Bringhurst, Alan Cole, Jim Emmett, Leonard Hashimoto, Michael Jones, Dennis Lee, Art Liebscher, Jon Minami, Dave Nollar, Glen Oshima, Danny Stearman, and John Wyatt.

I am also grateful to proofreaders Don De La Mare and Tom Harman for their valuable suggestions with the manuscript, fly fisherman Tom Ganz for his expert help with regional fly patterns, and to my wife, Linda, for her superb editing and illustrations.

Great Books

Fishing in Northern California,

Marketscope Books publishes the bestselling **Fishing in Northern California** (8 1/2 x 11 inches, 240 pages). It includes "How To Catch" sections on all freshwater fish as well as salmon, steelhead, sturgeon, shad, kokanee, lingcod, clams, sharks, rock crab, crawdads, stripers, etc. Plus, there are sections on all major NorCal fishing waters (over 50 lakes, the Delta, Coastal Rivers, Valley Rivers, Mountain Trout and the Pacific Ocean). All these waters are mapped in detail!

Fishing in Southern California,

Marketscope Books also publishes the bestselling **Fishing in Southern California** (8 1/2 x 11 inches, 256 pages). It includes "How To Catch" sections on all freshwater fish as well as barracuda, bonito, calico bass, grunion, halibut, marlin, sea bass and yellowtail. Plus, there are sections on major SoCal fishing waters (45 lakes, the Salton Sea, Colorado River, Mountain Trout and the Pacific Ocean). All these waters are mapped in detail!

Bass Fishing in California,

At last, a bass fishing book just for Californians -- both beginners and veterans. This book explains in detail how to catch more and larger bass in California's unique waters. But, most valuable, it includes a comprehensive guide, with maps, to 40 of California's best bass lakes, up and down the state. This classic has now been expanded to include scores of advanced bass-producing techniques. 8 1/2 x 11, 240 pages.

Trout Fishing in California

Trout fishing is special in California and now there is a special book for the California trout anglers. It covers, in detail, how to catch trout in lakes or streams, with line, bait or flies, by trolling, casting or still fishing, from boat or shore. And even better for California anglers, this is a guide to the best trout waters all over the state. Detailed info and precise maps are featured. 8 1/2 x 11, 224 pages.

Saltwater Fishing in California

California is blessed with over 800 miles of Pacific Ocean coastline. This is a marvelous resource for all Golden State anglers. And now there is a book that covers it all. Surf fishing. Kelp fishing. Harbor and Bay fishing. Poke poling. And more. Don't go saltwater fishing without it. Both veteran anglers and beginners are finding this book a necessity. It explains, in detail, how to catch albacore, barracuda, bass, bonito, halibut, rockfish, sharks, salmon, stripers, yellowtail and striped marlin. And there is a large "How-To and Where-To" Guide for hot spots all along the coast. And don't be without the Saltwater Sportfish I.D. Section. This book has become a standard because it explains in simple, straightforward language how to catch fish in the Pacific, off California. 8 1/2 x 11, 256 pages.

Pier Fishing in California

There are many marvelous ocean and bay fishing opportunities on California's piers. And now there is a book that covers each and every one of them—from San Diego to San Francisco Bay to Crescent City. Learn how to fish each pier, the species, best baits, proper timing, the underwater environment, fishing tips, and more. Plus, find out about the best techniques, baits, lures, and necessary equipment from an expert who has fished all these piers all his life. There is also an extensive pier fish identification section and cleaning and cooking info. 8 1/2 x 11, 256 pages.

Order your Copies Today!

	Price	Sales Tax	Total Price	Qty	Total Amount
___ **Fishing in Northern California**	$14.95	$1.20	$16.15	___	_____
___ **Fishing in Southern California**	$14.95	$1.20	$16.15	___	_____
___ **Bass Fishing in California**	$14.95	$1.20	$16.15	___	_____
___ **Trout Fishing in California**	$14.95	$1.20	$16.15	___	_____
___ **Saltwater Fishing in California**	$14.95	$1.20	$16.15	___	_____
___ **Pier Fishing in California**	$16.95	$1.40	$18.35	___	_____

Postage & Handling (1st book $2.00; no charge on 2 or more books) . . . . _____ *

Check Enclosed . . . . _____

*Special Offer (order 2 books, any combination, and we'll pay **all** postage & handling)

Name _____   Address _____

Send Your Order To: **Marketscope Books, Box 171, Aptos, CA 95001**
(Permission is granted to xerox this page.)

Contents

Contents *(continued)*

Contents *(continued)*

CALIFORNIA TROUT WATERS

All of the Best Trout
Lakes and Streams in
Each of These Zones are
Featured in This Book

Take a Kid Fishing

Northeast Corner

Eureka

Red Bluff

Northern Coast

Northern Sierra

Sacramento

Central Sierra

San Jose

San Francisco

Fresno

Eastern Sierra

Central Coast

Southern Sierra

Bakersfield

Santa Barbara

Ventura

Los Angeles

San Bernardino

Mid South

Far South

San Diego

California Trout

Rainbow Trout—Native of California, found in nearly all lakes and streams where water temperatures do not exceed 70 F for any length of time. Dark, bluish-green back, black spots on back and tail, red stripe on sides, silvery belly. Spawns on gravel bars in fast, clear water. Most suitable of all trout for artificial propagation and highly regarded as a game fish for its fighting qualities.

Brook—Native of Atlantic coastal area, found in many mountain lakes and spring-fed streams throughout the state. Dark olive, worm-like lines on back and sides, red spots along sides, belly reddish-orange to lemon, lower fins red tipped with white. Well suited to hatchery production. Unlike other species, it may spawn in shallow areas of lakes having spring seepage.

Brown—A native of Europe, generally the hardest of California inland trouts to catch. Plentiful in many Sierra streams and scattered elsewhere throughout the State. The record fish in California weighed 26 pounds. Dark brown on back with black spots, shading to light brown with red spots on sides. The only trout with both black and red spots on its body.

Golden—State fish of California, the golden trout is native to the high country of the Kern River watershed, and now is found in many lakes and streams in the Sierra from Mt. Whitney north to Alpine County. Medium olive back, shading down the sides to brilliant golden belly and reddish-orange stripes from head to tail, crossed with olive vertical bars. Lower fins golden-orange.

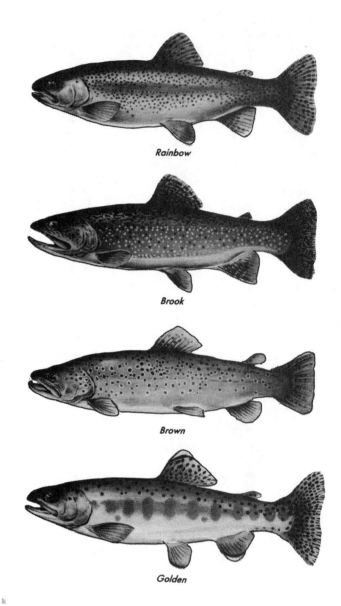

Rainbow

Brook

Brown

Golden

CalTrout

In this book we highlight such outstanding trout waters as Hat Creek, Fall River, Martis Lake, the McCloud River, Milton Reservoir, Yellow Creek, the San Gabriel River and Heenan Lake. These are special regulation waters where trout habitat is protected and restored, trout reproduction is maximized and the impact of anglers on the wild trout population is minimized, all resulting in great trout angling now and into the future.

California Trout, or CalTrout, an organization of anglers, has worked closely with the state and is primarily responsible for the outstanding wild trophy fisheries in California. The author and Marketscope Books would like to encourage readers of this book to support CalTrout. Our only motive in doing so is to enhance California's trouting. CalTrout supports both fly and lure angling programs. And other exciting programs, like the Mammoth Trout Park, are progressing. If you'd like to join CalTrout or get more information, they are at 870 Market St., #859, San Francisco, CA, 94102, (415) 392-8887.

BOOK I

Catching Trout
in
California

The California Troutin' Scene

Of the millions of anglers who annually try their luck in the Golden State, more fish for trout than any single species of game fish—fresh or saltwater. Many fishermen get their first taste of this great sport in the form of a weekend trout fishing trip, often as young children. California has a diverse "menu" of trout fishing waters to choose from for the freshwater angler, whether he is a fly fishing "purist," or a weekend "bait-dunker."

At the southern end of the state near metropolitan areas from San Diego to Los Angeles, numerous man-made impoundments are within an hour's drive for the recreational fisherman. These lakes have received the unfair reputation of being simply "put'n take" reservoirs, whereby hatchery raised trout are "put" in one week and "taken" out the next. In reality, there are some very innovative stocking programs that occur in this portion of the state which result in many quality trophy trout topping the five pound mark being caught annually.

Some lakes like deep San Vincente in San Diego, for example, sustain a trout population all year long. Many planted rainbows that "holdover" from the winter to the fall season will grow to healthy proportions here. The trout lazily feed on the abundant threadfin shad populations in this type of inland reservoir. They are not restricted to the shorter optimal growth period of trout in the colder climates and higher elevations of the northern part of the state. But even these trout with their hatchery origins can grow very wary and can pose quite a challenge for the Southern California angler.

Similarly, privately owned waters, such as Irvine, Anaheim, and the Santa Ana River Lakes, probably yield more lunker-class trout annually than the entire High Sierra fishery combined! A recent experiment in biological engineering has lead to the introduction of rainbow "triploids" in these lakes. These are a genetically superior strain of trout that grows at a dramatically increased rate, particularly in these milder climates. Specimens over 13 pounds are caught here with some frequency, and it is only a matter of time before some mammoth triploid rainbow tops the scales at over 20 pounds! But here again, don't take this level of trouting for granted. These fish, too, can become very hook-shy, and it will take some measure of skill to catch that lunker rainbow. There are also "urban" lakes in the San Francisco Bay Area, such as San Pablo, Merced, and Parkway, that produce a large quantity of both pan-sized and trophy trout each year.

As we move up the state, the complexion of the trout fishery changes somewhat. You will find more lakes where trout share an important niche in the lake ecology with warm-water fish, and on a permanent basis—not just put'n take. Lakes such as Castaic, Casitas, Cachuma, and Isabella, for example, have strong trout populations that provide year-round angling opportunities.

Further north, on up through the Central Valley and into the High Sierras, trout become the primary sport fish found in most of these waters. Their dominance in a particular lake system increases with elevation.

Put simply, the higher up you travel, the more likely the lake will be populated primarily by one or more varieties of trout. High Sierra lakes such as Crowley, Bridgeport, and Twin have become almost legendary for their historically excellent trout fisheries. Some of the largest rainbow and brown trout caught in the country have consistently been taken from these mountain lakes.

You will also find a great proliferation of little creeks, streams, and larger rivers—many sustaining great trout fishing—the further north you travel. Hot spots like the Owens, Truckee, and Walker Rivers, for example, have been bonanzas for California's fly fishing fraternity for years. This type of water is distinctively absent in the southern portion of the state.

In the northern portion of the state, there are many lakes in a semi-alpine setting that, although they are primarily trout fisheries, also support warm water game fish. Lakes such as Trinity, Almanor and Shasta are prime examples of waters that have both excellent trout and bass populations. Here also are great trout streams such as the Upper Sacramento, Hat Creek, McCloud, and Fall River as well as thousands of pristine mountain lakes and streams.

Thus, as you can see, in California there are a myriad of possibilities awaiting the venturesome trout fisherman. In the ensuing chapters, I will take you step by step, showing you how to improve your chances of not only catching a limit of trout, but also of catching larger, quality fish. There is much more than meets the eye to becoming a competent trouter in California. There are many little tips and tricks and "secret" tactics that I will present here which should dramatically improve your trout angling no matter where you fish in this great state!

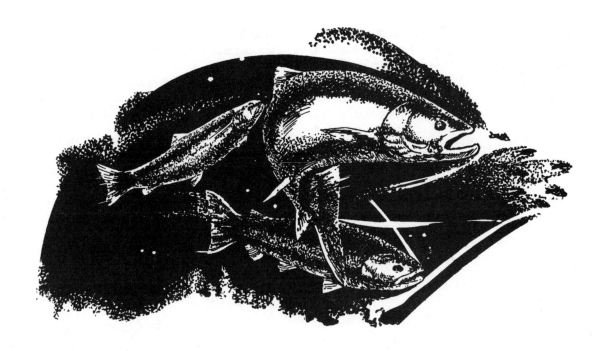

Our Trout: 'Bows, Browns, Brookies, Cutts and Goldens

There are five dominant species of trout available to the California angler: rainbow, brown, brook, cutthroat, and golden. All of these trout are members of the salmonidae family of fish which also includes varieties of salmon, mountain whitefish, arctic grayling, and char. There are a few lesser known members of this family that are also found in some isolated waters. These include the Kokanee (Sockeye) salmon, silver (Coho) salmon, and lake (Mackinaw) trout. In the individual lake and stream section of this book, I will talk more specifically about these species and the waters where they are found.

For now, I just want to give you a very brief descriptive breakdown of the five major varieties of trout. For a more elaborate discussion, I recommend two excellent source books: McClane's *Standard Fishing Encyclopedia*, and *Freshwater Fishes of California* by Samuel McGinnis. These texts are available at local bookstores and will give the reader seeking more in-depth information a scientific view of trout and other fish.

Rainbows

'Bows are far and away the most abundant of the five species found in California. They have been extensively studied in both hatchery and natural environments, more than any other type of trout. They comprise the bulk of trout in the daily creel totals throughout the state.

The rainbows are an exceptionally strong, hearty fish. They can survive in water temperatures ranging from 32 to 80 degrees. 'Bows are a true native American, indigenous to many of the lakes and streams in California. These trout are excellent swimmers, but in creeks and rivers look for them on the downstream side of large rocks or boulders. Rainbows will locate here both for an ambush point and as an energy conserving measure. They are very territorial, seeking good cover among logs, roots, and tree stumps in lakes and rivers, and especially the shady undercut edges of little streams.

Rainbow trout feed primarily on insects in streams, preferring stonefly and caddisfly larvae. In many of our man-made lakes, threadfin shad minnows comprise the major portion of their diet. Thus, 'bows are susceptible to both fly fishing techniques and casting artificial lures that represent the shad bait fish. Rainbows are also the easiest to fool with bait offerings. Garden worms, nightcrawlers, marshmallows, cheese concoctions, grasshoppers, crickets, live shad and, of course, the ubiquitous salmon egg will all take a share of these fish on most lakes or streams. 'Bows are probably the least wary of all the trout family and thus the easiest to catch.

Browns

The brown trout is actually not a native to the western hemisphere. It was imported here from Europe in the late 1880s. It gets its name from a dominant golden brown coloration. Browns will also have large reddish-brown or black spots on their sides, backs, and dorsal fins. These fish are overwhelmingly the most voracious and territorial of the five primary species, whether they are found in lakes or rivers.

Browns are not quite as adaptable as rainbows. They thrive in slightly cooler waters, preferably 54 to 64 degrees. These fish are also very touchy feeders. Biologists note that because of their basic diet, you will see little surface action from brown trout. Unlike rainbows, browns will usually not feed on insects, although I have discovered that they do find grasshoppers exceptionally tasty! They will seek out larger larvae and bigger prey including crayfish, frogs, newts, and worms. Brownies are also piscivorous—i.e. they are fish eaters—consuming both forage bait fish and smaller trout.

Figure on catching browns at greater depths than other trout. They like deep pools and steep banks in rivers as well as steep alpine lakes. Thus, I suggest throwing somewhat larger and deeper running lures for browns including spoons and medium- to deep-diving plugs. Most of the bigger brown trout caught annually in the Golden State will be taken by faster trolling methods. Flashers with bait trailers will work, but forget about using small spinners—they will twist too much. Browns will also hit artificial flies, but prefer more of the "wet" patterns that represent larvae and larger aquatic insects or small bait fish. For bait fishing, it is hard to beat live worms, 'hoppers, or nightcrawlers.

One more thing—browns are primarily nocturnal feeders. This makes early dawn and late afternoons near dusk the optimal (legal) times during the day to fish these tough fighters. Some veteran brown trout anglers estimate that 90 percent of the trophy class browns are caught in the last half hour before darkness sets in.

Brookies

These scrappy fish are technically not a true "trout" in the strict sense, but rather are a member of the char group. They are characterized by the brilliant red and blue spots on their sides. Brookies are second only to rainbows in sheer numbers. They have exceptional reproductive capacities, often spawning under rather diverse conditions not conducive for other trout. This is both good and bad.

On the positive side, brook trout will be found in a wide variety of higher elevation lakes and streams. The negative aspect of this proliferation is that they often overrun other species and the water becomes crowded with a population of stunted brookies.

In streams, look for brook trout in the more sheltered areas, particularly in the shady undercut banks. They can be found in the shallow sections of alpine lakes, preferring gravel banks and downed timber for shelter. Brookies can actually actively feed down to 34 degrees, which makes them a prime candidate for the ice fisherman's creel. This trout is most active, however, in water temperatures ranging from 57 to 61 degrees. They are rarely found in ponds, lakes, or streams where summer temperatures reach 68 degrees or above. Interestingly, this species is very short-lived, seldom exceeding four years of age.

Brookies are similar to rainbows in their preference for lures and baits. Smaller spoons, spinners, and occasionally even scaled down minnow-like lures will be effective. Live red worms have to rank right at the top as far as favored baits go. However, salmon eggs, Velveeta Cheese, and floating cheese mixes will also work quite well, especially in lakes and small ponds. Fly fishermen can test their prowess with a dry fly, as brook trout will readily rise to an insect hatch on the surface.

Cutthroats

There are actually three separate sub-species of cutthroat trout found in California. The coastal variety is the most common; it has feeding patterns and a life history most closely resembling rainbow trout. The other two types, the Lahontan and Piute Cutthroats, have very limited distributions. Most cutthroats will be found in coastal streams from Humboldt County north.

Cutthroats are often mistaken for rainbows. Upon closer examination, you will see prominent double red-orange stripes underneath the lower jaw, giving this trout its unusual name. A more subtle feature separating them from 'bows is that rainbow trout do not have teeth on the back of the tongue as do their cutthroat cousins. You can stream fish cutthroats in pretty much the same way you would rainbows. Spoons and spinners are productive, along with red worms, nightcrawlers, and especially, salmon eggs.

Goldens

Golden trout have been designated the official state freshwater fish of California. These are spectacularly colored trout, identifiable by the carmine red stripe down the lateral side, the yellow-white side portions, and the brilliant bronze belly. Goldens are found primarily in the southern portion of the High Sierras, mostly in Fresno and Tulare Counties, at elevations between 8,500 and 12,000 feet. Because the feeding and growing season is dramatically restricted with the cold winters and ice, a golden over 12 inches in length is truly a trophy catch.

These high country residents have a tremendous appetite for insects and larvae. Mosquitoes, ants, caddisflies, midges, and damselflies, in addition to small leeches and freshwater shrimp, comprise the bulk of the golden's diet. Hence, both dry and wet fly patterns that replicate this menu will definitely work on many of the remote lakes and streams where goldens are found. Both traditional fly rods and spinning fly'n bubble combinations are effective in these back country golden haunts. A wide range of spoons and spinners primarily in gold finish are also dynamite on golden trout.

Compared to the rainbows and brookies also found at these higher lakes, goldens are the most touchy of all. They primarily feed in the morning and late in the afternoon towards dusk. It requires some very stealthy maneuvers to approach these wary little trout in either shallow streams or crystal clear lakes.

Summary

This section has provided a very broad overview of the five dominant types of trout found in the Golden State. Although these trout are members of the same family of game fish, each has its own unique feeding and behavioral patterns.

Trout anglers should keep this in mind when they set out to do some fishin'. It is important to familiarize yourself with the different species that are in a particular lake, the kind of terrain where they are typically found, favorite natural baits, and the preferred water temperature they seek. The techniques used for bigger hungry browns, for example, on Lake Crowley will not be effective for small back country brookies. In subsequent chapters I will outline in greater detail some of the more specific methods used to catch these California trout.

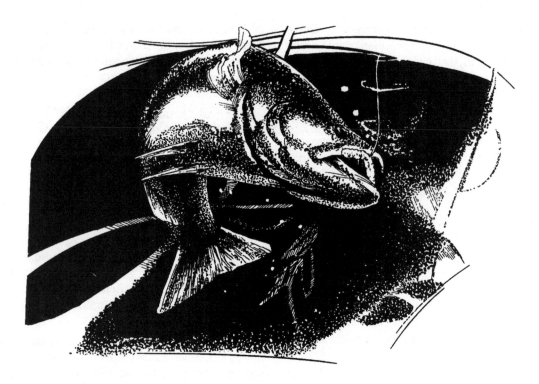

Bait Fishin': 'Crawlers, Christmas Trees and Crickets

There is an amazing array of baits—both prepared and live—that can be tossed to catch trout in the Golden State. Let's start with the most common offerings and then later talk about some of the more esoteric choices available.

Salmon Eggs

Day in and day out, you can always count on salmon eggs as a good trout bait. The biggest mistake trouters make in fishing this bait comes not so much from their presentation but from their selection off the shelf. Novice anglers sometimes see all salmon eggs as practically the same and hence opt for purchasing the cheapest jars available.

Cheap eggs are usually a waste of money and more often than not will result in an unproductive day of fishing. Better grade salmon eggs are cured longer. Some are typically larger and firmer; others are made to "milk" more in the water. The "milking" aspect is an important feature, especially if you still-fish with eggs. You want the egg to slowly soften up under water, but not totally dissolve off the hook. As it softens up, it discharges its contents, creating a film or milky cloud in the water that "calls" the trout in for a look. Cheaper salmon eggs do not milk that well, are often overly soft, and dissolve too quickly. Super firm, premium eggs are not necessarily larger, but are made for faster currents such as rivers and streams so they stay on the hook longer.

Pautzke's has become the generic name for salmon eggs in California. Even this brand has a series of grades available. The "Green Label" is their basic spread and is very suitable for most Western troutin'. The "Premium" label is Pautzke's best with a larger, firmer egg. Other equally viable salmon eggs are marketed under the Cossack, Mike's, Uncle Josh, and Atlas brand names. Take the time to inspect the contents of the jar before you purchase it and try to buy the best-looking, firmest eggs available.

As for colors, fluorescent red is still overwhelmingly your best choice in salmon eggs. There are times however, for whatever reason, that a whitish or cheese-yellow egg is the hot ticket. Interestingly, cutthroats often prefer an orange egg. But changes in water action, weather, and/ or light conditions can also have the effect of "turning the fish off" to one color of egg and "on" to another. You might consider carrying a jar of one of the more exotic colors for such situations. You can also combine these lighter colors with the red versions or with other baits such as marshmallows to field your own unique creations. Similarly, many brands are now manufactured with scent added such as cheese, garlic, or corn. Scented salmon eggs are often terrific baits when the traditional versions fail.

Small gold salmon egg hooks with the short shank and pronounced curve hooks are the most popular ways to fish this bait. Using a size 10 to 16, you can embed the small hook into a single egg, or sometimes through two smaller eggs. Often, the one large egg is preferred over two smaller ones.

Drawing again from my own experiences fishing many of Southern California's heavily pressured lakes, I have found that trout sometimes go crazy for a cluster of eggs. Instead of using the more conventional salmon egg hook, I will switch to a bronze, long-shank baitholder, preferably in size 8. I then thread on three or four premium grade eggs, fishing the cluster on a single leader.

That is one part of the trick, now here is the rest of the secret. Take some Berkley Strike in the trout scent or Dr. Juice in their trout flavors and add a few prominent drops to this cluster before you cast it out. The combination of the Strike or Dr. Juice dissolving and the eggs milking creates a sort of "vapor trail" under water that seduces trout even in the toughest conditions.

No matter how you fish salmon eggs, it is critical to always keep the hook embedded so it is hidden in the egg. It is truly amazing how even the basic stocker trout in put'n take waters will shy off from the egg if the tiniest hint of hook is exposed. So, take the time to carefully cover the hook as cleanly as possible before casting. Hold the baited hook up in the light and inspect it, to make sure that the shaft, barb, point and even the eye of the hook are totally encased in the salmon egg.

Velveeta Cheese

The Kraft people probably never realized that they would have such a satellite market for their processed cheese when they first introduced it. But, when you talk about fishing for trout with cheese, Kraft Velveeta is what comes to mind. You can buy it in small boxes with the cheese conveniently wrapped in foil at almost any supermarket.

The Velveeta is soft and fishes best when molded onto a treble hook. I recommend a size 12 to 18 depending upon how large and how touchy the trout are in the waters you are fishing. You might also try that little trick with the Berkley Strike or Dr. Juice, adding a drop or two on a gob of cheese. There are, from time to time, commercially made "cheese gobbers," that will actually let you mold a ball of Velveeta around a hook without touching the cheese. I remain from the "old school," preferring to "roll my own" Velveeta on the hook.

Floating Baits & Cheese Concoctions

Like Pautzke's for salmon eggs, and Kraft for cheese, Zeke's has become the hallmark for floating baits. These preparations are whipped into a variety of flavors and allow you to fish bait off the bottom. This is done for two

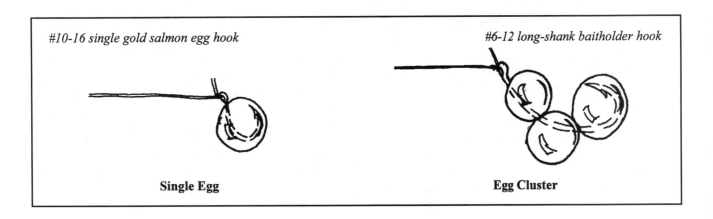

#10-16 single gold salmon egg hook

#6-12 long-shank baitholder hook

Single Egg

Egg Cluster

reasons: (1) sometimes the trout suspend off the bottom, feeding in a particular strike zone, and (2) getting the bait off the bottom lets it stand out from rocks, weeds, and similar obstructions.

Zeke's is available in the original (anise scented) flavor, garlic, salmon egg, and corn scents. I have observed on numerous occasions that the trout will go into a frenzy for one flavor and will pass on the others. A few hours later, they switch preferences and key into yet another scent. So it is best to carry at least 2 or 3 jars of this prepared floating bait with you if you are going to do some serious bait dunking. I might add that you can also mix the flavors together, creating a marbled effect that sometimes works amazingly well. Mold the floating bait onto a #12 to #18 treble hook.

The Targhee brand of processed cheese bait is another alternative to consider. It is similar to Velveeta in texture but comes in flavors more closely resembling Zeke's. There are times, particularly in stained water and lakes with bland muddy bottoms, where the Targhee spread really works.

You might also try experimenting—coming up with your own private concoction of a moldable trout bait utilizing such diverse kitchen ingredients as cheese, oil of anise, vanilla flavor—and who knows what. Sometimes by adding a small portion of cotton from a cotton ball you can get a variety of interesting substances to adhere together so that the final "blend" sticks on the hook better.

Marshmallows

As with cheese, Kraft found still another avenue for sales of marshmallows to the California trout fishing community. Using Kraft Miniature marshmallows, West Coast anglers invented a simple floating bait before commercial compounds were ever sold. For a long time, trouters would impale a small white marshmallow onto a treble hook for some really hot results. Later, the marshmallow fad evolved into using the more exotic colored versions. Sometimes, anglers put a white with a pink or yellow marshmallow on the same hook for an interesting twist on this bait. Here too don't overlook adding commercial scents such as Dr. Juice or Berkley Strike in trout aromas to your basic marshmallow bait.

Christmas Trees, "Shasta Flies," and Other Combos

Working with a base stock of salmon eggs, Velveeta, floating cheese and marshmallows, trouters in the Golden State have devised some rather "bizarre" combinations that often produce striking results!

One popular combo is called the "Christmas Tree." Take three quality salmon eggs and plant them on each point of the treble hook. Now, using either Velveeta, Targhee, or Zeke's, mold it over the eggs to cover the remainder of the hook. Use a variety of "toppings" to determine what the trout prefer that day.

A variation of this theme is to run a small #14 to #18 treble hook all the way through a miniature marshmallow. Temporarily slide the marshmallow above the bare hook. Next, put a single red salmon egg on each of the three hook points. Then slide the marshmallow back down, molding it above the eggs. This is humorously known as the "Shasta Fly."

Another very unusual combination is to thread a miniature marshmallow onto a long-shank #8 baitholder hook. Then lace a live meal worm onto the tip of the hook. The marshmallow floats the "mealie" and it must present one heck of an edible package to the trout—because it really works!

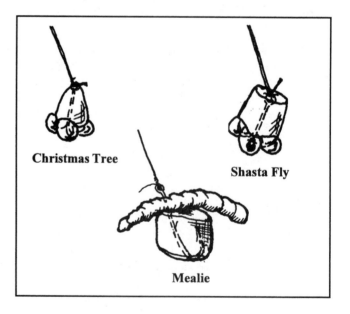

Christmas Tree

Shasta Fly

Mealie

Garden Hackles and 'Crawlers

Basic, run-of-the-mill earthworms (also known as "garden hackle") continue to catch trout, but more so at higher elevation waters than at lower, municipal reservoirs. The best way to fish these is using just one or two on the hook, making certain to cover the point and the shank. Rig the worms through the sex collar, using a #8 to #12 baitholder hook. For still-fishing from the bank, I prefer a more subtle offering of just one or two instead of an entire "gob." This presumably looks more natural to the trout.

Nightcrawlers present another situation all together. Fish the 'crawler with a #6 to #10 long-shank bronze baitholder hook. Run the hook through the sex collar and then back through, re-embedding it into the 'crawler, creating a weedless effect.

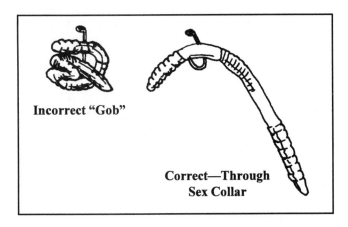

Incorrect "Gob"

Correct—Through
Sex Collar

Another option is to do the same thing only this time fill the nightcrawler full of air with a worm blower (basically a crude syringe sold at tackle stores). This will force the bait to float off the bottom depending upon the length of the leader line.

Both red worms and nightcrawlers can be still-fished with the traditional sliding egg sinker rigs. However, with nightcrawlers, you might consider using a 4 pound test leader. Bigger trout chomp on these jumbo worms and are often not that particular about the diameter of the leader material. Hence, the heavy leader will give you a little more leverage against larger fish. But if the 4 pound test doesn't get bit, go back to fishing the 'crawler on 2 to 3 pound test.

Be sure to inspect the bait before you leave the tackle shop. Most stores allow you to empty the contents into a metal or cardboard trough to determine that the bait is alive and represented in the proper amount. Nightcrawlers especially are often graded by size in area bait shops. You might find the big worms in regular, jumbo, or even snakelike "combat" lengths and thickness. Sometimes the trout–and even the trophy specimens at that—do not always want the largest 'crawler you can buy. Inquire with the tackle store regulars as to what size nightcrawlers the local trout are keying in on.

Finally, keep nightcrawlers chilled for best results. You can store them in an insulated "Bait Canteen" or buy an inexpensive styrofoam ice chest with a lid containing coolant solution that you can freeze. You can keep 'crawlers alive in this chest all day, even through the hottest summer months.

'Hoppers and Crickets

In some areas grasshoppers and crickets produce fantastic results when more conventional offerings fail. Some bait shops sell crickets in little cages. As for grasshoppers, you can easily catch your own. Take a woman's nylon stocking and stretch it over a wire coat hanger frame. Attach a broom handle and you have a simple grasshopper net.

Hook live 'hoppers and crickets right under the collar again, using light leaders and #6 to #10 baitholders. Large browns and 'bows seldom see these morsels and jump on them like a rare treat. So be prepared for possibly tangling with a larger-class trout when you use either live grasshoppers or crickets!

I want to strongly encourage the reader to try these two insects as really hot baits for trophy rainbows and browns. Only a handful of anglers ever catch a trout in California topping the five pound mark. I guarantee that there would be more lunker fish tallied if fishermen—especially shore anglers—would switch from prepared baits to either crickets or grasshoppers. Also, I want to emphasize that, for the squeamish, these two kind of "bugs" are relatively harmless and will not bite.

Other Bait for Trout Streams

There are some subtle tricks that help catch trout with bait when stream fishing. Locally collected baits can be deadly on rivers and creeks. These topics are explored in detail later on in the "Spin Fishing in Rivers and Streams" chapter.

Summary

As with all forms of troutin', bait fishermen must be willing to "mix it up" as far as presentations are concerned. Sometimes, just when it seems that the fish are annihilating one bait, the bite shuts off and you have to switch to another. In our highly pressured California streams and lakes, light, delicate leaders and small hooks are a must when soaking baits. Western trout can be super finicky, so be certain to take the time to discretely hide the hook in the bait.

Spoons and Wobblers: Popular and Versatile

Of all the lures used for trout fishing, the metal spoon has to be the most popular and versatile. Spoons come in an awesome array of colors, shapes, and sizes. There are some models, like the traditional red and white Daredevle, for instance, that are practically lifetime members of fishing's all-time "Deadly Dozen" list of freshwater lures. Other spoons such as the uniquely designed Z-Ray enjoy more of a regional following among Western trouters. Most good tackle stores will stock a very comprehensive assortment of spoons to choose from, but to the recreational fisherman, selecting the right ones can be a mind-boggling decision. There are, however, some very definite features to look for when selecting which spoon to throw. Let's start with size and weight.

Spoon Size and Weight

The spoons for most California trouting range in size from miniature ultralight versions in 1/32 ounce on up to about 1/2 ounce for casting or trolling for lunker-class fish. Manufacturers sometimes describe these super small spoons as "fly rod" models. In reality, few of these are ever used with traditional fly rods, per se. Most of these diminutive spoons are cast with ultralight rods and reels with 2 to 4 pound test line. They are excellent at times in the back country lakes on small rainbows, brookies, and even goldens. Spoons this size are difficult to cast even with the ultralight gear. Often, the angler will trail these spoons behind a clear plastic float known as a "bubble." Or, he will crimp a lead split-shot or two about 24 inches above the little lure to get that extra weight for casting.

The most popular sizes for spoons are 1/8 to 3/8 ounces. These will cast very adequately with 4 to 6 pound test line, and are good all-around choices for most generalized lake fishing and even for some of the larger streams. Heavier spoons, 1/2 ounce or more, are best suited for big fish on large lakes worked slowly on the retrieve or trolled.

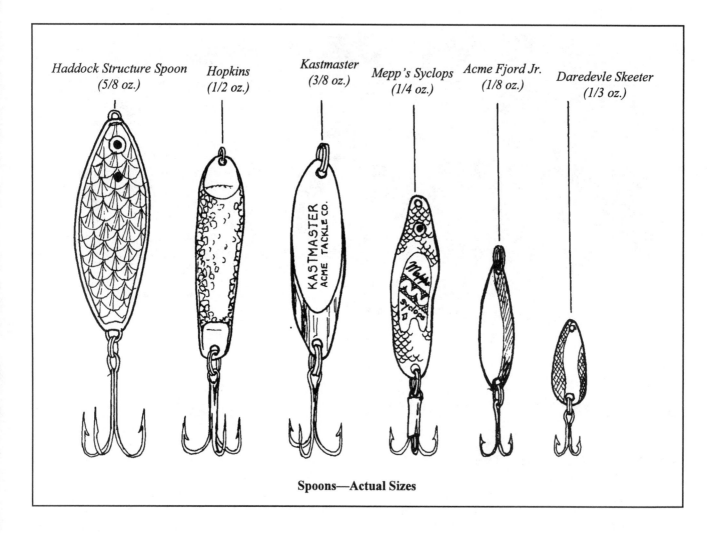

Haddock Structure Spoon (5/8 oz.)   Hopkins (1/2 oz.)   Kastmaster (3/8 oz.)   Mepp's Syclops (1/4 oz.)   Acme Fjord Jr. (1/8 oz.)   Daredevle Skeeter (1/3 oz.)

Spoons—Actual Sizes

Spoon Shapes

Trout spoons can be divided into three basic styles: wide-body, slim-profile, and flat wobblers. The first type of spoon is typically wide across the midsection. Sometimes, the actual thickness of the metal is "fatter" than average with this type of lure. The wobble effect with this style of bait is also characteristically "wide" in action. That is, for its size, the spoon will produce a prominent sweeping wobble on the retrieve. There are times when the trout are definitely "tuned in" to this particular type of radical side-to-side movement. Spoons such as the popular Wob-L-Rite, Hot Shot, Little Cleo, and Daredevle exemplify this type of wide-bodied spoon.

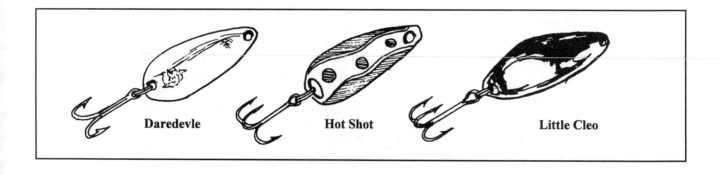

Daredevle   **Hot Shot**   **Little Cleo**

Like other game fish, trout will at times "shut off" on one particular pattern (i.e., a lure, color, retrieve or any combination thereof) and "turn on" to another. With spoons, the fish may switch from a preference for wide-body spoons to a slim-profile model. The latter presents a very sleek, subtle silhouette in the water. Often anything more dramatic than this style bait will actually scare the fish.

The action on a slim-profiled spoon is distinctively "tight" with minimal lateral wobble. Popular spoons like the Krocadile, Acme Fjord, Phoebe, and Mepps Syclops are prime examples of this slimmer spoon design.

The third type of spoon pattern moves away from the rounded utensil-like shape that gives these lures their descriptive name. Instead, this group—the flat wobblers—have thinner more angular forms. There is very little cupped effect in their surface area as they are designed primarily to flutter very seductively with a minimal amount of effort. Popular models used for California troutin' are the Kastmaster, Z-Ray, and Super Duper.

Spoon Colors and Finishes

As a general rule, a spoon in a predominantly silver or nickel finish is your overall best choice in bright sunlight. Copper surfaces, or painted combinations of red and white, black and white, black and green, chartreuse, frog, or mixes with some orange or yellow spots are good for cloudy, overcast days. Spoons with either solid or half-tone finishes in gold or bronze fall somewhere in between as far as natural sky light conditions are concerned. I want to remind you that these are broad generalizations and it doesn't hurt to be somewhat unconventional if the traditional pattern seems ineffective on a particular day.

There are also a few other rather exotic color schemes that are also very productive when spoon fishing for trout. I have found, for instance, that a black scale finish can be dynamite in the wee daylight hours around dawn and dusk. Apparently, this very dark pattern casts a more visible silhouette in the water against a dimly lit sky.

Natural trout-colored finishes on spoons are also very effective at times, particularly in the rainbow or brown

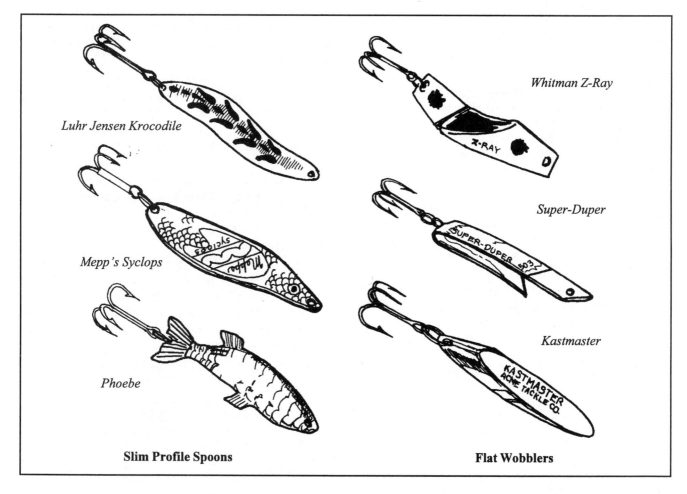

Luhr Jensen Krocodile

Mepp's Syclops

Phoebe

Whitman Z-Ray

Super-Duper

Kastmaster

Slim Profile Spoons   **Flat Wobblers**

trout patterns. Similarly, other manufacturers use brilliant, prism-like, flect-o-lite finishes, for example on the Super Duper, to generate an exciting luster effect as the spoon is pulled through the water. One other interesting alternative is a natural pinkish salmon egg effect found, for instance, on the Seneca Little Cleo spoons. This raised egg-like surface gives the spoon the illusion of a cluster of salmon eggs drifting lazily by—a favorite natural food for hungry rainbows!

You will find trout spoons are made with smooth or hammered metal surfaces. The smooth finish will generate a very subtle "flash" in the water. The hammered version refracts a tremendous amount of light which bounces off the multitude of dimples or indentations on its surface. Sometimes the trout want the more subdued, smooth finish spoon; other times they home in on the more vibrant hammered models. It is important to keep some spoons with each type of surface in your box, if only in simple nickel or gold versions.

Custom Color Your Spoons

Carry some self-adhesive flect-o-lite or reflective prism-lite paper with you. Cut a thin strip and add it like a pinstripe along the edge or down the center of a spoon; or coat an entire side with it. Sometimes just a single, sparse little dot added to an otherwise bland surface does the trick. Experiment a little and come up with your own secret, customized spoon. This prism material can really be a super secret weapon when you want to give the trout a completely new, radical spoon to look at.

Similarly, you might try scratching a small blotch or an entire stripe of sorts along the existing painted finish of the spoon. For some reason, trout will sometimes key in on this effect as if it draws more attention to the lure, possibly making it appear to be a scared or crippled bait fish.

You can also use colored marking pens to custom paint a particular spoon in the field. Be sure to use these with permanent, waterproof colors. Stripes, dots, or entire surfaces are all possibilities for unique coloring schemes. Hot pink nail polish is another valuable resource for doing similar custom work on your spoons. Paint a snake-like stripe down the center of a solid nickel or gold spoon for a really dynamic optical effect.

Working the Spoon: Be Creative

The biggest mistake novice fishermen make in using a trout spoon is attaching it to a snap-swivel combination.

Almost without fail, this will measurably reduce the necessary wobble that these lures are supposed to generate. Some spoons come with either a simple snap or a small split ring. In either case, these lures are ready to go as is. Do not add anything else—just tie to either the snap or split ring, whichever is stocked with the lure.

With some other spoons, for example the tiniest Daredevle and Hot Shot models, it may actually be best to tie directly to the hole in the spoon without adding a snap or split ring. These lures are just too small, and any additional machinery sometimes restricts their actions.

Most spoons that do not come with either a snap or a split ring will usually benefit by having one added. This extra link between the metallic spoon and the monofilament gives the lure more of a hinged effect, and it is able to swing from side to side more freely allowing for greater action. Here again, experiment but avoid adding the more restrictive snap-swivel to your spoons.

As for retrieves, many anglers are clearly not imaginative enough when working a trout spoon. They simply throw it out as far as they can and begin a straight retrieve back once the spoon hits the water. There are a number of little tricks you can add to this presentation that may generate a few more hookups.

First, whether you are casting the spoon from the bank or from a boat, let it sink to varying depths. Don't just grind it back wobbling a few inches beneath the surface. Trout will stratify along different thermoclines and strike zones on a given lake and may move up or down in depth during the day.

If you have sophisticated electronic fish-finding equipment on your boat, it will be easy to pinpoint precisely at what depth the trout appear to be active. If you do not have these instruments or are walking the shoreline, you will simply have to experiment by retrieving the spoon through different strata. So, let the spoon sink somewhat before you start reeling. Vary the sink from all the way to the bottom to a few feet below the surface.

On this note, be prepared for a strike while the lure is fluttering down on the fall. If you see a "tick" in the line, or if the line seems to go unusually slack, quickly re-engage the reel, pick up the slack, and set. These are often the telltale signs of a trout that has inhaled the spoon "on the sink."

Sometimes another simple retrieve will also generate some good strikes when the more mundane straight grind fails. This is called a "stop'n go." Here, once you begin your retrieve, stop suddenly every so often, allowing the spoon to fall. Again, be especially ready for strikes on the sink.

If you don't get bit after the spoon falls a few feet, start the retrieve again. Continue this stop'n go action all the way back in. It is theorized that this presentation attracts the trout because it mimics a wounded bait fish as it struggles through the water.

Another technique I have found to be particularly effective is to sporadically twitch the spoon with your rod tip while reeling it in. This imparts a lot of erratic darting action to this lure and causes it to more closely resemble the way natural bait fish swim. Many recreational fishermen are unaware of this "hot" little tip.

Summary

Spoons have been used for catching trout perhaps longer than any single artificial lure. Day in and day out, they will continue to be effective for California trout. However, keep in mind that even the hatchery fish can become quickly "educated" and quite finicky when it comes to attacking an artificial bait. So try to stay one step ahead of the next guy and be a little creative with these otherwise simple little lures. Learn to vary your retrieve with regard to depth and action. Switch off from style to style, mix up the finishes once in a while, and try some of your own customizing ideas. Be innovative with these simple spoons and watch your catch increase!

Spinners: Good Vibrations

Next to spoons, spinners account for the greatest number of trout caught on artificial lures. Spinners work primarily on sight and sound. The flash of the spinning blades, combined with the bright metallic body and colored feathered treble hook, makes this lure very tantalizing in appearance to a hungry trout. As the blade whirls through the water, the spinner generates a great amount of vibration that can literally "call in" fish to strike.

A trout spinner thus functions primarily as a "reaction" bait. It is made to imitate a minnow or similar bait fish scurrying to escape from a larger predator. The trout will react and strike at the little spinner for any of a variety of reasons: hunger, curiosity, annoyance, or even territorial protection. Spinners can be effective under a wide range of conditions. They can be productive in little streams, larger rivers, reservoirs, or back country ponds.

Spinner Styles

In-line Spinners: Most trout spinners sold in California are known as in-line spinners. This is the typical lure with a straight wire shaft, cylindrical tube, treble hook, and blade that rotates around the body. In-line spinners can have three blade arrangements: clevis, through-blade, or swivel.

The clevis design is overwhelmingly the most popular. The clevis is a U-shaped metal bar to which the blade is affixed. The blade is thus allowed to spin around the wire shaft which runs through the clevis. Standard clevis-style spinners include the Mepps line of baits, Luhr Jensen Bang Tail, Rooster Tail, and Shyster models.

Through-blade spinners do not utilize a clevis fitting. Instead the blade slides directly over the wire shaft, spinning quite freely. Spinners with this blade configu-

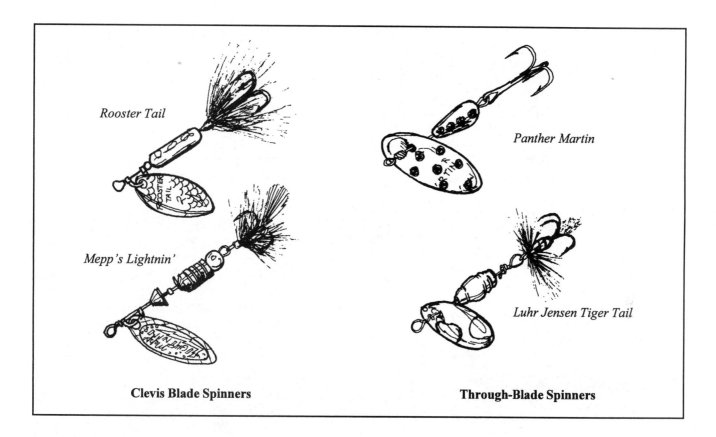

Clevis Blade Spinners

Rooster Tail

Mepp's Lightnin'

Panther Martin

Luhr Jensen Tiger Tail

Through-Blade Spinners

ration typically generate a lot of sonic vibration. This is because in contrast to the clevis-style models, the blade meets greater resistance when pulled against the water. Common models of through-blade spinners are the Panther Martin and Luhr Jensen Tiger Tail.

The simplest of all and the least used in-line spinner is the swivel model characterized by the old-fashioned Colorado spinner. This lure is made by joining two swivels together with a ring in the middle where the small

blade is also attached. The blade wobbles rather than rotates along the swivels, generating a very slow, subtle flash.

Safety Pin Spinners: The other type of trout spinner design is termed a "safety pin" model because of the way the wire frame is formed. This type of lure is widely used among bass fishermen and is commonly referred to as a "spinnerbait." However, some enterprising anglers have discovered that these spinnerbaits work equally well for

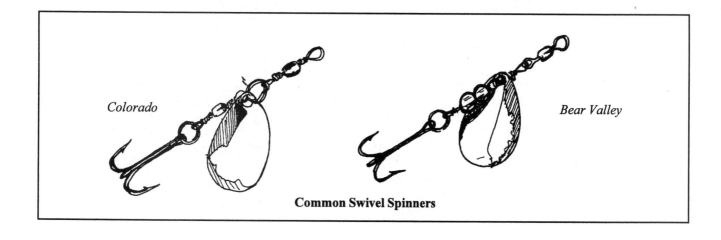

Colorado

Bear Valley

Common Swivel Spinners

trout. The safety pin spinner has a blade that is offset, attached to the upper portion of the wire frame. The lower section of the frame has the main body and weight of the lure, usually a small lead-head and some type of plastic or feathered trailer. The Bass Buster Beetle Spin and Chumm'n Minnow, the Super Rooster Tail, and the Mr. Twister Li'l Bit Spin are excellent examples of small, safety pin spinners suitable for California troutin'.

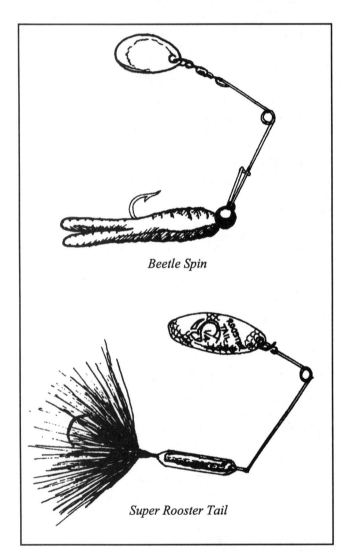

Beetle Spin

Super Rooster Tail

Spinner Blade Size

Many manufacturers use the blade size as the main variable to classify their lures. Blades range in size from the smallest #00 (about a 1/18 ounce spinner) up to a #5 (almost 1/2 ounce). This size range is fairly standardized among the different lure makers. As a general rule smaller,

#00 and #0 size blades are scaled down to fish with ultralight 2 to 4 pound test line on small clear lakes and streams. Spinners with #1, #2, and #3 blades vary in weight from 1/8 to 1/4 ounces. These are the most universally used spinners out West. They are very adequate for all of our man-made, flatland reservoirs, some of the bigger High Sierra lakes, and our wider streams and rivers. Larger #4 and #5 blades can be matched with 1/3 to 1/2 ounce spinners and are used on expansive waters where trophy-sized trout are found.

Spinner Blade Shapes

Spinner blades are made in three primary shapes: Colorado, willowleaf, and Indiana. The long, thin willowleaf-style blade will rotate the fastest, in a tight pattern, giving off the most flash. The Colorado blade is characterized by its wide, rounded surface. It generates the greatest amount of vibration as it "thumps" its way through the water. The more oval-shaped Indiana blade is somewhat of a compromise between the willowleaf and Colorado designs.

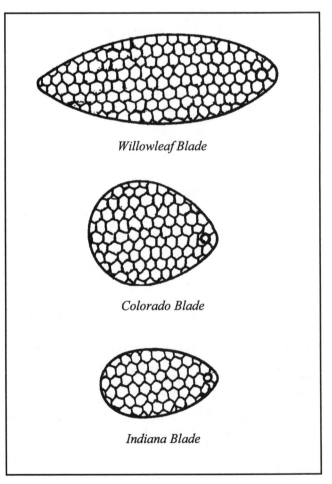

Willowleaf Blade

Colorado Blade

Indiana Blade

There are also some other rather interesting innovations that are variations on these three basic blade designs. For example, some manufacturers add a rippling effect to either Indiana or willowleaf blades. This creates a bit more erratic light reflection than does a smooth surface. Blades can be cupped a little to generate more of a throbbing vibration in the water. Some manufacturers also use blades with holes or vents cut into them to produce greater sonic effects.

Finally, there is a somewhat novel blade used by Mepps spinner. This is actually two blades in one. You can open the blade portions to make them spin more slowly with maximum flutter. This allows you to fish the Double Cross near the surface. Close the blade sections and they spin very rapidly, making the spinner sink faster for fishing in deeper waters.

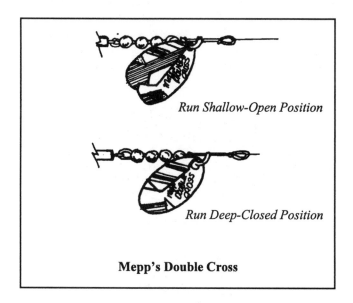

Run Shallow-Open Position

Run Deep-Closed Position

Mepp's Double Cross

On this note, a rough rule of thumb is that a larger blade will make the lure sink more slowly. It will also displace more water than a smaller blade and will spin the most freely if a slow retrieve is used. Hence a spinner with a bigger blade would be an excellent choice for fishing the lure slowly just under the surface on feeding trout. On the other hand, a narrower thinner blade spins faster and yields greater flash. It will sink faster and would be a good pick for fishing deeper in lakes or in larger river pools.

Two other points regarding the sinking qualities of different trout spinners are worth examining, especially

when you need to fish deep. First, you should always try to vary your presentation in any body of water, retrieving the lure through various depths until you locate the trout. Keep in mind that this family of game fish can stratify or "suspend," as bass pros term it, from the surface to the bottom of the lake, river or stream. And, to complicate matters more, they may move from different strike zones on a given body of water all through the day! The problem is how do you make repeated casts to that particular strata once you find the right depth where the fish are feeding?

The answer is simple: learn to "count down" to a given depth. Make your first cast letting the spinner sink all the way to the bottom while counting how many seconds it takes. Retrieve it from as near to the bottom as you can. On subsequent casts, subtract two seconds for each new toss, working an area from bottom to top. Once you find the fish, simply remember how far you counted down when you got bit. This will allow you to make repeated casts to the same approximate depth. I might add that this will also work with spoons and sinking plugs. Another trick is to take a marking pen and color a small section of the line if the trout seem to be striking your offering at a specific distance on the cast.

You can also intentionally slow the sinking of most in-line spinners by adding a feathered treble hook. The feathers create a lot of drag and resistance in the water. This makes it possible to fish slightly larger spinners somewhat more easily, if models with the bare treble hook seem to be sinking too fast and are getting hung up.

Spinner Retrieves: Mix 'em Up!

I will provide a more detailed description of how to retrieve these popular lures in separate chapters on lake and river fishing. However, there are some very basic rules you should follow to help maximize the effectiveness of spinners no matter where you throw them.

As I mentioned with spoons, most recreational trout fishermen also make the mistake of casting the spinner out and retrieving it straight back almost the instant it hits the water. Apart from not exploring different depths by letting it sink, there are some other oversights that occur in employing such a boring retrieve. Think for a second about how bait fish—particularly scared or wounded minnows—move. Rarely will you see them swimming in a steady straight line. Bait fish move in a more erratic fashion, often fluttering, darting, and frantically swimming to escape hungry predators.

Try to imitate this natural action by mixing in a few "creative" movements to your spinner retrieve. For example, try the "stop 'n go" technique I talked about with spoon fishing. As with the spoon, pause once in a while to let the spinner seductively fall and then start reeling it in again. Next, twitch the rod tip occasionally to make the spinner jump or dart about more. Another possibility is to crank the lure very quickly for a few feet and then slow it down, only to speed it up again.

There are numerous other possibilities with which the innovative trout fisherman can experiment. Just be creative. Let the fish see something different with your spinner in contrast to all the "sameness" the trout have seen with the legions of other spinners thrown at them. This will often be the key to triggering a strike, particularly on lakes that have tremendous angling pressure on weekends.

It is also important to get the proper "feel" for each different spinner you use to insure that your retrieve is the right speed to make it work properly. Make a few warm-up casts to get the feel of how the blade is meant to turn. If the blade does not seem to be rotating steadily, speed up your retrieve. If the lure starts to plane, slow it down a little. Each spinner will have its own particular "speed threshold" so to speak, so take a few practice casts before you waste a prime pool or hot spot on the lake by using the wrong retrieve.

Spinner Colors

As for the spinner blade colors, the same holds true for these lures as with spoons. On clear days, nickel blades will be your best bet. On cloudy days or in dirty water typical of early season runoffs, switch to bronze, brass, gold, or copper blades that the trout can see more easily. Blades with fluorescent colors are also sometimes effective under these darker conditions as are those with flect-o-lite prism finishes under clear skies. I have also found that a black blade with some contrasting white, red, yellow, or orange spots will sometimes produce outstanding results in California when traditional metallic colors are not working. This holds true in both clear and stained water.

With regard to the spinner's primary body color, consider the natural forage baits available in the water you are fishing. For example, white or yellow patterns seem to always work on lakes where threadfin shad make up a major portion of the bait fish population. Similarly, in streams there are many small aquatic and terrestrial creatures tumbling around in the water. These include worms, newts, hellgrammites, grasshoppers, and waterbugs. Darker pattern spinners in black, brown, frog, and crawdad-orange shades would be solid choices here.

Once again, none of these rules are etched in stone, so be flexible enough to try some of the more esoteric colors available when the bite gets tough. Often a radical change of pace like this will arouse new interest for an otherwise hook-shy trout.

Pluggin': An Overlooked Approach

Most trouters are somewhat remiss in that they minimize the importance of plugs in their tackle arsenals. Many anglers tend to think of these lures as being restricted primarily to warm-water lakes and bass fishing. The truth, in fact, is that there is a wide variety of these "hardbaits," as they are often termed, which have tremendous application to California troutin'.

Plugs are distinctively expensive when compared to spinners and spoons, often retailing for three times as much as these simpler lures. There is more technology in the way of design engineering and finishing involved in the production of these hardbaits which dictates higher costs. Still, the committed trout fisherman in California should have at least a modest array of plugs handy, particularly for fishing the big, flatland reservoirs. As you will soon see, many magnum-size lunker rainbows and browns are caught each year on this type of lure by dedicated trophy fishermen. Put simply, hardbaits can produce BIG trout!

Trout Plug Design: Different Shapes for Diverse Conditions

Plugs that are suitable for Western troutin' are available in three basic configurations: banana plugs, minnow-shaped lures, and crankbaits. Each offers a unique action that distinguishes it from the others. Depending upon prevailing conditions, you will sometimes find that one style is dramatically more effective than another.

Banana Plugs

These are the lures that most of us used when we first tried a plug as an alternative bait for trout fishing. The old standby, Helin Flatfish, best typifies this banana-shaped pattern along with its latter day cousin, the popular Kwikfish lure. These lures are designed to shimmy slowly from side to side when pulled through the water. They are noticeably light and, from an aerodynamic standpoint, are tough bets at best for free-casting. Novice anglers make the mistake of trying to toss the Flatfish or Kwikfish with standard spinning gear and become very frustrated, particularly when casting into the wind or when distance is needed.

The best way to fish this lure is to troll it. The key is to really throttle down and move the boat very S-L-O-W-L-Y. The Flatfish and Kwikfish and other similarly styled lures can be trolled with either straight monofilament, lead-core line, or downriggers.

Many serious trouters feel that the overall best size to use in the Flatfish is the X-4. This model has the counterbalanced dual treble hook rig that allows the lure to gently wobble from side to side when trolled deep at super slow speeds. This particular model is a real "hawg hunter," especially when teamed with lead-core line.

The smaller "F" series in this lure is also effective, trolled slowly and on smaller lakes for smaller trout. The tiniest size, the F-4, presumably was scaled down for the fly-rodder. You can actually spincast this lure with its single treble hook if you crimp a split-shot about 18 inches above it and retrieve it slowly.

The other regional variations of the Flatfish design also enjoy considerable popularity in California. The Kwikfish and Fire Plug are very lightweight, slow-wobbling banana lures. They are a good alternative to the Flatfish series since additional color patterns are available. Both of these plugs can be fished in much the same manner as the Flatfish.

Other lures in this genre of banana-shaped hardbaits include the Lazy Ike, the Heddon Tadpolly, Eddie Pope's Fishback, and Luhr Jensen's Hot Shot Plug. The Lazy Ike and the Tadpolly have not enjoyed widespread success in

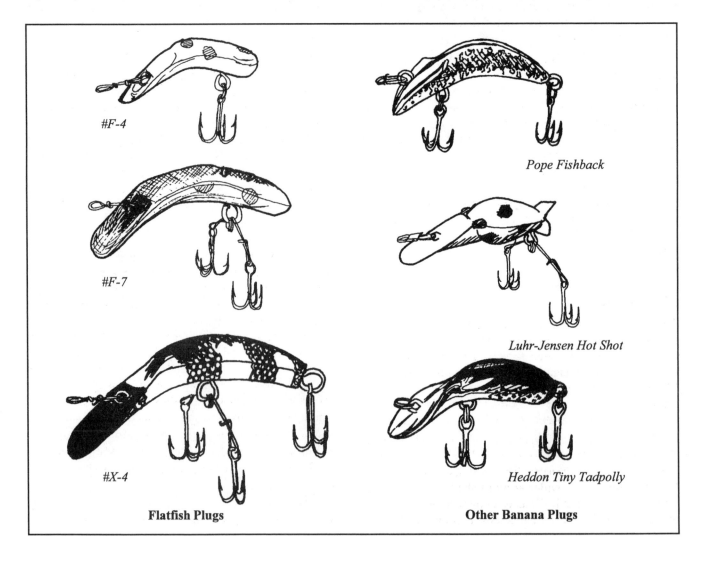

#F-4

#F-7

#X-4

Flatfish Plugs

Pope Fishback

Luhr-Jensen Hot Shot

Heddon Tiny Tadpolly

Other Banana Plugs

the West although each is built along the same lines as the Flatfish but is proportionately heavier.

These plugs, in contrast to both the Kwikfish and the Flatfish, have greater wind resistance and cast easily with basic spinning tackle. They can be very productive lures when a faster retrieve or troll is needed from a banana lure.

The Pope Fishback is a real "sleeper." This lure had considerable popularity in Southern California bassin' circles many years ago. I have discovered that this plug also performs very admirably as a deep-diver for trout in the warm summer months. The Fishback in the smaller sizes can be free-casted with relative ease. It "digs" down into the water and has a much "tighter" vibration pattern than the lighter Flatfish-type plugs with minimal side-to-side action. The lure really looks like a frantic minnow high-tailing it through the water. I have found that the Fishback sometimes excels as a late season trolling lure at a slow-to-medium speed, fished directly tied to 6 to 8 pound test monofilament.

Luhr Jensen's odd-looking Hot Shot Plug is similarly a quiet producer of sorts. It is better known for its prowess on steelhead in the Pacific Northwest. The smaller sizes in this bait, however, can be exceptionally effective on California trout. It can be slow-trolled just under the surface, again at fairly slow speeds. But you can also use this lure in another rather unusual fashion. During windy periods, let out about 50 feet of line and drift the Hot Shot. Its longer, more protruding diving lip keeps the plug down as it seductively wiggles from side to side. Hot Shots also come in a wide range of colors that let you augment your selection of banana-shaped plugs even further.

Minnow Baits

These thin, streamlined lures are meant to imitate a variety of smaller, forage bait fish that are indigenous to our lakes. These include threadfin shad, pond smelt, shiner minnows, mosquitofish, sculpin, chubs, and daces. Minnow-shaped plugs are also designed and colored to replicate small brown or rainbow trout—a favorite morsel for bigger browns and 'bows!

Imitation minnows are usually plastic or balsa wood. The plastic models are somewhat less expensive than their wooden counterparts. They are also more durable and are painted in a wider array of shades and patterns. However, I find that it is easier to impart more dynamic and erratic action into a balsa bait than one made from plastic. The wooden lure has greater buoyancy and seems to "swim" with a little better action. Still it is best to carry an assortment of both plastic and balsa minnows, especially if you are looking for that trout of a lifetime to hang in your den!

Minnow baits come in either floating or sinking models. The sinking versions, most commonly the "CD" or countdown balsa series made by Rapala, are weighted to sink immediately after hitting the water. These baits are proportionately heavier than the same size in a floating model. They are very suitable for free-casting from the bank or from a boat. Many recreational anglers often overlook this technique. They assume that since the Rapala sinks, it must be designed primarily for trolling.

Trouters who specialize in walking the shoreline should always carry some of these countdown Rapalas! You can make long casts with 4 to 6 pound test mono and cover a lot of lake with this popular plug. The #7, #9, and #11 models are best for lake fishing. You might also consider scaling down to a #5 or #7 for working deep pools in larger rivers or for high country lakes.

When you think of floating minnows, probably either the Rebel or Rapala models come to mind. Rebel manufactures an extensive line-up of plastic floating minnows ranging in freshwater sizes from 1 1/2 inches long up to 7 inches. Many of these models are made with small diving lips which will take the lure down just a few feet. Other Rebel versions are built with long "spoonbills" which allows this type of floating plug to dive fairly deep. Rapala, on the other hand, markets its freshwater floaters in shallow running models from 2 inches to 4 3/8 inches in length.

Another recent addition to the trouter's floating minnow collection is the Luhr Jensen Minnow (originally marketed as the Sea Bee). In contrast to some of the other styles on the tackle shop walls, the Luhr Jensen Minnow offers the angler a series of floater-diver baits with brilliant metallic finishes. This type of finish is especially effective in darker, stained or muddy water, or under low-light atmospheric conditions. The Luhr Jensen Minnow will give off a much more erratic "flash" than other models with more subtle finishes.

Unlike those used, in say, largemouth or striped bass fishing, floating minnows used in trout angling are rarely ever thrown as top-water surface baits. Rather, floaters are used as deadly trolling lures, especially on big trout.

The floating minnows generate considerably more lateral action when trolled as compared to sinking models. The secret here is to troll moderately faster than you

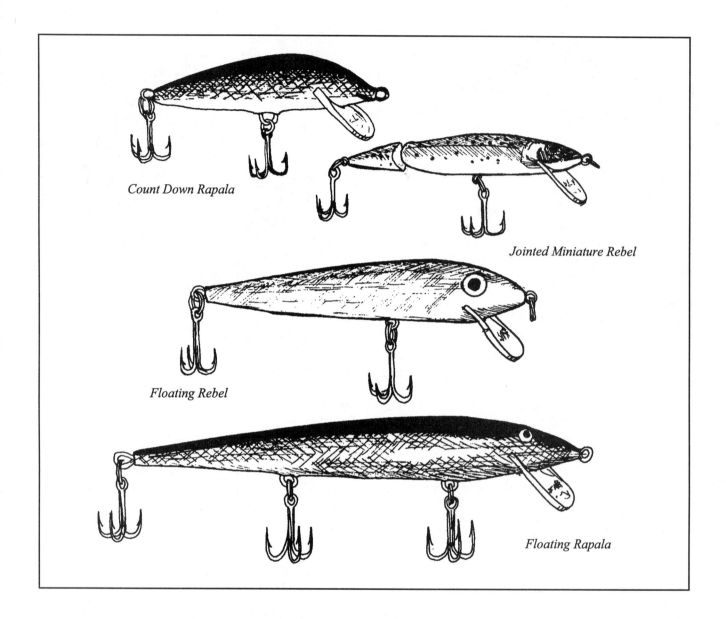

Count Down Rapala

Jointed Miniature Rebel

Floating Rebel

Floating Rapala

would with a banana plug. I've often been amazed at how these floating minnows can sometimes be trolled at a modest speed without results. The minute the pace is picked up and the trolling speed is increased—wham!— a vicious strike results.

I recommend that you experiment somewhat with regard to both trolling speeds and retrieves in using the floating Rebels or Rapalas. Don't be too intimidated about trying a "fast grind." However, if you go too fast, the bait will start to plane or "water ski" to the surface. After some practice increasing the troll or retrieve you will develop a feel for just how fast you can pull different floaters.

A compromise between the more dynamic floating minnows and the less active sinkers is to use a jointed model. Rebel sells them in both shallow and deep-diving versions while Rapala stays with a shallow style. Two other manufacturers also market some tiny plastic jointed minnows that are not tossed as much as they should be.

I have personally used the L & S Mirro Lure and Harrison Hoge Rocky Jr. on 2 to 4 pound test line and ultralight gear and have had terrific results when larger, more conventional minnow baits failed. These little 1 1/2 to 2 1/2 inch jointed minnows can be absolutely sensational on smaller trout in streams and back country lakes.

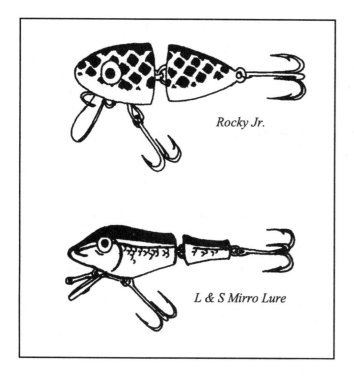

Rocky Jr.

L & S Mirro Lure

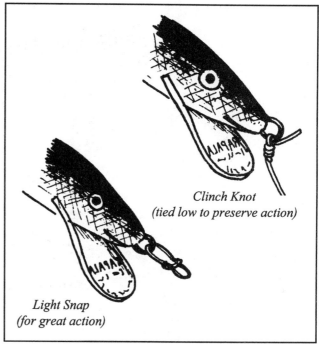

Clinch Knot
(tied low to preserve action)

Light Snap
(for great action)

I have always preferred free-casting them from the bank, but they will also produce when trolled. The key is to use light line to allow these miniature plugs to really vibrate on the retrieve.

Here I should note, particularly when using the balsa minnows, that you should try to stay with lighter 4 to 10 pound test line. Heavier lines dampen the action considerably. So scale down to get better action from these baits. With premium monofilament, a good drag system and a decent sized landing net, you'll be surprised at how big a trout you can take on the lighter line.

The way you tie the line to these minnow-style plugs can also be critical for the proper swimming action. With plastic baits, the only thing that is essential is not to add a snap-swivel to the existing split ring. This will really kill the action. Instead, tie directly to the ring.

With the Rapala minnows, use either a loop knot or tie a clinch knot lower on the lure's metal line. Few anglers pick up on this little tip. The manufacturer notes that it will maximize the action on the Rapala if it is tied in this manner.

If you feel more comfortable with a snap to connect the line to the eyelet, that is all right—but just use a snap and not a snap-swivel combination.

Crankbaits

Fat, chunky hardbaits became the "alphabet" craze of the bass fishing fraternity some years ago with the introduction of Cordell's hand-carved wooden "Big-O" plug. These lures, in plastic, foam, and balsa patterns are typically referred to as "crankbaits."

Commonly used models out West include the Storm Wiggle Wart and Wee Wart, Bomber Model-A, Rapala Fat Rap, and Rebel's "R" series of baits. Alphabet-style cranks are made to replicate an assortment of minnows, small trout, and crawdads.

Other crankbaits are designed along thinner, narrower silhouettes to imitate threadfin shad. Their actions are much "tighter" than the side-to-side wobble of the alphabet models. Popular patterns include the Rapala Shad Rap, Storm Thinfin, and Rebel Fastrac Shad.

A third, distinctive crankplug design is the so-called "lipless" models exemplified by the Rapala Rattlin' Rap, Luhr Jensen Sugar Shad, Cordell Spot, and Rat'L Trap Models. These lures are made for serious crankin', yet do not have any diving lips like the alphabet or thin (shad-like) profiles I discussed. Lipless crankbaits are designed to be either trolled or wound in F-A-S-T! Although seldom used by most recreational trouters, there is a

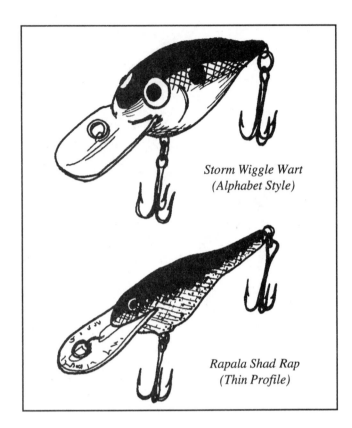

*Storm Wiggle Wart
(Alphabet Style)*

*Rapala Shad Rap
(Thin Profile)*

particular method for employing lipless "cranks" to catch some phenomenal 2 to 5 pound summertime rainbows at lowland reservoirs. More on this secret shortly . . .

The same basic maxim holds true for cranks as for minnow lures: balsa wood models have the most action, foam and plastic versions are more durable. Again, it is recommended that the trouter carry a modest assortment of styles.

Michael Jones is a prominent outdoor journalist in the Golden State, and he is also an accomplished angler. Jones has been a long-time proponent of using crankbaits for trout and has written many articles illustrating that they indeed produce. He points out that trout are predators just like their warm-water cousins, the large and smallmouth bass.

Predatory species like the bass react very strongly to intruders who swim into their territory. Jones further observes that if the recreational angler can develop some fundamental knowledge of trout movement (shallow in the morning, deep by mid-day) there is no better lure than a crankbait to quickly locate these fish.

Crankbaits induce many "reaction strikes" and can be retrieved at faster speeds than spinners or spoons. As

Jones notes, it is not that revolutionary to have members of the salmon family strike this type of artificial lure. Steelhead fishermen in the Pacific Northwest have been using crankbaits for years dragged behind their drift boats.

The trick is to scale down in size from the larger bassin' baits to smaller cranks for California trout. Furthermore, don't restrict their application to simply trolling on the bigger lakes.

Crankbaits can be phenomenal weapons cast from the bank on not only smaller lakes, but also on large rivers such as the East Walker or the Owens. Always keep in mind the adage that bigger baits such as cranks will catch the bigger trout!

As with most other plugs, avoid adding that unwarranted snap-swivel. It will really cost you a lot of action on these lures. Instead, tie directly to the split ring or add only a quality snap to the ring. Both strategies will work since they allow the crankbait to swim with optimal action.

Trout Plug Colors

Each of the three major styles of trout plugs are effective in their own, specific color schemes that are not necessarily productive for the others. For example, with the banana-shaped plugs, the following patterns seem to consistently catch their share of trout in the Golden State: frog, gold plate, silver plate, red, fluorescent, perch, pearl, black scale, and silver blue scale.

With minnow baits, the selection is somewhat narrower. The traditional silver with black back and silver with blue back are staples. These colors are especially good if the lake has large numbers of threadfin shad. On the other hand, switch to a gold minnow with black back if there is a dominant chub minnow population in the impoundment. Fluorescent red and blue anchovy will also work at times. Most importantly, don't overlook the natural rainbow trout finish. This is an essential color to throw for those big browns and 'bows.

Crankbaits present yet another range of colors from which to choose. The standard silver and gold foil finishes are time-proven winners. But also consider some of these other patterns that come close to resembling natural forage baits: shad, crawfish, perch, and rainbow trout. Bright metallic finishes such as chrome, gold, and red can be remarkably productive especially when more traditional colors seem flat.

A rather interesting color scheme is what is sometimes termed a "ghost" pattern. Storm manufacturers their Wiggle Wart series of plugs in a smokey clear finish, replicating the natural, subtle shades of shad bait fish. Similarly, Luhr Jensen markets the "clearwater flash" pattern as a variation of the ghost effect in its classic Hot Lips Express plugs. This is an excellent coloration to use on lowland metropolitan reservoirs, where planted rainbows and even brown trout annihilate schools of shad minnows.

Using the Color-C-Lector for Trout

In recent years the advent of the electronic Color-C-Lector has opened up an entirely new dimension for selecting lure color for most species of North American game fish. This relatively uncomplicated instrument is basically a photo sensitive light meter. It tells you which color, from a spectrum of 26 shades, the fish can most easily see under specific conditions. The meter is divided into three distinct bands that describe water clarity: muddy, stained, and clear. The meter will tell you what color to use depending upon the clarity of the water in which you are fishing as well as a variety of other conditions.

The Color-C-Lector operates with a nine-volt transistor battery and is totally portable. This is a real "plus" for the rental boat fisherman. You simply lower the light sensitive probe below the surface to the depth at which you feel the lure will be retrieved.

In order to get the most from this device you must have some idea of the depth you will be fishing.

For instance, if you are working a spinner about three feet below the surface, the probe should be lowered to that strata. You will probably record a different color reading if, for example, you lower the probe to the bottom where the spinner is not travelling since the amount of light which penetrates to that depth will be less. Similarly, if you are trolling a crankbait that dives about eight feet, the probe should be dropped to that depth for the appropriate color selection.

More and more anglers are finding that this instrument will work for a wide range of fish—including trout—and is applicable to an extensive assortment of spinners, spoons, and plugs.

One final point: it is important to intermittently take readings throughout the day. Color selections will vary independently of the lure you are using as atmospheric, surface, bottom, and even wave conditions fluctuate during the day. This may also provide some insight into why trout may strike a lure on one side of the lake but "shut off" when the same lure is tried on the other side. All of these conditions may vary from one spot on a lake to another.

Pluggin' for Trout: Vary the Retrieve

Although most of the plugs I've discussed here have good built-in actions right from the factory, it definitely helps at times to impart some of your own style to the lure. I am basically reiterating here what I emphasized with spoons and spinners—be creative!

If you are free-casting the plug from either the shore or from a boat, try that "stop'n go" retrieve I mentioned earlier. Be prepared for strikes to occur on the "stop" or right after you start up the retrieve again. Or, rather than just winding after the lure has stopped, give it a few tantalizing little twitches with the rod tip to make it look like an erratic, wounded bait fish.

A similar tactic will work when trolling. Many times I have induced trout to strike a trolled plug by adding some of my own action. I will give the lure a few twitches with the rod while underway or I will "stroke" the bait with a couple of intermittent longer sweeps of the rod. Sometimes this is all it takes to get the trout excited into hitting the plug.

Now, let's get back to that secret strategy I mentioned using lipless crankplugs. During the heat of the summer, rainbow trout planted in many lowland reservoirs, such as Lake Perris in Southern California, will hold over, yet seek deep, cold water in the 30-60 foot range. Also at these depths, schools of threadfin shad may be found, which are prime targets for these bigger 2-5 pound 'bows.

The trick is to meter the schools of bait and trout using your electronics. Then, vertically lower a 1/4 to 1/2 ounce "lipless" Rapala, Rattlin' Rap, Cordell Spot or Sugar Shad down into the bait fish schools. Throw your reel into gear and dramatically lift your rod tip from the three o'clock to twelve o'clock position.

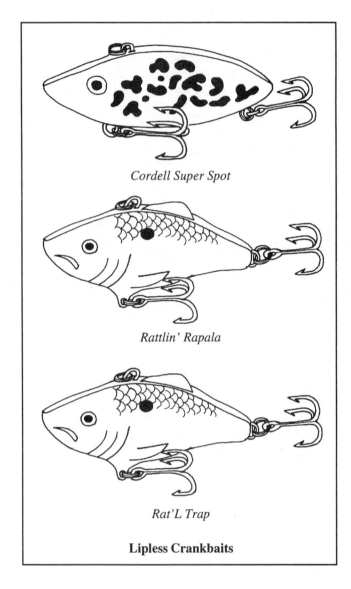

Cordell Super Spot

Rattlin' Rapala

Rat'L Trap

Lipless Crankbaits

Keep "jigging" the plug in this manner. As you lift the rod quickly, the lure vibrates tremendously, mimicking a wounded shad minnow. Many strikes occur as the crank-plug sinks back down on the "drop" phase as you lower the rod tip. Big rainbows and sometimes bass mixed in have been quietly tallied with these unique lipless crank-baits!

Summary

If you want to catch the trophy rainbows and browns in California, then you should consider using plugs more often. These lures are engineered to mimic the actions of larger forage baits that these bigger trout prey upon. For certain, troll them, but also don't hesitate to cast these baits from the bank. You can cover a lot of territory with these plugs under the toughest conditions.

Lake Fishin': Tactics and Tackle

An overwhelming number of recreational anglers try their luck on lakes when it comes to trout fishing in the Golden State. A wide range of lakes are readily accessible to the weekend warrior just an hour's drive from most metropolitan centers. Larger streams and rivers require a little more angling expertise than the average trout lake. In addition, many streams are not as easily reached as lakes, and as noted, they are conspicuously sparse in the southern portion of the state.

Thus, since so much trout fishing in California occurs on lakes, I want to spend some time in these ensuing chapters focusing on the ways to "read" this kind of water, the lures and baits to use, and the techniques employed to fish them. Let's start, however, by examining the basic ecological cycle of a typical trout lake through the four seasons.

Understanding Seasonal Patterns

Each trout lake, whether it is man-made or naturally formed, has its own particular "ecological picture."

However, there are some very broad generalizations that can be made which will help you better understand the basic lake environment and give you a better idea as to how and where to proceed.

Let's start with the spring season. Depending upon which part of the state you are fishing, the complexion of a trout lake can vary significantly. For Southern Californians, the hatchery stocking programs will be in full swing by mid-March. Low, flat-land reservoirs like Irvine, Poway, or Miramar still have water temperatures below 60, and weekly trout plants keep the action hot and furious. Higher elevation lakes such as Hemet or Big Bear, for example, may be showing signs of icing out if the winter was especially cold. Look for bigger trout to start marauding near the shorelines, hungry for those first springtime meals after their long winter nap.

Lakes in more mountainous terrain such as Casitas, Cachuma, and Isabella, will also have solid trouting with fish being caught on a variety of baits and lures worked near the surface. Lakes in the more northern locales from the High Sierras north, will also be in stages of the early thaw and by April should be fairly ice free with a lot of action available.

As the summer weather sets in, most trouting in Southern California grinds to a halt. By late June, weekly stocking programs have ended, and any fish that remain are normally found deep. Trollers will pick up a few fish on lead-core line techniques (more on this later). But most trout caught in Southern California from June to August will be on bait fished very deep, sometimes down to 90 feet. Only a few fish will hold over at lakes such as San Vincente, and Silverwood, and again, they will be found at greater depths.

More northern lakes will still occasionally kick out some summer trout on deep-trolling and bait-dunking presentations. Cachuma, Casitas, Castaic, Piru, Isabella, and similar reservoirs will have some modest early summer trouting. However, your best bet will be to head further north into the Sierras to take advantage of emergent insect hatches and more moderate weather at lakes like Grant, Crowley, and Lower Twin. Other semi-alpine lakes such as Almanor and Shasta will evince good summer troutin' from top-to-bottom with both trolling, casting, and still-fishing with bait. At these latitudes, trout most commonly will be up near the surface in the morning, deep by midday, and then back surface-feeding at dusk.

With the cool autumn weather, many California lakes experience major changes. As the surface temperature of the lakes declines, cold water in the upper level of some impoundments begins to sink, displacing the bottom water which rises to the top. When a lake "turns over" like this, the ecosystem pretty much falls into a biological state of disarray. Plankton and similar aquatic plant life decays and breaks from the bottom rising to the surface, leaving some lakes with a rather characteristic pungent odor during this two to ten week period. This turnover phenomenon may occur much later on some lakes, particularly in the northern part of the state. Lakes like Shasta, Trinity, Siskiyou, and Lewiston may not actually turn over until early winter.

Dennis Lee is a freshwater biologist for the California Department of Fish and Game. His studies indicate that certain species of game fish seem to become "confused" or go "off feed" as they wait for the water to stratify into more prominent comfort zones or thermoclines during the turnover period. This is often the case with bass; however, this does not seem to occur with trout.

Lee and other fisheries biologists have studied the turnover phenomenon and have observed that the thread-

fin shad seem to follow the protoplankton as it rises from the bottom. Interestingly, the trout will actually move with the shad and be in a feeding mode near the surface during this turnover period. After the turnover, the trout in the central and northern regions of the state will be even hungrier, aggressively feeding to "bulk up" before the winter doldrums set in. Top-line trolling in particular will be very effective on these post turnover fish.

During the fall, the trout will be feeding on larger prey and all techniques—fly, spin, trolling, lures, and bait—can be highly productive. Crowds are also dramatically diminished from the summer throng and the fish are much less spooky.

In Southern California, the "put'n take" programs have not yet started, and the only action is slim, on limited numbers of holdover trout. Lead-core trolling and bait fished deep are still your best options. By Thanksgiving, weekly plants begin and lakes such as Vail, Henshaw, Irvine, and San Vincente, will be in high gear again.

The colder winter weather continues to stimulate trout action for the Southern California reservoirs. Top-line trolling, casting, assorted lures, and a variety of baits will all be effective now. Similar action will be found in the central regions, but the bite in the Sierras and far northern trout fisheries will be on the decline. Fish can still be caught, but as their metabolism slows down so should presentations. Bait dunking will be overwhelmingly your best option for catching some of these winter fish. In the harshest climates, some lakes will freeze, yet there is still the possibility of taking trout through the ice. This is a rather recent innovation in California and can be effective with both lures and bait. I'll discuss this unique approach in a separate chapter.

Sierra foothill lakes like Folsom, Don Pedro, and New Melones actually offer their best trouting in the winter months. Trout are near the surface and feeding actively. Top-line trolling, bait fishing with a bobber, and casting lures are all good approaches. This is also true in coastal mountain lakes such as Sonoma and Berryessa.

Natural Variables Affect Lures for Lake Fishing

Before I get into a detailed discussion of the different types of trout spoons, spinners, and plugs to use on specific lakes, it is important to consider some of the natural factors that affect proper lure selection. There is an adage in fishing circles that states, "big baits catch big fish." After spending many years as a tournament angler and professional guide, I can attest that there is a lot of truth to this equation. However, don't go overboard! It simply doesn't make sense, for example, to toss large 5/8 ounce spoons in little municipal lakes like Merced, Poway, or Anaheim, where the average fish is not much more than 1 to 1 1/2 pounds in size.

The larger spoon in this case will overwhelm the little trout. This heavy lure does not in any way, in terms of shape and size, replicate any of the natural forage baits that such small planted trout would feed on. Hence, the selection of such a lure will "spook" the fish and most likely be totally unproductive.

In contrast, if you are going "hawg huntin'" in expansive, deep lakes that are known for kicking out some big lunker-class trout, throwing a tiny 1/32 ounce spoon may be similarly frustrating. These trophy fish are keyed to feeding on chubs, shad, other indigenous minnows and—baby trout. For the most part, fish like these are just not going to get excited about such a mini-morsel when larger, natural offerings are accessible.

Thus, to borrow an expression from the fly fishing community, try to "match the hatch" with regard to lure selection. Just as the expert fly fisherman attempts to select a fly that will most closely "match" with the natural terrestrial or aquatic insects found near the water, the lure fisherman be aware of the kind of forage and size of trout typically found in a specific lake.

There are some very rough rules of thumb that might be helpful here. Keep in mind that these are just basic guidelines and there will always be exceptions to such rules. So be open-minded enough to change lure presentations and experiment if the traditional methods fail to produce during a given trip.

First, figure that there is some correlation between fish growth and the size of the body of water they inhabit. Ichthyologists and biologists have proven this to be the case with even the most rudimentary aquarium environments. The larger the container, the greater the potential for the fish to grow to maximum size. Hence, little alpine and urban lakes, for example, will most likely have smaller trout that will key on miniature lures.

Second, trout growth rates diminish with increases in altitude. As the higher elevation lakes freeze for the winter, opportunities for continued feeding and bulking decline significantly with the entire ecosystem of the lakes going into a metabolic slow down. So again, expect to find smaller fish at the colder, uppermost snow levels.

Third, bigger lowland impoundments can have tremendous populations of forage bait fish (usually thread-fin shad minnows), thriving insect hatches, and a rich food chain that is not as affected by extreme winters and icing of lakes. Larger artificial lures are in order for lakes like these where trout are able to grow to greater proportions.

Finally, if in doubt, try to rely upon local sources of information. Tackle stores, bait shacks, grocery marts, and even filling stations serve as centers for exchanging fish reports from nearby lakes. Local people are usually more than happy to give the visiting angler reliable information about the lakes and streams near their businesses. As a matter of fact, so much of their annual commerce is predicated on securing this fishing trade that it is in their interest to give up-to-date, detailed reports whenever possible. Many of these people can tell you all about the species, size, and feeding habits of trout in the particular lake that they cater to. Don't hesitate to ask for help!

I also make an effort to pick up a local newspaper from any of the mountain outlets I visit. Local outdoor writers for these smaller tabloids seem to provide remarkable, lengthy details of where the trout are bitin' and, more importantly, how area experts are catchin' them.

Lake Fishing Gear: Keep It Simple

There are some very basic rods, reels, and lines suitable for lake fishing. In this day and age of high technology products, fishermen, like audio buffs and shutterbugs, have a tendency to overly complicate their array of "necessary" equipment. I have been involved in the California sporting goods industry for over a quarter of a century, so I can speak with some accuracy when I tell you that trout fishermen are a retailer's dream come true! More monofilament line is sold to trout fishermen in California than to any other group of anglers.

More rods, reels, lures, and gadgets are also bought by trouters than any other fishermen. The very nature of the sport, which requires using primarily gossamer light 2 to 6 pound test line, means that a lot of lures, hooks, sinkers, and bait will be lost on a few big trout, and even more likely, on snags on the bottom. Walk into almost any tackle store in California, and you will see a predominance of trout fishing gear.

Trout fishermen are thus seen as having excellent sales potential to tackle shop owners, since they know you will have to replenish your terminal tackle (i.e. hooks, sinkers, baits, and lures) from time to time. With lake usage fees, boat rentals, food, lodging, and travel expenses, the costs for even the simplest weekend trip can add up. So, let's look at the essential equipment needed to get started lake fishing, keeping it simple with minimal investment.

The Typical Trout Rod

In contrast to other types of fishing in California, you can get by with a lot less in the way of technology when selecting an adequate trout rod. To begin with, unlike bass fishing, there is not a significant need to look for a trout rod made from either highest quality graphite, kevlar, or boron fibers. This type of rod was made for repeated tournament-style casting so it has to be super light. Hi-tech rods like these also have to be ultra-sensitive to feel even the slightest bite and then stiff enough to make a powerful jaw-yanking hook set. For most California trouting, you won't require this level of sensitivity or power (with perhaps the exception of fly fishing which I will discuss later).

Hi-tech rods are usually expensive and simply not that essential for typical West Coast trout fishing. However, if you shop around carefully, you may come across a light action graphite composite rod at a sensational price. Like microchip technology, as graphite rods have become more fashionable, and production levels have expanded, prices have decreased. Some of the new, light action graphite models are very suitable for trout fishing and are much lighter in weight than standard fiberglass rods. Watch for an end-of-season sale staged by a large retail operation. You could find a sensational graphite rod for as little as $25.

If you can't find a "steal" on a graphite rod, opt for a less expensive fiberglass model available in a number of styles. For those who prefer spincast reels, look for a baitcasting rod with the traditional trigger-grip handle in 6 foot lengths. The popular 5 1/2 foot models are better suited for bass fishing. The 6 foot rods should have a medium-light to light action, with a semi-soft tip section to allow for casting light lines and small lures. There are several pros and cons regarding one-piece versus two-piece rods. Without a doubt, single-piece models are generally stronger. Whenever the rod blank is interrupted and the two sections are ferruled together, a flat, weak spot results. However, single-piece rods are somewhat more cumbersome and are not as easily storable as two-piece models.

I find that a good compromise is a quality two-piece rod with a glass-to-glass ferrule system. Better quality two-piece models will join the two sections with a male and female fiberglass ferrule. This design minimizes the flat spot in the rod, allowing the blank to bend more naturally, very close to a single-piece action. Avoid rods that use a metal ferrule. This construction is very out-dated and is typical of only lower quality blanks.

If spinning is your preference, consider 5 1/2, 6, 6 1/2 or 7 foot lengths. The 5 1/2 to 6 foot rods are best suited for ultralight reels and 2 to 4 pound test lines. These will give you considerable sporting enjoyment while playing the fish, but your casting distance is somewhat restricted with the shorter rod. A more versatile choice would be either a 6 1/2 or 7 foot model. Again, a two-piece rod is fine.

I would recommend avoiding more esoteric mini-spin rod and reel combos, or 4 to 6 piece backpacking rods if you can afford only one outfit. These more specialized rods certainly have an important niche in the trouter's tackle collection, but are probably better suited for high country fishing where space and weight are prime considerations.

Also, if you prefer the ease of a push-button reel (I'll review spincast versus spinning in a moment) but feel restricted with the shorter 5 1/2 to 6 foot rods, consider using a 6 1/2 to 7 foot spinning rod. You will have a wider range of spinning models to choose from as compared to spincasters. And, as mentioned, the longer rod will generate further casts, particularly with light lures. The only thing you give up is the convenience of a trigger-grip handle which is not built into the typical spinning rod. I have used this spincast reel-spinning rod combination many times with terrific results. It really combines the best of both worlds!

Trout Reels

Many beginners will enter the sport with a spincast or "push-button" reel. There are many of these models on the market in a variety of price ranges. I recommend starting with at least a medium-priced reel. Cheaper spincast reels are made of plastic. They have dubious drag systems at best, and often cannot be set lightly enough to respond to a 2 pound test leader or monofilament. This can result in many broken lines and lost fish.

Shop instead for a more dependable push-button model, preferably one made with an anodized aluminum or chrome-plated "cone" or hood. The reels made in this style are tough, good casting models. The better ones will feature either one or two strong pick-up pins on the inner revolving spool. You can usually check for this feature by unscrewing the cone and looking for the line pick-up

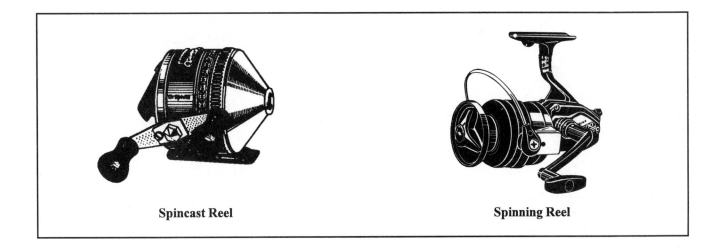

Spincast Reel   Spinning Reel

mechanism. So often, the spincast fisherman gets frustrated and angry because the reel has jammed. Sometimes a loop develops inside the cone because the line pick-up mechanism failed to work properly. This happens infrequently with higher quality, spincast models.

There are a few other tips worth remembering should you decide on a push-button model. First, be aware that almost all of these reels come prespooled with monofilament line. Unfortunately, regardless of what quality line the manufacturers use, invariably, it is too heavy for this brand of trout fishing. Usually, the spincaster comes with 10 to 15 pound mono. Now, you could fish this line if you used it in combination with a 2 to 4 pound test leader. This would be all right for bait fishing, but it is very restricted for casting 1/32 to 1/4 ounce trout lures. So, be prepared to strip off most of the factory stocked line and replace it with a good 4 to 6 pound monofilament for California trouting.

Second, as mentioned, novices often encounter problems with even the best spincast reels created by the formation of a loop inside the cone. The secret here is to keep tension on the line as you retrieve. Let the line pass between your left thumb and index fingers (right for left handers) as you cradle the rod in your hand. This keeps the line from developing a loop that quickly prohibits proper casting.

Finally, check the drag system on the push-button model before you leave the store. The reel should have a smooth, non-jerking drag. The better reels will have greater precision built in, allowing you to set the drag under the breaking test of even the lightest lines.

The old "coffee grinder" or open-faced spinning reel is the number one choice of the California trout fishing fraternity. You have a large variety to choose from. Look for a reel that features a smooth drag and quiet ball-bearing gears. It is not that critical to have an ultra-fast retrieve. A spinning reel with a steady 4:1 gear ratio will be plenty fast enough for California troutin'! The better spinning reels are also made from either strong anodized aluminum or graphite frames. The metal frames are perhaps a bit more durable than the graphite models, while the latter are much lighter.

Some of the higher quality spinners also come with an extra, interchangeable spool. This can be a great advantage if, for example, you like to free-cast lures from a boat but also want to occasionally troll. A reel filled with 2 to 4 pound mono is perfect for handling most light trout lures. Fill the other spool with 6 to 12 pound line depending upon lure choice, for trolling bigger baits and flasher combinations.

Above all, stay with a name brand reel regardless of whether you prefer a spincast or spinning model. "Cheapie" off-brand styles simply won't hold up season after season. The drag mechanisms are also usually inadequate for this style of light-line fishing, where playing a trout out until it has tired is so critical to a successful catch. Spend a few more dollars and make a solid, long-term investment in your tackle—you will not regret it!

Premium Monofilament—Another Good Investment

It is often said by professional fishermen and veteran guides that the line—not the rod, reel, or hook—is the most important link between themselves and the fish. All too often, the recreational angler will spend good money on a rod and reel only to scrimp on line. Premium grade monofilament is definitely more expensive than cheaper bulk line. For example, you can purchase a 1/4 pound spool of bulk low grade monofilament in 6 pound test that will measure sometimes over 1,500 yards for just a few dollars. That same amount of line in the identical weight in a premium grade monofilament could cost up to ten times the retail price of the cheaper grade. Why is there such a discrepancy?

To begin with, lower quality monofilament lacks uniformity. Its breaking test will vary throughout the spool. What you are purchasing in essence is the "average" breaking strength that is marked on the label. For example, that bulk spool of 6 pound bargain mono may have spots that break at closer to 4 pounds and others near 8 pound test. Premium grade monofilament, in contrast, is extruded with precise uniformity in breaking strength.

Cheaper monofilament also lacks some other key properties found in more expensive lines. The bargain brand line usually has only fair abrasion resistance, knot strength, and suppleness. Better grade lines are built to withstand exposure to sunlight, temperature, and contact with rocks, brush, and similar obstructions, while maintaining a soft suppleness on the reel for maximum casting distance.

Similarly, wherever a knot is tied, some of the strength of the monofilament has to be reduced regardless of how good the line is. With premium monofilament, this knot strength is reduced only slightly from the original breaking test of the line. With cheaper mono, the knot strength may be reduced almost 50 percent in some cases. Thus, after you tie a knot with that low-priced bulk 6 pound line, the point where the most pressure is exerted could test out at closer to 3 or 4 pounds, dramatically reducing the effectiveness of the line.

Change line every so often. Don't expect the monofilament you used at the end of last season to be adequate months later at the start of trout opening weekend. Also, here is another little tip that may save you some anguish in using brand-new monofilament. Many times, the fisherman finds that his new line will spring off the reel in uncontrollable coils as if it has a life of its own.

To avoid the coiling effect, remove the reel spool after you put on the new line and soak it in a bowl of water for about 10 to 15 minutes. Much of that springiness is dissipated by the water, making the line more supple and allowing it to lie on the spool more easily.

Another little trick worth trying is to color the first few feet of line or leader with a black marker pen. Some serious trout aficionados firmly believe that the darkened line or leader may actually show up less in clear water and bright skies than colored monofilament. If the fish are real "twitchy," experiment with this idea.

Summary

Well, now you should be armed with not only a elementary knowledge of how to "read" a particular trout lake, but also with the basic gear to successfully fish it. So, let's get more specific and focus on the different techniques used to catch trout in these California lakes in the following chapters.

Bank Fishin': Troutin' from Shore

For many California trout anglers, that occasional week-end odyssey to their favorite lake will usually take the form of fishing from the shore. Trouters who either own their own boats or who rent boats at the lake are clearly in the minority when compared to the herds who pound the bank.

Whether you fish small nearby municipal lakes with extensive planting programs or larger impoundments, there are certain key tactics you can employ to maximize your chances from the bank. In this section we will focus on walking the lakes, leaving streams for another chapter.

Reading the Shore—Look for Potential "Hot Spots"

Without having access to either a boat or a topographical map, the shore angler can still rely upon his visual instincts to locate potentially good stretches along the bank.

One of the first things I look for when I stalk trout from the shore are areas that have moderately sloping, gravel, or sandy bottoms. Trout gravitate to this type of terrain. It is rich in the availability of assorted aquatic creatures (snails, hellgrammites, freshwater clams, insect larvae, small minnows, etc.). This is also prime territory to find larger females as they engage in the spawning ritual.

Banks with shallow gravel bottoms are also excellent bets first thing in the morning. As the sun's rays begin to heat the shallower water, the trout are frequently stimulated into a more aggressive feeding mode. This is also a good time and place to try lures for these more active fish. On the other hand, after a rain storm steeper banks are a good place to investigate. As these banks erode, terrestrial insects, worms, grubs, etc., will wash down into the water creating a natural "feeding slide."

If you look carefully—and here, dependable polaroid sunglasses help—you can actually see drop-offs or ledges where the water off the bank gets dramatically deeper. You don't need sophisticated electronics to find these breaks into deep water. Just look for a significant change in water color. Typically, as the terrain slopes off, the water will often appear darker in color. During the midday heat, a longer cast into this drop-off water can be very effective on trout that have moved away from the shallows.

Feeder creeks, stream inlets, man-made spillways, or even the base of a waterfall can serve as cool resting spots for most species of trout. Many of these areas are also easily accessible with a cast from shore. The water in these locations is richly oxygenated and the turbulence stirs up a lot of insects, minnows, and similar sources of food. Any time you see current in a lake in the form of miniature eddies or whirlpools, count on these to be good fish-holding areas.

Long sandy or rocky points that extend out into the lake are also excellent places to try. Fish along the sides all the way out to the end. Sometimes one side of the point is better than the other. For instance, in the morning, the side receiving sunlight first can often be the best, as the warm rays again "activate" the trout. However, during the day, the trout may instead prefer the side that receives the least sunlight. Also, at times, the side of the point that has wind blowing directly into it can be sensational. Although the wind often makes shore angling very uncomfortable, trout can become very aggressive along these banks as they search for food sources funneled into the shore by the wind and current.

Points also allow the bank fisherman greater access to deeper water, which can be very valuable during the heat of the summer months. Similarly, boat docks and piers that permit public fishing also give the angler additional deep-water opportunities.

Some alpine lakes also have flat, shallow areas that are laden with sawed-off tree stumps. These "stump fields" seem to always be a haven for insect hatches and, hence, are good spots to try some evening fly fishing from the bank.

Similarly, lakes with overhanging tree limbs are often natural feeding spots where trout anxiously wait for caterpillars and other insects to fall into the water. Tree-lined banks also provide needed shade and sanctuary from the summer heat for the trout.

Other lakes have large boulders intermittently strewn along the shore, many reachable with a modest cast. Quite frequently, trout will seek out the shady side of these boulders for midday shelter. These boulders also serve as the perfect ambush haunts for bigger trout waiting for a wayward bait fish.

The facings of concrete or rocky dams are yet another choice spot to consider for bank fishing. Count on losing some lures or baits if there are lots of rocks, but also be prepared for action on bigger, marauding trout that hide among this structure. Here, you might think about throwing a lure from the face of the dam, rather than trying to fish from the bank.

Another possible area to try, particularly in lakes that feature a primary stocking program, is the spot where the hatchery trout are emptied into the lake. Some trout will often migrate only a short distance from this spot and/or eventually return to it within a few days of their original stocking.

Thus, by being somewhat calculating and deliberate, you can actually eliminate a lot of potentially "dead" stretches of shoreline, while zeroing in on some of these potential "hot spots."

Here is one additional interesting observation to keep in mind. Dennis Lee, the fisheries biologist, notes that there are actually different strains of trout within a particular species to be found in California. For example, there are rainbows that are raised in separate culturing facilities that clearly behave differently as a result of diverse hatchery conditions. Some strains of rainbows are nurtured to be very domesticated. These are your typical "put'n take" 'bows. They are used in many stocking programs since the Department of Fish and Game hopes they will be easily caught.

Fish in this genre show the poorest ability to survive in the wild. Often they will pack together in small schools. Heartier strains of rainbows that are raised in an environment similar to that of wild trout will quickly disperse throughout the lake upon planting.

Now what happens is that especially in many of the man-made reservoirs that rely upon the domesticated strains, the trout, due to the hatchery conditioning, will often circulate around the lakes in these small, compact schools. This migration is similar to the way dancers move around the perimeter of a ballroom floor.

Sometimes you will see that suddenly after a certain dull, inactive period, rods lined in picket fence fashion along a particular piece of shoreline start getting bit right down the row. This occurs because one of these conditioned schools of trout are moving through. Sooner or later, you should intercept these fish along their circular route. They pass through, you get bit, they move by, and the bite quickly shuts off.

So, in many man-made lakes that cater to this put'n take fishery, you might consider being more mobile while bank fishing. Try to relocate from spot to spot during the day if you fail to get bit. The object obviously is to be in the right area, with the proper bait, when the fish make their pass through your station on the shoreline.

Working Lures From the Bank

Quite often the fisherman tossing a lure from the bank will thoroughly trounce the guy in the fancy boat trolling or still-fishing many hundred yards off shore. Why would this be the case? Well, to begin with, in a lot of lakes much of the water richest in food is located just off the bank. Crawdads, aquatic insects, snails, and many styles of bait fish are found in this shallow water.

There is another reason why lure fishing from the bank can be so productive. When you are casting toward shore from a boat, invariably your lure is being dragged "down hill." However, in many cases, that prime strike zone is just a matter of feet above the bottom. Thus it is difficult to keep the lure in that strata as you retrieve it back into deeper and deeper water toward the boat.

In contrast, by presenting the lure from the bank and working it "uphill," the water gets shallower as you retrieve close to the edge of the lake. Hence, you are able to more easily keep the lure running fairly close to the bottom all the way throughout the retrieve.

When bank fishing, try to be more precise and work lures parallel to the bank instead of just throwing them toward the center of the lake. Sometimes other anglers—particularly those soaking bait—inhibit fishing a shoreline in this fashion. But, when you can do it, you will often be keeping that lure in the strike zone longer. This is a very important tactic, particularly following ice out on some lakes, when large voracious trout are cruising along the shallow banks.

Here is something else to consider: after the first thaw trout will "wolf pack" in schools moving along the bank. Sometimes you may see a "free-swimmer" following a hooked trout all the way to the edge of the shore. Quickly, toss the fish you just caught on the bank for now and fire off another cast. So often that "free-swimmer" will be waiting just a few feet from the shore, still in the mood to strike!

Use the wind to your advantage while throwing lures from the bank. Too often, fishermen "psych" themselves into thinking that it's time to pack it in once the wind starts blowing. Ironically, this may be one of the premier occasions to catch quality trout from the shore! The wind and ensuing wave chop stir up a lot of nutrients and valuable oxygen. This can often get the trout worked up into a feeding frenzy. Switch to a lure if you were dunking bait and try to key in on more aggressive fish.

I remember one trip to Gold Lake in Plumas County where I had been bait fishing without much luck for many hours. All of a sudden, a wicked wind began to whistle across the lake creating a white cap condition. I changed from bait to a spoon, and casted directly into the wind, slowly grinding the lure back through the waves.

In the span of less than one half hour I caught my ten fish limit of browns—all 15+ inch trout! The wind died down to practically nothing almost as fast as it had risen. Just as quickly, the trout action turned from fantastic to zilch. Make no doubt about it, that freak wind momentarily turned those fish on during what was otherwise a very slow day.

Spoons, spinners, and either minnow, alphabet-style or even lipless crankbaits are all viable lures to throw from the bank. However, if I had to pick just one lure to fish from shore under difficult windy conditions, I would select the Acme Kastmaster. This long-time favorite is one of the most wind-resistant spoons you can own in 1/8 to 3/8 ounce. Its super flat surface makes long distance casts on light line very easily. Sometimes I will add a strip of flect-o-lite tape to my favorite color, the gold version of the Kastmaster.

Here is a tip I stumbled across. Because this spoon has such a flat design, I would often have trout easily throw the lure with that initial jump. I just couldn't seem to get the proper hook set or leverage due to the lure's shape.

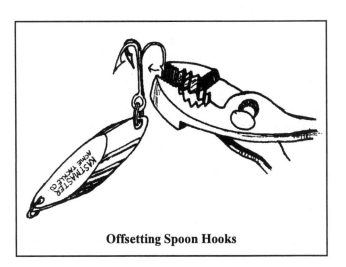

Offsetting Spoon Hooks

So, borrowing a trick from saltwater jig fishermen, I began to offset the small treble hooks that are stock issue with the Kastmaster. You can do this with a set of pliers in the field. Fewer trout will dislodge the treble hook now, since the barbs are more exposed with greater hooking power and penetration.

Observe the basic guidelines presented in previous chapters as far as picking the right lure color to use from shore: nickel, chrome, foil, silver on bright days; and copper, gold, bronze, fluorescent, black in darker, overcast conditions. You might also consider using more frog, yellow, orange, or chartreuse patterns for fishing the typical stained waters found in many Southern California lakes.

When you are pitching lures from the bank, particularly on clear-water lakes, try not to cast a shadow on the water. Similarly, make longer casts away from the shoreline under clear-water conditions, since the fish will be spookier in the shallows.

I cannot emphasize enough the importance of mixing up your presentations—especially when troutin' from the bank. Try different lures, colors and, most importantly, retrieves. Fish parallel to the shore when possible, but don't hesitate to work different strata retrieving your lures throughout various depths.

Still-Fishing: Soaking Bait

A vast number of recreational trout fishermen will focus their efforts on still-fishing from the bank with an assortment of baits. This type of angling is the most relaxing and is a lot less demanding than, say, wading or tossing lures.

Before I get into an extensive discussion of what types of bait to try, I want to mention some very subtle ploys you can use to enhance your catch while still-fishing.

To begin with, the label "still-fishing" is a restrictive misnomer. You will find that your best bait dunkers are those guys who continually move their bait a little in between casts. As I have noted, the trout in our California lakes are not sedentary creatures. For the most part, they continue to move, if only small distances throughout the day.

As a sinker rig is moved, the weight plows along the bottom creating small "puffs" of mud. Most game fish, including trout, can't resist investigating to find out what all the commotion is about. Once their curiosity draws them into the vicinity of the sinker, a strike may follow as the unassuming bait moves past.

Thus, what some of the more proficient bait fishermen do is to cast out the offering and inch it back in a few feet every five minutes or so. In this way, they also cover much more territory instead of just leaving the bait to soak in one location. But you can't always tell if the bait has landed in a bed of weeds or some similarly inaccessible underwater spot that the trout can't get to. By moving the bait a little bit every few minutes, you also eliminate having it inadvertently lodged in a bad location.

A very common mistake made by the novice trouter is to use leaders that are simply too heavy. I have recurrently seen unaware anglers fishing from the bank totally stymied while the guy next to them is hauling in trout left and right.

Both fishermen are using the same bait, but only one is having success. The key often is the difference in the leader, not the fisherman.

The successful angler is probably fishing with 2 to 3 pound test leader, while the unlucky man persists in tying the bait directly to his 6 to 10 pound line. This is an important consideration even in lakes that exhibit a stained water condition or in fishing for the less wary hatchery-bred trout. It is essential to scale down those leaders and try to finesse these fish a little more.

Now then, you can "hedge your bet," as they say, when using ultralight, gossamer thin leaders by applying a tiny "dot" of Superglue to the knot. This will insure minimal slippage. Superglue can also be used in tying monofilament to lures as well.

Other issues to consider are whether or not to hold the rod and whether you should fish with a slack or a tight line. I believe you will find different theories with regard to these questions. Some trout fishermen are adamant that it is best to leave the rod in a rod holder or propped on a rock—but, whatever you do, don't hold it until you are going to set the hook. The idea here is that by holding it, you may transmit some unnatural movement or "vibrations" down through the line to the fish. This is pretty much poppycock. Many of the cagiest bait fishermen around hold the rod and, as noted, move the bait back to the bank as they fish. I think the main thing to keep in mind if you prefer to still-fish holding the rod is to avoid any dramatic or jerky movements. This conceivably could spook more wary trout.

I like to leave the rod in a holder or on top of a rock and reel the line in a few feet every few minutes. I feel more comfortable this way, standing back a couple of feet and watching the line. It also makes me a bit more patient. Too many times when I've held the rod, I've swung on the tiniest indication of a strike and invariably missed the fish. I was just too "trigger happy" and didn't let the trout swallow the bait far enough.

As far as tight versus slack line bait fishing goes, both techniques will work. Many anglers prefer to still-fish with a tight line, reasoning that as the trout pulls the rod tip down (the "action"), the "reaction" of the tip springing back will automatically set the hook. Sometimes this works, especially on smaller fish. Tight lines are also somewhat easier to watch when you have a lot of wind and wave action crashing into the bank.

However, far too often, a lunker strikes the bait and snaps the light leader line with this strategy. It is probably better in the long run to fish with some slack. For one thing, the trout feels minimal resistance and is thus likely to inhale the bait better. For another, by giving the trout some slack before you set, you will have a little more to work with as far as absorbing the shock of the set. Here, I recommend just using a short, quick flick of the wrist, rather than a jaw-breaking set. This is one of the keys to

fishing light 1 to 3 pound test leader material without snapping it on the hook set.

Using Line Markers

Some enterprising trouters have devised ways to mark their lines to observe the strike more easily when still-fishing from the bank. One method is to rest the rod in a spiked rod holder and then pull down about a foot of line between the reel and the lead guide. Take a miniature red and white bobber and snap it to the swivel end of a snap-swivel. Next, open up the snap portion of this rig, and just hang the snap in the center of this slack line. It is important to leave the snap open. When the trout strikes, the float-swivel marker "jumps." Quickly unhook the open snap from the line and be prepared for the set. Even if the strike is quick and vicious, you can still set with the line moving freely through the open snap. Thus, the float-swivel marker maintains the slack line in addition to letting you visually pick up the slightest strike very easily.

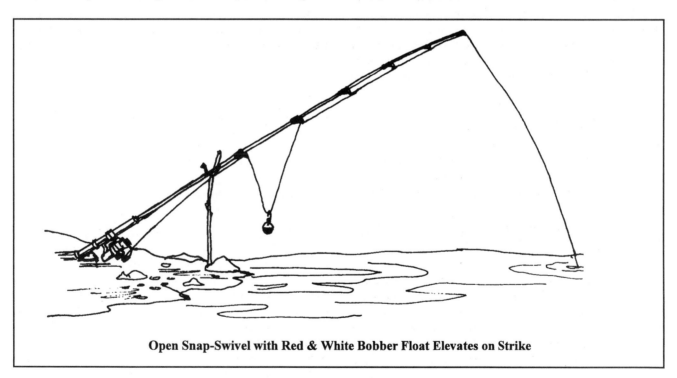

Open Snap-Swivel with Red & White Bobber Float Elevates on Strike

A variation of this can be improvised by taking a pinch of some sticky floating bait. You have to mold a little wedge of the bait to the slack line between the reel and the first guide. This forms a superb line marker and it quickly breaks off on the set. Other devices such as rod holders

with built-in bicycle horns or even the attachment of commercial "rod bells" that clip to the rod tip will also work. Keep in mind that some fellow bank fishermen may find these obtrusive, especially on more pristine, isolated lakes.

Common Bait Fishing Rigs

There are some simple, basic bait fishing leader and hook combinations that are time-proven for California-style troutin'. Most of these are available as pre-tied rigs sold at tackle shops throughout the state. You can also tie them yourself by purchasing the hooks and swivels separately along with spools of quality 1 to 3 pound test line.

Standard Cheese Rig. Many California trout are caught on either Velveeta cheese or some other floating or cheese mix bait. The principle setup for fishing these kinds of baits is two gold treble hooks tied to a four foot 1 1/2 to 4 pound test leader. One hook is tied to the end, the other is offset on a shorter dropper line from the main leader. At the other end, there is a monofilament loop that lets you conveniently attach the entire rig to a snap-swivel. This double cheese rig is fished with a sliding egg sinker — usually 1/8 to 1/2 ounce depending upon distance needed — joined by the snap-swivel.

As the fish strikes the cheese, the line passes through the egg sinker without any resistance. This is the basic sinker combination to use for even the touchiest trout.

Cheese-Egg Rig. A variation of the double cheese rig is to switch the second treble hook off the dropper leader and use a gold salmon egg hook instead. Fish this combo

identically to the double cheese setup, again using the sliding egg sinker.

Single Hook Setup. This is the most rudimentary of all terminal rigs and yet it is sometimes overlooked or not used properly. There are many situations, where due to excessive weed growth or rocks, it is better to bank fish a lake using just one hook rather than a double-hook combination.

You can rig this setup with the sliding sinker and choose from either a treble hook, a single salmon egg hook, or even a bronze baitholder hook depending upon your selection of bait. This is a simple rig to tie and you can customize the length of the leader to your own liking.

For example, if you are using a floating bait or an injected nightcrawler in a heavily weeded bottom, you can fish the bait with a 2 to 4 foot leader, suspending it out of the weeds.

The Spreader Rig. This combination must be hand-tied, yet it is simple enough to do even in the field. Run your line through the egg sinker and butt it by tying it off to a three-way swivel. Then affix your own desired length of line and the particular style of hook you prefer to each end of the swivel. The three-way swivel keeps the leaders, hooks, and bait separate without much difficulty in casting.

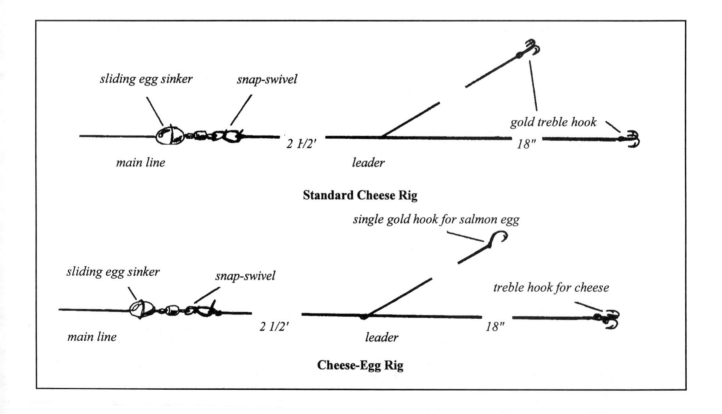

Standard Cheese Rig

Cheese-Egg Rig

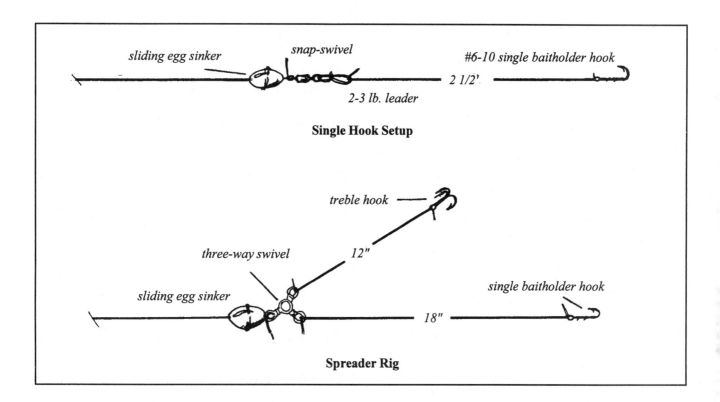

sliding egg sinker   snap-swivel   #6-10 single baitholder hook

2 1/2'

2-3 lb. leader

Single Hook Setup

treble hook

three-way swivel   12"

sliding egg sinker   single baitholder hook

18"

Spreader Rig

These four rigs are the most widely used for fishing bait from the bank here in California. But here is one further point that trouters often fail to account for which results in few or no bites: make sure the leaders on your snelled hooks are correctly sized. Too often, the manufacturers tie these hooks with leader line that is way too heavy for California troutin'. The hooks may be small enough, but the leaders are too thick and opaque.

Many anglers purchase these hooks because they are convenient to use. You can attach them to a snap-swivel or cinch them through the eye of a barrel swivel. But it doesn't matter how easy they are to use if the leader spooks the trout.

An exception to this is the delicately hand-tied snelled hooks that were originally sold under the European Allcott brand. These are gold salmon egg hooks that are intricately snelled with the line almost "fused" to the hook for maximum concealment. To my knowledge, the Allcott hooks are no longer marketed in the West due to their exorbitant cost per pack. However, you may still be able to find the Asian counterparts that are excellent for fishing salmon eggs in crystal clear lakes.

A further point: pre-sharpen all the hooks you use for bait fishing yourself. As a professional guide, I hand-hone even the smallest of my bait hooks for my custom-ers. I have found over the years that it really makes a difference on the strike-to-catch ratio compared to using hooks straight from the box.

An exception to this might be the American-made Eagle Claw Lazer Sharp series hooks that are needle-sharp right from the package. They also sell their salmon egg hooks in this style, colored red to really disguise the hook. The Lazer Sharp series of bait hooks require no pre-sharpening and are remarkably inexpensive compared to their Asian counterparts.

Removing the Hook

Trout can really swallow the bait deeply when you still-fish. You can try to extract the hook with one of those so-called "disgorgers." This inexpensive little plastic probe is made with a ball-like knob on each end into which you can insert the leader line.

Follow the line running through the ball to where the hook is embedded. When you get to the hook, twist it back and forth until it dislodges. Keep in mind if you use this device that this is a major operation and the patient will probably not survive all that rough handling.

A better option is a surgical hemostat, marketed by Berkley, or a similar instrument sold under the name of

Izorline's "Dr. Fisherman." As the commercial says, *if you decide to bait fish for trout 'don't leave home without one!'* This handy little tool lets you get those tiny treble and salmon hooks out without totally destroying the trout. In lieu of Dr. Fisherman, a long-point needle-nose plier will work almost as well.

When to Use Floats and Bobbers

many weekend trouters make the mistake of thinking that a float or bobber is used primarily as a visual aid to help detect a strike. That is only partly correct.

In many lakes, the weed growth right off the bank can be very prohibitive to typical sliding-sinker fishing. This is a prime situation in which to use a float. By attaching a bobber a number of feet above the baited hook, you can keep the bait suspended over the weed beds. Use live offerings such as nightcrawlers or salmon eggs, or use Velveeta cheese.

If you have heavier 4 to 6 pound line on your push-button or spinning reel, add a 4 to 5 foot leader of 2 to 3 pound test connected by a little barrel swivel.

Snap the colored float right above the swivel and you're ready to cast.

Another possibility is to use one of those clear, sliding plastic "bubbles." Many fishermen prefer these over the traditional red and white bobbers. They reason that the trout will have a harder time seeing these bubbles in contrast to colored floats, especially on clear lakes. With this type of float, your line passes through an inner plastic sleeve so that the bubble slides unrestricted up and down the line.

You can also take the tube out to fill the clear bubble up with water if you desire more weight for a longer cast. Under severe windy conditions, using a spinning reel with a 6 1/2 to 7 foot rod and four pound test mono and a clear bubble filled with water will allow you to make a cast pushing well over sixty yards in length. This could put your offering out into the lake where only boaters and float tubers normally venture.

There are a couple of different ways you can fish the bubble. One technique is to run the line through the inner sleeve and tie it to a snap-swivel. Then connect a 5 to 7 foot leader line to the snap-swivel with your baited hook.

Throw the rig out toward the center of the lake and the strand of leader line will slowly sink to the bottom as it passes through the bubble. This can be deadly with a live nightcrawler as it tantalizingly drifts down to the bottom. As you would expect, many strikes occur on the sink. You

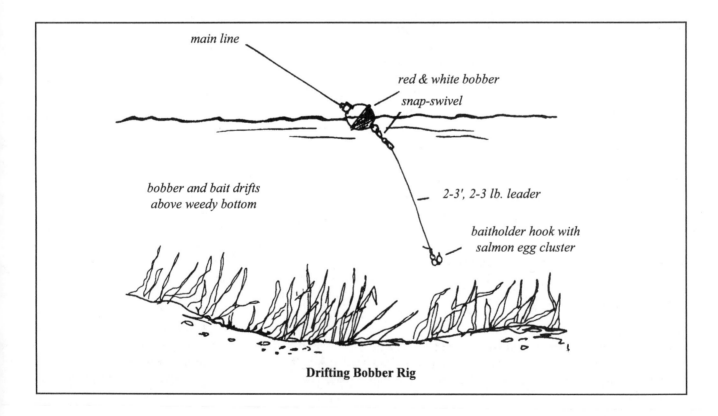

Drifting Bobber Rig

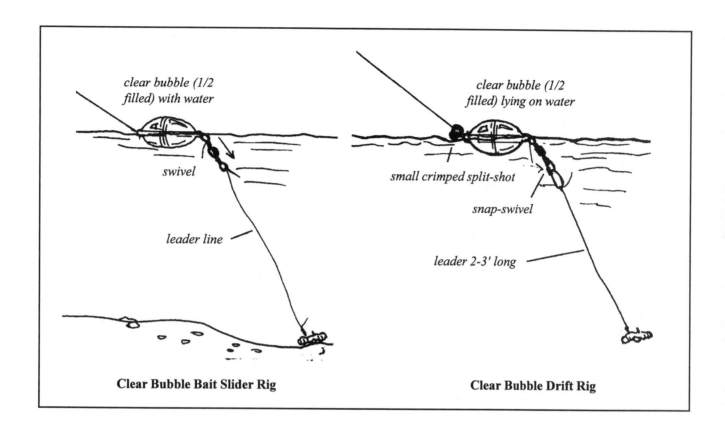

clear bubble (1/2 filled) with water

swivel

leader line

clear bubble (1/2 filled) lying on water

small crimped split-shot

snap-swivel

leader 2-3' long

Clear Bubble Bait Slider Rig

Clear Bubble Drift Rig

can reel up the line after the bait hits the bottom and move the float in toward the bank a little, stop, and let the leader sink to repeat the process.

Another variation in using the clear bubble is to rig it as mentioned above, but instead of letting it slide unrestricted, pinch a small BB-sized split-shot right behind it. This will secure the bubble so that only the length of the leader line will dangle underneath it.

There are many days when the trout prefer a bait that is faintly moving with the current. Using these floats or bubbles while working the shore at your favorite lake will often produce remarkable results when conventional still-fishing fails!

The Fly and Bubble Combination

Another very potent approach that you should consider when shore fishing for trout is using a wet or dry fly. Novice trout fishermen sometimes cringe at the thought of "fly fishing," figuring that they will have to make yet another expensive investment in equipment and related paraphernalia. But with the advent of the clear, plastic bubble, an entirely new dimension of fly fishing opened up to fishing enthusiasts.

It is very easy to rig up a fly and bubble combination. Simply set it up as you would for bait fishing, leaving the bubble to slide freely up the line. However, try to use as long a leader as possible. A rough rule of thumb is to measure the leader material from the tip of the rod to the reel—about 5 1/2 to 7 feet in length. It is important to keep as much distance as possible between the bubble and the fly.

Fill the float about half full with water. These bubbles come in different sizes so you can weight them depending upon the distance desired. Try to keep them just about 1/2 filled to minimize the noisy "plop" as it hits the water.

The leader material should be premium, 1 to 3 pound test monofilament. I emphasize premium, because you want to use as invisible a leader as possible. However, there is no need to purchase extravagant tapered leaders. These are more suitable for fly rod usage and will be discussed in a separate chapter.

Now we come to the hard part—how to select the proper size, style, and pattern of fly. There are some simple guidelines I can offer here for those who have absolutely no familiarity with fly fishing.

First, buy quality flies. Avoid the cheap "discount house" brands. It is probably easiest to stay with some basic dry fly patterns. These are made to imitate tiny insects landing on the water following a hatch. Purchase them in small size 14 to 18 patterns. The diminutive sizes will work best at higher elevation lakes where the trout are smaller and the water clearest.

Second, limit your choices to some of the proven winners among California fly aficionados such as the Ginger Quill, California Mosquito, Red Ant, Renegade, Royal Coachman, Black Gnat, White Miller, El Capitan, and Adams. These dry flies in gray, brown, or black shades work well on Western lakes.

Dry flies were meant to be fished "dry" or on top of the water. You can make the fly stay on the surface by putting a light coat of silicoat spray or a little bit of muslin on it. You will also get some temporary flotation by whipping the leader back and forth in the air to dry out the moisture. But I might add that rarely have I found making the fly totally "dry" absolutely necessary with the bubble rig in order to get bit. Most action seems to occur with the little fly just barely being dragged under the surface. As a matter of fact, in some cases, I have intentionally added a small split-shot midway on the leader to sink the dry fly. Often the trout prefer the dry fly fished "wet" in this manner.

Larger flies tied to represent minnows (streamers) or larval insects or hellgrammites (nymphs) are also worth trying at times. Another favorite is the Wooly Worm which most closely resembles a caterpillar. Two other patterns that fish well "wet" behind a fly and bubble combination are Joe's Hopper (an excellent grasshopper look alike) and the Muddler Minnow (made to appear like a sculpin minnow).

This is a good, basic menu to start with which will keep your occasional fly fishing uncomplicated. However, it is always best to check with regional tackle shops near the lakes you fish to obtain accurate recommenda-tions on the hot local patterns of flies working in those areas.

Besides selecting the right fly, the actual retrieve is probably just as important in using a fly and bubble setup. It is essential that you really go into a total slow-down mode in fishing this rig. The trout will most commonly strike the fly on a slow steady retrieve. Other times, a stop'n go technique works better, with many strikes occurring as the fly rests and starts to sink.

Another common mistake is trying to set too hard with the small fly. A lot of strikes will appear as nothing more than a dull pressure on the end of the line, or at best a very gentle tugging action. Use a very short set when you feel the strike. If you miss the fish, keep reeling slowly. Quite frequently, the trout will come back for a second look and a more vicious follow-up strike.

Trout can be very acrobatic when hooked on a fly, especially rainbows and brookies. It is important to keep constant pressure on the line to cut down on the possibil-ity of the fish throwing the small hook. If you want to minimize the chances of the trout becoming airborne, here is a little tip worth noting. Try to keep your line and rod tip near the water. This creates a lot of surface tension between the line and water which makes it harder for the trout to leap with both the weight of the bubble and the wet line. A precision, perfectly adjusted drag is very critical for properly playing out trout hooked with the fly and bubble outfit.

Study this form of fly fishing closely. It can become an incredibly productive strategy for catching trout on many of our large Western lakes. So often, the fish will be rising for flies, dimpling the surface a considerable distance off shore. The traditional fly rodder simply can't reach these trout. Here is where the bank fisherman who is proficient with a fly and bubble rig can really excel at putting on a show!

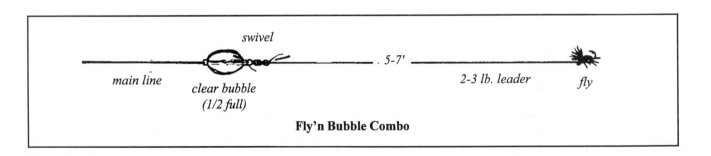

swivel

main line *clear bubble (1/2 full)* . 5-7' 2-3 lb. leader *fly*

Fly'n Bubble Combo

Wading and Tubing

One of the most enjoyable forms of bank fishing a lake is to put on a set of hip or chest waders and venture out into the water. Wading is not permitted on all trout lakes, especially on some of those used as "No Body Contact" drinking water reservoirs. Be sure to check local regulations. On that note, some lakes that have extensive boat traffic, require "belly boaters" to wear a fluorescent orange vest like they would when deer hunting to increase their visibility at such a low point in the water.

Wading allows the shore fisherman just that much more access to the lake. By moving off the bank, the angler can more easily work the shoreline in a parallel presentation or fan-cast to open water. There is also something of a distinctively different thrill in playing out the trout in his own environment as you wade in the water. Any of the aforementioned techniques will apply to wading, but most anglers prefer to toss lures or flies with this approach.

You can purchase waders in a wide range of styles. The hip waders are available primarily in rubberized canvas or the more expensive rubberized nylon. You can buy very inexpensive chest waders in the "stocking foot" models. These are lightweight and are made to slide into an old pair of athletic shoes. The shoes thus form the hard outsoles for this type of wader.

Better stocking foot waders are made of nylon; cheaper ones, from plastic. The higher quality stocking foot waders are excellent for most California waters in the late spring through fall. They have minimal insulating qualities but are very safe. Because they are so lightweight, you could probably swim in them if you had to.

Better quality chest waders are made from rubberized nylon or neoprene. These will provide the greatest warmth and are predictably more expensive. The investment may well be worth it if you plan on wading all through the year.

With chest waders, it is a good idea to cinch an old belt around the chest area. The belt will reduce the chance of water filling up the wader should you slip into a deep hole. The Berkley Fishin' Partner box makes an excellent companion for wading. The web belt serves to keep the waders tight to minimize leakage, plus you have a mini tackle box easily accessible carried right on your chest.

And a landing net is also imperative for wading in case you hook that whopper trout.

Tubing takes the wading experience one step further. These "belly boats" are made to use in conjunction with lightweight chest waders. You can even purchase miniature swim fins used to provide greater mobility while fishing the tube. Prices vary depending upon the quality of the materials and whether the tube has a back rest and/or accessory pouches. Some diehards prefer the traditional circular tube, while other belly boat enthusiasts are now fishing from the newer u-shaped models.

Many float tube models are also designed with special straps to secure an extra rod. This setup is gaining a lot of interest, especially on big, expansive lakes, whereby the belly boat trouter might want to switch back and forth with two fly rod combos. The two different rigs allow the angler to attack "big water" with, say, floating and sinking lines, depending upon prevailing conditions which might switch during the day. The same option would apply to the spin fisherman using two different combos from the float tube.

On big lakes, like Crowley, legions of tube fishermen can be found quietly approaching water holding lunker trout that might otherwise shy off from an intruding boat. But sometimes the wind can play havoc with the neophyte tuber who inadvertently gets caught too far off the bank. The struggle to paddle your way back to shore through the waves and wind chop can be an awesome experience.

Some rather creative tube fishermen have devised a unique scheme to fish their belly boats under windy conditions. As they leave the bank, they secure a stake in the ground with a good 100 to 200 yards of lightweight rope attached. They then can use this line as a sort of "umbilical cord" tied onto their tubes. When the wind comes up and they decide to return to the bank, they simply pull themselves back in by gathering up the rope. A truly novel idea!

To top this, don't be surprised if you see a belly boat trouter on your favorite lake moving along with a small trolling motor and a portable electronic fish finder! It has been done already!

Boat Fishin': Anchors Away

No doubt about it, fishing for trout from a boat will often give the angler a tremendous advantage over the bank fisherman, particularly at highly frequented lakes. But this "edge" is only possible if the trouter fishing from a canoe, inflatable, or larger boat learns to: (a) properly read the water, (b) select the appropriate gear, and (c) understand the basic rules of boat handling and safety.

Before we actually get into the ways that expert trout anglers fish from their crafts, it is important to discuss briefly how to set up the boat properly.

How About Trolling Motors?

To begin with, an electric trolling motor is an excellent investment to supplement a larger gas engine. These little dynamos work off a standard 12 or 24 volt battery and can quietly propel a medium-sized boat or canoe for the entire day. If you prefer to work plugs, spinners, or spoons up and down a shoreline, the electric motor is an absolute prize piece of equipment!

Fishermen mount these motors on either the stern or the bow of all kinds of canoes and boats. Models are available which can be steered by hand or by a remote foot pedal. Better quality trolling motors have multiple speed settings, allowing you to conserve "juice" on calm days as well as to increase the power when pushing through wind.

Although these electric thrusters art termed "trolling" motors, they are not really necessary for this type of fishing. As noted, they perform best when the angler wants to move very quietly over a stretch of lake. On larger bodies of water, smaller air-cooled standard outboard engines, or even larger inboard-outboard engines, can actually be throttled down to troll even slow-moving lures such as cowbells without spooking the trout.

Spot-casting a lure while the engine idles or "putts" along is also quite possible with these motors. The key is to let out a good 50 yards of line if trolling to keep the bait or lure away from the wake and immediate disturbance, or to make long casts if throwing to the bank or to open water.

I might add, however, that on larger popular lakes that evidence a lot of boater traffic, the trout seem to become acclimated to all the noise and commotion. Such pressure seems to rarely affect fish on such waters. But if I am stalking big trout in the shallows or trolling on the smaller, quieter lakes, I use an electric trolling motor.

Should I Invest in Electronics?

Electric depth finders can be a very valuable tool, even for the weekend angler. Your best option will be one of the streamlined, thin-profiled L.C.R. (liquid crystal recorder) units. They can be mounted on either the bow, side, or console of most boats. Portable versions are also available for the rental boater.

The L.C.R. measures a variety of things helpful to the trout fisherman. It meters depth and shows the angler where drop-offs, ledges, canyons, submerged pinnacles, and creek channels are located—all potentially good trout-holding spots. It also displays the thermocline layer and the trout themselves.

But equally important, the L.C.R. will indicate precisely where bait fish are schooled, particularly the dominant threadfin shad minnows. So often the trout will follow the forage fish to whatever depth they are located. Put simply: if you find the bait, you find the trout.

Another often overlooked instrument is a simple thermometer. When fastened to a cord and lowered into the lake, it can be used to locate colder water areas such as underground springs. During the summer months these submerged springs, for example, can be fantastic deep sanctuaries for a lake's trout population.

Boat Fishing Gear

The basic rods and reels itemized for bank fishing will certainly work for most troutin' from a boat. Ideally, three primary outfits would be perfect. Carry one spincast or spinning combination filled with 4 to 8 pound test for fan-casting lures or still-fishing. A 5 1/2 to 6 foot baitcasting rod and matching reel is ideal for top-line trolling, vertical spooning, or casting larger lures for trophy fish. Stay with 6 to 12 pound monofilament. Back up these two outfits with either a much larger freshwater reel or a small saltwater baitcaster (preferably with level winder) and stouter rod for lead-core trolling.

If you own a wood, fiberglass, or aluminum boat or canoe and want to set it up for some serious troutin', make sure the floor is lined with carpeting. The inexpensive indoor-outdoor type is fine! Insulation like this will stifle unnecessary sound and prevent extraneous vibrations from being transmitted through the water. These sounds can really scare off the fish.

Next, try to carry two anchors instead of one. The weight of the anchor depends on the size of the craft. They will range from about 10 to 20 pounds and come in all shapes. I like the plastic-coated mushroom variety, since they won't mar the boat and are fairly quiet. However, if you are typically fishing on big lakes with strong winds, definitely use the old standard, galvanized fluted marine-style anchor. And don't shortchange yourself with regard to buying an anchor with adequate weight. For example, you will need a solid 15 lb.(+) for anchoring a 16-17 foot boat in rough weather.

Always try to keep the bow pointed into the wind as you set out your bow anchor. If your boat is pointed down swell and you attempt to anchor from the stern, look out—you may soon take water over the side and swamp! A lot of weekend fishermen do not realize this. Now, if you want to do some "professional-style" bait dunkin', after you anchor the bow tight, drop a second anchor off the stern. This should now keep your boat from swiveling back and forth in the wind—an aggravating effect with only a bow anchor.

If you are renting a boat at the dock concession, request that the landing operator give you a backup anchor. Quite often they will do this without much hassle. This will allow you to still-fish much more easily in the wind.

As for rod holders, you can keep it simple and use the basic metal models that clamp onto the boat's gunwale. These will work for both still-fishing and trolling. More elaborate styles such as the Fish-On holder can actually be pre-cocked to snap back and set the hook as the fish takes line and pulls the rod down.

Another accessory item worth considering is a wire fish basket. Trout, like most game fish, will not stay alive very long in even the best aerated live wells. As a matter of fact, it is technically illegal to possess live trout in a boat according to Department of Fish and Game laws. This is to keep anglers from unlawfully using live trout as "bait" for larger game fish such as largemouth or striped bass.

An alternative way to keep the fish fresh is to place them in a wire fish basket. Water is allowed to pass through the wire frame as the basket hangs from the side of the boat. It is also possible to drag the basket through the water while slow-trolling without damaging the fish.

New Areas to Fish

All of the principle "hot spots" listed in previous chapters (e.g., points, weed lines, dam walls, etc.) are accessible to boat as well as shore fishermen. However, troutin' from a boat will allow the angler to key in on the fish in one particular way not possible when fishing from the shore. By using electronics, the boat fisherman can monitor the particular depth where the trout are holding. Quite often, the trout will suspend or school in a narrow band of water. They can indeed be caught if the lure or bait is presented through that strata. So, the smart trouter will use his electronics during tough times to isolate that band of fish. Next, he will try to either troll or cast a lure or lure/bait combo through that strip of water hoping to find aggressive fish. Along this line, let's examine more closely the art of "fan-casting" and other casting methods that can be used from a boat.

Special Casting Techniques

Armed with a handful of popular spinners, spoons, and alphabet- or minnow-style crankbaits, the boat fisherman can cover a lot of territory by methodically choosing a particular target and fan-casting the area. As you zero in on the spot (e.g., a point, gravel bank, boulders, etc.), make casts not only to the primary target but also "fan out" to patches of water adjacent to it. A lot of times game fish will move on and then off of a specific holding area. By fan-casting you may be able to intercept trout that are in the migration path moving toward or away from the main resting spot.

At other times, especially on known big fish lakes, lunker-class trout will often "boil" on the surface in a manner similar to saltwater game fish. These explosive swirls on the water are usually the sign of an actively feeding fish! The trick here is to throttle down to a near standstill so as to not spook these larger trout and glide into casting range or switch to the electric motor.

Select a lure from your box that you can throw a long way—remember, the object is to keep the boat as far away as possible from the boils. It is best to cast the bait slightly beyond the surface disturbance again, so as to not scare off the fish. Then, grind the lure back through the swirl all the way to the boat.

Veteran "hawg hunters" stalking trophy browns in this manner will throw large 1/2 ounce or larger spoons such as the Hopkins, Haddock Structure Spoon, Kastmaster, Crippled Herring, Champ, Krocadile, or even the aluminum Schurmy Shad. It is best to let the spoon sink a little and to be prepared for a strike on the fall.

For shoreline activity, try to keep the boat moving parallel to the bank. Be courteous to the shore fishermen and, when possible, toss a variety of baits up and down, especially in the early morning and at dusk.

Spoonin' for Trout

Although vertical spoonin' for trout in lakes is not too commonly done here in the West, there are times when it is worth a try. In some impoundments, the trout will "stack up" along ledges and/or cluster near schools of bait fish. By using your electronics, you can readily see these trout when they are suspended off the bottom "packed tight" like this.

Occasionally, if you position the boat above the fish, you might have a chance at vertically spoonin' some of these trout. With this technique I recommend a baitcasting outfit. Spoons will drop faster with less restriction using a baitcasting reel because the revolving spool turns so quickly and freely. In contrast, with spinning or spincast reels, the line pays out after it slowly uncoils off of a fixed spool.

Be prepared for many strikes to occur on the drop as the spoon is sinking. "Thumb" the line as it is going out, putting just a little resistance on it to decipher a slight "tick" signaling a strike. Use your thumb pressure to quickly stop the spool and set up on fish.

Once the spoon sinks to the desired depth, engage the reel and lift up with the rod a good 3 to 4 feet. This makes the spoon "jump." As the lure falls back down, it will resemble a dying, fluttering minnow. Many strikes will occur on the "fall," as it is termed, on a slack line. Watch for that telltale "tick." Or you may just feel dull pressure as you go to lift up again.

As the line is sinking, all of a sudden it seems to just stop short of falling all the way back to where the lift was started. This is another indication that the trout has inhaled the spoon and has started to swim off with it. In all these cases, swing and set on anything that seems unusual in interrupting the descent of the spoon.

There are a number of good spoons to try with this technique. As previously discussed, the ever-popular Crippled Herring and Kastmaster in 1/8 to 3/8 ounce, along with the 1/4 to 3/4 ounce Hopkins, and the 3/8 and 1/2 ounce Haddock Jig'n Spoon or Structure Spoons will work. Smooth or hammered gold are my favorite colors. But also try those that have a rainbow trout pattern in flect-o-lite along with other prism-like finishes.

I recommend using either a split ring or a single snap if the spoon is not sold with one. This will impart additional erratic action to the lure as well as providing a good point to tie a firm knot.

Drift Fishing

Trolling, casting, and still-fishing with bait are typically the most common types of troutin' done from boats. However, one further technique that should be attempted is drifting. A lot of times, when the wind really starts to whip across the lake, drifting may actually be the best overall way to comfortably continue to cover a lot of water. Trolling with heavy wave chop or wind can often be a problem when you have to fight the elements. Drifting down wind can be just the right alternative when the weather changes. Keep in mind that this unique approach should be explored even under mild conditions.

The easiest presentation is to line the boat up in an imaginary drift route where it will be pushed by the wind and current. This can be parallel to the shoreline, between two points, along a ledge or drop-off. An ideal bait is a live nightcrawler.

Drift the 'crawler laced on a #6 or #8 baitholder hook. Thread the hook through the sex collar once, leaving a tiny bit of barb exposed. Sometimes it is best to let out 50 feet or so of line and lazily drift the 'crawler weightless behind the boat. Hold a good 2 or 3 feet of line in your hand as the bait drifts. This is similar to the way saltwater live-bait fishermen "fly line" an anchovy.

When the trout hits, let the fish have some free line. Often, the strike is vicious; other times it may be more of a cautious nibble. The trout will tend to eat this big bait

better if it feels no resistance as it strikes on the drift. This method can be very productive on subsurface feeding fish.

At times, it may be better to add a small split-shot weight about 18 to 24 inches above the 'crawler when the trout are feeding deeper. Again, "fly-line" the bait allowing the fish to run a little with it before setting the hook.

Another variation on this theme is to use a very small spinner without hooks, preferably with a Colorado blade. Attach an 18 to 24 inch, 4 to 6 pound leader line behind the spinner with a live nightcrawler threaded on a small baitholder hook. The small blade will revolve enough under a slow drift to provide a subtle "flash" ahead of the nightcrawler. This mini-lake troll rig is excellent on back country lakes or when the trout seem particularly skittish.

Live minnows can also be drifted in the same manner. An alternative is to drift these baits beneath a float. This method is superb for subsurface feeding trout, and it has the advantage of letting the angler follow the strike more closely. Minnows can be either hooked through the back under the dorsal fin or through both lips. Hook size can vary depending upon the species and size of bait fish you are using. Baitholder hooks in sizes #1 through #8 will usually suffice.

Lake restrictions on the legality of using live bait varies. It is best to check with local lake authorities to make certain that live minnows are permitted where you are fishing.

Another rather unusual possibility for drifting involves using floating baits or marshmallows. Trout will often "puddle" around near the surface, casually slurping in insects or other aquatic fare that have landed on top of the water. Sometimes these fish will strike a floating bait drifted on the surface. Use very light line—preferably 2 to 4 pound test—and try to keep the bait some distance from the boat. You will have to manually help let out the line since the baits have such little drag. "Fly-line" the baits as mentioned and watch for visual attacks as the

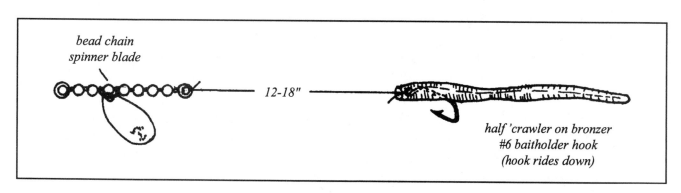

bead chain spinner blade

12-18"

half 'crawler on bronzer #6 baitholder hook (hook rides down)

trout suck in the Berkley Power Bait, Zeke's or marshmallow offering.

Similarly, a single salmon egg drifted on light line in open water can produce outstanding results. Once again, remember to keep that line light! Anglers skilled at ultralight fishing will use gossamer two pound test monofilament, while anything larger than four pound test will inevitably spook the fish. Also, the hook must be completely hidden in the egg.

Drifting with lures can also yield outstanding results. As was previously mentioned, small banana-shaped plugs such as the Hot Shot Kwikfish or Flatfish have enough tantalizing subtle wobble to generate strikes when fished on a drift pattern. Sometimes adding a single lead shot above these lures makes them dive a little deeper without inhibiting the action on the drift. It is imperative, however, to keep the line as light as possible or the lure's action will be restricted. Premium grade monofilament in 4 to 6 pound test is recommended.

It is also possible to drift fish for trout with a spoon. This is known as "spoon jiggin" and can be very effective when the fish are deep. The principle is the same as vertical spoonin' (i.e., let the lure sink to the desired depth and work it in a series of lifts and drops. Note that you may often have to reel the spoon up and make a series of drops if the drift is fast and you are fishing deep.

Otherwise, you will have too much belly in the line to impart the proper action to the lure and the spoon will tend to rise out of the strike zone. Having too much line trailing behind the boat also makes it tough to detect strikes with the spoon drifting technique.

Another innovative drifting approach is to work a dropper rig with a minnow plug. As is often the case, many of our lakes here in California are relatively clear—and deep. During certain times, schools of threadfin shad will migrate to these deep environments sometimes below the 60 foot level. Game fish such as trout will follow the schools of shad to these greater depths. Outside of vertical spoons, downriggers, or planing devices on a troll, about the only other way anglers try for these trout is to still-fish them with bait.

But a dropper rig can be a very viable alternative! Tie your primary line to a standard three-way swivel. Next, take about 12 to 14 inches of 10 to 12 pound line to form one leader. Attach a one ounce spoon sinker—the kind normally used for surf fishing. Attach a one ounce spoon sinker—the kind normally used for surf fishing. Take another 24 to 30 inches of 6 pound leader material and tie it to the swivel with either a #5 or #7 floating Rapala on the other end.

It is probably best to ease this setup below the boat until you hit the bottom. Then let out another 30 to 50 feet of line to keep the rig away from the boat. I might add that a skilled caster can easily pitch this awkward setup way from the boat without too much trouble—the key is to use a longer 6 1/2 to 7 1/2 foot rod.

The reason a floating minnow plug is preferred is simple: (a) the small thin size matches closely with the silhouette of threadfin shad; (b) the plug will float off the bottom to avoid getting hung up in obstructions; and (c) floating minnows usually have better action than sinking versions.

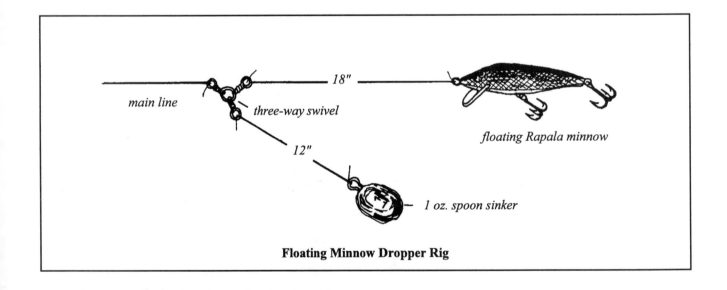

main line

three-way swivel

18"

floating Rapala minnow

12"

1 oz. spoon sinker

Floating Minnow Dropper Rig

In tough windy conditions, when the bait and trout are deep, you can drift this dropper rig behind the boat. Every once in a while, give the rod tip a few exaggerated twitches to make the plug frantically dart from side to side. (You can also slow-troll this dropper rig.) On a cold winter outing at Lake Perris, I was introduced to this innovative technique by veteran guide Dave Nollar. We found shad just off the bottom in 60 feet of water. Using the dropper rig, I was amazed to actually feel trout hit the plug really hard at such great depths. After you detect the strike, set the hook and reel the trout in with a steady, constant retrieve. These plugs have small treble hooks and it is a long way up to the surface.

The enterprising boater can also drift with a fly. This is similar to slow-trolling with a fly rod or a bubble and fly combo tied to a spinning outfit, but without the use of power. Tie a fly directly to monofilament providing it is 2 to 4 pound test. Otherwise, a light leader is recommended. Dry flies, wet flies, streamers and even nymphs are all possible choices for this form of drift fishing. This method can be sensational on high country lakes while drifting out of a small inflatable boat.

Trollin': Cowbells, Lead Core, Downriggers and More

Serious trout fishermen in California have come to realize over the years that trollin' produces BIG fish! I've noted that chuckin' an artificial lure such as a minnow plug from the bank or delicately still-fishing a 'crawler will take its share of trophies. But day in and day out, if you had to depend upon just one method to catch lunker trout—trolling off shore would be your best bet.

Proper Trolling Tackle

Since most recreational trouters in the Golden State depend upon either spinning or closed-face push-button reels, let's consider for a moment how to troll with this tackle.

First, I would recommend scaling up in line size if you want to use spinning gear for trolling. If you purchase a spinning reel that comes with an additional spool, leave one spool filled with 4 pound mono for light lures, free-casting, or top-line trolling (more on this later). Fill the other spool with either 6 or 8 pound mono for dragging bigger lures and/or a lake trolling blade setup. (You will usually use a lighter leader of 6 pound mono behind the blades.)

However, if you only own one reel, or have a push-button model with nonchangeable spools, stay with 6 pound test for general all-purpose trolling. Lighter 2 to 4 pound test which you may have been using for smaller trout or ultralight presentations simply won't continuously withstand the impact, stretch, and shock should a bigger trout strike on the troll. Your basic 6 to 7 foot light to medium action spinning or spincast rods will suffice for most trolling applications here in California.

I would also recommend that if you are really serious about your troutin' and want to approach trolling from a more sophisticated angle, by all means invest in a modestly priced baitcasting rod and reel. The baitcaster features a level wind mechanism that automatically lays the line evenly along the spool upon the retrieve.

Monofilament lines have a tendency to twist as they uncoil off the spin or spincast spools when they are combined with a lure that is made to revolve. This effect is dramatically minimized with a baitcasting reel since the line is not coiled around a stationary spool and instead is neatly laid onto a revolving spool.

Baitcasting reels also have one other commendable feature that is worth considering—a star drag system. The star drag (so termed because of the star-like wheel used to adjust the tension) is much smoother and more precise than drags found on even the best spinning reels. This allows you to make very fine adjustments and settings with the baitcaster. This can be particularly advantageous using lighter 6 to 8 pound mono to play out lunker trout.

These lightweight level wind reels are made from either graphite or anodized aluminum frames. The best come with either graphite bushings or stainless steel ball bearings. They hold a lot of line and have a fast 5:1 (or faster) retrieve ratio. The higher gear ratio is another nice feature to consider. This is especially true if you want to quickly reel in a lot of line when you are trolling far behind the boat.

Quality baitcasting reels are usually more expensive than better spinning or push-button models. However, they are built with considerable strength and precision and will last many years with minimal maintenance. They are clearly worth the investment.

As for a matching rod, my preference would be to opt for a medium action, 5 1/2 to 6 foot single-piece baitcasting model. I like the single-piece blank because it is stronger than a ferruled rod. I feel more confident with this extra-strong construction in fighting a big fish. Also, sometimes two-piece models have a tendency to twist or turn at the ferrule, especially with the amount of torque and pressure which is constantly exerted during the troll.

For serious trolling, it won't make that much difference whether you select a fiberglass or a more expensive graphite baitcasting rod. If you want a more versatile outfit that you can also use for freshwater bassin', purchase the lighter, more sensitive graphite blank.

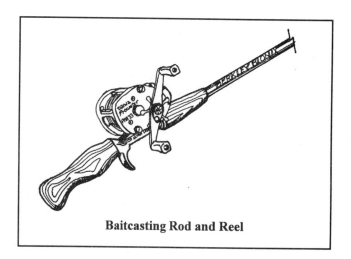

Baitcasting Rod and Reel

Where to Troll and What Patterns to Use

Quite often novice anglers make the mistake of conceptualizing trolling as a random approach. They take a quick glance at a particular trout lake as they leave the boat dock, figuring, "It all looks the same. Anywhere is a good place to start." In reality, accomplished trollers employ a very scientific game plan as they set out to fish a lake. As with shore fishing, there are some very key areas to look for as potentially good trolling water in order to increase your probability of tying into some trout.

Any drop-off or ledge characterized by darker water color has to be considered as a prime trolling target. Often these ledges signal the presence of an underwater canyon, old creek channel, or river bed. Trout will suspend and feed both along the edge and in the center of such drop-offs.

The outer fringe of weed lines can also be very productive for trollers, particularly in the early morning hours. More active fish will play hide 'n seek in this cover and will be on the alert for any tempting prey passing near the edge of the weeds.

Outside points, the facings of rocky or concrete dams, and areas that are known to have submerged underwater springs are also good possible trolling areas. Similarly, the water near any feeder streams that dump water into a lake are also viable trout-holding spots awaiting the patient troller.

One of my favorite spots to troll, which is often overlooked by anglers staying more to the center of the lake, is the mouth of a sheltered cover or bay. This location can be "red hot" with trolled bait or lures, especially in the wind. The combination of wind and wave action blows a lot of insects and bait fish back into these coves so the trout often "stack up" waiting for an easy meal.

Just as it is important to remain fairly mobile while tossing lures or bait from the bank, trolling patterns should also be varied. Too often recreational anglers get into a rut by trolling back and forth through the same area, with the same baits, at the same speeds.

Sometimes by zigzagging or trolling in a figure "S" route, a lot of needed action can be imparted to your troll. Remember what I said about lure presentation and how bait fish swim in erratic motions. This should hold true for your trolled bait, too. With an "S" pattern, as the boat turns inside, lure action decreases in speed due to the greater slack in the line. But as the boat moves through the curve and pulls towards the outside, the line tightens and lure action increases. Quite often, this is all it takes to get the trout excited into striking the trolled offering.

You can also add some twitches with the rod tip as the bait is being trolled. As noted, this can be very effective with minnow-style plugs. Similarly, you can occasion-

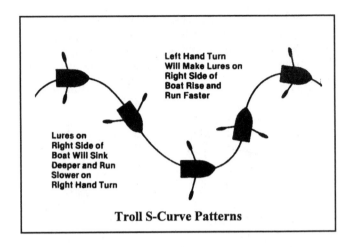

Left Hand Turn Will Make Lures on Right Side of Boat Rise and Run Faster

Lures on Right Side of Boat Will Sink Deeper and Run Slower on Right Hand Turn

Troll S-Curve Patterns

ally move the boat with a few quick bursts of speed, then slow down. This gives the trolled bait the illusion of a frantic bait fish trying to flee. You can employ this particular technique regardless of whether your craft is powered by a gas motor, an electric trolling motor, or even with oars or paddles.

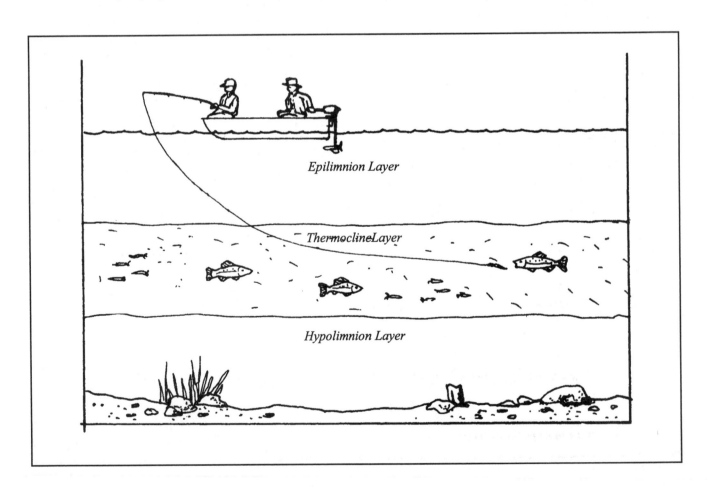

Epilimnion Layer

ThermoclineLayer

Hypolimnion Layer

Finally, it is also important to note that most of our lakes are divided into primarily three layers from spring through fall. The uppermost (epilimnion) and lowermost (hypolimnion) are the most devoid of aquatic life. So always try to troll your baits through the thermocline which stratifies at 15 to 50 foot depths.

The thermocline layer has the greatest concentration of food sources, particularly in terms of forage fish, and contains the highest oxygen levels. Keep this fact in mind to avoid trolling in extraneous "dead water" that is either too shallow or too deep extending beyond the thermocline.

In this next section I want to focus in greater detail on some of the primary trolling techniques that are used for California troutin'. Let's start by examining the simplest of all: flat or top-lining.

Flat-Lining

This type of trolling requires very little in the way of equipment changes. The same spinning or spincast outfit used for casting lures or bait will suffice for flat-lining. Although here again, a lightweight baitcasting rig can readily minimize line twist while providing a superior drag system. In either case, scale down to 4 to 6 pound mono as a good all-around line weight.

With flat-lining, you will be trolling without the help of flasher blades (also known as "lake trolls"). The object is to let out about 50 to 100 feet of line with a favorite lure tied on directly to the light mono. The more line you let out, the deeper the lure will go. But remember, also, the more you let out, the greater the drag or resistance will be through the water. This makes for more difficult hook sets. Also consider adding a small, quality ball-bearing swivel about 36 inches above the lure to minimize line twist.

Most anglers will flat-line not much more than a few feet below the surface, looking for exceptionally aggressive dawn or early evening trout. However, consider adding a variety of weights to your flat-line rig to make the lure travel at deeper levels during the rest of the day.

You can affix a Bead Chain torpedo or keel weight about 18 inches above the lure to add a little more depth. Sometimes a 1/2 to 3/4 ounce sliding egg sinker butted with a snap swivel ahead of 24 inches of leader line will also work quite well. With very tiny spoons or spinners in the 1/32 or 1/16 ounce range just crimp on a medium-sized lead shot about 24 to 30 inches above the lure for extra depth without hurting the little lure's action.

Another option available to flat-liners if they want to drag a lure deeper without getting involved in a lot of paraphernalia is to use a Troll Ease rudder. This handy little device is a rudder or keel constructed out of a wire frame. You can conveniently adjust the necessary weight for the Troll Ease by adding or subtracting egg sinkers that slide onto the frame. Use a 6 pound leader line behind the rudder with your choice of spoons or spinners.

There are actually some very specialized spoons that are so light and thin that they are sold primarily for trolling. The Needlefish and the Triple Teazer dance erratically through the water when pulled on a slow, flat-line troll with 6 pound mono. Both of these thin bladed spoons produce absolutely remarkable results all season long when trolled for California trout. The whole secret to the success of these two lures is to troll them very S-L-O-W-L-Y.

The Needlefish and the Triple Teazer are made with a single hook instead of the traditional treble hook. Some anglers balk at buying a spoon with only this single hook. Ironically, you may actually get better hooking power from this configuration over a treble hook. This is because the single hook allows you to apply greater lever-

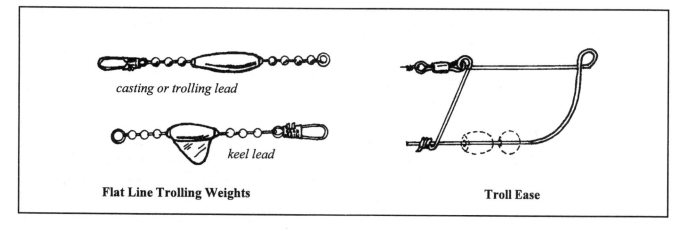

casting or trolling lead

keel lead

Flat Line Trolling Weights

Troll Ease

age on the fish without having the trout throw the lure — as often happens with a treble hook. Also, these spoons are so incredibly light that a treble hook would restrict the action too much.

Here is another little tip: take about half of a night-crawler and thread it onto these single-hook spoons. This extra amount of scent and attraction can produce fantastic action, again on a flat-line troll! The best colors to use in these super thin spoons are chrome, bikini, rainbow trout, frog, perch, and black scale.

Other viable lures to use when flat-lining include almost any of the popular in-line spinners and a variety of spoons such as the Krocadile, Phoebe, Z-Ray, Lil' Cleo, or Super Duper. As previously mentioned, those lightweight banana plugs such as the Flatfish or Kwikfish lures also excel as flat-line offerings.

Diving Planes

Luhr-Jensen's Pink Lady and the Les Davis Deep Six are two popular diving planes used for deep trolling. Although these are also affixed directly to monofilament line, they simply dive too deeply to be categorized as a flat-line technique. These devices allow the angler to fish fairly deep but without having to drag heavy sinkers as with downriggers or sinker-release rigs.

The planers themselves are made from plastic and weigh just a few ounces. Yet, they can take a lure down to over 100 foot depths, which is otherwise only possible by using a pound or two of lead.

Diving planes like these are relatively simple to use. You tie your main line to the planer. Then tie a leader line to the device with a lure attached to the other end. After the planer is cocked or "loaded," it is tilted at such an angle that it will dramatically dig down into the water with its pronounced diving lip.

The device automatically trips out of the diving angle when a trout strikes and planes to the surface. This permits the fisherman to fight the fish with minimal resistance from the light plastic planer.

For general troutin', the smaller planers are recommended. Because of the tremendous drag and stretch on the line generated from the deep-diving effect, gear up and use heavier 10 to 15 pound line to pull the planer along with a little stiffer rod. Your leader material should remain about 6 pound test.

If you want to really get "scientific" in using a planer, add a Grizzly Line Counter to your rod. This nifty little measuring device will actually tell you how much line

you have out when the trout strikes. By using this monitor, you can repeatedly let out the same amount of line in between fish to guarantee that the lure remains in the strike zone.

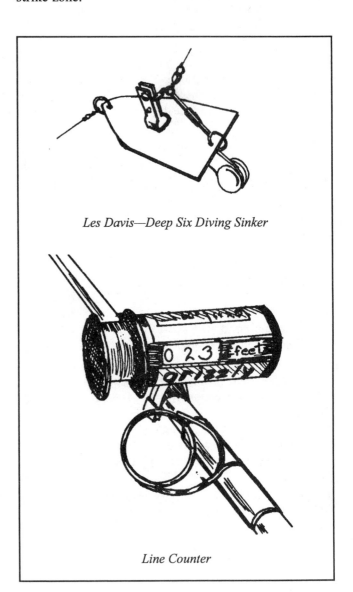

Les Davis—Deep Six Diving Sinker

Line Counter

Lake Trolls

These lures are made up of a series of brightly polished reflective blades connected in tandem by a strand of lightweight wire. Lake trolls are made to imitate a school of trout feeding on forage minnows.

Lake troll blades must be fished in conjunction with bait, a lure, or a lure tipped with bait. These are followed by a 6 to 8 pound test leader, 18 to 36 inches in length.

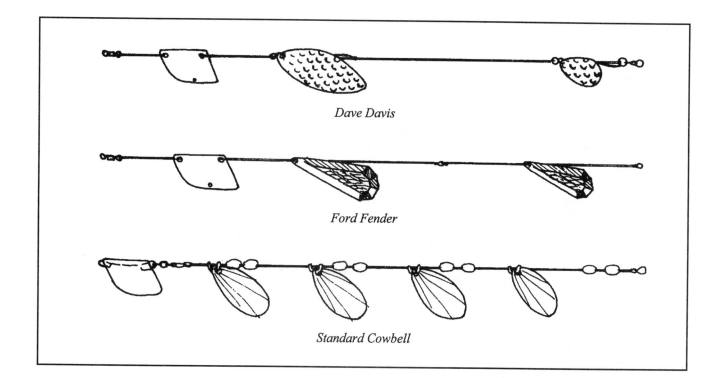

Dave Davis

Ford Fender

Standard Cowbell

Your main line can actually range from 6 to 15 pound test, since the trout will key in on the lighter leader material.

Some trout fishermen refer to lake trolls as "cowbells." This is a catch-all term which is technically incorrect. Cowbells are only one generic type of lake troll system. Other popular designs include the Dave Davis, Bolo, and Ford Fender models. Each of these styles have unique blade configurations that have application to some lake conditions, but not to others—just like any other artificial baits.

Anatomy of Lake Trolls: The first major component to consider in selecting a lake troll is the shape of the blade. Rounded blades such as those found in Cowbells, swing slowly with a wide tracking movement. Narrower, willowleaf-style blades spin in a tighter pattern and are best suited when a faster troll is desired.

Compared to the rounded models, the narrower bladed rigs put out considerable vibration. The Bolo-style blade

generates the best sonic effects and would be a good choice for darker, murky water.

Next, examine the size of the blades. Pick the larger blades for trolling on deep, big lakes. Select a much smaller set of blades for little impoundments or clear, high elevation lakes. The more blades that come with a troll, the deeper it will work. Use trolls with fewer blades for shallow, clear lakes.

For dark water, use blades in a brass or copper finish or what is termed a brass and nickel combination. In clear water conditions, switch to either nickel, prism, flect-o-lite, or hammered finishes. It is best to carry at least two or three different blade combinations in your tackle box to accommodate diverse conditions.

Sometimes you will need to use a "snubber" to absorb the shock and avoid having the leader break when you drag a lake troll rig. A trolling snubber is basically a piece of surgical tubing with a swivel at each end. Inside the

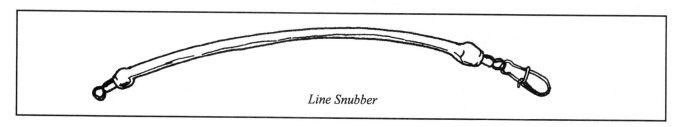

Line Snubber

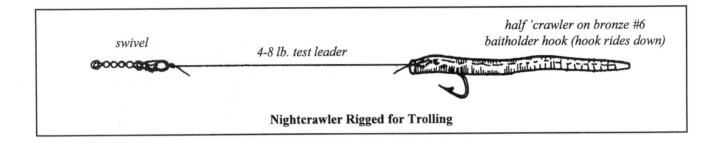

swivel   *4-8 lb. test leader*   *half 'crawler on bronze #6*
baitholder hook (hook rides down)

Nightcrawler Rigged for Trolling

tubing is a heavier, coiled line. When the trout strikes the offering, the line stretches out to absorb the impact.

For most put'n take lakes featuring hatchery trout rarely exceeding 2 to 3 pounds, a snubber will not be essential. However, in fishing a trophy lake with bigger 'bows and browns, tie on the snubber as extra "insurance" if you decide to use a lake troll combination.

After you have selected the proper set of attractor blades, the next thing to consider is what to troll behind them, if I had to pick one single offering that is productive under a wide variety of conditions, it would be a chunk of nightcrawler laced on a baitholder hook, tied to about 24 to 36 inches of 6 pound leader material. Interestingly, the key here is to use about a half section of the 'crawler. But more importantly, here is the inside scoop on how to really make this bait work: the half 'crawler section must be carefully threaded onto the bronze #6 or #8 hook, covering the shank with the barb and then exposing it as you push it through the worm.

When the nightcrawler is hooked in this manner, it will seductively wiggle through the water behind the flashing blades. Trout go crazy over this presentation! In contrast, if you use a whole 'crawler, it seems to either intimidate the fish or sometimes just produce "short strikers." Similarly, if you thread the 'crawler into a "gob," hooking it many times, much of that sensuous action is lost.

Another little trick is to put a few drops of Berkley Strike on the nightcrawler and even on the blades themselves. This strike stimulant compound slowly dissolves in the water and will actually leave a "vapor trail" around the bait. This often precedes strikes when the trout simply seem to be in an otherwise non-feeding mood.

Small spinners and wobbling spoons will also work trolled behind attractor blades. The Needlefish in particular seems to consistently get bit when combined with a set of lake trolls. Again, add a nightcrawler trailer onto the Needlefish for "double coverage." A six pound test

monofilament leader will also be very adequate with this setup.

Another interesting option you might want to try some time with a lake troll is to drag a large streamer fly behind the flashing blades. Some excellent patterns to use include the Wooly Worm, Wooly Booger, Girdle Bug, Hornburg, Muddler, and Joe's 'Hopper.

More on Fly Trolling

On the above note, consider expanding your repertoire to include other ways to troll a wet or dry fly. (I'll discuss the principles of traditional fly fishing in a separate chapter.) With just a spinning or spincast outfit, you can actually take some pretty nice trout by slow-trolling a variety of flies.

Some anglers will tie a fly—either wet or dry—directly onto 2 to 4 pound monofilament. Then they will strip off a good 40 to 80 feet of line by hand since the fly weighs practically nothing and therefore can't be cast. The trick is to very lazily slow-troll the fly just under the surface. Traditional dry and wet fly patterns, streamers, and nymphs can all be effective at times.

Another variation is to slow-troll with the versatile bubble-and-fly combination previously discussed. I want to emphasize that the boat must really be slowed down to troll flies in this fashion.

Conventional fly-fishing gear with a floating line and a 7 to 8 foot dry fly action rod is even better and, I feel, more sporting with this unique trolling tactic. The floating line will accommodate all styles of flies—even those meant to be fished "wet." Most strikes will occur just at sub-surface depths and the floating line is easy to monitor.

Fly-trolling can be a dynamite approach when fishing out of small inflatable boats or canoes on high elevation lakes. Either oars or paddles will provide you with ample speed to properly fish flies in this way. Furthermore, you do not have to be an accomplished fly fisherman to fish flies in a trolling situation. This is a remarkably easy technique, but it is seldom used by most recreational anglers in the Golden State.

Lead-Core Trolling

One trolling strategy that has gained wider popularity in the past few years has been to use lead-core line, especially during the warmer months. Using lead core is a somewhat technical type of fishing that requires its own unique tackle program.

Lead core is basically a linen-like line with a metal wire core. It was designed solely for the purpose of trolling—and dragging the lure deep. Every 10 yards of lead core is color coded in a different shade. Anglers often refer to "how many colors" they are fishing while trolling this specialized line.

This kind of line is characteristically much, much thicker in diameter than conventional monofilament. It is sold in 12, 18, or 27 pound test spools by such popular manufacturers as Izorline and Gudebrod. I strongly recommend purchasing 18 pound lead core for most California conditions. The lighter, 12 pound version just won't sink fast enough. In contrast, the 18 pound test has a larger lead core in the center, yet with approximately the same amount of fabric braid as the lighter 12 pound test. Hence, it sinks much faster.

The heavier, 27 pound test is simply too large in diameter, requiring a bigger conventional reel just to store 100 yards. This is the basic amount required for most lead-core fishing in the Golden State.

Because all lead-core line is bulkier than monofilament, you will need to use a casting reel with a fairly large spool capacity just to house the bare minimum 100 yards of 18 pound test. Most veteran lead-core fishermen resort to using a light-to-medium saltwater rig for this rather esoteric style of troutin'. The Penn #209 reel with the convenient level wind feature is a popular favorite. More and more anglers are taking this lead-core technology seriously and are investing in better, lighter reels with sophisticated drag mechanisms used to fight double-digit weight rainbows, browns or mackinaws that might be nailed with this setup. Penn now has an entire series of light graphite frame level-wind reels with stainless steel components to cater to the hard-core, lead-core trouter. The new Penn 310GT and 320GT graphite frame models also have the important level-wind feature which is essential for using 200 yards of lead-core line. Other

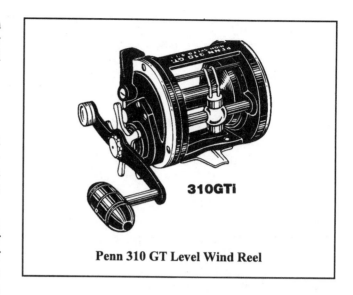

Penn 310 GT Level Wind Reel

scaled-down saltwater reels made by Daiwa, Shimano, and Penn without the level wind device will also suffice. Make certain they are matched with the deeper, stronger metal spool instead of one made of plastic.

Some lead-core aficionados prefer shorter 5 1/2 to 6 1/2 foot popping rods or live bait (anchovy) sticks primarily in one-piece blanks. Others like a lengthier rod with a softer tip in 7 to 8 foot models. These are slightly stiffer than the whippier, more parabolic steelhead rods and were designed for lead core or downrigger trolling.

Some trollers feel that the longer rod more easily keeps the line and lure out of the boat's wake.

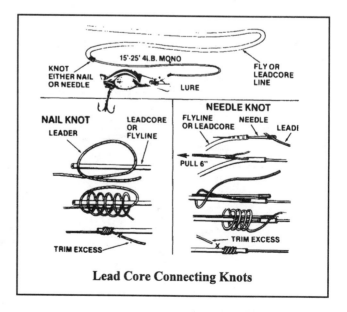

Lead Core Connecting Knots

Most California anglers will typically troll about 6 or 7 colors, or about 70 yards of lead-core line. Tie a 6 pound mono leader about three feet in length, to the lead core with either a nail knot, or more conveniently, to a barrel swivel. On the other end of the leader line, troll any of the popular spoons, spinners, or even minnow or banana plugs. Many local trouters prefer either the Needlefish or the Triple Teazer as their "bread'n butter" lead-core lure.

I might note that the strike with lead-core line is actually quite pronounced. This is because there is very little stretch with this type of line and every bit of action is transmitted through the rod. After you feel the trout is hooked, it is best to retrieve the lead core in an even steady fashion. Invariably, the trout will plane to the surface. Also remember that you must have your star drag set more closely to the breaking test of the leader (i.e. 6 pound test) rather than to the lead core itself (i.e. 18 pound test).

For many anglers living in California where the waters warm quickly, lead-core trolling has virtually saved the day on many mid-season outings when the trout moved to deeper strike zones. There isn't anything very complicated to using this technique and it is definitely worth considering as a secondary approach when the water warms.

Downriggers

In contrast to past years, you will now see more and more fishermen using downriggers. This takes deep trolling one step beyond lead-core line. The idea of using downriggers for Western trout was actually borrowed from commercial and sport boats fishing salmon in the Pacific Northwest.

From midsummer through early fall, many California lakes have surface water temperatures soaring to over 70°. Trout must seek the more comfortable thermocline usually found somewhere between 25 and 50 feet. A downrigger will conveniently bring your trolled offering down to that strata.

Many novice anglers balk at using a downrigger for two reasons. First, all the machinery appears to be overly technical which scares off a lot of people. Second, that 3 to 7 pound sinker just doesn't seem too sporting to a lot of trouters. But, let's "debunk" some of the misconceptions that surround this key trolling method.

To begin with, the setup itself is not that complicated to understand. Your selection of trolling baits (e.g. a lure or lake troll combo) is tied directly to your main monofilament line coming off your spin, spincast, or baitcasting reel. The mono is then clipped to a line release located near the heavy sinker.

As the line is let out, the sinker is also dropped down to the desired depth. The sinker itself is tied to a heavy wire cable that runs along a pulley, extending out on a metal boom and coiled on a downrigger wheel.

Quality units will also have a monitoring device that measures how deep the heavy sinker is riding. When the trout strikes the lure or bait, the mono releases from the line clip and you fight the fish directly on the monofilament. Many anglers make the mistake of thinking that

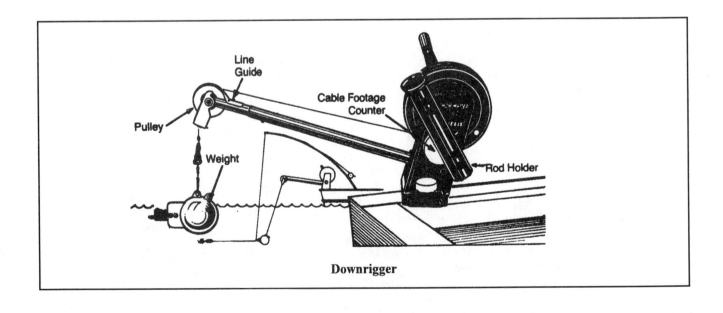

Downrigger

Penn Downrigger

you have to play the fish with that magnum-sized weight being dragged at the same time.

To emphasize, the sinker remains stationary as the mono is released from it upon the strike. So, in contrast to using a diving plane, adding weights, or pulling lead-core line, downriggers allow the angler to actually fight the fish without all this encumbrance while still trolling deep.

After the trout is hooked, the trolling weight and cable are cranked up (either by hand or electrically on the more expensive models) onto the wheel. By examining the line monitor, you can then drop the sinker down to precisely the same depth as where the previous strike occurred.

Veteran downrigger fishermen will use this machinery in conjunction with electronic fish finders. The electronics help them to find the depth that the trout are holding and the downrigger then makes it possible to fish that depth. This unique trolling methodology has proven to be productive on a variety of trout species including browns, brookies, and 'bows.

Technically speaking, just about any type of rod or reel can be used with a downrigger. Many anglers feel most comfortable with a medium action blank that will not bend so easily at the tip while it is in the rod holder. But still others enjoy the thrill of hooking trout deep and playing them on an ultralight outfit which will also work with a downrigger.

Almost any of the popular spoons, spinners, or plugs can be trolled with a downrigger. Experiment a little should you decide to install a downrigger on your boat. Quite often trout will be seeing a lure for the first time in a deep strike zone because of the downrigger technique. For this reason you might consider selecting slightly larger lures. Big fish will be less wary at deeper depths and they will definitely strike a larger bait.

Other "Exotic" Trolling Rigs

There are numerous other types of trolling schemes derived from combining two or more conventional presentations. For example, take a popular trout spoon and remove the treble hook, leaving the split ring. Add a small bearing swivel to the split ring. Run anywhere from 18 to 24 inches of leader behind it and tie on a smaller spoon (with treble hook attached). This combination can be trolled very slowly and has the appearance of a larger fish being trailed by a smaller minnow.

A similar effect can be obtained by using a diving plug instead of a bigger spoon. Remove the treble hooks from a larger banana plug such as the Fishback and run a leader line behind it. Again, attach a small spoon to the leader.

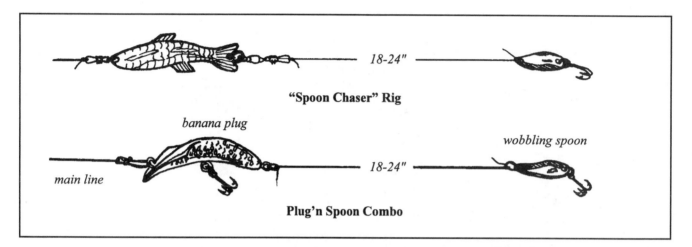

"Spoon Chaser" Rig

banana plug

wobbling spoon

main line

18-24"

Plug'n Spoon Combo

The thumping action of the plug can often "call in" trout to investigate. They simply can't resist the little fluttering spoon slowly drifting by.

One other method is to use a three-way swivel and troll two different lures at the same time. The important thing is to keep the leader lines different lengths to avoid crisscrossing or tangles. A favorite combination is to use a minnow plug on the longer, lower dropper leader such as the Rapala CD-7. Then tie a small spoon like a Phoebe or a shorter leader to ride above it. This gives the overall appearance of a smaller game fish chasing a tiny minnow.

There are endless other "exotic" combinations that you can experiment with on your own. Sometimes these trolling rigs can be the "hot ticket" after the trout have been bombarded with more traditional setups!

Trolling for Kokes—A Special Case

Kokanee, or landlocked sockeye salmon, present a special case for inland trolling. These fish have been planted

only in selected lakes including Camanche, Bullard's Bar, Pardee, Bucks, Whiskeytown, and Huntington. Additional lakes may be included for future programs as the popularity of this fishery grows.

Kokes do not grow as large as most other trout found in flatland impoundments. They average about 8 to 20 inches in length. These members of the salmonid family feed more on plankton than insects, nymphs, or bait fish minnows. When they do feed on such natural offerings, they will usually select smaller samples. Hence, the first thing to consider in trolling for Kokanees is to scale down in lure size, presenting nothing more than an inch in length.

Kokes prefer water temperatures of 50 degrees or less, orienting near the bottom, in deep channels or around underwater springs. Trolling is considered by far the best method for catching these fish since it allows the angler to cover a lot of deep territory. Weighted lines (e.g., Troll Ease rigs or downriggers), deep planers, and lead core are the best options for tying into some quality Kokes.

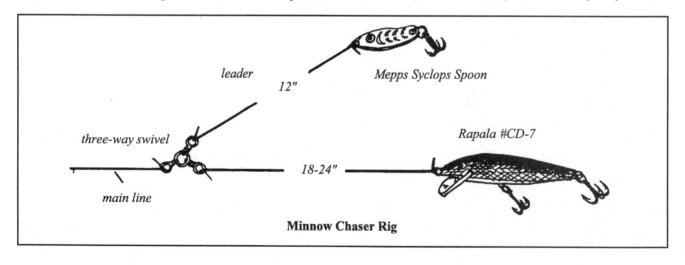

leader

12"

Mepps Syclops Spoon

three-way swivel

Rapala #CD-7

main line

18-24"

Minnow Chaser Rig

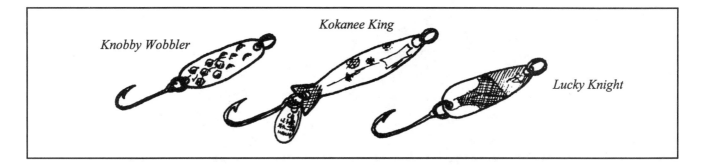

Knobby Wobbler

Kokanee King

Lucky Knight

However, you can sometimes flat-line troll Kokanee in the spring and fall months when they come nearer to the surface during the spawning period.

Veteran Koke fishermen have found these little game fish to historically respond to some very precise color combinations as far as artificial lures are concerned. These include: pearl, pearl with fluorescent red, rainbow, and nickel with a red head. Popular lures for California Kokanees include the Red Magic, Super Duper, Nobby Wobbler, Needlefish, Kokanee Killer, Teazer, and Kastmaster.

One hot tip is to put a small piece of red worm, nightcrawler, or even a single kernel of white corn onto a small spoon or spinner as a trailer. Interestingly, sometimes a nice, firm red salmon egg or a piece of red yarn similarly affixed will also work as a lure trailer for Kokes. Because these fish have super sensitive mouths, most expert Kokanee anglers recommend using a snubber for the best hook set. Also these are touchy scrappers so stay with slightly longer 4 to 8 pound leaders up to four feet in length.

Other Trolling Tips

To round out this chapter here are a few other little tips that will lead to more productive days trolling. First, use bigger trolling lures in the fall when the natural bait fish in the lake are largest.

Second, don't hesitate to troll FAST as an alternative to a slow-troll approach. It is estimated that bait fish swim one mile per hour per inch of length. Therefore, you can troll a 6 inch minnow plug up to 6 mph. Lunker trout will aggressively bushwhack a big, moving lure like this. By trolling fast there will also be fewer misses and short strikes. When a trout decides to eat a lure on a fast troll he crunches it hard!

Finally, if it's big browns you're after, remember this species is pretty wary in big reservoirs. Thus, let out a good 75 to 100 feet of line to keep some distance between you and the touchier brown trout.

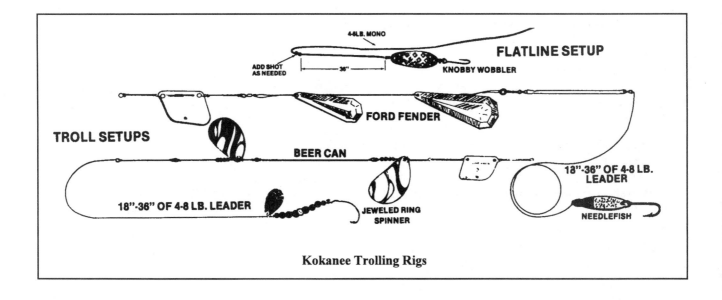

4-6LB. MONO

FLATLINE SETUP

ADD SHOT AS NEEDED

36"

KNOBBY WOBBLER

TROLL SETUPS

FORD FENDER

BEER CAN

18"-36" OF 4-8 LB. LEADER

18"-36" OF 4-8 LB. LEADER

JEWELED RING SPINNER

NEEDLEFISH

Kokanee Trolling Rigs

Stream Fishin': Reading Tailouts, Whitewater and Quiet Pools

Although many weekend anglers try their luck at fishing trout in California's rivers, streams, and creeks, only the most knowledgeable learn how to consistently catch quality trout from these waters. It's not overly difficult to catch planters, but trying to land a trophy brown or a chunky 'bow from one of these rivers or streams is another story.

Whether you prefer spinning or more traditional fly fishing gear, it is essential to know how to "read" a stream in order to have a halfway decent chance at tying into one of these bigger trout. There is much less luck involved in fishing this type of water in contrast to a lake or pond.

Aquatic life in this underwater world tends to move quickly—both predator and prey alike. Thus, it is important to make precise casts with precise offerings to a precise location.

Differences Between Lake and Stream Environments

The fundamental feature that separates the "environmental picture" of a stream from that of a lake is the presence of current. In lakes and ponds nutrients ranging from microscopic life to larger crustaceans and forage bait fish filter down from the surface. This "fallout" of food inevitably results in trout orienting toward the lake bottom. (This of course is assuming that proper temperature and oxygen levels are also established at that depth.)

Crawling or swimming forage such as crayfish or threadfin shad found in lakes do not have to fight current. Crayfish can be found all over the lake as long as there is some underwater structure with access to the bank. Similarly, schools of minnows can stratify through different depths without the major effect of current.

In rivers the moving current pushes nutrients downstream. These food sources can be collected or funneled into deeper, quieter pools where they then settle down to the bottom. This is one reason why pools are key fish-holding spots in a river or stream.

In this environment, small sculpin and minnows will seek sanctuary among rocks and boulders. Crayfish, freshwater clams, and snails will be found in calmer deeper pools and shallower backwater areas. There is also an assortment of insects whose larvae assume an aquatic form during this stage of metamorphosis. These include mayflies, caddisflies, damselflies, dragonflies, and stoneflies. These larvae hatch from the bottom and float to the surface. These, combined with other terrestrial and flying insects that have landed in the water, comprise "drift," another source of food for river trout.

It is essential for the trout fisherman working a stream to understand where such natural food sources will be found. He or she should then try to use either bait, artificial lures or flies to match this selection of prey both in terms of size and coloration as well as their natural movements through the water.

Climate also affects the stream ecology differently than it does lakes or ponds. For instance, in winter through early spring, some streams have water temperatures falling into the mid-30 range. As cold-blooded creatures, trout demonstrate a certain metabolic lethargy in super cold water like this. Don't expect the fish to swim very far to attack your bait or lure during the colder periods of the year. The trout will not expend much energy to hunt down food and fight the current at this time. Under these conditions, the wise trouter won't look for fish in rushing water, turbulent pools, swift riffles, rapids, or swirling eddies.

Instead, he will focus his attention on places in the steam where the trout will have to exhaust the least amount of energy. He will try slower-moving water, undercuts near the bank, brush, logs, boulders, and rocks: locations where the trout can find winter solace near the bottom and out of the fast current. Put simply, look for early season trout in water that is both slow and deep. Too often, the recreational angler makes the mistake of stalking the opening day trout in the swifter moving water. Remember—these fish are coming out of the winter thaw and want that slower current they can catch up with.

Similarly, don't make the error of simply grinding your lure or fly across the surface. This may work well for fish later in the season. But for winter and early spring, trout will orient primarily to the deeper bottom dwelling areas of the stream. Therefore, you will have to utilize lures, baits, and presentations that will be suitable for working this deeper, slow-moving water.

From late spring through mid-fall, the trout will move into faster current. It is in these riffles that the fish will find the richer oxygenated water necessary to sustain them in the hotter months. The roily, high muddy waters of the early season have now subsided and California's rivers, streams, and creeks are typically much clearer by summertime. This however means that the trout will now be touchier both because of water clarity and increased angling pressure.

By fall, water levels will typically be low. Trout will be very wary so be cautious in your approach into the water. Make the extra effort to minimize any excessive "splash" as your bait or lures enter the water. There will be fewer hatchery trout left in the fall as stocking programs now come to a standstill. Bigger browns and rainbows are now more accessible as they prepare to make a final, aggressive feeding foray before the winter cold arrives. Evening hours toward dusk will be your best time to fish for big river browns.

On this note, let's examine in greater detail how to "read" a stream to increase your odds of catching greater numbers of quality fish from these waters.

Looking for Stream "Hot Spots"

There are a number of key fish-holding areas to look for in approaching a river or stream. Some are very obvious, natural-looking "hot spots," others are more subtle. Ironically, some of the best places are where you initially make contact with a stream. For example, there are numerous bridges and overpasses that allow you to drive over the water.

Many anglers pull off to the side of the highway adjacent to these structures and hike down to the water. Quite often the bridge pilings have been seated in deeper water. These are natural or man-made pools where bigger trout may be found. The bridge and the concrete or wooden pilings themselves provide considerable shade and are also excellent possibilities.

Whether you prefer to wade or fish from the shore, some of the best water may be lying right at your feet as you prepare to fish the stream. Be sensitive as you walk toward the water so as to not spook the fish. Check to see if there is some type of overhanging brush, shady trees, larger rocks, boulders, or major undercuts to the bank. These could all be promising spots that you don't want to spoil by simply plunging into the water.

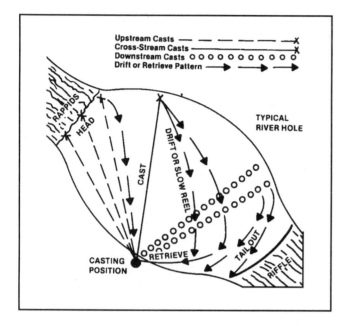

Upstream Casts — — — — — — x
Cross-Stream Casts ————————— x
Downstream Casts o o o o o o o o o o o
Drift or Retrieve Pattern → → → →

RAPIDS

HEAD

TYPICAL
RIVER HOLE

CAST

DRIFT OR SLOW REEL

RETRIEVE

TAILOUT

RIFFLE

CASTING
POSITION

As a matter of fact, if you are in waders, consider fishing the water close to the bank from the shore before entering the stream. Veteran stream and river fishermen will tell you time after time that some of the largest trout caught during the season are nailed right next to the bank. All of the cover and obstructions provide excellent hiding spots for lunker-class browns, brookies, and 'bows!

You might consider using a pair of binoculars to scope out a stream from above the bank. Occasionally it is possible to actually see large trout—especially browns —through field glasses. Sometimes it is best to leave these larger fish until evening when they will be less wary. Brown trout are very territorial and larger specimens will often remain near their particular haunts throughout the day.

Similarly, a good pair of polarized sunglasses can be an indispensable aid in reading a stream, particularly under bright, sunny conditions. The polarization effect cuts down the glare from the water and allows you to actually see fish puddling near the surface or lying in clearer pools and shallower spots. There are many other features to look for as potentially good areas even if you can't see any trout milling around.

Far too often, the recreational angler takes the "easy way out," so to speak, when it comes to sizing up a river or stream. They play it "safe" and primarily stay with locations that have good, easy-walking access.

Sometimes the more difficult hard-to-get-to spots hold the largest trout to be found in the stream. You may

have to do some walking upstream, for example, to find a shallow place to cross in order to fish that good-looking area back down stream.

Similarly, by carefully maneuvering down a steep bank—one step at a time—you may get to a pool or a riffle that the average weekender feels simply isn't worth the effort. Believe it or not, some of the most industrious trout fishermen will actually approach a small creek or stream on their knees or bellies so as to not spook off ultra-wary fish.

Trout feed head-first into the current most of the time. That is to say, they will face upstream in the direction the food is flowing in order to intercept it. But there are exceptions to this rule. In some cases, trout can find calm or "slack" water that is actually downstream.

Technically then, the fish could be working downstream while still facing the current when feeding in these backwashes, pools, or eddies. Thus, the best technique overall is to cast in an upstream direction and let your offering drift naturally in the current.

Pools are a major location on a stream to find big trout. This is especially true at the top of the pool where the water is deepest and most turbulent. These are prime conditions for trophy fish. The base of a waterfall with the richly oxygenated water in the resulting deep pool is similarly a choice hot spot to consider for lunker trout.

Along with the more obvious spots, such as pools, eddies, rock, undercuts, and shady banks, calm backwashes (tailouts) are still another major fish-holding area on a river or stream. You will find this "whitewater" at the tail end of the riffles forming a hole or a little pocket where the stream becomes shallower. This is also where the current really begins to pick up speed. A lot of natural food gets trapped in these tailouts and many of the major species of trout will be found here.

Tailouts have to be fished either upstream or downstream. The water is simply ripping too fast to try to work the area with a cross-current cast. In contrast, sometimes a cast across the current through a large pool is more effective than a typical upstream-to-downstream drift. Here the angler may want to keep the fly, lure, or bait retrieved more through the middle of the pool where the trout may be holding.

In keying in on a pool it is probably best to initially try an upstream cast. Often the trout found in the center of the pool will "spook" quickly if a cast plops right on top of them or the lure or bait is being retrieved across the pool. By throwing above the pool, the offering is allowed to more naturally drift down into it. If nothing happens, then switch to throwing across the pool as an alternate approach.

In reading a stream, the angler may indeed find a potential hot spot but blows his chances by making a hasty presentation. The biggest problem facing the novice—spin or fly fisherman alike—is how to get that lure or bait down deep into those pools, rocks, boulders, undercuts, or eddies. The remedy is simple: fish more upstream under these conditions. This will allow you to gain more control over the lure, fly, or bait and to slow it down in order to sink it deeper.

Here is the secret. Try to angle your cast upstream, slightly off to the side somewhat rather than directly into the current. This gives you more slack or "belly" in the line so that the bait or lure will then tumble a little more slowly and drift closer to the bottom. On a taunt line, the bait lifts too quickly off the bottom, rapidly drifting out of the strike zone.

When you find that stretch or pool of slower water, don't hesitate to try to "slow grind" your fly or lure across the bottom. Only this time, start fancasting across the area to cover as much depth as possible.

Summary

Although I will discuss more precise techniques to fishing a stream with fly or spinning tackle shortly, the angler must first learn to "read" the water before such presentations are attempted. If there is one common error the weekend trouter makes in fishing moving water, it would be overworking the more obvious, best-looking, deeper pools. This is where most recreational anglers will be fishing so these spots really get hammered through the peak of the season.

Spinnin' in Streams: Walk Silent-Fish Deep

Most of us have our first experience stream fishing using a spinning outfit. This type of gear has terrific application for California troutin'! The single most important thing to keep in mind in setting up your tackle for stream fishing is to keep it light. Too often trouters try to use some of the stiffer rods and reels more applicable to big lakes.

Stream trout tend to be smaller in size than those found in reservoirs. As was noted in the previous chapter, our streams and rivers can also run very shallow, with very high water clarity.

Proper Stream Tackle

Simply stated, even in a fast-water environment, trout can be very spooky. The 6 to 8 pound test monofilament you were using to troll for bigger browns on Lake Crowley might be too heavy to, say, catch rainbows on Rush Creek. So, if possible, try to use a lighter, 5 1/2 to 7 foot rod with a little whippier action for most typical stream conditions.

The lighter rods will match better with a 2 to 4 pound test line. This finer diameter monofilament is preferable for streams. The mono will also serve a dual purpose, functioning both as the leader and as the primary line. It is better to fish a stream using the lighter monofilament than to tie knots and use swivels and leader materials since this extra paraphernalia has a tendency to get hung up more in rivers or streams.

The combination of lighter lines and sensitive rods also goes hand-in-hand with small spinners, spoons and plugs suitable as stream offering. Similarly most of the natural baits are best fished in the moving water with minimal, if any weight. This keeps the bait from snagging on the bottom while maintaining the appearance of food naturally flowing with the current. A lightweight spinning combo is the easiest way to present these baits, maximizing both casting distance and sensitivity.

Stalking the Stream

Try to work the stream from the downhill side. Keep low and avoid throwing your shadow on the water. Minimize your casting motion. A quick, tight, and precise pitch or loft is best. An exaggerated motion can spook the trout.

Another rule of thumb is to fish big baits with this tackle early in the season. The trout are hungry following ice out and will definitely strike a large offering such as a nightcrawler, bigger spinner, spoon, or plug. Spin fishermen—even the most novice—can easily toss these larger baits with this equipment.

The best overall presentation with spin tackle is the upstream cast. The bait or lure can then tumble downstream with the current. Turn the reel handle every so often to keep the line a little taunt. It is much easier to detect strikes with the tighter line. Keep in mind that any sudden stop in the drift of the monofilament can signal one of two things: (a) the lure or bait is hung up on the bottom; or (b) there's a trout on! If you feel resistance on the end of the line and it pulls back, make a sharp set. If it's a snag, try to gently shake it loose.

To reiterate once more—and it's crucial to understand this—whether you fish bait or lures with spinning gear, try to let the offering settle somewhat so that it reaches the bottom or is just above it. Sometimes a presentation made on or near the surface will indeed produce. Far too often, the angler makes the mistake of dragging the spinner, spoon, plug, or bait too quickly, well above the deeper spots that hold fish.

Working Baits Downstream

A good maxim to follow when fishing bait in rivers, streams, and creeks is to use only enough weight to get the proper cast and drift. This is very important. Too much weight results in either the bait snagging on the bottom or having the natural drift inhibited. Again, if you can get by tying directly to 2 to 4 pound test line, this will help to minimize any drag that you would otherwise get from a swivel used as a leader link.

The simplest technique with bait fishing a stream is to not use any weight at all. By leaving the bail of your spinning reel open following a mid or upstream cast, the bait can naturally cascade downstream. Since the monofilament weighs practically nothing combined with bait, it will take some practice making even the shortest casts with this method. You may also have to help pay the line out by hand, at least initially, until the current starts to sweep the bait downstream.

Occasionally, I might add, throwing downstream then skittering the bait upstream across the surface can also work. Bigger, more aggressive and hungry 'bows and browns will sometimes strike the bait fished this way. It is as if the trout sense that a tasty morsel is quickly escaping upstream. If the weightless tactic doesn't seem to keep the bait properly in the drift (especially true in very swift flows) then add a small BB shot about 18 inches above the hook. This minuscule weight will surprisingly add quite a bit of casting distance, particularly in the wind.

Use a larger split-shot as needed depending upon the distance and/or depth necessary to keep the bait in the strike zone. Here is another little tip: buy the old-fashioned split-shot that has to be crimped on with pliers. The more recent innovative style has protruding "ears" that allow you to pinch the shot by hand. This type of lead is convenient because it is removable but the little lead ears have a greater tendency to get hung up than the simple, rounded variety.

For faster, more turbulent water, particularly on larger streams and rivers, some anglers prefer to fish bait with a sliding egg sinker. Use the technique described for fishing a basic bait rig when still-fishing in lakes. However, for rivers and streams, use the sliding sinkers in much smaller weights, usually under 1/4 ounce.

If you seem to be hanging up with the egg sinkers, here is another little trick to try: use a bullet weight designed for bass fishing. These cone-shaped sliding sinkers hang up minimally on rocks and brush. They are also available in weights under 1/16 ounce. If you prefer a more stationary sinker without the hassle of a leader line, just crimp down on a bullet weight which is tied directly to the primary line, usually 2 to 4 pound test. Use pliers to crimp the weight about 12 to 24 inches above the hook.

In very swift current, it may be necessary to increase the sinker weight to keep the bait from rapidly sweeping downstream. Another technique is to use a pencil weight. This unique sinker is basically a very soft piece of lead

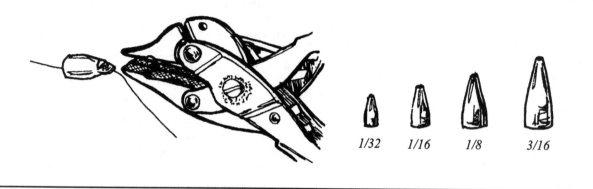

tube similar in appearance to a fat pencil lead. It has a hole drilled through it and can be fished like a sliding weight.

Use a barrel swivel to butt the pencil weight and keep it from sliding any further. Then attach a separate leader line and hook to the other end of the swivel. This is similar to a sliding egg sinker rig used for still-fishing.

Another option is to use the pencil lead attached to a dropper leader tied to a three-way swivel. The shorter dropper leader can be of much lighter line than either the primary line or the other leader with the bait. This way, if the lead gets hung in the rocks while drifting or with a trout on, it will break off from the lighter leader. You can then at least get most of the setup back without retying everything, or you can play the fish out without restriction.

The secret to the pencil weight is its extreme softness. This makes the lead sinker very malleable, bending back and forth as it crashes into the rocks. The extreme thinness of this sinker also permits the weight to slither over and between obstructions in the stream where other sinkers would get snagged.

One other ploy should be considered in fishing deep pools. Believe it or not, you can actually use a small red and white bobber to effectively fish this type of area in the stream. Trout will often stratify or suspend some distance from the bottom in deep, quiet pools. By attaching the tiny bobber 3 to 4 feet above the hook, you can keep the bait "suspended" in the pool. This strategy works well for fishing salmon eggs, red worms, crickets, or grasshoppers. It is especially effective with Velveeta cheese, which is tough to keep on the hook while stream fishing.

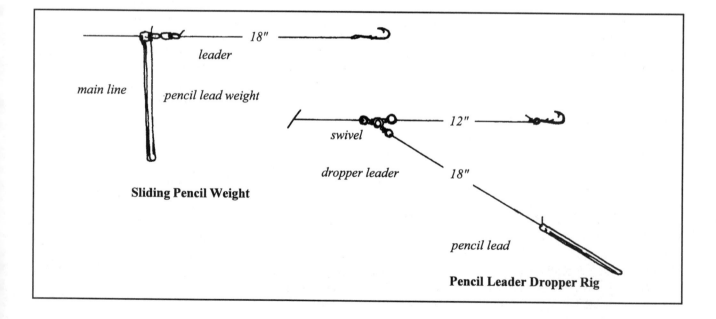

Live Baits

Now let's look at the baits themselves and how to fish them with spinning tackle in a stream. To begin with it is hard to beat common garden worms. Thread these smaller red worms on to a size #10 to #14 bronze baitholder hook. The clearer the water and/or the smaller the trout, the tinier the hook. Use a pinch or shot or toss the worm weightless, if conditions permit.

Cast upstream and let the worm tumble in the current. And, remember, you are trying to create the effect of bait that has naturally rolled into the current.

If you are working a stream known for big trout, then consider switching to a larger offering such as a nightcrawler. Like red worms, these can be fished whole, with or without a weight. Some trouters prefer to cut the nightcrawler in half sections which eliminates the possibility of a smaller fish striking "short" and getting only the end of the bait. With 'crawlers, scale up to a #6 to #10 hook.

Another option is to inject the nightcrawler with air and fish it totally on the surface without any weight. This has an effect similar to a small water snake drifting temptingly along. Quite often this tactic can be dynamite on lunker brown trout.

Both red worms and 'crawlers are excellent early season bait choices, especially when the streams, rivers, and creeks are high and roily with dirty water. Both baits will take their share of quality fish, particularly because they can be fished deeper and nearer the bottom where the bigger fish stay.

Grasshoppers and crickets make excellent baits for stream fishing. They too can be fished either weightless or with a minimal amount of weight. Hook size is dictated by the insect itself but usually a size #6 to #10 baitholder will suffice.

Collecting Natural Baits

More enterprising anglers will don hip boots and gather one of the all-time primo trout baits around—the caddisfly larvae. These are also termed "caseworms" because of the inch-long hardened protective cases that surround the larvae body. Look for caseworms in the shallow, slow-moving portions of the stream. Turn over flat rocks where you will find these twig-like casings.

Carefully peel away the casing to expose the yellow-ish, six-legged larvae. Thread it onto a #8 to #10 short-shanked hook. Fish the caddisfly larvae either weightless or with a small BB shot added above the bait.

Some fishermen like to work in teams while wading to collect other esoteric natural baits. One angler works upstream turning over flat rocks, while the other mans a wire mesh screen a little downstream. The larvae and nymphs of caddisflies, stoneflies, or hellgrammites drift downstream after being dislodged from submerged rocks. They are then easily collected in the wire screen.

There are a few other "exotic" natural baits that will produce solid results for the spin fisherman. Terrestrial insect larvae, caterpillars, bees, and beetles will all work. So will the pine or stump grubs gathered from downed timber. It is estimated that insect forms make up over 90 percent of a trout's daily diet. So, just about anything that flies or crawls is fair game! Similarly, the "meaty" portion of aquatic snails, some indigenous minnows, and even smaller crawdad tails can be sensational at times.

With a little imagination and ingenuity, you may be able to find other natural baits which are easily collected alongside of and in the stream itself.

Prepared Baits

As for prepared baits, it pays to buy a firm, premium grade jar of salmon eggs. These fish best on a gold salmon egg hook in sizes ranging from #10 to #16. Use either one or two eggs together—sometimes one way works better than the other, so experiment a little here. Salmon eggs can be gently tossed without any weight or with only a small amount.

Prepared cheese baits or just plain Velveeta cheese can also produce in streams. Depending upon the current, terrain, and depth fished, a variety of hooks should be utilized. Baits can be molded onto either a gold salmon egg hook or a longer-shanked bronze baitholder. A small #14 to #18 gold or bronze treble hook is best for securing the cheese, but will obviously get snagged more easily. Consider saving the treble hooks for the deeper, quiet pools.

Lures for Stream Spinning

If you prefer to throw some "hardware" in your favorite stream, there are a few helpful tips to keep in mind. To begin with, as with any type of lure fishing, make a few casts to determine the proper speed of the retrieve to generate effective action from the lure. This is more important to do when attacking streams, since the current can play havoc with the lure as it is retrieved through the water.

It is best to cast slightly upstream and try to let the spoons or spinners drift on a relatively slack line. These lures should ease by the undercut banks and be allowed to flutter down into the deeper pockets. Keep in mind, however, that you must maintain somewhat greater tension on the line with a spinner in contrast to a spoon. This is necessary to keep the blade turning.

Also, make a very precise, concerted effort to slow the retrieve down enough to have the spinner or spoon lazily drift down into the deeper holes. This is where the bigger bows and browns live—and they will definitely bushwhack a wayward lure if it gets down into their lair. As the lure moves through the current, slow the retrieve when it cuts across deeper pockets and pools. Then let it settle, gently fluttering down, before starting up the retrieve again.

Switch to larger spoons and spinners in the summer to fish these deep pools. Consider changing to a single hook if the treble hook keeps getting hung up on the bottom or on brush. Spoons usually tend to take bigger trout in streams than spinners. The theory is that bigger browns see a spoon as a larger meaty morsel that needs to be eaten! Spoons can also be vertically "jigged" in little white water pockets, often inducing a vicious strike.

If you are getting bit "short" on a spinner while stream fishing, switch to the more subtle, flashing action of a spoon. Similarly, if you persist in snagging along the bottom too much, replace the treble hook of the spoon with a single hook. If the action slows, spice up the single hook with either a red worm or nightcrawler chunk trailer. This often produces spectacular results.

Darker spinners are good for dirty, cloudy, early season conditions. In high water like this, many terrestrial baits will have tumbled off the banks into the water. The darker spoons most closely match the drab shades of these land-based critters.

Similarly, a gold colored Kastmaster or Phoebe spoon, or a small Mepps, Rooster Tail, or Panther Martin spinner with a gold blade can be excellent for early season trout. The gold tone shows up best in the muddy, high water conditions.

Plugs for the Stream

Just as with lake troutin', plugs are often overlooked for larger stream or river applications. I was introduced to plugs as a possibility for this type of fishing quite by accident while fishing the Merced River below Yosemite National Park. This stretch of river has some deep pools but great angler pressure. There were a number of us working one large pool soaking assorted baits.

You could see the fish sulking in the clear water, including some hefty sized rainbows. Out of sheer desperation, I threw a gold #7 Countdown Rapala minnow across the pool. I let it sink a few feet then started my retrieve.

Wham! A nice pound-and-a-half rainbow smacked the little minnow plug and was soon in my creel. I repeated this scenario a number of times in similarly impacted pools along this very popular river.

To emphasize again, the situation is really no different for rivers and streams than for lakes—big fish like big bait! A properly tossed plug will definitely fit this need in contrast to a more diminutive spoon or spinner. This is especially true with stream-bred brown trout.

The minnow-shaped plugs such as the Luhr Jensen Minnow Rapala or Rebel models are viable possibilities. The sinking versions perform especially well for working those deeper pools. They are fished best by casting slightly upstream but then retrieved across the current.

If you cast too far upstream, the current will tumble the plug or drift it too fast to properly engage its diving action. As the crankbait moves with the current, keep a tight line. The water against the diving lip may provide most of the action you need from the lure, so consider slowing the retrieve down a little in swift current.

If the slender profile minnow-style lures tend to snag in the river or stream you are fishing, don't give up too quickly. Instead, switch to a smaller alphabet plug. These chunky little baits "plow" along the bottom while hanging up less than the minnow models.

Popular choices in the alphabet design include the Rapala Fat Rap, Storm Wiggle and Wee Wart, and the Rebel "R" and Humpback models. Gold, silver, foil, and rainbow trout patterns will be your best bets for pluggin' in California's rivers and streams.

If the water is exceptionally cold and the current not too swift, try the more subtle banana-shaped Kwikfish or Flatfish plugs or the Hot Shot. Fish these lures with a small split-shot crimped about 18 inches above the knot. Stream and river trout will often strike these slower-moving plugs when other lures fail to draw any interest.

Fly and Bubble Combos for Streams and Rivers

The popular fly and bubble setup will also work on larger streams and rivers. Cast slightly upstream and maintain some tension on the line following the downstream drift.

Be prepared for strikes on either the drift or even the retrieve back upstream. Day flies, wet flies, streamers, and nymphs can all be fished with the fly and bubble combo. Light 2 to 4 pound leaders are recommended.

Similarly, in super-turbulent water it may sometimes be nearly impossible to fish either a conventional fly rod or a spinning outfit with a fly and bubble. Instead, rig up a three-way swivel and a pencil lead as previously described. Run a dropper leader with 2 to 4 pound mono, about 18 to 24 inches long, and trail it with a popular fly. Nymphs and wet flies in particular can be fished deep in the fast currents with this rig.

Fly Fishin': Hackles and Feathers

Of all the ways to catch trout in the Golden State, fly fishing with traditional gear is held by many to be the most challenging. The serious fly fisherman—or "purist" as he is sometimes termed—is perhaps the most "cerebral" of all the members of the trout angling community. Dedicated fly fishers attempt to fool their quarry with minuscule replicas of insect or other aquatic life forms. It is this continual struggle to "match-the-hatch" that makes this sport both frustrating and rewarding.

In this chapter I want to "de-mystify" some of the basic techniques used for catching trout on flies. Too many novice trout fishermen automatically assume that they have to be either an expert caster or amateur entomologist to use this tackle properly. In fact, it is not that overly complicated to gain some respectable proficiency with this gear.

But let me also say that this particular section will only serve as a "primer" of sorts. It will hopefully give the reader a brief foundation in order to get started fly

fishing. There are a variety of other fine resources to turn to if your interest remains high.

For example, there are excellent detailed texts and specialized magazines delineating the finer aspects of this sport available at bookstores and libraries. Similarly, there are a number of fine educational videos illustrating the basics of fly casting. Finally, there are a variety of highly organized fly fishing clubs and instructional classes which can be located through California's outdoor press. These are great places for the beginner to hone his or her skills under expert supervision.

Basic Fly Fishing Gear: Rods, Reels, Line and Leaders

It takes a little more planning and forethought to come up with an ideal package in the way of a fly rod, reel, and line in comparison with other outfits. To begin with, unlike other forms of fishing, the artificial fly you will be casting is extremely light. In a strict sense, you will be casting the line, not the fly. It is thus very important to team the line with a balanced rod.

Fly lines come in 25 to 35 yard coils and are made in a variety of tapers. The simplest construction is a level line that has no taper at all. This style of line has the same diameter from end to end. This is the cheapest line available and it is rarely used by more serious anglers. It is difficult to cast and offers minimal wind resistance.

Double-tapered fly lines are tapered at each end of the coil and can be reversed to maximize usage. This tapered effect makes the line much easier to cast by minimizing wind resistance. Many beginners opt for a double-tapered line as a good, multi-purpose line for a modest investment.

Another alternative is to carry an extra spool filled with a weight-forward fly line. This style has a considerably larger diameter at one end then tapers down for the remainder of the coil. It is sometimes termed a "torpedo taper." The wide diameter enhances "castability" since there will be that much more weight being pushed out for the first part of the cast. A weight-forward line is very good for making distance casts with either large bulky flies or directly into the wind. This would also be a good choice for working large impoundments.

Most fly fishing in California can be mastered by using a floating line. This is true even for most "wet" presentations with flies, streamers, or nymphs. Highly visible floating lines in yellow, orange, or white make it easy to observe the strike. The key to fishing "wet" is that the leader sinks. For lakes and rivers where greater depth is critical, switch to a sinking line.

Fly lines are delineated by how many "grains" the particular type weighs. These range from #1 (60 grains) all the way up to a heavy #12 (360 grains). Most lines sold for California conditions are between #5 and #7. A #5 to #6 line is suitable for most back country situations or small creeks and streams. A #6 to #7 line is considered the best all-purpose weight for most of our waters. The weight, the taper, and the flotation properties of the line are built into its descriptive nomenclature. For example, a weight forward, #7 floating line is marketed as "WF-7-F."

As for fly rods, I highly recommend investing in a two-piece graphite model. In fly casting, you have to put the fly into motion by "pushing" the line out, using the combination of the power of the rod butt and the "whippiness" of the tip. A series of "false casts" are usually made as the angler strips out more line between each successive motion, trying to obtain the proper distance.

I suggest graphite because it is both light and powerful for making long, repetitive casts. It is also very sensitive which is important for strike detection with this finesse type of trout fishing. A quality graphite fly rod should last for many years.

Proper rod length is in part a matter of the terrain you are fishing matched with a bit of personal preference. For example, most veteran fly fishers prefer a 7 1/2 to 8 foot rod for small brush-lined streams and an 8 to 9 footer for working big rivers and lakes. The longer rod is made to handle heavier line needed to obtain the greater distance required on these larger waters.

The lengthier rod also keeps more line off the water, thus spooking the trout less when a distance cast is needed. A longer blank also helps to minimize drift, giving the fisherman better control over the line in contrast to a shorter model.

In contrast, the lighter, shorter rod offers more sport and better balance for presenting flies to smaller trout on little creeks and streams. The shorter rod also balances nicely for delicate presentations. It is better for creepin', crawlin' and pokin' through brush around the stream. Most fly rods now have the recommended line weights with which they balance best marked on the blank near the butt section.

As for reel selection, the choices are relatively narrow: either single-action or automatic. The single-action reel is very simple and essentially just stores line. Some have built-in drags that can be very useful for fighting larger trout. The single-action reel has a very slow gear

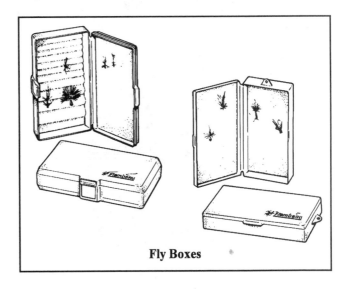

Fly Boxes

ratio, somewhere around 1:1. When the angler retrieves the fly line coiled at his feet, he must quickly and tediously reel the single-action model to gather it up.

Although the single action type of fly reel is simple to operate, they can range in price from under $30 to over $100. As the price increases, the quality of the metal or graphite frame improves as well as the quality of the gearing and drag mechanism. A medium-priced single-action fly reel will last for many years.

The automatic fly reel makes it possible to gather in line very quickly. As the angler strips off fly line, he is basically "winding up" a spring built into the reel. When it is necessary to retrieve the line, simply touch the trip handle and the spring "unloads," recoiling the line on the spool. For every foot of line stripped off the reel, the spring is "loaded" to retrieve that amount.

These reels are usually heavier than single-action models. For this reason, many purists prefer the better balance possible with the single-action reels when they are matched with a graphite fly rod.

However, for fishing big waters where trophy trout are known to lurk, the automatic does have some strong applications. It makes it possible to gather in line very quickly on lunker fish that may have made a long run and

are now tiring. The automatic fly reel lets you gather up slack very rapidly while maintaining tension on the line.

Some novices simply do not feel comfortable stripping-and-reeling in the coiled line as is done with a single-action model. The automatic reel simplifies this procedure.

One more point: it will be necessary to "back" either type of reel with some additional line. This can be either dacron or some other linen line, or heavier 12 to 20 pound monofilament. You might also consider using one of the new "non-mono" lines with ultra-small diameter, and hardly any stretch. These include Berkley Fireline, Izerline Spectra, or Spider Wire. Use this backing material to "build up" the spool. This keeps the fly line from compacting too tightly which would occur if the backing is not used. In this way the fly line will maintain its maximum qualities without becoming too compressed or kinked. Rarely for most stream conditions will a trout strip off enough line to reach the 50 to 100 yards of backing material.

Tapered Leader

Fly fishermen must use a leader of tapered monofilament to properly make their presentations. A leader that tapers from a heavier base to a finer diameter tip greatly facilitates casting.

The fly fisher must "shoot" the fly out into the water, laying it and the leader down as straight as possible. A standard piece of monofilament that is not tapered like this will often land in a coiled, jumbled mess with the cast.

Tapered leaders are gauged by the "tippet." For California troutin', a 3x to 5x tippet is usually adequate. The overall leader length can range from 7 1/2 feet to 12 1/2 feet. The smaller 7 1/2 foot leaders are suitable for 20 to 30 foot casts on small streams. Use a longer tippet for low water conditions, when the trout are real "twitchy," and the water typically very clear.

The corresponding size fly that matches best with each tippet is as follows:

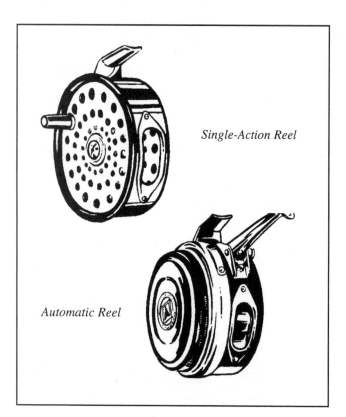

Single-Action Reel

Automatic Reel

Tapered Leader Gauges	
Tippet #	Fly-Size Range
0x	#2 to #1/0
1x	#4 to #8
2x	#6 to #10
3x	#10 to #14
4x	#12 to #16
5x	#14 to #18
6x	#16 to #22

More Paraphernalia

There are numerous other accessory items that augment the basic fly fishing outfit. For dry fly fishing always keep some floatant material handy to keep the fly on the surface. Polaroid sunglasses are great for spotting fish in clear water.

A vest and fly box are also essential gear. They help to keep things organized and consolidated to make movement along a river or stream easy. A hook hone is another valuable accessory that is often overlooked. The hook on a fly can become dulled very quickly from being snagged on the backcasts. Examine your fly often and re-sharpen the hook as needed.

Hemostats are excellent for disgorging the small fly. A fingernail clipper keeps the knot which attaches the leader to the fly trimmed tight. Sometimes it helps to trim the hackles or feathers to make a more compact presentation. On this note, a miniature scissor can also be helpful.

No-knot eyelets are also a neat little timesaving device. These eyelets are designed to be embedded into the fibrous core of the fly line. The leader is then tied directly to the tiny wire eye. This eliminates using the more cumbersome and hard-to-tie nail knot.

Other accessories should include a creel, landing net, and interestingly, a smaller aquarium dip net. The aquarium net can be useful for scooping natural insects from under rocks to properly match-the-hatch. Finally, don't forget a belt to wear around your chest waders. This piece of gear is often overlooked but it can be a real safety device for wading deep streams as it will help to prevent the waders from filling with water.

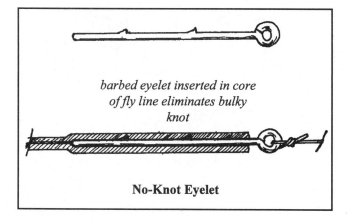

barbed eyelet inserted in core of fly line eliminates bulky knot

No-Knot Eyelet

"Matching the Hatch": The Foundation of the Sport

It is estimated that terrestrial, flying, and/or aquatic insect life comprises 90 to 97% of the trout's daily diet. It is for this simple reason that fly fishing can be so deadly as compared to other techniques when it comes to stalking California trout. To become a modestly accomplished fly fisher, it is necessary to master a rudimentary knowledge of insect ecology as it relates to the lake or stream.

Some insects are primarily terrestrial or land-based 'crawlers or flyers. They mature from eggs to larvae to adult stages while on the shore. Bees, wasps, ants, many beetles, and grasshoppers exemplify this type of metamorphosis. Other insects such as caddisflies, stoneflies, or mayflies develop in larval form primarily while under water. Many aquatic insects which have this immature nymph-like state can be found crawling along the bottom toward shore just prior to hatching into the adult form. The terrestrial base then serves as a "launching pad" for the mature flyer. Other insects emerge from the lake or stream bottom and eventually become airborne adults as they reach the surface.

It is then up to the fly fisherman to try to duplicate or "match" his little artificial lure with the species, size, color, and life stage of the insect on which the trout is currently feeding.

Flies are primarily divided into four major categories depending upon the basic type of terrestrial or aquatic creature they are tied to represent. They are classified into either "dry," "wet," nymph, or streamer patterns.

Dry Flies

When neophyte anglers think about "fly fishing," the image of the lure they usually have in mind is a small dry fly softly dancing upon the water's surface. Dry flies are designed to imitate mature, hatched insects that have either floated to the surface or have landed upon it. In either case, the dry fly is presented to the fish on the surface of the water where it presumably stays "dry." Hence the term "dry" fly.

The hackle on a dry fly is commonly made from the neck feathers of a rooster. They are tied and spread around the head or tail section of the fly to imitate the legs of an insect. The hackle feathers also help to keep the dry fly afloat. Some dry fly patterns are constructed with very delicate hackles, sparsely tied to the bottom. These are best fished in clear water conditions where the trout can closely scrutinize the lure. Dry flies with bulkier, more prominent hackle feathers can be fished in stained water or overcast and dim light conditions. Patterns with the "bushy" effect will also float best when a surface presentation is paramount to getting the trout to strike.

Perhaps the most critical consideration for successful dry fly fishing is learning to match the fly to the corresponding size of the natural insects that are landing on the water. Proper coloration and pattern matching to the species of insect are obviously important, too. But many expert fly fishermen agree that, above all, it is most important to present a silhouette that most closely resembles the natural insect's size and shape.

Dry flies are tied in larger #12 sizes down to tiny #26 patterns. For most California conditions, the beginner can usually get by with a light assortment in size #14 with some #16's for super clear water. Popular patterns for our waters include the Adams, Black Gnat, Caddis, Cahill, California Mosquito, Coachman, Dusty Miller, Ginger Quill, Gray Hackle, Humpy, Light Cahill, Peacock, Renegade, Royal Wolff, and Royal Coachman. Another style to keep handy, especially when grasshoppers fill the mountain meadows, is Joe's Hopper — a larger specimen that fishes great as a dry fly.

Obviously, the best time to fish dry flies is when the trout are "rising" to the surface and feeding on the insect hatch. Interestingly, though, a rise on the water does not always mean that the trout are actually feeding on the surface.

Quite often the fish are chasing emergent larvae floating up or hatching from the bottom. This gives the angler the illusion of surface-feeding trout. Under these circumstances, it might be better to fish a nymph or a wet fly rather than a dry fly (more on these variations shortly).

Wet Flies

These styles are made to duplicate insects hatching and rising to the surface. They are also sometimes termed "emergent flies" since many patterns replicate insects emerging from the larval stage. Wet flies can also mimic downed insects following a major hatch that is sinking after landing on the surface. They can also be tied to look like mature aquatic insects or even small forage bait fish. Wet flies are fished under the surface of the water often on the bottom of a stream. Since the fly is under water it is termed a "wet" fly. Wet flies are almost always weighted so they will sink under the surface of the water. In contrast, dry flies are never weighted.

Wet flies for Western waters are generally sold in sizes #10 to #12. The larger hook allows them to sink more easily. Many pros prefer to use a larger #10 pattern early in the season when waters are high and often muddy. Later in the year they will shift to a smaller #12 wet fly when water levels are low and clear.

Popular patterns for California troutin' include the Black Gnat, Brindle Bug, Coachman, Ginger Quill, Gray Muskrat, Hare's Ear, Peacock, and Wooly Worm. You may recognize some of these names as common dry fly varieties. The wet fly versions are simply made on larger, usually heavier hooks with several wraps of fine lead wire around the hook shank and sometimes with less hackle material. Wet flies are typically tied in much drabber colors than dry flies. Tan, brown, black, cream, and green make a good assortment of wet fly colors for your fly box.

Joe's Hopper

Black Gnat

California Mosquito   Royal Coachman

Dry Flies

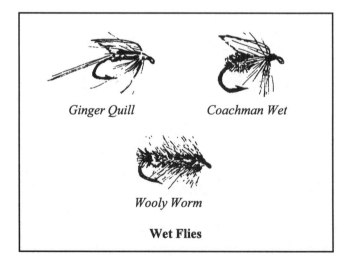

Ginger Quill   Coachman Wet

Wooly Worm

Wet Flies

Nymphs

Strangely enough, the hatched or adult stage of life for an aquatic insect exists only for a short time along the stream or river. However, aquatic insects in larval form exist all year long and comprise a more abundant food supply, hugging the bottom in lakes and streams. It is estimated that trout feed on this subsurface forage 90% of the time. This accounts for the potent fish-catching properties of nymph style flies.

Not enough recreational fly fishers use these flies. They are extremely bland looking, for the most part, and are more difficult to fish than the other varieties of flies. But at certain times, nymphs can be deadly; for instance, in between insect hatches, in super cold water, or even during a hatch. Trout will feed on insects near the bottom of a stream as well as those that are rising to the surface.

Nymphs are tied on hooks similar in size to those used on wet flies, although occasionally some jumbo versions will be sold all the way up to a #4. Some patterns have copper or lead wire wrapped internally around the body to provide for greater sinking action. In contrast to wet flies, nymphs do not have wings.

Just as the dry fly fisherman collects insects flying around or landing on the water to "match-the-hatch," anglers working a nymph will often turn over rocks in the stream to examine what larval forms are present in the waters they are fishing.

Similarly, a "match" can be made by opening up the stomach and checking the contents of the first-caught trout. Popular nymph patterns include AP Timberline, Caddis, Gold Ribbed Hare's Ear, Gray Nymph, Light Cahill, March Brown, Olive Nymph, Stonefly Nymph, and Zug Bug.

Streamers

These elongated flies are designed to portray larger bait fish such as shad, daces, pond smelt, chubs, or sculpin. They can even be tied to look like a small, baby trout. Working with the maxim that "Big Baits Catch Big Fish," you should rely on your streamer flies when you want to do some serious hawg huntin'!

Streamers are tied on longer shank hooks and are made to sink. Feathers or long strands of natural bucktail hair are used to give the fly the minnow-like action. Surprisingly, they can be fished in a variety of ways. Above all, streamers can be worked fast in contrast to the other three basic flies. This feature allows the trouter to cover a lot of water to locate feeding fish when visual signs such as rises are absent.

For this reason, a streamer would be a wise choice when confronting unknown water for the first time, especially when fishing for big fish in the spring. Some of the more commonly used patterns are Black Ghost, Gray Ghost, Hornburg, Muddler, Olive Matuka, Olive Leech, and White Marabou.

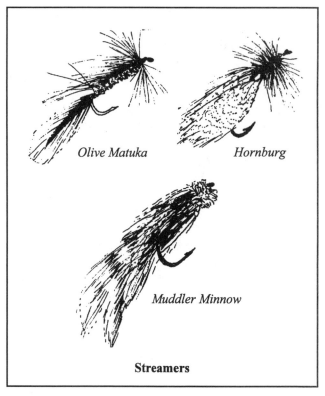

Olive Matuka   Hornburg

Muddler Minnow

Streamers

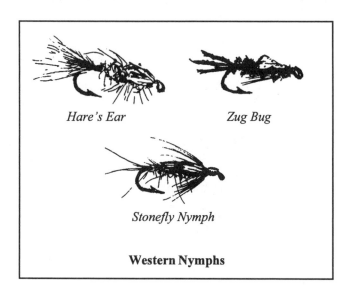

Hare's Ear   Zug Bug

Stonefly Nymph

Western Nymphs

Dry Fly Tactics

There is an awesome amount of literature regarding the proper way to present an artificial fly. Let's start with the "basics" of fishing the dry fly. It is with this style of fly that most weekend anglers will get their first "taste" of troutin' with a fly rod.

Under most conditions, the object to fishing a dry fly is to present it with minimal drag. It is the weight of the line that drags the little fly unnaturally in the current while working a stream. Because the line weighs so much, it can drag the fly under the surface of the water and give the fly an unnatural appearance. Trout will not strike unless the fly looks natural (i.e., without any drag). There are a variety of tactics even the novice can employ to minimize drag so the dry fly floats very naturally. To begin with:

1. Make shorter casts to control the line better.
2. Cast with a tighter line, "snapping" the rod tip with a quick flick of the wrist in order to take out the slack at the end of the cast.
3. Make your cast either slightly up or downstream which will help to take up the slack more quickly.
4. Avoid casting across the current—this type of cast generates the greatest potential for slack and ensuing drag.

Traditional fly fishing lore has recommended using an upstream cast for proper dry fly presentation. This casting technique allows for the most natural drift. Trout always face into the current or upstream, so when the upstream cast is used the angler will be hidden behind the fish.

This can be an especially important ploy in gin-clear water with spooky fish. The upstream cast also provides maximum hook setting capabilities. When the fisherman sets up on the trout with this presentation, he actually pulls the hook back into the fish's mouth.

Also, by working a dry fly upstream, a hooked trout that wants to put on some aerial fireworks can be quickly lead downstream out of the area. In this way other trout rising to the hatch nearby won't be scared off by the hooked fish.

More current theory, however, now considers certain applications for a downstream cast when working a dry fly. This type of presentation works well in swift or convergent currents. You may also have to use it when confronted by headwinds, making an upstream cast difficult to execute. With the downstream approach, you will have less "belly" in the fly line which makes it more manageable.

There is minimal leader and fly line on the water with a downstream cast—i.e. the trout gets to see the fly first, not the leader and line. But there is the problem of pulling the fly away from the trout on the set with a downstream drift. Put simply, plan on missing more strikes with this downstream tactic.

Trout seem to "suck in" the dry fly when it is floating naturally, starting upstream and then drifting down with the current. If possible, try to actually create a little slack by stripping out line if you are shooting the line in a downstream cast. This will let the fly drift more naturally and give the trout a better chance to suck in the bait rather than just getting a mouthful of water.

Another little trick is to use a fluffier dry fly with more prominent hackle material. After making the downstream cast try to "skate" the bulkier dry fly across the surface, while stripping in line at the same time. This tactic can often result in explosive strikes as the trout senses that the errant bug is escaping.

The main problem with the downstream casting approach is that it may spook the trout. The total number of casts an angler can make to one spot in the stream is limited. A dry fly that gently floats by on an upstream cast can often be presented a number of times without necessarily spooking the fish.

However, with the downstream cast there is always the chance that when you pull the fly line back towards you, it will slap against the water and really scare the trout —or worse, shut down an entire area. So, precision and careful forethought is necessary with this technique.

Dry fly fishing is very "visual" in contrast to other fly presentations. You must learn to set the hook on sight and feel. Don't snap the rod back too dramatically. Just a short, gentle, quick snap is all that is needed once the fish inhales the fly. Also, it almost always is best to cast slightly past the rise and have the fly float more naturally into the fish.

The tippet leader must actually sink with this type of fishing although the fly and the line both float. You can rub saliva or even mud along the tippet portion to make it sink. Similarly, use any of the silicone sprays, dry fly "dope," or muslin preparations on the little fly to make it float. As a general rule, use a light-colored dry fly in dim light, switching to a dark-colored pattern when facing a low-setting sun.

Here then is a summary of the little tips that should help the novice improve his or her catch when dry fly fishing:

1. Buy quality, hand-tied flies. Check with local tackle shops in the area you are fishing for current, regional patterns that are producing.
2. Try to use balanced tackle—this is very critical with this delicate form of fly fishing.
3. Be certain to match the size and coloration of the fly with the natural insect hatch. Worry less about using a dry fly that is the precise replication of the bug—size and shading are more important.
4. Maintain proper flotation with the fly. Don't "splash-land" the fly on the surface. A soft, delicate landing is best.
5. Use the least amount of leader possible. Make sure that the tippet sinks.
6. Present the fly beyond the rise when casting, so as not to "spook" wary trout.
7. Minimize drag—try to maintain a natural drift with a dry fly.
8. Enter quietly and move cautiously when wading the stream. Avoid making extraneous surface noise along the bank or banging into rocks on the stream bottom. Keep the casting action smooth—eliminate exaggerated movement.

Wet Fly Tactics

The angler has a lot more latitude in using a wet fly. These baits can be cast upstream, downstream, or across the current. You can fish the wet fly on a drag-free line, allowing it to drift into deeper pockets. It can also be skittered across the surface retrieving on a downstream cast. Sometimes it is best to retrieve back with short, rhythmic jerks of the rod tip. This gives the appearance of a free-swimming, immature insect or a smaller minnow swimming upstream.

At other times, either quick little twitches or longer more exaggerated pulls may be more productive. Thus, you can be creative fishing the wet fly with a lot more room for error than with dry fly fishing.

To detect wet fly strikes, aim the rod where the fly lands and follow the line. Any sudden jerk, hitch, pause, or jump in the line is very likely a trout on the fly. Basically, any time you encounter an interruption in the natural drift of the wet fly, set up!

Western trout fishermen have devised a unique way to fish wet flies to create the effect of a dynamic active caddisfly hatch. They will use two wet flies rigged on a dropper leader and on the main tippet. Tie one fly to the end of the tippet, the other on a 6 to 12 inch dropper line coming off 30 to 48 inches above the bottom fly.

This double rig can be twitched, pulled, skitted, or jerked underneath the surface. The dropper leader rigs are commercially made and available at your local fly shop. As with dry fly fishing, be flexible and change patterns regularly until you find a wet fly the trout prefer.

Nymphing Nuances

As with wet flies, not enough recreational trout fishermen use nymphs as an alternate, lethal approach to catching subsurface trout. Nymphs usually produce best with an upstream cast in order to fish a dead drift with the fly heading downstream. These flies can be dragged, twitched, jerked, pulled, or even fished nearly motionless in ultracold water.

Veteran fly-fishers hand down the following as rough rules of thumb for fishing nymphs:

1. To imitate mayfly larvae, drift the nymph near the bottom.
2. For stonefly or caddisfly larvae, fish the weighted nymph so it tumbles in the current.
3. To mimic either dragonfly or damselfly larvae, use quick jerks in a stop'n go retrieve.

Of course these are broad generalizations so don't hesitate to experiment with other approaches.

Nymphs are also an excellent choice for stalking big trout in deep pools. A sinking fly line will help to keep the fly down deep. A small split-shot can also be added to work the nymph near the bottom.

Here is another simple tip: put a little silicone paste on all but the last 12 to 18 inches of leader to keep the nymph just at subsurface level. This helps the presentation of the fly when the trout are feeding on emergent insects.

Many Western nymph fishermen prefer to fish two nymphs at a time using the basic dropper rig described for tandem wet fly fishing. The trick is to use a smaller, lighter-weight nymph on top with a heavier, larger pattern on the bottom. A popular California combination is the Hare's Ear in #10 to #14 representing an immature caddisfly with a #8 Zug Bug on the dropper line.

Other variations on this theme, I might add, include a Hornburg or Muddler Minnow, streamer fly trailer, a #12 to #16 nymph pattern, or a Wooly Worm wet fly teamed with a smaller caddisfly nymph.

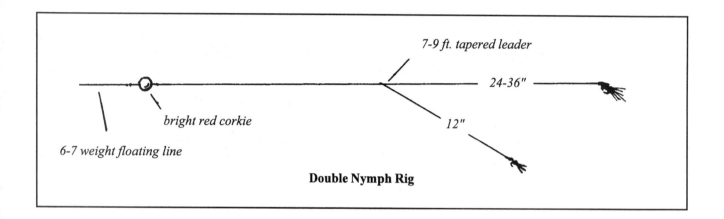

7-9 ft. tapered leader

24-36"

bright red corkie

12"

6-7 weight floating line

Double Nymph Rig

The pervasive problem confronting nymph fishermen is being able to detect the strike. Because nymphs are often fished deep, there can often be a lot of "belly" in the line which makes it hard to determine when a fish has taken the fly. Similarly, as these flies are worked over the bottom, invariably they will get hung up on brush, rocks, etc. But often what seems to be a snag can in reality be a touchy trout just mouthing in the nymph.

Expert fly fishers have a few tricks up their sleeves, however, that help them to monitor strikes more easily when working nymphs. To start with, even though these baits are fished from subsurface to the bottom, try using a floating fly line. The high visibility variety in orange or yellow is especially good for nymphing. Even with the sinking leader you can still detect many strikes by watching the fly line twitch or move on the surface. But, at times, even the greater visibility available from the floating line won't be enough.

The next step is to use a "strike indicator." I remember the first time my guide on the Madison River in Montana showed me one the these attached to his leader. I looked at the little float and said to myself, "You've got to be kidding!" My first impression was that this "strike indicator" was pretty much reminiscent of the ole' cork bobbers I grew up with when fishing for warm-water panfish. It seemed distinctively out of place in the world of sophisticated hi-tech fly fishing paraphernalia.

But these little chunks or balls of styrofoam or cork really do work! They are ultra light and are affixed anywhere from 18 to 36 inches above the nymph. Commercially made strike indicators available are the Cortland Striker, Betts, Evasote, Pulsar Pinch-On-Float, Corkie, or Bungie Butt.

Some anglers prefer to make their own strike indicators. You can use a small piece of brightly colored yarn wadded into a ball and wrapped onto the leader. Or put a hot needle through a small section of cork and pass the leader through. To finish, paint the cork with fluorescent red or orange enamel.

Yes, to some extent this is basically "bobber fishin'." But, don't expect the tiny strike indicators to "go under" like a bobber when the trout hits the nymph. If you wait for this type of dramatic movement from the float, it may be too late since the fish may quickly exhale the fly.

Instead, be sensitive to any slight twitch, unusual lateral movement, or bobbing action from the indicator. This type of subtle motion often signals a trout taking the nymph.

Also, look for many strikes to occur as you begin to lift the fly from the water. This is when the trout's natural instincts trigger it into intercepting the insect before it becomes airborne. This same effect may occur as the nymph is lifted from the water in preparation for the next cast.

Here is one other helpful insight that veteran fly fishermen use to determine if conditions are right for a nymph. While using a dry fly or a wet fly (or a dry fly that has lost its buoyancy and is now wet) occasionally the trout will make a lateral "flash" on the bait. Some pros feel that in contrast to a surface-feeding rise, this is the telltale response from a fish keying in on nymphs.

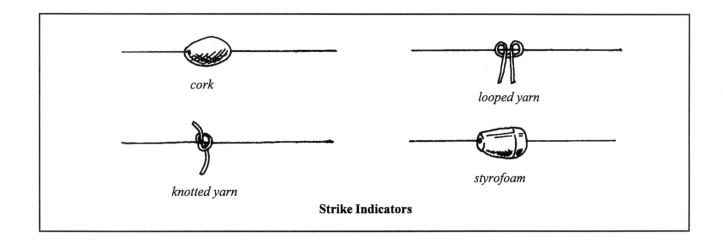

cork

looped yarn

knotted yarn

styrofoam

Strike Indicators

Streamer Tactics

Streamer flies are large flies intended to imitate bait fish. Since bait fish make up a substantial portion of the diet of a "big trout," these flies are effective when fishing for trophy trout in large bodies of water.

Streamers are presented in much the same way as smaller wet flies and nymphs. They can be worked upstream, downstream, or cross-current. A variety of retrieves can be effective at different times. You can strip, jerk, twitch, pull, stop'n go, or even skitter a streamer across the surface. Many fly fishermen prefer to use a sinking fly line to keep the streamer in the deeper strike zones. However, as long as the leader sinks, a floating fly line will suffice for many occasions when using a trout streamer.

Interestingly, trout will often flash or "roll" over a streamer without actually striking the fly as was previously noted with nymphs. If this happens several times, take a break for a moment and retie, forming a shorter, 6 to 12 inch dropper leader off of the main leader. Attach a smaller dry fly or even a nymph to the dropper.

Often, the large-scale silhouette of the streamer will draw the trout out to investigate. As it makes an investigative "pass" at the larger offering, it simply can't resist the smaller tidbit moving just ahead. This double rig has the appearance of a minnow (the streamer) chasing a smaller bug (the dry fly). It can be a deadly combo.

"Dapping"

There is one very specialized tactic for fly fishing a stream that should be mentioned. This is affectionately known in fly fishing circles as "dapping." This technique is terrific for fishing in little pockets. It also works well for presenting the fly around concentrated brush, down steep ledges, or near fallen logs.

Keep the fly about a rod's length away from you and be prepared for some spectacular close-range action! The object is to poke the fly into a confined area and jiggle it up and down a little. This gives the fly the appearance of an insect struggling to break away from the water's surface to fly.

Wet flies, dry flies, and nymphs can all be "dapped" in this manner. This technique is analogous to the way anglers on California's central coast "poke pole" in the rocks for marine fish. Its freshwater counterpart is easily recognizable as the "flippin'" technique popularized in professional bassin' tournaments.

It is best to use longer 8 to 9 1/2 foot rods for stream conditions that are suitable for dapping. Try to keep the leaders off the water as much as possible—this is basically a vertical presentation of the fly. At times, a quiet entry will work, but often a more radical "splash" produces.

The amount of noise should correspond to the size of the insect the fly represents: less noise with small flies, a little more commotion with larger varieties. If necessary, add a small split-shot to the leader to keep the fly in the pocket.

Remember, too, you will be fishing in tight quarters with this approach, so keep your own movements to a quiet minimum. Trout that are holed up in these hard-to-get-to spots are often large, territorial, bruiser-class fish. They have reached this size because they are smart and have lairs that offer considerable protection as well as an ambush point. So approach with caution and make precise, calculated presentations when dapping a fly!

Fly Fishing in Lakes

We have already discussed two popular ways to use flies on larger bodies of water: the fly and bubble combination and a fly drifting from a boat tied directly on light monofilament. But fly fishing from the shore or from a boat with a traditional fly rod and reel opens up an entirely new avenue for troutin' on California's lakes.

One of the major differences between lake and stream environments is that the trout will be moving more in the lake as they hunt down prey. They won't be fighting current or competing for the limited prime spots necessary for sanctuary in a stream. Trout in a lake will be orienting to places where fallen insects can funnel into during the wind. Or, they will locate in areas where forage bait fish congregate.

The best time to attack a lake with a fly rod is in the early morning. This is usually the best time to observe rises and make casts to viable feeding targets. Once the winds kick up, it will be much more difficult to discern such surface activity. This would be the time to shift to either a wet fly, streamer, or nymph.

Look for sheltered bays, inlets, springs, ledges, etc.— all the places previously mentioned that can hold lake-bound trout. Consider using a sinking fly line to fish deeper in these lakes. Longer 8 to 9 foot fly rods are also commonplace for extensive lake fishing where heavier lines are used and longer casts are often needed.

In windy, choppy conditions, the weather can actually work to the fly fisherman's advantage. In contrast to the rushing, turbulent water of a stream, many lakes have very deep clear water when the weather is calm. This means that the trout can "study" your offering a little longer than they can if it is drifting by in a stream.

When the water becomes more agitated on a lake, clarity is reduced and the trout are thus not so finicky as they would be in calm clear conditions.

Some expert fly fishermen theorize that you can actually tell the type of insect on which the trout are feeding by closely observing the kind of rise they make on the lake's surface. Although evidence is not hard and fast, there appears to be some truth to the following:

1. Rises that just dimple the surface indicate trout feeding on small terrestrial bugs.

2. When the trout seem to be crashing the surface, it is likely that they are chasing larger flying or aquatic insects that they sense are trying to get away.

3. If there are "bulges" on the surface, this may be the sign of some major nymph activity.

By keying in on such observations, the skilled angler may be able to second guess the trout and more quickly "match the hatch" to the insects currently available to the fish.

A Note on Catch and Release

As angling pressure intensifies on our Western waters, more and more streams are being designated catch-and-release areas. Some streams allow only artificial lures and others are reserved for strictly flies (sometimes only with barbless hooks). More and more anglers prefer to release their catch even on "open" lakes and streams as a gesture of conservation for future generations. If you decide to release trout here are a few guidelines to follow:

1. Make every attempt to keep the trout in the water. Try to release the hook without touching the fish, preferably underwater.

2. Wet your hands first if you have to handle the trout out of the water. This will help keep the fish's protective anti-bacterial slime from coming off.

3. Use hemostats to quickly and gently twist the small hooks from the trout's mouth. You can often do this procedure without touching the fish.

4. Release the trout into quiet water if it has been handled. With hands submerged, give it only a little assistance to start it swimming again.

5. Trout that have been hooked deeper can still be saved in some cases. Cut the line and leave the hook lodged in the gullet. The fish's natural enzymes should eventually dissolve the hook.

Summary

Fly fishing with traditional equipment can be both frustrating and spectacular. It will indeed take some time, effort, and patience to master this facet of California troutin'. The attempt to "match-the-hatch" has to be one of the more mind-challenging dimensions of the sport of fishing. Fly fishing, above all other forms of troutin', has a strong conservation bent to it. With this technique, the angler has the greatest opportunity to catch fish and release them uninjured back into their natural environments. This feature alone has a great appeal to many American sportsmen who share a strong ecological concern for our delicate fisheries.

Wilderness Troutin':
Back Country Solitude

For the more adventurous angler, California's expansive alpine wilderness offers literally thousands of lakes, ponds, streams, and creeks accessible only by packing in on foot or by horseback. Much of this water requires less than an hour's walk from the trailhead. Others involve an even more extensive safari into the back country, spanning a few days worth of travel.

Wilderness waters differ from lowland streams and reservoirs primarily in the short growing season for trout. This is precipitated by the extreme cold and icing-over of the lakes. For the most part, you will find smaller, pan-sized rainbows, browns, brookies, cutts, and goldens at these elevations. But there are dramatic exceptions to this rule.

Back country lakes that have excellent food sources in the way of nutrients, insect life, and forage bait have the greatest populations of trout.

Unfortunately, though, competition among the alpine fish community is extreme in such environments, resulting in large numbers of stunted trout.

Bigger specimens can be found in deeper lakes where smaller populations of fish reside. The food stocks in such lakes are less abundant which results in depleted numbers of fish. But those that do survive from year to year have the potential for growing to larger proportions. These lakes are typically steeper, heavily bordered with rocks, and offer a challenge as far as access is concerned. However, the lake may well be worth the effort if you are interested in larger back country trout.

In this chapter, I will highlight some of the tips used to catch wilderness trout. Many of the methods noted are simply variations of tactics previously described for lower elevation troutin' with bait, lures, or flies. The key difference here is that the backpacker will have to scale-down in tackle to fool these touchy upper elevation fish.

High country trout will undoubtedly be more wary than their lowland cousins. The water is usually crystal clear and the fish spook easily. It will take a very stealthy angler, using super light lines and diminutive offerings, to trick these trout.

High Country Tackle

Much of the same gear used for fishing the lower level lakes, streams, and rivers in the Golden State will also work for back country troutin'. Light action spinning rods in 6 to 7 foot lengths, 5 to 6 foot spincast rods or 7 1/2 to 8 foot fly rods will all work for high elevation trout fishing. These rods are exceptionally light and can be tied to a backpack frame quite easily.

I personally prefer to pack in these rods broken down into the two-piece sections. The two-piece fiberglass or graphite blank provides better, more natural flex to the rod in contrast to a blank broken down into 4 to 6 smaller sections. Also look for backpack rods that have the glass-to-glass ferrules instead of the older metal-to-metal ferrules. You will find that a rod whose different sections are joined glass-to-glass, or if you can afford it, graphite-to-graphite, creates an overall rod blank that is smoother and more flexible than one that is put together with metal ferrules.

For the "hard-core" backpacking enthusiast, there are a variety of rods specifically designed for this type of fishing. You can select 4 to 6 piece spinning rods or spin-fly combos. These have reversible reel seats to accommodate both spinning and fly reels. They come packaged in a variety of protective cases and can be stowed inside the backpack if necessary.

Team these rods with small reels to keep your pack-in weight minimal and to enhance balance in the outfit. Ultralight spinning reels, low-profile push-button models, and single-action fly reels are in order. Another option is to invest in one of the compact "mini-combos" that feature miniature spin or spincast reels with a matching multi-sectioned rod.

Avoid so-called "telescopic" models. These are short rods with sections that compact down by sliding into each other. The "action," and I use this term loosely here, is extremely stiff and segmented with this type of construction. Half the joy of catching these high elevation trout is fighting the little scrappers on lightweight gear. Stiff, heavy action telescopic rods simply overmatch the fish.

As for lines, premium grade, 2 to 4 pound monofilament is your best bet for spin or spincast outfits. For fly fishing, stay with a floating fly line (proper weight is printed on the fly rod), and an assortment of light tippets.

Artificial Baits for Wilderness Trout

When it comes to assembling an arsenal of lures and flies for a backpacking expedition, think small! A wide array of metal hardware in the form of ultralight spoons and spinners will work for these fish. Popular spoons such as the Daredevle, Kastmaster, Needlefish, Phoebe, Wob-L-Rite, and Z-Ray will produce on waters at this altitude. Spinners, including the Mepps, Metric, Panther Martin, Rooster Tail, and Shyster, can be equally effective.

The simple Colorado spinner with its slow, subtle flash should also be included in any assortment of backpacking lures. Both silver and gold spoon patterns will work along with spinners in yellow, black, white, brown, or frog.

Small minnow-shaped plugs such as the Rebel floater, Rapala CD-5 and CD-7 and the tiny Rocky Jr.'s will also perform well at times, especially on larger fish. The Count Down Rapalas, particularly in gold or rainbow trout pattern, can be terrific for covering some of the deep, clear, high country lakes.

Work these lures from the bank, or consider sharing the load with a partner and pack in a small inflatable boat. Either drift or slowly paddle-troll the small spoons, plugs, or spinners in primary fish-holding areas as you would on lower elevation lakes.

Small, scaled-down lake trolls can also produce phenomenal catches in the back country. A little #10 Dave Davis with either a lure, red worm, or nightcrawler trailer can be "hot" at times. Slowly dragging blades on these alpine lakes can also account for some of the larger trout not always accessible from the shore.

When it comes to fly selection, the most spectacular fishing at this altitude will be on dry flies during a wide-open insect hatch. Whereas sizes #12 to #14 were most suitable for lower, flatland lakes, smaller #14 to #16 (and sometimes even #18) patterns are necessary in this gin-clear water. The following patterns are time-proven winners on these uppermost lakes and streams: Black Ant, Black Gnat, California Mosquito, Quill Gordon, and Royal Coachman.

As was mentioned in the previous chapter, nymphs are too often overlooked as a choice by recreational fly fishers. This also holds true for those venturing into the back country. Definitely pack a tight election of dam-selfly, dragonfly, and caddisfly larval imitations.

The Caddis Pupa, Hare's Ear, and Zug Bug nymphs should all work great in sizes #10 to #14. Similarly, a smaller Wooly Worm in a dark shade can be sensational on a drift or when fly-trolled at this elevation.

Because these waters are so clear and the trout are very skittish, it is imperative to make long casts away from the bank when fishing the high country lakes. The versatile spinning fly and bubble setup has really had an impact on this style of Western troutin'. Now, even the most neophyte anglers—as well as seasoned pros—have a chance at catching some of these hook-shy wilderness trout.

A smaller bubble that minimizes the loud "plop" when it lands on the water is recommended. Similarly, stay with dark black swivels when possible to minimize unnatural flash on these crystalline lakes.

Packing Bait

The same basic prepared baits that work at lower impoundments and streams will usually produce in the high country. Salmon eggs, Velveeta cheese, Zeke's Floating Bait, and miniature marshmallows will take their share of high country trout. Light sliding sinkers and very fine diameter leaders in 1 to 2 pound test are essential. Similarly, keep the treble, salmon egg, and baitholder hooks on the small side, scaling down to match the size of the trout indigenous to the wilderness waters.

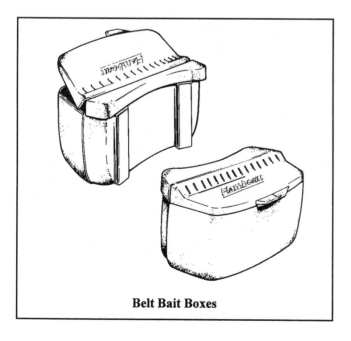

Belt Bait Boxes

Salmon eggs and floating baits can be packed very easily in the jars in which they are sold. Use foil to prevent the Velveeta from excessively melting in the pack and store marshmallows in a plastic zip-lock bag. Above all —and I'm a real strong proponent of this—take back all the containers, plastic bags, and foil you brought into your campsite. It is essential to preserve the pristine nature of this wilderness territory.

Natural baits will consistently catch more fish than prepared offerings in the back country. Pine grubs, ants, hellgrammites, crickets, grasshoppers, caddis larvae, and beetles will be the "hot tickets" for the enterprising angler willing to take the time to trap his bait.

One of the best natural offerings is a red worm fished on a light leader, a 1/8 ounce sliding sinker, and a small #12 to #14 bronze baitholder hook. Another option is to fish one or two of these laced onto the hook, dangling three to four feet below a tiny red and white bobber, snapped directly to 2 pound test monofilament as your main line. Let the mountain winds gently drift the little float and worm along the outside shore ledges. Red worms also excel when drifted in the small creeks and streams in wilderness areas.

Larger browns seem particularly fond of nightcrawlers at these higher elevation lakes. My preference is to fish them with a sliding cast-a-bubble float letting the 'crawler gently sink to the bottom, casted some distance from the bank. (This technique was described in the earlier section on bank fishing basics.)

Another tactic is to use the small red and white bobber but try to cast the longest leader possible between the float and the nightcrawler. With a 6 to 7 foot rod, you can manage to cast a leader line of equal length with some practice. Watch your backcast, particularly around heavy brush-lined lakes.

Both red worms and 'crawlers can be purchased at tackle stores on the way to these mountain lakes. They usually come stored in styrofoam containers which provide adequate insulation during the colder months. In the summer season with warm temperatures even at the higher elevations, the nightcrawlers can pose somewhat of a handling problem. These jumbo worms require cool temperatures to stay alive. Keep them shaded as much as possible.

When the temperature soars, you may be able to salvage them only for the first day of fishing. Without necessary refrigeration, the 'crawlers will usually perish very quickly.

Here is another tip for using these baits. Be selective when you buy nightcrawlers at the tackle shops. Invariably you will find samples that are slightly larger and thicker than red worms while others resemble baby snakes. I have found that the smaller 'crawler works best at higher altitudes. The larger baits are super on lowland reservoirs and on bigger rivers, but they seem to be too large for most high country trout. Sort through the containers and chose the smaller 'crawlers.

Wilderness Gold–California's Golden Trout

Of all the species of trout found in the great state, there is none more revered or treasured by anglers than the golden trout. This species has an interesting past. Biologists theorize that goldens evolved from native rainbows trapped in the state's major glacial basins during the last ice age. Through this natural isolation, they evolved into their present state.

Most goldens are caught in selected lakes between 8,500 and 12,000 feet. Although most fish taken will be between 6 and 10 inches, with a 12 incher considered to be a real trophy, the state record is a whopping 9 pound, 14 ounce monster. State fish and game authorities speculate that there is compelling evidence that even larger goldens exist here in California!

They recommend looking for the larger lunker fish in the French Canyon, Humphrey's Basin, or Bear Creek regions in the John Muir Wilderness Area. Large predator goldens in this class will most likely be found in the deeper, rocky, more isolated high country lakes.

Goldens can be caught on both live and prepared baits. But the major interest has been to fool them with artificials. In selecting spinners and spoons stay with gold finishes and blades. Experts seem to agree that golden trout prefer this shade over nickel, silver, and red and white finishes. Kastmasters, Mepps, Panther Martins, Phoebes, Rooster Tails, and Wob-L-Rites will all work with goldens—in the gold metallic finishes.

For the dedicated fly fisherman, almost all of the popular patterns of dry flies described earlier for wilderness trout will produce catches of goldens. But, here again, the prudent angler would be smart to have a good selection of smaller nymphs handy when venturing into golden country.

Some lakes, for instance the Cottonwood Lakes out of Lone Pine, will have a reduced limit on this precious fish.

Here a five-fish limit applies and only artificials with barbless hooks may be used. Thus, be certain to check current angling regulations if you are particularly interested in pursuing goldens in the high country.

Additional Pointers for High Country Troutin'

Perhaps the most overlooked piece of equipment in many backpacker's supply selections is an item that has nothing really to do with fishing itself—insect repellent. You can figure that if there is a prominent hatch, the bugs will be thick. The mosquito problem at these higher elevations can be absolutely awesome at times during the warmer months. Pack plenty of repellent to last the duration of your stay in the back country.

Wilderness trout are spooky. Long casts, smaller offerings, and light lines are in order. You may have to do more creepin' and crawlin' in stalking these fish in this mirror-like water. Be careful about casting long shadows on the water. Keep your movements to a minimum.

Finally, be especially alert to cruising or rising trout that are extremely visible in this clear water. Wear polarized sunglasses and try to cast beyond the fish so as not to scare them off with a cast placed too close.

Summary

The back country can offer some of the most sensational troutin' available in the Golden State for the angler willing to trek into these areas. The ecology of this alpine environment is very delicate. Take every extra measure to protect and nurture it for future generations. Camp only in areas that are designated by forest service authorities.

Be aware of the fact that you may have to secure a wilderness permit before venturing into these remote areas. These can be easily obtained at regional ranger stations. In more popular areas, it is a good idea to obtain your permit before your trip as the number of persons allowed into a wilderness area is limited in order to preserve these fragile environments.

Practice catch'n release whenever possible, keeping only those trout that you can consume while in the wilderness. And remember to remove all of your trash. Leave your camp in better shape than when you arrived!

Ice Fishin': Cold Foot Troutin'

In the past, ice fishing in California was a fairly well-kept secret among a small group of dedicated "cold footers." Today, more and more West Coast anglers are partaking of this unusual type of troutin', making the pursuit of this game fish truly an all-year sport, even in the Sierras.

Midwesterners have enjoyed ice fishing for a variety of species such as northern pike, pickerel, perch, walleye, and trout on large, expansive lakes. In contrast, our lakes are typically much smaller, and our winters shorter, with icing being more problematic. Here in California, the seasonal climate is simply too unpredictable. Whether or not a lake freezes over becomes a hit-or-miss proposition from year to year.

The likelihood that a lake will freeze over increases with elevation. The dominant species in these higher lakes are trout, which are thus the fish most sought through the ice in California. Rainbows, brookies,

browns, Mackinaw, and Kokonee salmon are all taken by ice fishermen in the Golden State.

Some southland lakes such as Big Bear in the San Bernardino mountains will occasionally ice over in the winter. Further north, a number of other lakes become better candidates for this type of wintertime troutin'.

Along the popular Highway 395 stretch, Convict and Rock Creek Lakes are strong possibilities. As you hit the June Lake Loop, June, Gull, and Silver often freeze solid during a severe California winter. But opportunities really increase in the Mammoth Lakes Chain and along the gateway to Yosemite Valley with Sabrina and Virginia Lakes. On the northeastern side of the Sierras in the Reno-Tahoe basin, other ice fishing hot spots include Davis, Gold, Frenchman, Boca, Stampede, Prosser, and Donner Lakes. To the far north out of Mount Shasta City, Siskiyou, Castle, and Scott Lakes are popular with the "cold foot" crowd.

Ice Fishing Tackle, Bait and Lures

Californians are not quite as sophisticated with their ice fishing gear as their midwestern cousins. For instance, you won't find too many fish shacks or vertical ice-jigging rigs on our lakes. Instead, western trouters stick with very basic spinning or spincast outfits spooled with 4 to 6 pound monofilament.

Many rod and reel companies now market unbelievably tiny mini-spincast combos with the scaled-down rods and super ultralight reels have become very popular with the ice fishing fraternity. A few anglers will keep it even more basic, resorting to simple hand-line rigs.

All of the standard popular bait fishing combinations discussed earlier have application to ice fishing. Salmon eggs, Velveeta cheese, and good ole "garden tackle" (red worms) are favorite fare for trout through the ice. However, keep in mind that trout under these super cold conditions will indeed be hungry but, because their metabolism is slower in the winter, they will need more time to eat the bait. So let these gentle feeders run a little bit further with the bait than you normally would in warmer months.

Accomplished ice fishermen have also discovered the benefits of fish-attracting compounds. They will add some "scent" to all the baits offered through the ice. One little tip is to use either a marshmallow, a ball of Velveeta cheese, or a firm salmon egg (firm to avoid having the trout "suck" them off the hook). Then work some of Berkley's Moldable Strike in the trout scent around the remaining exposed portion of the hook. This bait combination really lays a "chum slick" under the ice for these touchy trout.

Another trick that ice fishermen employ to discern very subtle bites is to use a small plastic bobber as a strike indicator. After you leave the bait at the desired depth, snap the little float onto the monofilament right at the surface water line. The bobber will signal even the faintest of strikes and is easy to monitor visually.

For the more adventuresome, there are a variety of popular lures that can be used under these chilly conditions. Action is critical here. The angler must impart a lot of vertical jigging to the lure to make it palatable to these fish.

Narrow jigging spoons such as the Hopkins, Haddock Jig'n Spoon, and Swedish Pimple are proven winners. More traditional casting spoons like the Kastmaster, Krocadile, and Phoebe will also perform quite well in 1 1/8 to 1 1/2 ounce versions.

Naturally, anticipate that a majority of strikes will occur on the "drop" as you initially let the spoon sink to the bottom or on the "fall" after the spoon is lifted off the bottom and is fluttering down again.

Rapala makes a specially designed minnow that is suitable for ice fishing in their "W" series of baits. This unique lure swims in a circle as it is vertically jigged up and down, making it very tantalizing for bigger trout.

This has been a popular bait in the North and Midwest and is receiving more recognition in California ice fishing circles of late. I should also add that you might need to actually visit a bass fishing pro shop to find these rather bizarre-looking Rapala ice jigs out here in the West. California bass anglers have found these lures to be dynamite at times on deep granite basin lakes when the bass are schooling on small threadfin shad minnows. But keep in mind, on lakes like Casitas, Cachuma, Skinner, San Vincente, and Perris, bass will often be mixed with rainbow trout and vice versa, as they seek out the shad bait fish. Give the Rapala ice jig a try on impoundments like these!

Other interesting baits to consider for ice fishing that are often overlooked are small jigs. Micro-jigs, Scroungers, Baby Gitzits, Haddock Twin Tails, Baby Kreepy Krawlers, and marabou-feathered crappie jigs are all good possibilities. Although most of these lures were designed for panfish or bass, they will often produce sensational catches of trout through the ice.

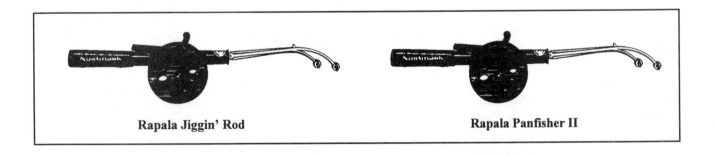

Rapala Jiggin' Rod   Rapala Panfisher II

Ice Jiggin' Rapala Minnow

The key is to team them with light, 4 to 6 pound monofilament line.

It is as important to mix up your presentations while ice fishing as when troutin' from the bank or from a boat. It really helps to vary the depth of the bait or lure you select, fishing it from top to bottom. Most wintertime trout in California will be taken in 4 to 25 feet of water. If anything, novice ice fishermen tend to fish way too deep for these trout.

A very rough rule of thumb to observe is to fish the upper 10 feet of depth on sunny days. On colder, overcast days, keep your offerings near the bottom where warmer water will be found. Remember that darker, muddy bottoms absorb and retain more radiant heat, making them good trout-holding terrain in the winter. Lighter colored, sandy bottoms are better spots after ice-out.

In sum, it is best to work the bait or lure at different levels, starting at the bottom. Then, keep suspending it a few feet higher on subsequent drops until the proper strike zone is determined. Also, in this icy, crystal clear water, the trout will be able to see your bait or lures from considerable distances. Thus, it is essential that you minimize your movement.

Setting Up on the Ice

Before you set out to cut a hole in the ice, it is absolutely imperative to assess whether the ice is thick enough to be safe for fishing. Too many Westerners are unfamiliar with the icing phenomena, having lived in warm environments most of their lives. Thus, when they walk out on the ice, they have little idea of what constitutes a safe condition and can quickly put themselves into a very hazardous situation.

This writer, a longtime Californian, fell victim to this inexperience on the ice one winter's day at Big Bear Lake. I attempted to walk across a shallow portion of the lake that was frozen over to a small, narrow inlet that had open water.

About 100 yards off shore, I fell through what was only about two inches of ice. I will never forget that feeling of sheer terror and "weightlessness" as the bottom literally fell out from underneath me!

Fortunately, a major tragedy was averted since I was only in three feet of water! I had read somewhere that if you can get back on the ice, you should lay down in spread-eagle fashion to more easily distribute your weight. I did this and was lucky enough to inch my way back to safer ground like a snake on its belly.

A good formula to follow is to have at least 6 inches of ice underneath you at all times. Better yet, look for ice about 1 to 2 feet thick for that extra measure of safety. Ice much thicker than this will be too difficult to cut through. Also, I might note that I was virtually alone during my ordeal. If you plan to fish in such potentially dangerous conditions, do so with a buddy or near other ice fishermen in case help is ever needed.

Veteran "cold footers" will have a game plan of sorts of where to start boring the holes. An area where a known creek exists with water that runs into the lake is an excellent spot to start. There is usually some kind of trout feeding activity along these cuts. Similarly, as noted, darker muddy bottoms are good, warm trout-holding areas to try.

Sometimes you can actually lie down on the ice and look through existing holes to see some trout. A better idea is to pack a portable electronic fish finder. To obtain a good reading, first pour salad oil over the smooth ice and then place the transducer on that spot. You will be able to measure not only the depth, but also the availability of any trout immediately in the area where the hole is to be drilled.

Ice fishermen like to cut out a series of holes, not just one. Do this in a wide circle, a straight line, or in a random pattern of your own design. There is a good reason for drilling so many openings: trout spook easily when the hole is bored as the sound is transmitted loudly through the cold water. By cutting a series of holes, you will give the trout time to return to a particular spot while you drill another.

Invest in an inexpensive ice auger to bore through the ice more easily. Holes should be only about 6 to 8 inches in diameter. Try to round off the sharp edges of the hole to avoid having the monofilament get cut upon contact. Keep a kitchen strainer or a slotted spoon handy to remove ice chips that will intermittently form on the surface water.

Here is another suggestion: bring a board to place under your feet. You will undoubtedly get very wet and cold standing around without something under your feet. Arctic-style insulated boots are another alternative. On this note, dress warmly for ice fishing. Students of wilderness travel point out that keeping the extremities warm is of paramount importance to avoid potential frost bite and hypothermia. Insulated socks, warm headgear, and quality gloves are a must for this type of troutin'. Consider packing an extra set of gloves, since invariably your original pair will get wet from drilling, handling fish, and so forth.

Finally, as a courtesy to other "cold footers," leave a mound of ice chips near the holes you have drilled just before you leave for the day. This way they will see these marked openings and avoid unintentionally putting a foot through a hole just recently frozen over!

Summary

Ice fishing in California can provide the Western angler with an entirely new and exciting dimension of trout fishing that only a few have explored. Trout caught under the ice tend to be bigger, better, quality fish with voracious appetites. They are less wary to some degree during these winter months due to significant decreases in angling pressure. Be careful on the ice, try to fish with a buddy, and enjoy a winter's outing in pristine surroundings!

Trophy Trout: And More Tips and Tricks

There is an old saying that goes: 10 percent of the fishermen catch 90 percent of the fish. This may be somewhat overstated in terms of sheer numbers since it does not take a rocket scientist to catch regularly stocked, planter-size rainbows; however, when it comes to fooling larger, quality trout, this adage may indeed be fairly accurate.

As with any type of fishing—fresh and saltwater alike—there is a small group of "hard-core" aficionados who put a lot of time in on the water in pursuit of their favorite game fish. This certainly holds true for the growing legion of California trouters who pound these waters year-round in search of large, trophy fish.

These anglers have devised certain little "tricks," so to speak, that they utilize to not only catch larger trout, but more fish than the average recreational fisherman. As has been mentioned, competition and angling pressure on our California waters is immense at times, especially on weekends. Let's examine some of the finer points of this sport which may provide you with even more productive days in the future.

Bait Dunkin' Tricks

Since a majority of Western trouters rely upon bait to catch their limits, here are a few special tactics that will make your offerings more appealing.

First, the advent of fish attractant scents has had a great impact in professional bass fishing circles, but most West Coast trout fishermen seem very wary of using these concoctions. On many guide trips, I have seen my clients outfish an entire flotilla of boats by using these scents.

Get in the habit of putting a few drops of specialized trout attractant on your bait before every cast. A few drops of Dr. Juice or Berkley Strike, for example, on a cluster of salmon eggs, a 'crawler, or miniature marsh-mallow can create a virtual "chum slick" in the area around the bait. When there are a lot of baits in the water on a crowded lake, you have to give the trout a reason to strike yours above all others. I firmly believe that there is no such thing as too much fish attractant when it comes to trout!

Some pros actually take the trout scents and squeeze a number of drops directly into a jar of salmon eggs before they leave on their trip. They let the eggs and scent sit for a while with the scent almost "curing" into the eggs. This does not affect either the firmness or the milking quality of the egg. It adds another strike-inducing element to the bait.

Another novel approach, mentioned in earlier sections, is to whip up your own "spread" featuring all natural ingredients. Take some garlic and mince it, placing the fine blend in a jar. Mix in Velveeta cheese to develop a thick and pliable paste-like compound. Next, add some cotton balls to the mixture. The cotton fibers keep the cheese and garlic spread adhering together so it won't fall off the hook. You may want to experiment, adding other ingredients, extracts, oils, etc., to come up with your own unique mixture. But this one is my personal favorite, and I can attest that it really works!

Another little secret maneuver is termed "sugar cubing." Often the angler will find trout that are super touchy. Almost any form of resistance in the way of a connecting swivel, split-shot, or even a sliding egg sinker seems to spook the fish. The first thing that comes to mind is to "fly line" the bait without any weight whatsoever on 2 pound test mono. However, too often greater distance is needed than is possible with a simple fly-line approach. The way around this is to cast with a sugar cube.

Using a main line of 2 to 4 pound premium grade monofilament (the lighter the better), tie on a small hook to the end depending upon the type of bait selected. Next, take one or two cocktail-size sugar cubes and affix them about 18 inches above the baited hook. The way to do this is to double about three inches of monofilament and wrap it around the cube, forming a slip knot.

The sugar cube(s) will give you all the weight necessary to make a distance cast. But—and here's the key—as the cube hits the water it starts to quickly dissolve, leaving the bait on a totally weightless line! Remember what was said about keeping the bait slightly moving even when "still-fishing"? Intermittently reel the weightless bait in, occasionally letting it rest for a few minutes to cover greater territory. Keep plenty of sugar cubes ready for subsequent casts. When the trout runs with the bait, the slip knot will pull free so that the fish will be played on a straight, knot-free line.

Northern California trouters have been using an interesting variation of the salmon egg bait that has produced remarkable catches of trophy rainbows and browns. Instead of using the traditional red salmon egg, they still-fish with steelhead roe. These eggs milk much better than salmon eggs and stay on the hook longer.

Steelhead roe comes in vacuum-packed containers in cluster form. The trick is to separate the eggs from the cluster and thread them on a bronze single baitholder hook in size #10 to #12. Try to get about 6 to 12 of the little eggs on the hook to form your own cluster. Here too, give the cluster a few squirts of Dr. Juice or Berkley Strike to spice up the offering.

Another subtle baitfishing tip involves bobber fishing. Many trouters have wondered how to fish trout at greater depths while still using a float. A conventional snap-on plastic bobber allows you to fish perhaps 6 to 7

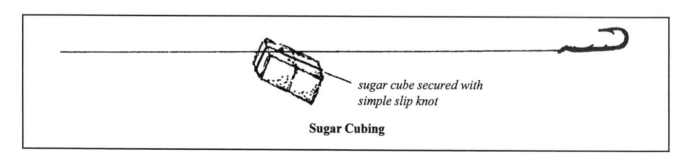

sugar cube secured with simple slip knot

Sugar Cubing

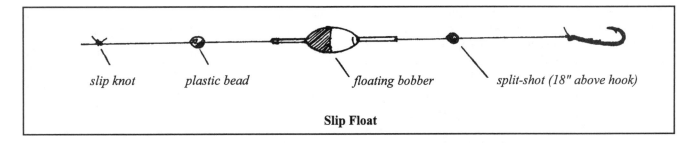

slip knot   *plastic bead*   *floating bobber*   *split-shot (18" above hook)*

Slip Float

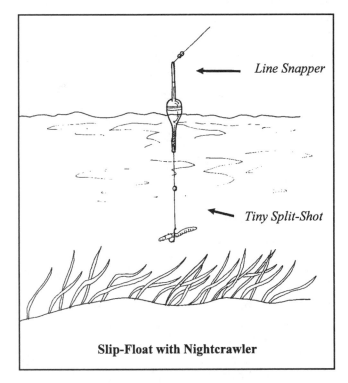

Line Snapper

Tiny Split-Shot

Slip-Float with Nightcrawler

INSTRUCTIONS

Search for the actively feeding big fish by setting your Eagle Claw Precision Turned Float to allow the bait to touch the bottom of the lake. (The float will rest on its side or tip to one side.) Then move the float down the line until the float rests in a straight up-and-down position. If fish don't bite after a reasonable amount of time, move the float down the line another foot or so. Repeat the process, if necessary, until you find the level that produces fish.

Slip Float
Rig to stop float at desired depth. For best results, use Eagle Claw Bobber Stops.

Stick Float
Slide spring up; insert line in slot; then let spring down.

Slip and Stick Floats

Insert line in wire loop. Hold bead between fingers and pull plastic ring. Adjust Float Stop to desired depth. Thread Slip Float, then rig sinker and hook(s) as desired.

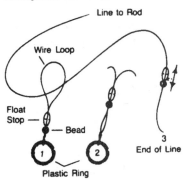

Line to Rod

Wire Loop

Float Stop —

Bead

Plastic Ring

3
End of Line

Rigging Bobber Stops

feet below the surface at best. The unique Float Hi Glo system lets you fish as deep as you want. This quill-like styrofoam bobber rig comes with a pretied slipknot. This knot basically acts as a bumper to keep the sliding float on the surface with the lengthy leader underneath it. The slipknot can be slid up onto your main line, and then actually reeled onto the spinning reel.

This sounds confusing but it really works! Simply cast the float out and the line will slide through it until it hits the slipknot. A plastic bead is used above the knot. A split-shot is also crimped about 12 inches above the baited hook to make it sink faster and align it vertically. You can fish any depth desired with this unique slip-float setup, all the way down to 35 or 40 feet if necessary while still essentially bobber fishing.

A final tip to consider in baitfishing for lunker-class fish is to learn how to "back-reel." A lot of real "hawgs" are lost on light lines and leaders. It becomes kind of a "Catch-22" situation. The angler wants to nail a big fish, but he has to use a fine diameter line to get them to bite. Then in the ensuing battle, the trophy is lost with one final surge that breaks the light leader material.

This scenario can repeat itself even with the best drag systems available on today's hi-tech reels. A way to minimize this is to back-reel, giving the fish line in conjunction with the mono played out by the drag. You can do this by switching off the anti-reverse mechanism on most open-face spinning reels. Some push-button and baitcasters also allow you to disengage the anti-reverse feature. By back-reeling, the angler can respond and give the fish line much more quickly than by just relying upon the drag. Too few trouters employ this technique when using light lines. It can really save that lunker from breaking off.

Keep in mind that the reels from yesteryear that our grandfathers used did not have the sophisticated drag systems of today's hi-tech spinners and baitcasting models. In those days, anglers had to master the art of "back-reeling" if they wanted to catch that lunker trout.

Similarly, this tactic will work when trolling for, say, big browns, using light 6 to 8 pound test line for fish scaling over 2 to 3 pounds. Also, keep in mind that on those particularly cold mornings or entire days, the reel drag you precisely set at home before departing on the trip may now have washers that are somewhat sticky or even frozen due to being in the weather. Check and readjust the drag once in the field. But remember, back-reeling on a trophy fish eliminates the need to really worry about drags. Success is now in *your* hands, not your reel's!

Other Spinner and Spoon Strategies

There are a few other things weekend trouters can do with spinners and spoons to enhance their fish-catching potential. For example, sometimes the factory-stocked treble hooks that come with these lures are not the best options available.

If you seem to be missing some strikes, take a pair of pliers and offset the hooks. By offsetting each of the three hooks, you will open up more space between them. This will make the overall treble hook somewhat more prone to getting hung up, but in open water it will also make the treble hook more effective for hook-setting.

Similarly, often the stock treble hooks are too small for the lure and many fish are lost. Replace them with

larger trebles—preferably in the more natural bronze finish instead of the flashy chrome versions.

Treble hooks on spoons and spinners can also be replaced with a sharper single Siwash hook. I mentioned earlier that this single hook arrangement actually provides better leverage and hook-setting qualities than most treble hooks. Add a chunk of 'crawler colored yarn, or even a tiny 2 inch plastic worm as a trailer to the single hook.

With trout spinners, you can bend out the blade a little to create a wider arc in the blade's movement. This results in greater vibration. Or, you can bend the blade in a little, cupping it, to generate more "thumping" action.

Above all, take the extra time and effort to sharpen all the hooks on the lures you throw, trebles and single hooks alike. Far too often a quality trout is lost because the angler relied upon the hooks right from the factory box. Carry a hook sharpener with you in the field and re-sharpen points as needed.

More Ploys with Plugs

Not only do Western anglers overlook using plugs for trout, they miss out on tossing some of the more exotic patterns that catch larger fish. An illustration of this is the small Rebel crawdad-shaped crankbaits. These plugs have been producing some lunker-size fish for shore fishermen for years on the lower Owens River and Pleasant Valley Reservoir.

No doubt, other imaginative trouters have used this little plug elsewhere in California but have pretty much kept quiet about it. Crawdads are a major forage food for these larger rainbows and browns. This small Rebel plug excels at replicating this natural bait.

On a similar vein, believe it or not, big trout will crash on a large top-water plug! Occasionally, some creative anglers have used plugs such as the distinctively cigar-shaped Heddon Zara Spook on magnum-size surface-feeding fish. This style bait is made to imitate a dying, fluttering minnow struggling on the surface.

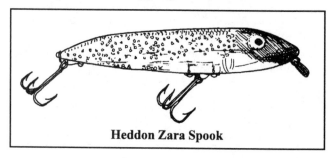

Heddon Zara Spook

It is no mere coincidence that these would work on a marauding cannibalistic brown trout on a big reservoir. Early morning and dusk are the best times to take a shot with these large surface plugs.

Other mainstream bass plugs can also be productive at times on bruiser trout. Arbogast Hula Poppers and Storm Chug Bugs can be fished on the surface. Or, where there are a lot of threadfin shad around, try a thinner profile crankbait such as the Storm Thin Fin, Bayou Boogie, Cordell Spot, or Rapala Shad Rap. Purchase these plugs in foil, shad, perch, or rainbow trout colors. You can also troll them fairly quickly on straight 8 pound monofilament using a top-line approach.

Plugs can also work on rivers as well as lakes. If there are a lot of obstructions to get snagged on, replace the treble hooks with single Siwash hooks. These will hang up much less in the fast-moving water.

Unusual Soft Plastic Baits

More and more recreational anglers are experimenting with soft plastic baits for Western troutin'. Many of these lures have enjoyed prominent success among bass and crappie fishermen, but not too surprisingly, they will often prove very effective on trout.

Tiny plastic panfish lures such as the Mini-Jig or Baby Gitzits can be dynamite on a variety of trout. Fish these directly on 2 to 4 pound monofilament and definitely add some scent to the lure. In the case of the tubular baits, put the scent directly into the hollow body. The fluorescent pink color in particular seems to be a "hot" combination with these small jigs.

The Scrounger is another intriguing lure that also has been a proven winner for California trout. This tiny plastic grub with the curl tail also features a unique plastic-lipped jig head. This pronounced lip results in a tremendous oscillating effect from the Scrounger even with the slowest retrieves.

The Scrounger is made to resemble a small forage minnow, erratically swimming from a hungry game fish. Fish the lure on ultralight gear either casting it or working it on a slow-troll pattern. Silver, clear, white, and yellow colors are suitable for troutin'.

Plastic knob-tail baits such as A.A. Worms Super Shads are similarly viable trout getters designed to have terrific tail-throbbing action. These should be rigged on either 1/16 or 1/8 ounce lead heads. They can be casted and steadily retrieved back to the boat or shore. Or, they can be slow-trolled like the Scrounger. Super Shads are available in a very realistic rainbow trout finish that can also be effective on larger, quality fish along with shad patterns.

One other soft plastic lure is a rather bizarre "sleeper" of sorts among the trout fishing experts—the plastic worm. My first encounter with this bait's application on trout waters occurred one evening at Big Bear Lake in the San Bernardino Mountains. Larger 1-1/2 to 3 pound rainbows were puddlin' near the surface, occasionally lazily rising to a weak insect hatch late in the afternoon.

After a few strikes with an assortment of regionally-favored dry flies, I threw a 6 inch plastic worm across the surface. This worm was in the natural nightcrawler color with both a front and "stinger" hook in the rear. With just a few twitches of the rod tip, I made the worm move sinuously just under the surface. In a matter of seconds, there was a vicious boil on the bait and a fat 2 pound rainbow quickly ended up on an otherwise empty stringer. Give these worms a try—especially fished with an open hook just under the surface. The results may surprise you! Usually, you will not find soft plastic worms rigged like this, so you must rely upon your own handiwork. However, I might add, that occasionally you might find some plastic worms that are actually rigged with a front and rear ("stinger") hook, as well as a couple of fluorescent beads and a small propeller blade at the head! As crazy as this lure looks, it does actually catch some nice rainbows

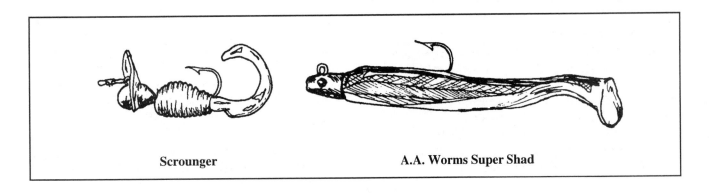

Scrounger   **A.A. Worms Super Shad**

for anglers working on subsurface fish on lakes or in deep river pools.

Secrets of the Trophy Hunters

There is an elite band of trout fishermen in California who are primarily committed to one endeavor: searching for trophy, world-class, brown trout. These men put tremendous time in on the water pursuing both line class and all-time record browns. They fish in some of the most inclement weather and pride themselves on being "first on" and "last off" the lake.

Bob Bringhurst and Jon Minami are two of these California "hawg hunters" with impressive credentials. Bringhurst was the former all-tackle world record holder for the brown trout category with an incredible 33 pound, 10 ounce behemoth! Minami is the previous California state record holder with a 26 pound, 5 ounce brown. Both of these men have spent hundreds of hours on California's trophy lakes such as Bridgeport, Lower Twin, and Crowley in quest of these lunker fish. Each is recognized as a true expert on how to catch record-breaking browns. Here are some secret tips they are willing to share with the reader.

To start with, they are very selective as to when to fish for trophy-size browns. They concur that the two best times of the year to look for big browns are at the start of the season or late fall. In early spring, the fish will be actively feeding following the winter thaw. Their appetites will be voracious with a penchant for large bait fish such as planted rainbows or small Kokanee salmon. Bringhurst and Minami then shy away from these lakes in the summer when vacation crowds and angling pressure increase. Their interest is rekindled by late October when the bigger browns start to move into the shallows to spawn. Hence, autumn is the other major period in which to concentrate when looking for a trophy fish.

The best time of day to fish for lunker browns is the early morning or late afternoon. Bringhurst notes that he will start in the morning and stop fishing when the shadows leave the water. After a midday rest, he will return to the lake at 3:00 p.m. and begin to work the darker water all the way until dusk.

Minami prefers to fish in the worst, most miserable weather in which he can safely maneuver his boat. He theorizes that big trout are extremely wary. With rain, wind, snow and wave chop, the water conditions become much more turbulent and the fish a lot less hook shy. Less dedicated trouters will also quickly exit from the lake under such conditions. This leaves the better spots open with virtually no angling pressure.

There are some prime areas on these larger bodies of water that will hold big trout. The pros will look for locations that go from deep to shallow. Points, ridges, and drop-offs will sustain a lot of forage bait. Larger browns will move up and down along these areas throughout the season. Spots where the hatchery trucks dump small stocked rainbows can also hold a resident population of big fish. The shallower weed lines in the fall will also harbor chub minnows in some lakes—another preferred food of larger brown trout.

Thus, Bringhurst and Minami rely upon their electronics to monitor the location of "bait fish" (chubs, shad, planted rainbows, and school Kokanees). This is where the largest specimens in the lake will likely be found. In a sense then, the experts will look for "structure," preferably with deep-water access that should hold bait fish and in turn attract big browns.

Strangely enough, our experts won't waste time fishing live bait or using lead core, downriggers, diving planes, or lake trolls in pursuing trophy browns. Instead, they rely upon one primary method—top line trolling with BIG baits.

Bringhurst likes to pull a minnow-shaped plug most of the time. The Bomber Model Long-A in gold chub-like finish is one of his favorite choices. When he senses the browns are feasting on kokes or small rainbows, he switches to a larger Rapala minnow in sizes #13 to #18 in rainbow trout pattern.

Minami, by contrast, will drag either a magnum-size #U-20 Flatfish in a frog finish, or a super long #18 floating Rapala. Using only 8 pound mono, he will troll these baits at subsurface depths, not much more than 10 to 12 feet. Occasionally, in rough water, Minami adds a small 1/4 ounce keel weight to hold the plug down and keep it from planing. With jumbo baits like these, it is also best to use a durable, black interlocking snap, and consider changing to stronger, sharper bronze treble hooks.

Trolling speed can be critical when pulling these extraordinary large baits. The first thing Minami does when he sets out on a lake is to take surface temperature readings. If the water temperature is real cold in the 35 to 40 range, a very slow troll down to as low as 1 1/2 mph will be used to drag the big plugs. In warmer water, a much faster troll can be employed (5 to 8 mph). It sometimes helps to add a series of twitches or jerks to these big plugs while trolling to present a more tantalizing action.

The pros will also custom color these hefty Rapala minnows. They purchase the stock plug in silver with black back. Next they use a permanent marker and etch a lateral red line. By then adding numerous black dots with another marker, they end up with some very fancy cosmetics, very closely resembling the Kokanee or rainbow forage bait. If the water is very stained, they will make the black dots extra large (about the width of the pen's tip) to enhance the lure's visibility.

Only occasionally will Bringhurst and Minami actually throw on boiling surface-feeding fish. This usually occurs with big spawners working the shallows in the fall. Even then they will opt for their favorite lures, the Bomber Long-A or the king-size Rapala minnow. Here they emphasize that it's important not to just toss it out and grind it straight back to the boat. Be somewhat inventive and instill a more dynamic erratic motion to the lure so as to mimic a frantic fleeing rainbow, chub, or Koke.

Summary

It will take a very creative and cunning approach to consistently catch the larger trophy trout from our crowded waters. Jon Minami summarizes it best when he says the major edge he maintains over the recreational weekend trouter is his dedication and perseverance. Too often the novice angler gives up when weather conditions turn sour or the action slows down. This is when the pros "gut it out," as they say, drawing upon past experiences and using their innovative techniques to make some spectacular catches!

Cleaning and Cooking Your Catch

Trout should be handled with care once they are taken from the water. Short of icing down a cleaned fish, it's best to keep the trout alive as long as possible. Interestingly, once the fish dies, the stomach fluids continue with the digestive process. It is this metabolic function that is the primary cause of spoiled meat. Also, if you soak a dead trout in water, bacterial growth is rapidly increased and the flesh softens in a matter of hours.

Storing Trout Properly

Some anglers prefer to simply string their trout on a cord stringer. Others opt for a fancier safety-pin style stringer with either metal or nylon clips to secure the fish. If you decide to string your catch, be sure to run the stringer through the jaw, not through the gills. Trout will survive longer if strung through the lower jaw. Fish will die very quickly if the gills are impaired.

Try to keep the stringer out in deeper, cooler water if possible. If you are fishing from the bank, tie an extra length of cord to the stringer to keep the trout further off the shore. The water closest to the bank is also usually the muddiest and most silt-laden. Leaving trout in dirty water for a number of hours causes them to die too soon.

For boaters, wire fish baskets, as mentioned, are good investments. These will keep trout in fairly good condition all day. Another option is to put the fish into an ice chest immediately after they are caught. Ideally it is best to clean or fillet them at this time and then place the trout on a bed of ice. Be sure to drain the water intermittently.

My experiences as a guide have shown this to be the best overall method of insuring maximum freshness for my clients' catch. The ice will also keep the flesh firm for some time. If you don't clean the trout at once, then at least try to store the fish whole on the ice. The worst thing you can face after a hard day of fishing is trying to fillet a soft, mushy trout that has been handled improperly.

During the winter season, you can conveniently toss trout up on to the snow bank. They will keep all day long in this natural deep freeze.

For a more traditional approach, a creel is still an excellent choice for keeping trout fresh while walking the bank. Avoid buying a cheap rubberized nylon-canvas version. These do not have the insulation qualities of the better Arctic-type creels. These are made with heavy evaporation canvas outer layers and an excellent plastic inner liner. The canvas absorbs water perfectly and will keep the trout very cool as the moisture evaporates through the fabric. The plastic inner lining is non-absorbent and will clean very easily.

The old-fashioned natural wicker creels are still sold more for sentimental value since they are relatively expensive. It's hard to beat the Arctic-style models.

Some trouters still persist in lining the inside pouch of the creel with wet shoreline grass. This adds a modest amount of insulation but is not that essential if the outside of the creel is kept wet. Every once in a while, take the time to wash the canvas creels out with warm water and a light detergent. This will help to keep the fabric from rotting prematurely.

Cleaning Trout

The overwhelmingly easiest way to clean trout is a process known as "gillin'n guttin'." This procedure is exceptionally suitable for planter-size trout and under field conditions.

Take the point of your knife blade and insert it into the fish's anal pore. Run the blade all the way up to the gills. Spread open the body cavity and remove the entrails. Next, grabbing the lower jaw, pull back, separating the

jaw and the gills from the head area. You will actually pull on the jaw with a tearing motion to rip out the gills.

Now, take your thumb and move it down the exposed dark dorsal vain that traverses the length of the body cavity. Pushing down with your thumb ruptures this vessel and clears out the dark blood line. Run cold water through the meat to clean out residual waste. This will keep the trout in good shape for being transported until you are ready to cook it.

Depending upon your sense of "culinary aesthetics," cook the fish "as is," or cut off all the fins with a knife, scrape off the scales, and remove the head when you get home.

Gillin'n guttin' works particularly well on smaller fish. To avoid bones, filleting is your best preparation, however. It requires almost surgeon-like skill to do this

with planter-sized trout. The key to filleting—whether on plants or larger fish—is to use a thin-blade razor-shape knife. The blade has to be extra thin and sharp to separate the meat from the skin. A dull blade has a tendency to tear the meat unevenly and ruin the fillet.

I prefer to hold the fish by the head as it is placed on a flat surface with the back (dorsal) side facing toward me. I'll make a diagonal cut behind the gill cover and run the blade all the way down to the tail. Next, I cut through the widest portion of the fillet (making a diagonal cut) but don't cut through the skin. Twist the blade to gently slide down the fillet separating the muscle fiber connecting the skin to the meat.

Turn the trout over on the other side and repeat the entire procedure. This will leave you with two fillets, minimal bones, if any, and no skin.

On super large trout—that lunker over 3 or 4 pounds—consider steaking it out in a manner similar to the way in which salmon is prepared. Gut the fish, then make a series of lateral cuts (crosswise) through the bone and meat, starting from behind the gill cover to the tail. Steaked sections like these can be grilled, baked, or barbecued.

Preparing Trout

Trout flesh is tender and delicately flavored. It can range in color from white to the deep pinkish orange most commonly associated with salmon. Trout are very good when prepared by most cooking methods. Smaller trout are best when freshly grilled over an open fire. They can also be pan-fried, oven-fried, or baked with butter or other light sauce. Larger trout are especially excellent when baked, stuffed, or broiled.

Over the years I have run across a number of tasty recipes for trout. Here are some of my favorites.

Grilled/Barbecued Trout

These following recipes for barbecued or grilled trout are especially great when camping. They are simple and quick to prepare but wonderfully tasty in the out-of-doors. Or, you can prepare them on your backyard barbecue with equal success.

Best Barbecued Trout

Fresh whole trout, cleaned
Butter
Fresh lime juice
Ground pepper
Paprika (optional)
Lemon wedges and sauce, if desired

Melt the butter and mix with the lime juice and black pepper to taste. Oil the heated grill thoroughly with vegetable oil to prevent fish from sticking. Place the trout on grill and turn frequently so the fish won't curl. Baste with the butter mixture every few minutes. When the skin begins to brown, lower the grill closer to the coals, cooking about 3 to 5 minutes on each side, depending on the size of the fish and heat of the flame.

Serve with fresh lemon slices. Total cooking time is 8 to 12 minutes.

Quick'n Easy Grilled Trout

Fresh whole trout, cleaned
Italian or other oil dressing

For an easy tasty treat, use the recipe above but substitute your favorite oil base dressing for the butter mixture. Be sure to brush the fish inside and out.

Pan-Fried Trout

The all-time favorite way to prepare trout when camping is pan-frying. It is easy to do and the trout are very tasty. Make sure you cook them slowly so they have a flaky tenderness while the skin remains golden brown.

Old-Fashioned Camp Trout

Fresh whole trout, cleaned
Flour
Seasoning (marjoram, dill or paprika to taste)
Lemon wedges
Fresh minced parsley

Wash and pat the cleaned fish dry. Roll in the seasoned flour. Heat the fat (oil, butter or bacon grease) in a heavy skillet , add the fish and cook over medium coals. Turn the fish often to prevent sticking. Cook the fish slowly until the inside is flaky and tender and the skin is tender and golden. Serve with fresh lemon slices and fresh minced parsley.

Panfish Fried in Batter

Fresh cleaned whole trout
1 egg, lightly beaten
1/4 cup milk or canned milk diluted with water
1/2 cup bread crumbs, cornmeal or cracker crumbs
Seasoning to taste
Lemon wedges

Combine the egg and milk. Dip the trout in the mixture then coat with the crumbs or cornmeal. Lay out the fish on a clean flat surface and allow to dry 3 to 5 minutes. Heat the oil in a large skillet. Add the fish and fry until golden brown on one side, turn and fry until the flesh flakes easily when gently probed with the tines of a fork. Serve with lemon wedges.

 **Poached Trout**

Here's a fancier recipe which requires a few more ingredients but tastes great on a camping trip. It is excellent with medium-sized trout.

Trout Poached in Wine

Fresh cleaned medium-sized trout (frozen may also be used)
Dry mustard
2 tablespoons butter or oil 1 tablespoon soy sauce
1 teaspoon honey
1/4 cup sherry wine
1 cup water
1 tablespoon or more flour

Mix 1 tablespoon butter and a pinch of mustard in a large heavy skillet until well blended. Add the remaining ingredients, stir well and heat to boiling. Simmer for 5 minutes. Add the fish, cover and continue cooking until the flesh flakes easily.

Remove the fish and cover to keep warm. Blend the flour with the remaining butter and add to the sauce. Cook, stirring constantly, until thickened. Pour the sauce over the trout and serve.

 **Battered Trout**

One of my favorite trout recipes uses a modified beer batter mix. This is a simple, delicious camp recipe.

Beer Batter Trout

2 cups whole wheat flour
Beer (your favorite light or dark brew)
Clear cooking oil
Trout fillets

Slowly mix the beer into the flour. The batter should be moderately thick so that it does not drip off the small pieces of fillet when dipped. Cut the trout fillets into about 1 x 3 inch pieces. Dip them into the batter and slide them into the hot oil. The whole wheat flour will deep-fry to a golden brown crust. Mat each piece dry with paper towels. Sprinkle with malt vinegar.

Note: You can also make a tempura batter to deep-fry your trout pieces. Tempura batter mixes are sold commercially and usually stocked in the ethnic food sections of bigger supermarkets. Make sure your clear cooking oil is very hot before frying your tempura-coated trout pieces.

The Amazin' Finger Jig

John Beale has become somewhat of a local fishing legend in Southern California. Like a pied piper of sorts, Beale is known as "Crappie John" among his followers. He routinely holds informal seminars at area lakes demonstrating the tiny lures that have made him one of the most extraordinary fishermen in the Southland. In 1989 alone, Beale personally tallied nine rainbow trout topping the ten pound mark, including two 16 pound monsters. Most of these lunkers were taken from put-and-take reservoirs like Irvine, Prado, or Santa Ana River Lakes. Hard-core trouters may snicker at Beale's accomplishments, noting that catching trophy fish of this magnitude is easy on such waters. The thousands of good fishermen who visit these lakes each year and never catch a double-digit rainbow might argue this point. Remember, Beale didn't do this once, but rather nine times that season!

But here is another interesting statistic that may temper the skeptics. One year, on a junket to North and South Lakes and Bishop Creek, Beale, and his party of four nailed 700 trout in three days! This included not only rainbows, but also brookies and German browns. I should add that almost all of these fish were released as Beale does with lunkers caught on local lakes. So what is the secret to this one man's success? It evolves around a minuscule bait Beale developed called the "Finger Jig." This lure, combined with a highly sophisticated methodology, makes the Finger Jig one of the most potent weapons trout anglers can add to their lure arsenals.

The Lure

Upon first glance, Beale's invention is a relatively unspectacular-looking bait. It resembles many of the various plastic skirted crappie lures used by pan fishermen throughout the West. One would hardly believe that these tiny 1/64 and 1/32 ounce jigs are serious hawg catchers. But Beale has put a lot of technology into these little lures. To begin with, the hollow tube itself is made from a special rubber compound, not plastic. Beale is emphatic that this is a critical distinction between his Finger Jigs and other crappie lures. He notes that, in contrast to similar looking plastic baits, the miniature tentacles in the tail portion of the Finger Jig always stay flared apart. This gives his little tube bait a lifelike, "breathing" appearance. Beale also points out that the Finger Jigs have gone through years of trial-and-error as far as balance and symmetry are concerned. He claims that many of the imitations of his lures will not rotate like a wounded bait fish. He also has a patent on the jig head he uses. It is completely balanced from the end of the hook to the nose of the lead head, and maintains its perfect balance when you put the skirt on. All the skirts used with the Finger Jig have the same weight.

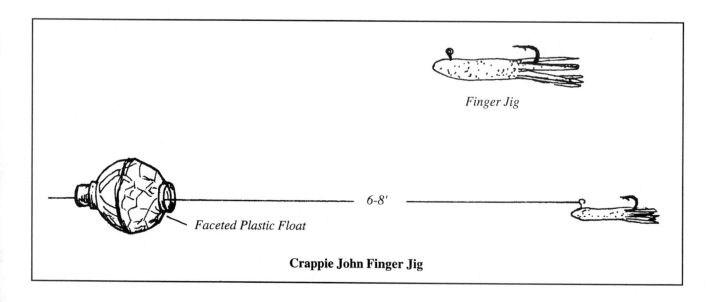

Finger Jig

6-8'

Faceted Plastic Float

Crappie John Finger Jig

It is also important to mention that upon close scrutiny, Beale's creation is distinctively rigged in a way that is different from most other lightweight jigs. If you examine it, you will observe that the tiny lead head is actually implanted inside the hollow tubular body instead of laced externally through the nose of the bait.

Freshwater bass fishermen will quickly observe the similarities between the design of the Finger Jig and the way bass pros rig the popular Fat Gitzit, Power Tubes, and Fatzee tube baits with an internal jig head. In both situations, the internal rigging has the effect of making the hollow-bodied lures 'swim" erratically through the water. Beale suggests using the smaller 1/64 ounce lure on higher elevation lakes or when the trout seem particularly spooky. Switch to the large 1/32 ounce version on larger impoundments or when you are trophy hunting.

As for color selection, a lot depends on water clarity according to Beale. He recommends using smoke/sparkle, rainbow, clear/silver, or brown and orange with red flake for clearer water. If the water is stained, he will switch to a brighter color. On one particular outing, I noticed that the water color at Anaheim Lake was a stained, greenish color. Beale immediately tied on a brilliant chartreuse Finger Jig. His success that day under tough conditions proved his color choice was indeed the right one.

The Rig

While fishing with Beale, I was amazed at how specific he is in terms of the tackle used to present the Finger Jig. He recommends a rod that is seven feet long with a parabolic shape and a soft tip. The rod should be made from high quality fiberglass rather than graphite. This is because the fiberglass composition is much more forgiving with the "soft" action than an ultra responsive graphite blank. Quite frequently, the trout will gently mouth the Finger Jig. The soft-tip rod allows for a smooth gradual set. A stiffer graphite model might inadvertently tear the little jig out of the trout's mouth with the slightest hook set.

Beale matches the rod with an ultralight spinning reel. He has used a variety of models and is emphatic that it must have a super-smooth drag. As for line, Beale is adamant that it must be green-colored two pound test. He firmly believes that on heavily pressured lakes like Anaheim or Irvine, this particular monofilament is the most invisible to skittish rainbows.

The Bobber

Surprisingly, the most intriguing component to Beale's system is the small plastic bobber he uses to suspend the tiny Finger Jig. These are basically the standard red and white or fluorescent floats used for pan-fishing. However, it is what Beale does to these stock bobbers prior to using them that is a fairly well-kept secret. First, his floats have to be re-worked to accommodate the gossamer two pound test mono. The trick is to make certain there are no sharp plastic ridges on the bobber from when it was molded. Trim down the plastic molded ridge with nail clippers, then sand it, round it off, and smooth it down to where it won't cut the line. Two pound test line is pretty easy to cut.

Next, select a float to match prevailing conditions. Beale recommends a 1/4 to 1/2 inch diameter bobber for most municipal lakes. Scale up to a one inch diameter maximum when distance is needed on larger impoundments or because of windy weather.

Here's another little ploy Beale and his disciples use to customize their bobbers. They will very carefully bore a small hole in the float and add a ball-bearing shot or strands of soft wire pushed down into the opening. Then the hole is resealed with epoxy. The extra weight facilitates greater distance when casting but it doesn't impair the overall balance of the setup. Beale stresses, however, that whenever possible use the lightest bobber you can. If the trout feel any resistance, they will drop the lure. The lighter the bobber, the less resistance they will have. They will pull the smaller bobbers under quicker than the larger ones.

One final tip is worth mentioning when it comes to selecting a plastic float for this unique tactic. Lately Beale has been experimenting with a new wave of compact, snap-on bobbers that are chrome-plated. These floats have faceted surfaces so that they reflect considerable light while rocking on the surface. Beale theorizes that on lakes which have a prominent population of threadfin shad, the more angular-shaped chrome bobber appears as a school of minnows darting near the surface. Presumably, this serves to call in big hungry rainbows to investigate.

The Presentation

It will take some practice to cast the Finger Jig rig with anywhere from 5-7 feet of dangling leader. Beale basically swings the leader in a circle over his head—as if it were a lariat. He releases the mono from his finger as the leader completes the circle. The momentum of the moving leader and float helps to sort of "slingshot" them off the rod. Once the cast is completed, the most intricate phase of the presentation begins—the retrieve. The trick is to extend the index finger of the hand holding the rod. As you start to wind in, the fine diameter monofilament slaps against the finger with each turn of the rod handle. What happens is that each time the mono bumps across the finger, the miniature jig hops or jumps underwater. This gives the illusion of a frantic minnow. But this is only part of the program.

It is equally essential to occasionally pause for a few moments, allowing the bobber to remain motionless. The jig actually swims in a circle. Even though it's on a bobber and you may have 5 or 6 feet of leader from the bobber to the lure, it will swim down as long as you don't touch the bobber. It you move the bobber, the jig will move in the opposite direction—it will dart back. Also, every time you move it, the tail is opening and closing. Thus, the slow stop-and-go retrieve generates a highly seductive swimming action in the Finger Jig. Wave motion and current can similarly make the little lure appear to be quite lifelike, mimicking an errant bait fish.

Another secret tactic frequently used by Beale and his cohorts is to thread a jumbo-size worm onto the 1/32 ounce Finger Jig and a smaller "mealie" onto the 1/64 ounce model. The addition of the live larvae can quickly stimulate feeding interest in the trout when the bare jig fails to produce. Beale also sometimes prefers to "fly line" his lures as he terms it. In this situation, he will not use a plastic float, simply casting the Finger Jig out tied directly to the two pound mono. Here too, he leaves his index finger extended close to the bait so the line will jump with each complete turn.

The trout do not always inhale the tiny bait. Sometimes, especially with the bobber rig, the strike will resemble that of a bluegill or crappie. The trout will bobble the float. It will take off to one side. Count 1, 2, and then strike. Other times, while fly-lining the Finger Jig, the strike may be nothing more than a subtle "tick" or merely a mushy pressure on the end of the line.

More Applications

Crappie John's method will also work on other freshwater species. For instance, Beale has staged convincing demonstrations racking up hefty crappie stringers at Southland lakes such as Henshaw, Silverwood, and Wohford. You can work the Finger Jig from the bank as Beale does, or from a boat, or even while wading or float-tubing.

Don't be surprised if some wayward largemouth, bronzeback, or spotted bass annihilates this little bait. Beale has caught many keeper-class bass with this technique. Although his specialized rig may not be as "hi-tech" looking as today's modern bass weaponry, tournament anglers may want to give Beale's Finger Jig a try. There is no question—it routinely produces under diverse conditions when other more conventional offerings fail.

Lunkers on the A.C. Plug and the Super Shad

Alan Cole is a painting contractor turned lure manufacturer, designer, and inventor, living in Southern California. Cole is also a member of the "Brown Baggers," an informal group of professional trouters who specialize in hunting double-digit weight rainbows and brown trout. Over the years, while tinkering in his garage, Cole came up with a design for a lure that would prove to be deadly on big Florida-strain largemouth bass, striped bass, and—you guessed it—lunker rainbows and browns.

Cole's original A.C. Plugs were handmade from wooden doweling, reminiscent of what you use to hang your clothes on in the bedroom closet. He carefully notched each head portion of the lure to form a rudimentary but effective diving lip. Each original plug had a tail portion, connected to the head piece with a joint. Upon first glance, Cole's invention was nothing more than a large, notched wooden plug similar to those used for northern pike or muskie.

But here's where Cole's invention differs. The wooden tail portion of these long, 8 to 12 inch plugs is also notched out. In the notch, Cole cemented a rather peculiar looking, soft plastic tail section with a prominent paddle on the end of it. (These soft plastic tails are similar to the Super Shads made by A.A. Worms but without the thicker torso design.)

It is this soft plastic tail section, mounted into the wooden, jointed plug that drives the big fish crazy! This magnum-size lure generates considerable action solely from the jointed wooden front and rear parts moving back and forth on the retrieve. This action is nothing compared to the sensual, throbbing movement that is produced by the thin soft plastic tail section, as the A.C. Plug swims through the water.

Cole figured that this slow-swimming seductive action mimicked the basic movement of typical hatchery-bred rainbows. As all veteran Brown Baggers know, these stocked 'bows are prime targets for trophy rainbows and brown trout topping the ten pound mark.

Once the action was narrowed down, Cole worked on the finish of the plug. The original versions of his big crankbait were hand-painted with many coats of lacquer, combined with a sprinkling of brilliant, scalelike glitter. Each A.C. Plug left Cole's garage-factory as a nearly perfect match to a planter rainbow, both in size, coloration, and most importantly action.

As the word quickly spread—especially among lunker bass fishermen and striper snipers whose target species also prey upon small rainbows—Cole could barely keep up with the demand for his homemade jumbo plugs. Local tackle stores in Southern California were retailing

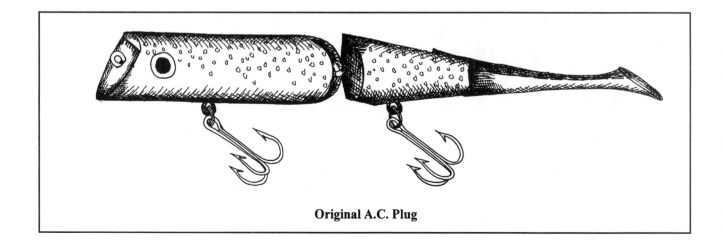

Original A.C. Plug

these original A.C. Plugs for up to $50.00 each and they were selling out at that.

Eventually, Cole's big fish killer caught the attention of the Arbogast Lure Company which now mass manufactures the A.C. Plugs at much more affordable prices. I should add that you might be able to find some of Cole's original creations collecting dust on tackle shop shelves. Each one of these handmade models has its own unique swimming action, so you never know what you might be getting until you pulled the plug through the water. This "surprise factor" has been, of course, eliminated, as the new Arbogast models are manufactured with high standards of uniformity.

Fishing the A.C. Plug

I spent numerous days on the water with Cole, observing the ways in which he most effectively fished his big lures. My impression is that there are fundamentally three techniques for working the A.C. Plug: casting, top-line and lead-core trolling.

Casting

It will take some real strength and stamina to toss this plug all day from either a boat or while walking the bank. My preference is to use light-to-medium saltwater tackle. Keep in mind, that casts over 60 yards are easily possible with this huge lure! I like to throw it with a 7 1/2 foot graphite poppin' rod combined with a Penn Levelmatic 93 0/940 baitcasting reel and spooled with 15 to 20 pound test premium grade monofilament. I emphasize using this 930/940 reel for one important reason: oversized, smooth, saltwater drags.

930 Penn Levelmatic

On my third cast with this plug, the very first day I used it at Lake Castaic, I got bit by a lunker fish! I wasn't sure if it was big holdover trout, a giant striper, or one of the legendary Florida-strain largemouth bass found in this metropolitan impoundment. What I nailed was a whopping 9 pound, 12 ounce largemouth with both of the A.C. Plug's big trebles lodged in its mouth!

I specifically rigged up that day with the Penn Levelmatic reel, with the idea and hope in mind that I would stalk a big fish with the big lure. I wanted that saltwater drag in case I was lucky enough to find a saltwater-size fish in this popular freshwater reservoir.

Now, as far as the retrieve goes, let me stress that the "toads" that are tallied on this bait—trout, bass and stripers alike—seem to strike it best on a slow wind. Don't expect the plug to dive too deep either. Most of the originals swam at about 2 to 6 foot, subsurface depths. So a faster retrieve won't necessarily pull the A.C. down deeper. In fact, if you reel in too fast, the big plug may start to plane and "water-ski" on the surface.

Also, you will quickly realize that it does not take too much retrieve speed to get that seductive soft plastic tail section to pulsate. Keep in mind, that Cole spent many long hours on the lakes striving to perfect his A.C. Plug so that it would closely replicate the action and swimming pace of a small, planted rainbow trout. So, for optimal action, maintain a fairly slow, steady retrieve.

Don't necessarily expect wallhanger-class rainbows or browns to make a scorching hit-and-run attack on these plugs. Many times big fish just stop the A.C. dead in its tracks, then turn and start a slow, steady run. This is a huge lure, and it creates a lot of water resistance as the trout takes it and makes that initial run.

If the fish nips at the seductive soft plastic tail or hits harder but misses the hooks—KEEP REELING! The most effective course of action is to maintain your retrieve, continuing to give the lure its lifelike, swimming, and now possibly wounded, appearance. That big trout may come back for a second look!

These plugs are now more readily available and affordable. Expect to see bank fishermen borrow a page out of the striped bass manuals, and actually walk the shorelines of trophy trout lakes throwing these big lures with surfcasting spinning tackle. That's right—long 10 to 13 foot saltwater surf rods and large saltwater spinning reels spooled with 15 to 20 pound mono. Striper enthusiasts have been nailing big striped bass from lakes like Silverwood, Castaic, Pyramid and Skinner for years making long casts from the bank with these jumbo plugs.

When you see that ten pound brown rolling on the surface at Convict, Crowley, Bridgeport or Twin, why not whip out the surf rod and feed that lunker the A.C.? Take it to the bank—this strategy works!

Flat-Lining the A.C.

Here, too, with this basic subsurface trolling program, I'm going to recommend saltwater gear such as a Penn 501 or 506 Jigmaster Junior, filled with 20 pound test mono. I probably cannot emphasize enough that this lure is simply a hawg hunter. You don't catch a lot of smaller trout with 8 to 12 inch lures. Why not be prepared and fish with gear that is more appropriately matched to ten-pound-plus rainbows or browns? On that note, combine the Penn Jigmaster Junior reels with a light tip saltwater rod, such as the Penn Sabre 195 or 196 Series.

Keep your trolling speed on the slow side. It won't take much boat speed to generate the trout-like action from these plugs. Tie the lure directly to the monofilament. No leader is necessary. If the A.C. starts to either plane or roll on the surface, throttle back and slow down.

I suggest letting out close to 50 yards of line before throwing the reel in gear. I feel that big freshwater game fish, unlike some of their more fearless marine cousins, are more wary of boat noise, prop vibration, and similar unnatural disturbances. For this reason, lay the big plug back some distance behind the boat. The twenty pound test monofilament has minimal stretch, even up to 50 to 60 yard lengths, ensuring a solid hook set with the A.C.

506HS Penn Jigmaster

As I mentioned before in this text, try to vary your trolling pattern somewhat. Avoid running in a straight point-to-point manner, and instead try that series of S-curve maneuvers I discussed in earlier chapters. Just remember, keep your speed modest and forget a stop-and-go ploy with the throttle. The A.C. Plug seems to perform best at that steady, methodical speed.

Lead-Core the A.C.

This strategy is especially effective if the big browns or rainbows are stratified or suspended in thermoclines between the surface and the bottom. The sinking, lead-core line helps to drag this large, buoyant wooden plug down to these mid-depth strike zones. You can pull the A.C. on 18 to 25 pound test, lead-core line, spooled on a Penn Levelwind model. Use a 5 to 8 foot length of 15 to 20 pound test monofilament as a leader tied directly to the A.C. Plug. Typically you will need to use your electronics to monitor for the suspended trout. Then letting out anywhere from 3 to 8 colors of lead core (10 yards per color), settle into your basic S-L-O-W troll pattern.

Look for this method to produce some real lunker rainbows and browns, particularly in the later spring and summer months when these fish suspend at greater depths seeking cooler, more oxygenated water.

The Giant Super Shads For Super Trout!

It has only been in recent years that Western anglers have discovered many more applications for soft plastic lures such as A.A. Worms' giant Super Shad lures. These lures were initially marketed for saltwater angling. Anglers have found that these shad-like soft plastic lures, characterized by their fat bellies and knob-tail designs, performed well on lunker Florida-strain largemouth bass, especially in a planted rainbow trout pattern.

These big plastic baits also work well for big rainbows and browns. In addition to the basic rainbow trout coloration, the lures are also effective in other patterns that mimic threadfin shad, chubs, Sacramento perch, and similar indigenous bait fish that a lunker 'bow or brown might find tempting to attack.

The Super Shads are basically rigged in two ways. The simplest strategy is to lace the 10-inch-long plastic body on to a 3/8 to 1/2 ounce wedge-shaped lead head. Then run a short 3 to 8 inch length of leader with a small treble hook tied on, attached to the base of the lead head's larger hook. The treble is planted into the tail section of the bait, embedding only one point into the soft plastic,

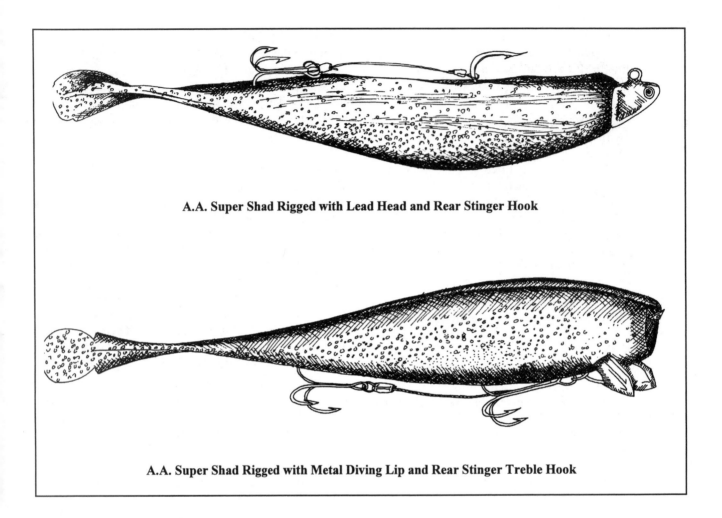

A.A. Super Shad Rigged with Lead Head and Rear Stinger Hook

A.A. Super Shad Rigged with Metal Diving Lip and Rear Stinger Treble Hook

leaving two exposed. This becomes the "stinger" setup for trout that might short-strike the big lure, nipping at the tail.

A variation of this stinger hook rig is marketed by A.A. Worms and is comprised of a metal diving lip and stinger treble hook harness. The bare metal diving lip is "implanted" into the head portion of the long piece of soft plastic. The treble hook portion of this harness setup is also embedded by a single hook point into the tail portion of the giant Super Shad to form the "stinger" effect.

Similar to the A.C. Plug, the A.A. Worms' Giant Super Shad can be either casted or slow-trolled for big trout. This lure is very soft, and when a lunker rainbow or brown strikes it, the hook set is typically strong and solid, as the trout chomps into the lifelike plastic! Try fancasting from either the bank or a boat. You may also pull the giant Super Shad on 12 to 20 pound monofilament with a subsurface flat-line approach, or slowly drag it tied directly to the mono or trolled 3 to 8 colors down with lead-core line.

A Special Note on Releasing Trophy Trout

It is becoming evident that even with heavily planted waters in metropolitan lowland reservoirs or High Sierra lakes, trophy class rainbows and browns in that 5 to 10 pound range remain incidental catches. Successful anglers are encouraged to both preserve their remarkable catch and yet still release these big fish to fight another day.

If big trout are weighed in fairly quickly after they are caught, brought to the scales in a plastic bag filled with water, handled with very wet hands to preserve the fish's slime coating, then chances of a successful release are good. Transport the trophy fish to the scales in the plastic bag filled with water. Quickly empty the water out, weigh the fish in the still wet bag, then quickly release it.

Next, contact one of the many taxidermists in the state that specializes in fiberglass reproductions. (Fewer and fewer taxidermists are still actually "stuffing" dead fish, opting instead for the fiberglass mounts.) Let the taxider-

Digital Scale

mist know the weight of your catch, the time of year, and the location where you caught the big rainbow or brown.

They will usually have molds already made to replicate trout that are practically identical in length, girth, and, most importantly, overall weight to your catch. If you took a snapshot of your trophy, that will also provide the taxidermist with some helpful information about your trophy's actual coloration.

As a long-term investment, these fiberglass replicas are terrific! They do not need to be routinely touched up as do most skin mounts which dry out over time. The paint jobs produced by top-notch taxidermists are incredibly lifelike. Most importantly, you are rewarded with the knowledge that your big trout swims another day thanks to your personal concern and efforts in this supreme conservation gesture!

(I should also add as a footnote to this important catch-and-release practice, both Rapala and Berkley market excellent, quality digital scales. This will help the lucky angler to weigh his trophy right after he catches it, making the release ever more immediate. These scales are highly accurate and a worthwhile addition to the Western trouter's tackle box!)

More Trout Catching Secrets

Do you sometimes wonder why it so often happens that a few anglers seem to be catching all the trout while everybody else is getting skunked? Maybe it's because the successful few use little-known trout catching secrets.

Natural Roe

Besides the Finger Jig , there is another rather obscure bait that has produced some trophy-size rainbows here in Southern California when fished under a small plastic float. After catching a fat chunky female 'bow while working the shoreline, gut the fish and remove the viscera. Then, carefully remove the pale roe and the surrounding mucous membrane. Next, place it in a small container with a tablespoon of salt and a tablespoon of sugar. This cures and sweetens the eggs, making them easier to handle and tastier for the trout. To fish this tidbit, take a small cluster of the tiny eggs and wrap them around a long-shank baitholder hook, tied to a two to three pound test leader, five to seven feet below a small bobber. This natural roe floating outside the weed line can produce spectacular results for big brood stock rainbows when more traditional baits fail.

As I noted in previous chapters, the light leader is crucial in using any bobber combo. If you have heavier four to six pound line on your push button or spinning reel, add a four to five foot leader of two to three pound test connected by a diminutive snap-swivel. Snap the colored float right onto the swivel and the leader to the snap. Now you're ready to gently lob cast the natural roe.

The most common mistake made in using a small bobber with roe in this manner is trying to set up on the trout too quickly. Usually the fish will gently "mouth" or even "push" this bait away from the bank or weeds. This is signalled on the surface by the bobber either tipping from side to side, intermittently going under or moving off in one distinct direction. Avoid the temptation to instantly set the hook. Instead, wait for the bobber to stay submerged longer and for your line to become fairly taut. When you set the hook, do it with a soft sweep of the rod. Remember, you will be using fine diameter leader with minimal breaking strength.

I have found that this setup is excellent all year long and particularly on highly pressured lakes where the trout have been bombarded with the full gamut of store-bought baits. Browns and rainbows cruising along the weed beds will readily annihilate a natural bait such as this when it is suspended at mid-depth in this fashion. Rarely does the colored plastic bobber ever seem to spook the fish. It can be fished from the shore or from a boat.

Clear Bubble Slider Tricks

One often overlooked variation of the sliding sinker bait-fishing rig is to fill a clear bubble all the way with water. Butt it against a swivel and add an 18 to 24 inch length of leader line with your favorite bait attached. The bubble will now sink. It is used in place of a sliding egg sinker. But, interestingly, I have found that compared to a lead weight, the plastic bubble seems to hang up less in thick weeds or underwater vegetation. The bubble has a certain amount of neutral buoyancy that may actually keep it slightly above the bottom when there is a modest amount of current in the lake.

Another trick along this same vein is to add a few drops of red food coloring to the water in the plastic bubble. An optically enticing "bait" which glows as it lies near the bottom is created. This colored bubble often attracts trout to the vicinity for a closer investigation and, hopefully, a strike at your nearby bait.

You can also bore small holes into the float and replace the water with liquid fish attractant. As the float rests on the bottom, the scent slowly seeps out, creating a "vapor cloud" of sorts that will call the fish in. This can be an exciting ploy, often generating a feeding frenzy when rainbows are schooled in tight near the bottom.

Hashimoto's River Secret

Leonard Hashimoto is the originator of the famous Salt-water Tora Tubes used all along the Pacific Coast. One of his other passions is fishing for trophy trout in fast-moving current. Working along stretches of the Colorado River, Hashimoto has taken scores of 5 pound beauties. His ingenious technique also involves using nightcrawlers; he notes, "the larger, the better."

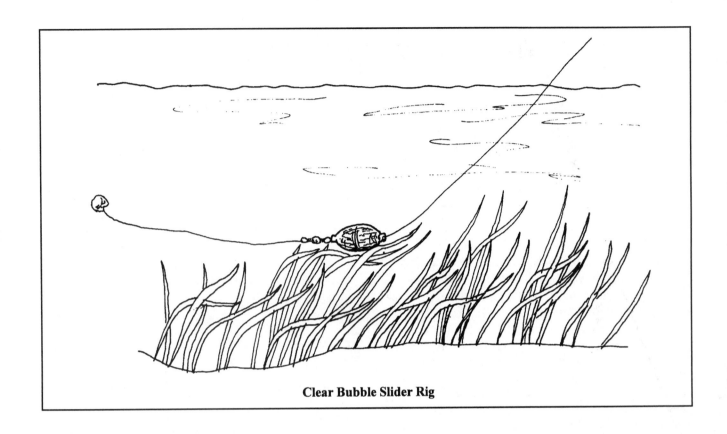

Clear Bubble Slider Rig

The object is to float the nightcrawler above the bottom while it tumbles through the swift current. Instead of using only a sliding egg sinker and a 'crawler, Hashimoto also relies upon a Glo-go or Spin'n Glow bobber. These attractors were originally designed for steelhead. But, used in conjunction with a sliding weight, they serve to both attract big river trout and keep the 'crawler bobbing along just above the bottom. The colorful, whirling blades on these specialized floats generate a very fast, tight vibration underwater as they spin ahead of the nightcrawler. Hashimoto observes that this too has the effect of bringing in big river rainbows to examine the 'crawler as it floats by. He recommends inflating the worm. Use an 18 inch 4 to 8 pound leader behind the Spin'n Glow, and thread the whole bait onto a #8 Gamakatsu needle-sharp short-shank egg hook.

Stearman's Record Catcher

Danny Stearman is the man who caught the 26 pound, 8 ounce German brown from Lower Twin Lake in 1987 to establish the state record. His trophy fish edged out Jon

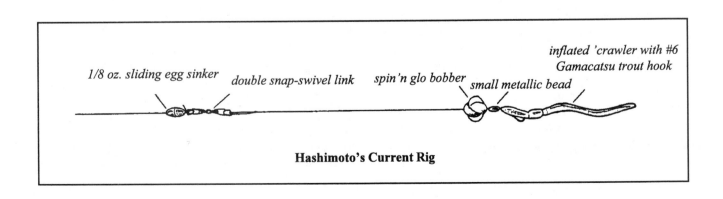

1/8 oz. sliding egg sinker   double snap-swivel link   spin'n glo bobber   small metallic bead   inflated 'crawler with #6 Gamacatsu trout hook

Hashimoto's Current Rig

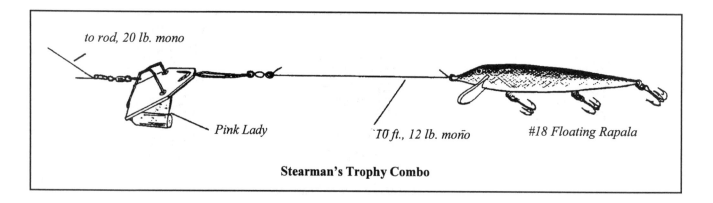

to rod, 20 lb. mono

Pink Lady

10 ft., 12 lb. mono

#18 Floating Rapala

Stearman's Trophy Combo

Minami's former record by 3 ounces. Stearman, like Minami and Bob Bringhurst, is a dedicated lunker trout hunter with a passion for browns. His particular methodology stands distinctively apart from these other two famous "brown baggers."

Stearman not only likes to troll slow, but also deep. He uses a rather novel setup comprised of an 8 foot saltwater live bait rod teamed with a Penn Jigmaster, spooled with 20 pound test monofilament. He ties the line to a Pink Lady diving plane. But then he adds a 10 foot length of 12 pound leader to which a large Rebel or Rapala is attached. Stearman used the Pink Lady to first get the lure down deep and also to serve as an attractant. The browns come in to investigate the diving plane then they hit the minnow plug as it passes by.

As I pointed out in previous sections, Stearman, like other "brown baggers," emphasizes that you have to fish big browns in nasty weather. He feels that the chilly early morning and sunset hours are optimal feeding periods for these fish. But he notes that the onset of stormy conditions can really stimulate world-class fish into a more aggressive feeding mode.

It is also interesting to note that like accomplished bass professionals, Stearman relies heavily upon his electronics to home in on these big browns. He first looks to see if plankton blankets any particular part of the lake. He feels that this is the food stuff that sustains bait fish minnows, and larger browns will be nearby. Then he may look for schools of shad, chubs, planter rainbows and kokanees. Once found, this is the area in which he commences trolling.

A Powerful Phenomena!

One of the most significant advances in trout angling technology has been the advent of Berkley Power Bait.

When this concoction was first introduced onto the market, there were stories about how it out-fished the competing floating baits by as much as 6 to 1 in the field.

Word spread quickly about how effective this new bait was. Initially there were rumors that it would soon be outlawed by the D.F.G. because it worked too well! Needless to say, these rumors proved to be false and sales of this trout bait continue to soar.

The secret of Power Bait is that it is impregnated with a time-release substance that literally attracts trout to it. Like other floating mixes, Power Bait can be prominently suspended off the bottom with a sliding egg sinker setup, making it even easier for the fish to home in on it.

As with any other trout bait, it is imperative that you rig the Berkley variety with a fine diameter, 1 to 3 pound test leader. I have also found that it sometimes helps to switch colors of the substance throughout the day as both climatic conditions and the trouts' preferences change.

For instance, I might start with the bright optically exciting fluorescent orange color in the morning under dark skies. I then switch to the more subdued pink or yellow colors later in the day.

I have also found two other little ploys worth mentioning when using this bait. Try mixing two shades of Power Bait together on a size 14 to 16 hook to form a marbled effect. This really gives the trout something new and different to look at. Or add a single drop of Berkley Strike in trout scent to a gob of Power Bait for extra effect.

Keep in mind that Power Bait is quite sticky and stays on the hook remarkably well. You can also use it to form a "Christmas tree" in conjunction with salmon eggs.

Carrying this scent technology even further, Berkley later introduced Power Nuggets and Power Eggs. These are basically marshmallow and salmon egg substitutes, again impregnated with fish attractants. These too should

Berkley's Power Baits

be fished on light leaders and are suitable for making the "Shasta fly" or salmon egg cluster rig I discussed in the baitfishing chapter.

Two other offerings in the Power Bait family are also worth trying for both rainbow and brown trout. The maggot-like Berkley Power Wigglers are great at times fished in lieu of a real meal worm on a tiny #12 to #14 long-shank baitholder hook. Or use them to form a marshmallow/mealie combo teamed with a Berkley Power Nugget. Better yet, lace a Power Wiggler on the back of a miniature Crappie John Finger Jig as the ultimate enticement for finicky rainbows!

Similarly, the little plastic Berkley Power Grubs fished on a 1/16 ounce lead head will prove at times to be a sensational big-fish killer in urban lakes with shad populations. These can be casted from the bank or on the slow-troll teamed with 2 to 4 pound test monofilament.

Advanced Power Bait Strategy

Berkley Power Bait was first introduced on the troutin' scene some years ago. Initial reports indicated that this floating concoction was a terrific alternative to traditional bait dunkin', but no one really knew how potent this stuff would be. Now years later with numerous limits of browns, rainbows, and brookies tallied on Power Bait, research indicates that this secret formula out-catches salmon eggs by a phenomenal 6 to 1 ratio!

Here are a few special tips on how to use Power Bait on not only lakes, but streams and rivers as well.

1. Try fishing deeper pools, eddies, tailouts, and even moderately flowing current with Power Bait. This mixture is easier to shape than cheese and will stay on the hook better than Velveeta. Use either a small split-shot crimped about 18 inches above a tiny #16

to #18 treble hook, or a dropper loop setup with the soft pencil leads I mentioned in the section on river tactics.

The nice thing about the Power Bait in this situation is that it floats up above the bottom while the cheese will sink. It will thus hang up less on rocky or brushy stream beds. Equally important, the Power Bait floating off the river bottom will also serve to target trout that might be suspended in deeper pools or in the current.

2. Along this same line of attack, Power Bait can also be fly-lined without any weight right on the surface gently casting with either a fly-rod or ultralight spinning combination. There are occasions when trout, especially hatchery-bred rainbows, will be rising or puddlin' on the surface and will actually

Power Nuggets

Power Eggs as a Lure Trailer

can be added to certain lures to improve otherwise absent scent quality in hard baits. Always make sure not to overload either treble or single hooks so you do not impede the built-in action of the spinner or spoon.

Custom Coloring

Sometimes it pays to make innovative changes in your artificial baits to provide some sort of new intriguing lure to hook-shy rainbows and browns. Many times while in the field, I have found that a spoon, spinner or plug which has been doctored slightly will all of a sudden dramatically increase the potency of the lure.

Scale-like Luhr-Jensen Prism-Lite finish tape is a valuable asset to any trouter's tackle box. You can cut this paper into any shape, peel back the protective backing, and stick it to any metallic or plastic surface. Quite frequently, a small piece of Prism-Lite applied to an otherwise mundane solid gold or silver spoon turns the lure into a spectacular one-of-a-kind offering.

You can also add this scale-like finish to minnow-shaped or banana-style plugs, or to the whirling blade of an in-line spinner. If you want to return the lure back to its original factory appearance, simply peel the prism paper off.

Fluorescent pink nail polish is another little trick I have used over the years. Sometimes adding a seductive

"slurp" down a tiny chunk of Power Bait more readily than they would bite a dry fly.

3. On many urban trout lakes a recent innovation is to team Power Bait with a live nightcrawler. Mold a small amount of Power Bait onto the remaining portion of the exposed hook shaft and even around the knot. The Power Bait adds additional scent to the live nightcrawler and makes the big worms easier to pick up off the bottom, especially in the stained or muddy water conditions so frequently found in urban reservoirs.

   If you scale down somewhat from fishing with those thick giant "combat" size nightcrawlers and use the smaller models, the chunk of Power Bait on the hook shank might actually serve to help float the worm off the bottom. This eliminates having to inject the nightcrawlers with air.

4. A final secret is to use the paste-like Power Bait as an attractant with your hardware. You can pinch a small amount of Power Bait onto the hackle-feathered treble hook found with many trout spinners. You can also try smearing some onto the rippled hammered surface of a metal spoon.

Power Bait is a time-release mixture so you can actually make quite a few casts with your hard lures before the scent wears off. You might also try this same strategy using both Power Eggs and Power Nuggets. Both of these variations on the floating Power Bait series

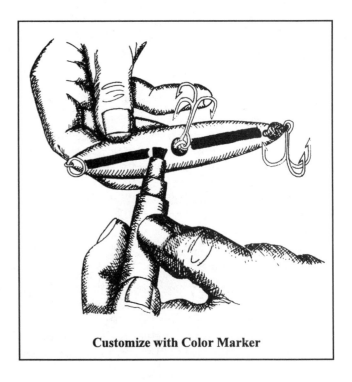

Customize with Color Marker

fluorescent pink fire stripe down the front surface of a spoon or plug can turn the lure into a more dynamic-looking bait.

Similarly, a black felt tip maker can be useful for adding a dark dorsal vein to a minnow or banana-style plug. A red marker can provide you with a lateral line or polka dots to replicate a small planted 'bow or Kokanee salmon with your lure. Or switch back to the black marker and shade an existing bright metallic surface to make the spoon or spinner blade more subdued, or to have it create a better silhouette against a darkened sky.

Finally, use a fluorescent chartreuse marking pen to add only a small "splash" of this color to make a spoon , spinner, or crankplug more visible in muddy or stained water, typically found on many of our lowland urban reservoirs.

Keep Your Baits Clean!

Trout—even those little 10 to 12 inch stocker rainbows—have particularly keen olfactory senses. Just as they can smell the fragrance of the different prepared and natural baits, they can equally detect unnatural human or other odors.

You will find that the best bait fishermen routinely take extra meticulous measures to keep their offering pure and uncontaminated with outside odors.

Here is where the Dr. Juice odor eliminator or a small tube of biodegradable soap comes in handy. Take the extra effort to wash your hands following eating or handling food. Similarly, do the same to wipe out the smell left on your hands from outboard motor oil, automobile gasoline, or other extraneous substances. All of these unnatural odors can spook the trout if they are inadvertently transferred to your bait.

Another little tip is to carefully check that the 1 to 3 pound test monofilament leader utilized with your floats or sinkers is perfectly clean. Some pros firmly believe that if you leave traces of Velveeta, salmon egg, or floating mixtures on this strand of mono, it will create an unnatural line of scent in the water. This may result in the fish failing to key in on the actual bait where the hook lies.

Also, there are times then the trout are so finicky they will eat only those baits that appear "100% pure" in the water. Hence take extra care to handle each different bait with clean hands, so again, foreign bait odors won't be transferred as you switch offerings.

Quite frequently, I will squirt a drop of Dr. Juice trout attractant or Berkley Strike in trout scent and rub it into my hands. This compound is not only an attractant, but will also serve as a "mask" to cover up extraneous outside odors.

More on Scent

Along this same vein, liquid fish attractants can also be applied to artificial lures at times to increase their potency. One of my favorite strategies is to saturate the feathered treble hook on a trout spinner with Dr. Juice or Berkley Strike. The liquid adheres fairly well to the feathers, creating a time-release "vapor trail" as the spinner is retrieved or trolled.

Dr. Juice Hand and Lure Cleaner   **Dr. Juice Fish Scents**

Borrowing a chapter from my bass guides' logs, I'll also sometimes add a teaspoon of scent into a plastic baggie. Then, the night before a trip, I may soak floating minnows, banana plugs, spinners, and even spoons in the attractant.

This creates both an oily fish-like finish on these artificial lures in addition to emitting those fish-attracting qualities as the lure is pulled through the water. When the scent is placed in the baggie like this, you are also able to fully re-coat your lures throughout the day without touching the liquid.

A more recent concoction is the paste-like "Smelly Jelly." This compound is especially effective when you want to apply an attractant to a hard metal surface found on spinner blades and trout spoons.

Protect Those Lures!

The metallic finish found on trout spinners, spoons, and trolling blades should be routinely cleaned or polished to maintain optimal effectiveness.

To begin with, try to wipe the nickel, copper, brass, silver, or gold finish of the metal blade dry with a soft cloth after a day's fishing. If you see that the lure's blade has become tarnished, this usually means that bare metal is showing from the lure being nicked which encouraged oxidation. Sometimes fine-grade steel wool will help to restore some of the luster; in other cases, the steel wool seems to actually dull the spoon or spinner blade surface.

You can polish many of these lure blades with silver polish to restore their luster. You also may have some trout lures in your box that have blades with a lacquered finish. To restore these lures, take off all the lacquer with nail polish remover, then proceed to polish it. Once this factory lacquer coat has been removed, however, it will be necessary to routinely polish the blades to keep the finish bright and shiny.

Quality trout spoons and spinners along with lake troll combos are becoming expensive to replace. It helps to keep these metallic-finish lures segregated as much as possible in your tackle boxes. Some anglers prefer to take their favorite lake trolls and place each one, with the wire cable coiled, into an old, soft cotton sock. This little ploy will insure that the metallic surfaces keep their brilliant flashy finishes while not in use.

Here's a few more quick tips to help you maintain your personal lure arsenal. First, try to also dry off all those treble hooks after a day's outing. This will greatly reduce the potential for rusting.

Secondly, when you return home from your trip, open your tackle box and let it air out for a few hours. This will serve to eliminate any residual moisture left inside from wet lures, hooks, and related paraphernalia.

Finally, as mentioned previously, carry some of those small sheets of Luhr-Jensen Prism-Lite lure tape in your box at all times. This glossy, scale-like finish can be easily applied to practically any spoon, spinner, trolling blade, planing device, and plug that has nicks, chips, scratches, or other cosmetic imperfections incurred from banging around in your tackle box or getting attacked by hungry trout. Use it like a "band-aid" over the "injury spot" to cover up the blemished surface of the lure!

Trolling the Weeds

Many trout fishermen often put away their tackle in the height of the summer, frustrated when their favorite lake is inundated with heavy weed growth. Davis Lake in the Eastern Sierras is typically weedy like this during the warmer months. Nevertheless, lake locals persist in taking hefty stringers of rainbows with a little innovation.

Art Liebscher is one of the veteran trouters who work Davis all year long. During the weedy periods, he recommends a meticulous program of S-L-O-W trolling.

First, Liebscher suggests using unusually light, parabolic 6 1/2 to 7 foot spinning rods matched with baitcasting reels. He claims that the light tip action lets him detect even the most subtle strikes. Although Davis's 'bows average 15 to 18 inches, quite frequently they hit the trolled baits in a very delicate manner.

Liebscher spools his reels in the summer with 6 to 8 pound test line, tied to a set of lake trolls. This is the integral component in his trolling system with specific models recommended over others.

The Les Davis Bolo series of flasher blades are Liebscher's time-proven winners. This heart-shaped blade configuration produces minimal resistance and drag so it can be pulled with light-tip spinning rods outside the weed beds with limited snagging. The #2 or #3 size seems to be the most productive for the weeds with four brightly polished blades on the wire cable.

On numerous trips I have watched while other anglers trolled the more popular Ford Fender, Dave Davis, or Cowbell series of trolling blades. The more obscure Bolo design seems to clearly out-fish these other models on many summer outings.

Liebscher alternates between brass and nickel finish blades depending upon prevailing conditions. As a general rule, the brass-colored blades seem to produce best in the early morning or on overcast days when light intensity is minimized. After the sun comes up, he switches to nickel-colored blades. Liebscher prefers this blade system to have a red scale-like center.

As a compromise, he will occasionally tie on one of the larger Les Davis Slim Jim lake trolls in the half-and-half, nickel and gold finish. Note that these are still two relatively narrow fluted blades that generate minimal torque and drag when trolled on light spinning rods, again over a lake surface with intermittent weed growth.

Attached to these flashers is a 24 inch length of 4 pound test leader and a #6 long-shank bronze baitholder hook. A short rubber shock snubber can also be added to protect against broken leaders should a big trout strike. Next, Liebscher laces on a nightcrawler to complete the "Davis Lake Special." But here is where he makes one subtle adjustment which results in outstanding limit catches. The trick is to avoid using a whole nightcrawler behind the trolling blades as is commonly done. Instead, cut the worm in half. Next carefully thread the chunk of 'crawler onto the baitholder hook. Leave the hook totally exposed with the nightcrawler extending out behind it. This is the secret to catching more trout up here at this lake.

As you slow-troll this setup, the half 'crawler sort of "corkscrews" in the water. This presumably replicates a summer caterpillar or similar larval creature indigenous to the lake. There is no question that it generates many more strikes than a whole nightcrawler that most anglers were taught to use. This was proven to me when Liebscher out-fished me 5 to 1 on two separate occasions using his half 'crawler strategy while I fished my whole worm trolled behind identical flasher blades.

Lake locals have devised a few other ploys to master the extensive weed growth at Davis. One way to fish the lake is to slow-troll large brown or black Wooly Worms tied directly to a 4 to 6 pound test mono. You have to kind of strip off line from the reel to get the Wooly Worm out behind the boat, since it weighs so little and you will not be using a float here. Similarly, the versatile clear plastic bubble-and-fly combination used with a spinning outfit works here—either trolling or drifting. Use any fly, nymph, or streamer. Area tackle stores can advise you as to which popular patterns are currently producing, but count on one of them to be the Wooly Worm. It is important to note that these tactics are not solely applicable to Davis Lake. Try them throughout the summer when troutin' gets tough due to weed growth at your favorite lake.

GPS Technology for Troutin'

Trout fishermen, like backpackers, mountain climbers, explorers, big game fishermen, and tournament bass anglers may want to take advantage of the new GPS electronic units made by Magellan. The Magellan GPS Trailblazer uses the most accurate and sophisticated navigation technology ever created—the satellite-based Global Positioning System (GPS). With GPS, you always know where you are and can get where you want to go—anytime and anywhere on Earth. The Global Positioning System was developed by the U.S. Department of Defense to provide worldwide positioning and navigation information to our military forces. GPS also has a broad range of civilian and commercial applications, including boating, surveying, mapping, aviation, vehicle tracking and outdoor recreation.

The Global Positioning System consists of 24 satellites, each orbiting 12,000 miles above the earth twice a day. Each GPS satellite constantly transmits its position in space and the precise time using atomic clocks which are accurate to one second every 70,000 years. The Trailblazer receives information from the satellites, solving complex mathematical equations based on the receiver's distance from the satellites to determine the

A Hand-held GPS

user's exact position, speed and direction. GPS is the ultimate positioning and directional system—one that guides on land, sea, and air, providing extraordinarily accurate navigation data anywhere in the world 24 hours a day. The hand-held Trailblazer is menu-driven and extremely easy to use. Simply enter the position coordinates of any destination—even a place you've never been —and Trailblazer will guide you directly to it. Or store your starting point in Trailblazer's memory and it will get you back there every time. Trailblazer will also track your course automatically, tell you what direction you're heading, how fast you're going, how much farther you have to go, and much more. All at the push of a button. Compact, lightweight (14 ounces) and self-contained, Trailblazer is completely portable and fits neatly into your pocket.

The GPS technology has great application for the serious trout fisherman electing to explore large bodies of water. The Magellan Trailblazer would indeed come in handy fishing big lakes such as Shasta, Bridgeport, Trinity, Twin, or Crowley. Rather than having to rely solely on your electronic fish finder to locate the precise dropoff, stream bed, rock pile, or underwater spring where you found trout on previous outings, the GPS unit will put you right back on the prime fishing hole every time. Similarly, alpine trouters might be wise to invest in these affordable Trailblazers as they backpack into the myriad of lakes found in the High Sierra back country. Also, you can easily use the portable hand-held Magellen units while fishing from your own boat or a rental skiff. And, the new boat console models feature very short antennas, similar to a transistor radio's.

A Rapala Trout System

Of all the classes of lures you might want to include in your troutin' tackle arsenal, none is perhaps more versatile than the Rapala family of lifelike minnow-shaped lures. Rainbows, browns, cutthroats, brookies, and, of course, big mackinaws feed naturally on indigenous bait fish. These might include threadfin shad, Sacramento perch, chubs, sculpins, and even small shiners. As I have noted in other sections of this book, trophy-size rainbow and brown trout will also maintain a rather cannibalistic posture at times, homing in on smaller planted 'bows on big lakes. Rapala has a series of plugs that accommodate each and every one of the general conditions outlined above. Here is a concise menu that will help you select the right lure from this diverse family of lifelike plugs.

Shad Raps

These thin, shad-profile lures are perfect for lowland reservoirs where rainbow trout often share the water with largemouth bass or stripers. Shad Raps can be either casted or trolled. I recommend trolling the small, SR-5 and SR-7 models either on a flat-line or lead-core program. Keep your color selection simple, matching the indigenous bait fish population with either the silver foil or shad finishes.

For major league trophy huntin' with big rainbows or browns lurking in the shallows, scale up in size and switch to the SR-8, SR-9, or even the saltwater class, SR-14 Super Shad Rap.

These models replicate either large shad minnows or perhaps small panfish such as perch. On that note, give the perch finish a try. This is a perfect match for the Sacramento perch that trophy trout gorge themselves on at Lake Crowley.

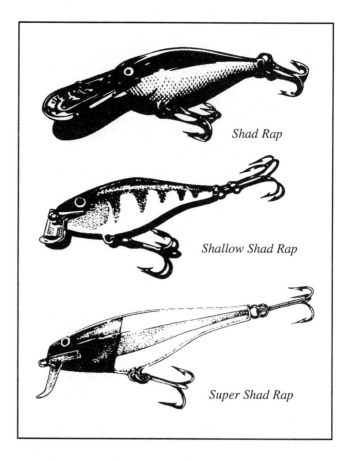

Shad Rap

Shallow Shad Rap

Super Shad Rap

Fat Raps

This basic alphabet-style plug also excels in lowland lakes where threadfin shad are found. However, the type of wobble that the Fat Rap generates also can drive the trout crazy at high elevation lakes. Stay with the basic SFR5 models but keep some of the MFR3 mini Fat Raps on hand. These 1 1/2 inch long miniatures are deadly at times on rainbows that are feeding on any type of small bait fish. The SFR5 models can be casted, or better yet, trolled on a flat-line. The MFR3 mini Fat Raps definitely should be trolled on 2 to 4 pound test monofilament. Consider trying silver foil, gold foil, perch, shad, or fluorescent chartreuse patterns in the Rapala Fat Rap collection.

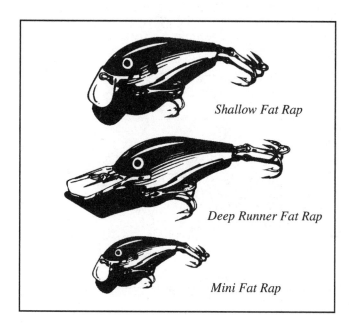

Shallow Fat Rap

Deep Runner Fat Rap

Mini Fat Rap

The Countdown

The Rapala Countdown minnow is properly weighted for a controlled sinking action. It is designed for holding at a predetermined depth or especially for casting into the wind. The Countdowns excel at targeting trout that are traveling in suspended strike zones. The basic Countdown sizes seem to produce catches of Western trout. They range from the tiny 1 1/2 inch CD3 all the way to the longer, heavier, 4 3/8 inch CD11. My personal favorites through the years have been the CD5 and CD7. I like to cast or flat-line troll these two models on four pound test line. The strike you feel when a decent 1 to 2 pound trout hits these plugs is also an unexpected jolt! They really try to annihilate this bait fish look alike lure!

Countdown

As for color selection, day in and day out you can't go wrong with silver foil, gold foil, or rainbow trout patterns. Sometimes the bright fluorescent gold/red combination also produces on overcast days or in roily water or windy conditions.

Original Floater

This is the plug that started it all. The Original Floater minnow is actually a floater-diver. When you retrieve or troll the lure it dives a short distance under the surface. The side-to-side action of the Original Floater is really what triggers the strikes. It closely resembles a frantic bait fish under attack by a marauding trout. There are clearly occasions when the rainbows, browns, and brookies want the Floater over any other Rapala lure style.

This model does not have much wind resistance in the smaller #5, #7, #9, and #11 sizes. For trolling, the more compact versions are recommended. Employ a flat-line, lead-core, planer, flasher blade, or downrigger technique combined with the Rapala Original Floater. These larger #13 and #18 models have become legendary among the "brown bagger" fraternity who specialize in stalking rainbows and brown trout exceeding the ten pound mark.

As was noted in separate sections on lunker huntin', you can also cast the bigger #13 and #18 size minnows or Rapala's new Husky Jerk minnows, along with the variety of trolling options.

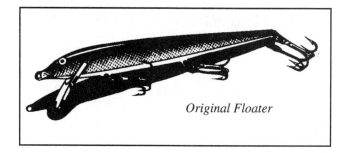

Original Floater

Rattlin' Rapala

This slab-shaped lure also nails trout when they are in a fairly aggressive feeding mode. The Rattlin' Rapala can be trolled at high speeds without planing out of the water. This lure mimics fast-swimming threadfin shad minnows and works particularly well at lowland lakes. Keep in mind the tactic I discussed in an earlier chapter regarding using lipless crankplugs such as the Rattlin' Rapala to vertically jig with a lift-and-drop rod tip sequence to tap into schools of rainbows holding over through the warmer summer months in 30 to 90 foot depths.

Try your Rattlin' Rapalas in solid chrome, chrome/blue, gold/black, or natural shad finishes. As with all these Rapala plugs, avoid the temptation to add a snap-swivel, or, for that matter, even a snap to these lures. Rapalas are all "pretuned" before they leave the factory for optimal motion and are designed to be tied directly to your monofilament.

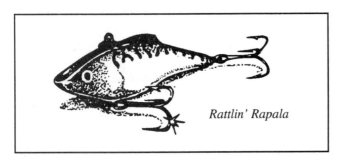

Rattlin' Rapala

Rapala Jointed

California trouters are somewhat remiss in not using this classic jointed minnow as much as other Rapala designs. Sometimes trout prefer the extremely "tight" vibration that the Rapala Jointed plugs produce combining the actions of the Fat Rap and the Original Floater models.

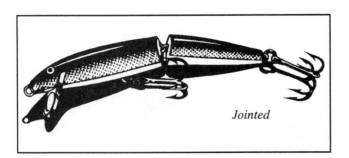

Jointed

Shrewd trout anglers know that a jointed minnow is an excellent option when the fish are especially wary and water conditions are tough. Again, the jointed feature of this lure generates considerable attention which may help to trigger strikes from finicky rainbows or browns.

As with the Original Floater model, try the Rapala Jointed series in basic silver, gold, perch, gold/fluorescent red, or silver/fluorescent chartreuse combinations.

Rapala Husky

This heavyweight model was designed with the California trouter in mind. It is perfect for the angler who wants to throw a minnow-shaped plug into the roughest water or strongest winds, looking for the bigger fish. The Husky is made for lakes such as Crowley, Bridgeport, and Pleasant Valley where the bank fisherman needs a lure that will give him the distance to target big cruising browns or 'bows.

I recommend casting the Husky in silver, perch, or even the crawdad finish while looking for lunkers from the shoreline.

Rapala Balanced Jig

This is the term the Rapala technicians use for the strange-looking ice jig extensively discussed in a separate chapter. Don't restrict the use of the Balanced Jigging minnow to ice fishing per se. This lure has application anytime you meter trout holding at 30 to 100 foot depths near the bottom feeding on schools of bait fish.

The lure is designed so that it swims in tantalizing circles right in the middle of suspended schools of trout. Try anywhere from the tiniest W2 1/8 ounce models all the way up to the largest W11 version weighing 1 1/8 ounces. Stock silver foil, gold/fluorescent red, and perch as your basic colors.

Polarized Eyewear

One often overlooked piece of equipment in the serious trout fisherman's repertoire is superior sunglasses. Over the years we have talked about the need for angler to invest in good sunglasses as perhaps the ultimate fish-finding device. Above and beyond this, keep in mind that eyes also need the protection from ultraviolet (UV) light that quality sunglasses can provide. Not all sunglasses provide these features.

So check out the sunglasses you own now. If they are not polarized—no matter how expensive or fashionable they may be—they aren't what you need for fishing. Pick a pair that will help out on the water. Polarization is the only effective method for removing dangerous and irritating glare.

Sunglasses also come in a variety of lens colors which filter out varying amounts of glare and light for a variety of situations. Select the color that works best under the conditions you will be fishing.

Color	% of Light Transmitted	Fishing Conditions
light gray	21%	maximum glare moderate sunlight
dark gray	10%	maximum glare intense sunlight
light amber	29%	maximum glare sight fishing low light, haze, or fog
dark amber	12%	(same as light amber)
light vermilion	21%	under maximum glare provides visual acuity and enhances color
dark vermilion	10%	(same as light vermilion)

Think about how many times you have tried to follow your cast, pick up your lure or fly as it hits the water, or tried to "sight" fish while casting to trout rising for insects? If you take this sport seriously then consider developing a repertoire of lens colors for such critical conditions as low light, intense sun, glare, fog, or haze.

Quality *polarizes* sunglasses are an essential addition to your freshwater tackle collection. These glasses also help to protect your eyes under extreme climatic conditions. The investment is well worth it!

A Systematic Trout Box

One of the most important pieces of equipment the accomplished trout angler should invest in is a tackle box which accommodates the fisherman's specific needs. Too often the weekend angler simply buys either the least expensive, smallest, or most basic box on the shelf without anticipating the further accumulation of tackle and related accessories.

Over the years we have been using Flambeau tackle boxes in our bass guiding business, on our Eagle Claw Saltwater Fishing Schools, and while fishing all sorts of California trout lakes, rivers, and streams. These boxes are extremely durable, but most importantly, they are designed by fishermen for fishermen. Here's how I would go about selecting and setting up a serious trout fishing tackle box.

First of all, if I am fishing primarily from banks, I would want a box that is lightweight, compact and easy to carry. I recommend one of the Flambeau satchel-style models. These boxes remind me of a "fishing briefcase." There are single-sided satchels, double-sided versions for twice the storage capacity, and larger tri-level satchels for the shoreliner who wants to pack everything. The Flambeau satchel boxes feature clear, see-through top lids which allow you to quickly inventory your stock of bait jars, plugs, spoons, spinners, hooks, and sinkers.

For the boater, I recommend one of the Force series of boxes or a classic Hip Roof model. The Force series has both a sliding drawer and removable trays. I like these boxes because they are still relatively compact and they hold a lot of tackle. They are deep enough to stack quite a number of salmon egg and Power Bait jars on top of each other. In addition there is ample room in the Force boxes to stash away an arsenal of lures including trays big enough to hold even the longer saltwater size #18 Rapala minnows.

Many boaters still prefer the more traditional Hip Roof tackle box characterized by its cantilevered multi-

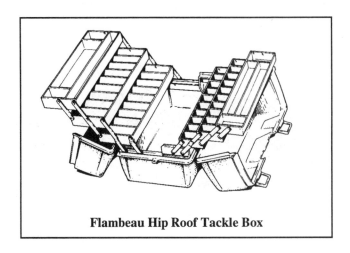

Flambeau Hip Roof Tackle Box

level trays that fold out from both sides. These trays hold about as many spinners, spoons, and plugs as you would ever need on a trip to your favorite California lake. Hip Roof boxes also have an advantage over traditional styles with its ultra-deep storage cavity under the trays. If you like to carry extra reels, spools of monofilament, lots of jars of bait or maybe even a lunch and a thermos, a Flambeau Hip Roof box is perfect.

A recent innovation in tackle box design from Flambeau is one of my current favorites. It actually has its origins with backpackers who use a modular system to efficiently fill their various backpack compartments with only the most usable equipment and provisions.

Flambeau's Soft-Sided Tackle System is not really a traditional tackle "box" per se. Rather it is a sturdy tote bag, constructed from heavy-duty nylon with well thought-out pockets, pouches, and compartments to hold your accessory items.

Most importantly, each Soft-Sided Tackle System comes with six separate large plastic boxes that slide into the top compartment of the nylon bag. Better yet, for the serious trouter, each of the six lightweight boxes can then be subdivided into a multitude of compartments. In this way each of the individual plastic boxes can be customized to hold the particular array of lures you select for a given outing.

For my personal tackle I have purchased additional plastic boxes which I have used to create customized boxes for a variety of fishing conditions. Specific items include "deep diving trout plugs," "High Sierra spinners," "spoons/spinners for streams," "magnum-size minnows," and boxes for other specific locales. The night before a fishing trip I pack anywhere from 3 to 6 boxes into the nylon tote bag. This creates a compact repertoire

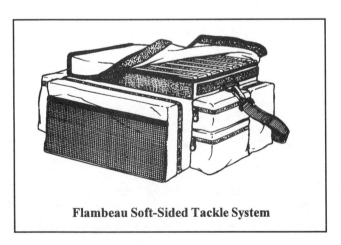

Flambeau Soft-Sided Tackle System

of tackle specifically selected for the conditions I will encounter the following day.

The Flambeau Soft-Sided Tackle System also serves as a convenient tackle box for the bank walker. The unit is comprised of fairly light, small plastic boxes and a nylon case. Velcro flaps, a sunglasses compartment, a mesh "wet" pocket, and a two-inch-wide adjustable shoulder strap crates a nifty tackle system for the trouter who works the shoreline.

Live Shad: A Lowland Secret!

Few recreational trout fishermen realize that many lowland lakes, especially those in Southern California, are populated with schools of threadfin shad bait fish. Even fewer trouters know that these minnows are excellent bait particularly for larger rainbows that have held-over for months—or even years—following their initial stocking.

On guiding trips to Lakes Skinner and Perris, located in Riverside County, for example, I have caught rainbow trout in late summer and fall at depths approaching the ninety foot mark.

Invariably these larger 1 1/2 to 4 pound hold-over 'bows school near concentrations of threadfin shad minnows. These lowland trout will definitely strike the live bait fish, but first we have to catch these minnows.

The shad can sometimes be seen "puddlin'" near the surface in the bait fish schools. Using a boat powered by an electric trolling motor, you can quietly gather up the shad with either a long-handled dip net or traditional throw net. These are not particularly hearty bait fish compared to shiner minnows, but they will stay alive for some time in either an aerated live well such as those found on bass boats, or in a bait container such as the Flambeau Floating Minnow and Flote-Rite Bait Buckets.

The program for rigging live shad is not too complex. Simply crimp a larger split-shot about 18 to 24 inches above a small #6 saltwater-style short-shank live bait hook, or a #4 to #6 long-shank freshwater baitholder model. The threadfin shad can be either hooked just behind the dorsal fin, or up through both the lower and upper lips sealing them shut.

Most rainbows caught on live shad at these lowland lakes are usually found at the more extreme 45 to 90 foot range. It will take some time for the split-shot setup to sink down to these depths. Once on the bottom, the shad will be fastened loosely enough to swim around and draw the strikes. Fish live threadfin shad on fine diameter 4 to

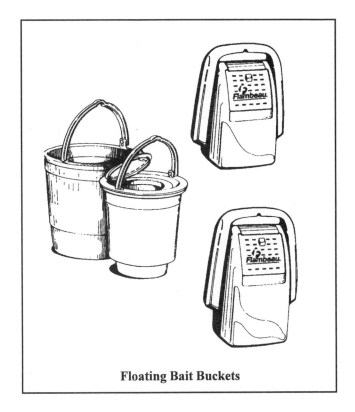

Floating Bait Buckets

6 pound test premium mono. Make a gentle lob cast, or simply lower the bait over the side of the boat.

Some real lunker size 'bows are caught with this relatively secret bait strategy using live threadfin shad minnows! These bait fish are not sold commercially. They must be caught by the angler himself.

The Crippled Herring—A Very Special Spoon!

Most of the metal spoons used for trout fishing are of the basic "cast-and-wind" variety. (A variation of this is the "pull-and-go" method used to "wind" these spoons while trolling.) The Luhr-Jensen Crippled Herring is a dis-tinctly different spoon compared to the cast-and-wind models. When using the Crippled Herring for trout, strikes occur on the "fall" as the lure is sinking. This makes the Herring a specialized choice for fishing rainbows, browns, or mackinaws when some sort of vertical attack is in order.

The Crippled Herring spoon excels on this vertical troutin' approach in two situations: fishing through ice or through suspended schools. When troutin' through the ice, the fish will hit the Herring either during or at the end of a downward fall as the lure is either first dropped, or on the lift-and-drop sequence employed with the rod tip. The lift or forward movement of the lure will attract early season, hungry, iced-in trout. It is the backward or downward fall created by slack line that triggers the strikes with this unique spoon.

Similarly, if you have electronic depth finders, you may be able to actually meter schools of rainbows, browns, or macks that are layered or "suspended" in specific strike zones. One of the ways to concentrate on these suspended trout, is to approach the fish with a vertical presentation such as spoon jigging. Dropping the Crippled Herring down to fish in these intermediate zones between the surface and the bottom is an effective way to target otherwise hard-to-get-to trout. Here again, in this situation almost all strikes occur as the lure is initially sinking or on the "drop" phase of the lift-and-drop rod tip sequence.

With this particular trout lure, do not expect vicious strikes as you would from a plug, spinner, or spoon retrieved or trolled along the surface. Usually, the trout will sort of "bump" the Herring as it sinks. Immediately set the hook hard if the lure is "bumped," the line suddenly goes slack, or you see a slight "tick" on the mono. These are all signals that a trout has inhaled this lazily, fluttering spoon! The Crippled Herring, unlike most trout spoons, is marketed with a single, Siwash-style hook, instead of the traditional treble. You will find that this unique hook configuration gives the Herring the

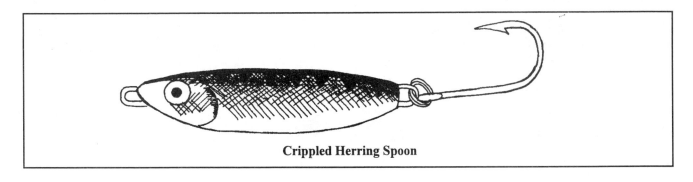

Crippled Herring Spoon

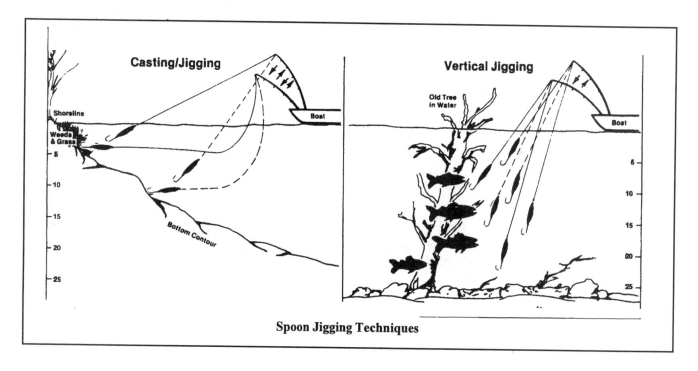

Spoon Jigging Techniques

erratic fluttering action it generates on the fall. As I have noted in many of my writings on saltwater and inland lures, a single hook often actually gives you better leverage, penetration, and overall hook-set than the more popular treble model.

A couple of other insiders' tips are worth noting when fishing for trout with the Crippled Herring. First of all, don't be tempted to bend the lure yourself. Some trouters believe that they will give the Herring more action if they bend the body of the lure. Don't do it! The Herring is balanced perfectly right from the factory.

Secondly, although this spoon works almost exclusively as a "drop" bait, don't overlook the need to match the finish of the Crippled Herring to prevailing conditions. Fish chrome or nickel patterns on bright, sunny days, or in clear water. Switch to gold, fluorescent and pearl-white combinations in typical early season turbid water. Use fluorescent green or yellow mixes if you work the Herring deep in the stained water of Southern California's trout reservoirs. Mother-of-pearl or pearl-white finishes with this spoon are excellent for darker water or after ice out on alpine lakes. When you fish lakes in the High Sierras, such as Crowley, Bridgeport or Twin, where bigger rainbows and browns feed on Sacramento perch or small, stocker 'bows, a Crippled Herring in either a metallic perch or a rainbow trout pattern might be deadly with the vertical attack.

Finally, you will find that the Crippled Herring's unusual single-hook rigging, allows you to trim the spoon with a variety of trailers that might be tough to do with basic treble hook models. A small chunk of nightcrawler, a jumbo meal worm, or a Berkley Power Nugget adds a tasty tantalizer to an otherwise quite simple lure. Be careful, however, especially with the smaller 1/6 to 1/4 ounce models, not to load the Crippled Herring up with too much trailer. Jig the spoon up and down a few times with your favorite trailer to make sure you have not altered the lure's critical, fluttering, falling action. Remember, like almost all other spoons, strikes with the Crippled Herring occur as the lure sinks.

BOOK II

California Trout Waters:
A "Where-to"
and "How-to" Guide

California Trout Waters: A "Where-to" and "How-to" Guide

The remainder of this book highlights the major trout fishing areas in the Golden State. With the tremendous number of lakes, rivers, streams and creeks that are found in California, it is impossible to include each and every one.

Instead, I have tried to focus on the primary waters with public access which will have appeal to Golden State anglers. For easy reference, this portion of the book is divided into nine geographic regions, and lakes and streams are organized alphabetically within each of these sections. See the State Map and listing of lakes and streams on page 9.

Information has been gleaned and assembled from a variety of sources. These include personal logs, filed reports from outdoor guides, conversations with marina operators and tackle dealers. Fishing patterns and water conditions can change dramatically from time to time in certain parts of the state. The following section is designed to provide the most accurate data available. But there is no substitute for the reliable reports that can be obtained at the local areas themselves. It is thus recommended that you check local sources for the most up-to-date information before you arrive at the lake or stream.

Northeast Corner Trout

In the far Northeast corner of the state, the trout angler will find some of the most incredible scenery anywhere in the West. The view is equally matched with outstanding troutin' opportunities. The immense and ever popular Lake Shasta complex is a year-round favorite. Shasta is unquestionably the central fishing focus in this part of the state. But often overlooked by the casual trouter is the tremendous potential of the streams, rivers and other lakes in this area.

Two of the truly stellar trout streams anywhere in the United States are right here: Hat Creek and Fall River. Wily, scrappy, native trout are found along some of these runs. Similarly, some of the best river trout fishing can be experienced right outside of the city of Redding as the great Sacramento River meanders its way into and out of Lake Shasta. Eagle Lake has its own mysterious, chunky strain of rainbow and then there are several other lakes and wilderness areas featured in this section that should not be overlooked.

Angling pressure is another factor to consider when planning a troutin' trip. There just aren't as many anglers, either living or driving, this far up in the Golden State. So the Northeast corner and the adjoining Northcoast region are good bets if you want a degree of solitude along with your trout.

Burney Creek and Lake Britton

Burney Creek and Lake Britton offer good fishing for planted trout. Bait, like salmon eggs, is usually the best way to take local planters. The McArthur-Burney Falls State Park (off Hwy. 89, near the town of Burney) can also be used as a base-camp to enjoy all the other fine trouting in the area. The park itself has over 100 developed campsites, a boat rental and launch ramp, swimming beach and the magnificant Burney Falls. But it is also centrally located for short drives to fish the McCloud, Hat Creek, Fall River, Baum Lake and the Pit River. Not that there aren't other campgrounds in the area, but this state park has so much to offer for the entire family. The anglers can go off and do their thing while everybody else enjoys all the park has to offer. For information contact McArthur-Burney Falls State Park, Route 1, Box 1260, Burney, CA 96013, (916) 335-2777.

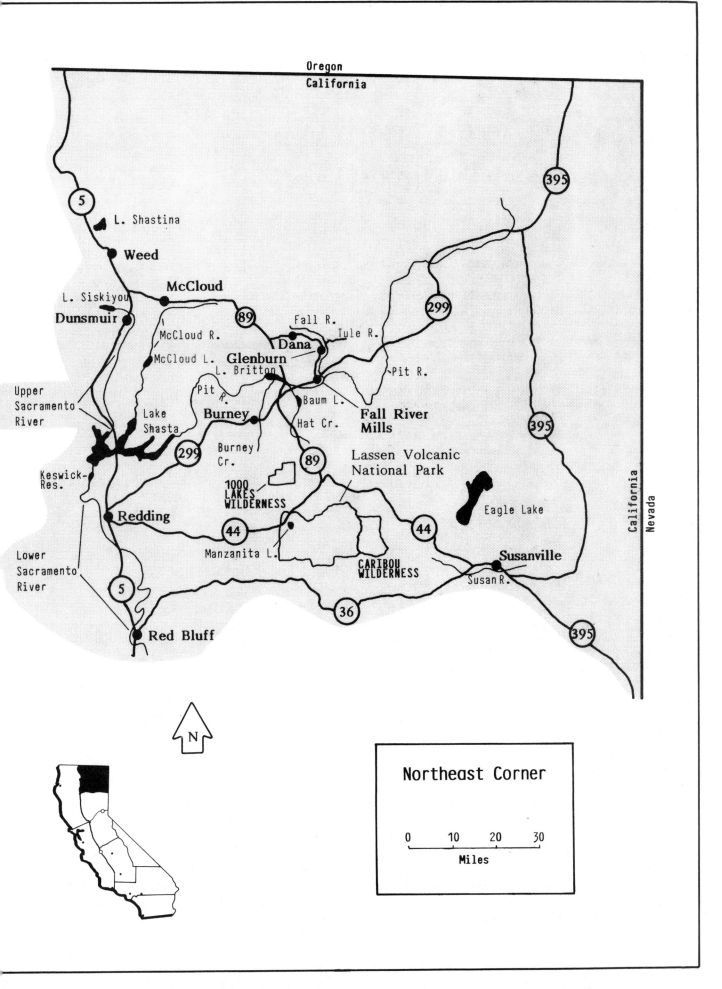

Oregon
California

⑤ 5

L. Shastina

Weed

McCloud

L. Siskiyou

Dunsmuir

McCloud R.

McCloud L.

Glenburn

L. Britton

Fall R.

Tule R.

Dana

Pit R.

Pit R.

Baum L.

Burney

Hat Cr.

Fall River Mills

③ 299

③ 395

Upper Sacramento River

Lake Shasta

③ 299

Burney Cr.

⑧ 89

Lassen Volcanic National Park

Eagle Lake

Keswick Res.

1000 LAKES WILDERNESS

④ 44

④ 44

Redding

Manzanita L.

CARIBOU WILDERNESS

Susanville

Lower Sacramento River

⑤ 5

③ 36

Susan R.

③ 395

Red Bluff

③ 395

California
Nevada

N

Northeast Corner

0   10   20   30
Miles

Eagle Lake

Just out of Susanville in Lassen County, the trout fisherman will find one of the most unusual fisheries in the world—Eagle Lake. At 27,000 acres, this is the second largest natural lake in the state. What makes it so unusual is the significantly high alkalinity of its water. Through careful management and selective breeding, fishery biologists have nutured the Eagle Lake strain of rainbows so they grow big and fat in this alkaline water. The lake opens around Memorial Day and closes December 31. This allows a long resting period for the solid trout population. By opening day, be ready for some dynamite action!

As the trout begin to spawn in the shallows at the north end near Pine Creek, definitely try some top-line trolling. When summer approaches, the fish will migrate south to the deeper, cooler, spring-fed waters near Wildcat and Eagle's Nest. Now is the time to use lead-core line or downriggers. Shore fishing can be good near Rocky or Wildcat Points. Don't hesitate to fish nightcrawlers on or near the bottom. Greater surface action will pick up in the fall as water temperatures decline.

Trolling is undoubtedly the primary method at this lake. A Ford Fender lake troll with a 'crawler trailer is hard to beat. Countdown Rapalas in the fluorescent orange finish along with silver and gold models are popular. A gold #K-5 Flatfish, gold Phoebe, Krocadile spoons, yellow Daredevle Pup, Kastmasters and Z-Rays comprise a good selection of other trolling baits for Eagle Lake rainbows. Lead-core enthusiasts would be wise to work 3 to 4 colors, pulling a frog or bikini Needlefish, Lucky Knight, or Finsel spoon.

Wading with fly gear early in the season is another alternative to consider. Fish a #6 to #8 Wooly Worm or the regionally favored Invitation Shrimp and J. Fair Fly. Interestingly, small crappie jigs in brown or black fished beneath a bobber have also been found to be very effective on Eagle Lake trout.

You can reach the Eagle Lake Marina by calling the Susanville operator. The Eagle Lake general store is at (916) 825-2191, and the U.S. Forest Service in Susanville is at (916) 825-3176.

Fall River

Fly fishing aficionados recognize the Fall River as one of the Top Ten trout streams in the United States! This river is loaded with rainbows and browns, but is heavily protected by stringent angling regulations. Artificial baits with single barbless hooks are the law, from the Tule intersection all the way upstream to its source at Thousand Springs. You will find minimal bank fishing opportunities along the Fall. Many trouters pack in boats (no motors) or float tubes. Two lodges (Lava Creek Lodge and Rick's Hunting and Fishing Lodge) provide access, if you stay with them.

Spin fisherman can compete with fly fishing purists; but, again, all lures must be replaced by a single barbless hook. Gold Kastmasters, Krocadiles in gold with fluorescent fire stripe, and the Li'l Cleo spoons in gold with bronze are time-proven winners in the fall. Fly fishermen have a wide variety of patterns from which to chose. Flies recommended by veterans who fish this river are the Zug Bug, Pheasant Tail Nymph, Black Aps, Olive and Gray Caddis, Spinner Falls, May Fly, Green Drake and Pale Morning Duns.

This is a deep, 21-mile-long stream with widths ranging from 150 feet to 250 yards. Springs feed it, so run-off has little effect on flow rate. Below the Tule-Fall River intersection there are no tackle restrictions. Boats can be put in off McArthur Road near Glenburn. Look for rainbows up to 7 pounds. For information contact Intermountain Fly and Tackle in Fall River Mills at (916) 336-6600. The Fall River Chamber of Commerce is at (916) 336-5840.

Hat Creek and Baum Lake

Few recreational anglers realize that Hat Creek is recognized as one of the premier native trout streams in the continental United States! As a matter fact, the lower stretch of water, 3 1/2 miles up from Lake Britton was the pilot site for California's Wild Trout Program initiated in the early 1970s. This area is heavily regulated, requiring only artificial baits with single barbless hooks. Check current regulations before setting out. It is estimated that rainbows outnumber browns in an 80/20 spread on the lower stream, with most fish ranging between 10 to 16 inches. But there are some lunker browns. Park where Hwy. 299 crosses the creek. In contrast, upper Hat Creek upstream of Baum Lake is populated primarily by planted rainbows with an occasional native strain fish mixed in. Access is good from 5 campgrounds along Hwy. 89.

Fly fishing is the name of the game along the lower run. Bigger dry flies, especially the #6 and #10 Salmon fly, can be outstanding at times. Other assorted favorites include Cahill, Olive, Tan or Yellow Paraduns, Humpies, Blue Dun, Black Fuzzy, Renegade, Adams, Sulphur Dun, Deer Hair, Spider and Joe's Hopper. This is a broad, meadow stream. Wading or using the bank works. In fishing a "wet" presentation, try the Pheasant Tail Nymph, Tricots, Hare's Ear and the Rusty Spinnerfall. Muddler Minnows and Marabous will be well*chosen streamer patterns.

Hardware slingers will find the upper Hat Creek water much to their liking. Spinners such as the Mepps, Rooster Tail and Panther Martin series are proven winners. Spoons, including the Wob-L-Rite and Super Duper, will catch fish along with smaller Rebel and Rapala plugs fished in the deeper water. Fishing baits on the upstream drift will also be very effective. Nightcrawlers, red worms, meal-worms, crickets, grasshoppers and salmon eggs will account for many planted 'bows.

Baum Lake can really be a "sleeper." The lake is populated by over 40 percent brown trout with fish recorded at over 20 pounds! It is open all year long, but no power boats are permitted. Float-tubing has been a favorite technique for tying into some of Baum's trophy-class fish. The fly and bubble combo along with standard fly fishing tackle is preferred by the float tubers. The same basic fly patterns outlined for Hat Creek will work on Baum Lake.

More information on these trout waters is available form the Burney Basin Chamber of Commerce at (916) 335-2111 or Vaughn's Sporting Goods in Burney, (916) 335-2381.

Manzanita Lake

This little 50 acre lake rests within Mount Lassen National Park. It is open all year, but can ice over during a severe winter. Manzanita is at 5,800 feet and is most accessible by boat or by wading. Floating tubes, row-boats, canoes, inflatable rafts, and prams are permitted—but no motors. There can be an awesome hatch of midges and mayflies on this tiny lake. Look for mid-June to be the prime time, with quality 12 to 20 inch rainbows and browns a strong possibility.

Fly fishers prefer to work a variety of nymphs and dry flies, many replicating the mayfly nymph at Manzanita. The Hare's Ear and Pheasant Tail nymph would be solid choices. Wooly Worms and Wooly Boogers also produce and can be fly-trolled or drifted from the small craft. Barbless hooks are required on this protected water. Spinning lures are all right as long as they too have single, barbless hooks. The Phoebe, Kastmaster and Mepps Syclops spoon, as well as the Panther Martin, Mepps and

Rooster Tail spinners in 1/16 to 1/4 ounce models are viable selections. Or use a bubble and fly combination.

At Manzanita, there is a two-fish, 10-inch maximum (that's maximum, not minimum) size limit, restricted to artificial lures and single barbless hooks. Most anglers never land a trout exceeding five pounds, but at this lake ten pounders are attainable! Of course, there's camping in the park, with one campground right near the lake. For information contact the Manzanita Ranger Station, (916) 335-4266, Powell's Fly Shop, (916) 345-3396, or Lassen Volcanic National Park, (916) 595-4444.

McCloud River and Lake

The McCloud River runs parallel to Hwy. 89 from Bartle toward the town of McCloud and then south to Lake McCloud and finally into Lake Shasta. This is an extremely scenic and prolific trout stream. And variety could be its middle name. It offers every type of water that holds trout. The McCloud is a great stream for the connoisseur angler, and for the youngster or beginner. Flies, bait and hardware (spinners and spoons) all can be effective. There are brook, brown, native rainbow and planted rainbow trout, as well as a few Dolly Varden (which must be released alive). And there is a complete spectrum of regulations, from 10 trout limits in one section of the river to a catch-and-release, barbless flies and lures-only section.

The upper portions of the McCloud f rom Bartle down to about a mile below Fowlers Camp is a planted section of stream (10-fish limit) that is easily accessible from campgrounds such as Fowler's, Big Springs, Cattle Camp, Algoma and several others. It you want to get away from other anglers and improve your chances of catching native and hold-over fish, walk the barely hikeable path along the stream to areas between camps. Both spinning and fly fishing is good. Top baits are salmon eggs and worms. Mepps spinners produce. Portions of this stream run through meadow for miles. Flow is gentle and fishermen wade here in summer without waders. Speaking of wading, the McCloud is a wader's stream. To fish it properly, in this stretch and also below McCloud Lake, you've got to get wet.

A second alternative is to fish the stretch just south of the McCloud Dam. It can be reached by taking Squaw Valley Road about 12 miles out of the town of McCloud. In this 6.5 mile stretch only artificial lures and flies may be used and the limit is two fish per day. Access is via Ash Campground about a mile downstream from the dam, on a road on the east side of the river. This is a canyon stream with more flow than in the Upper McCloud.

Finally, there is a catch-and-release stretch of the McCloud that begins at the mouth of Ladybug Creek and extends for about 2 miles. Take the road on the west side of the McCloud Lake Dam that leads to the Ah-Di-Na Campground. Only artificial lures and flies with barbless, single hooks are allowed. See the map below.

Fly fishermen in particular find the McCloud a very challenging spot for both dry and wet fly fishing. The dry fly action is primarily on an evening bite. Don't hesitate to try some larger patterns, even up to a size #10. Re-

gional favorites include the orange or yellow Humphy, Adams, Mosquito, Western Coachman and Yellow Cahill.

In switching to a wet fly presentation, consider using a double tandem fly setup. Area locals recommend the Pheasant Tail Nymph, Hare's Ear, Black or Brown Wing Fly, Caddis Larva, Yellow Jacket, Burlap or Peacock patterns. Dapping can also be a viable approach on the McCloud.

As for the reservoir, bait dunkers like to use the "Shasta Fly" marshmallow-salmon egg combo. Top-line trolling with lake trolls and 'crawler trailers, along with smaller spinners and spoons, produce with limited suc-

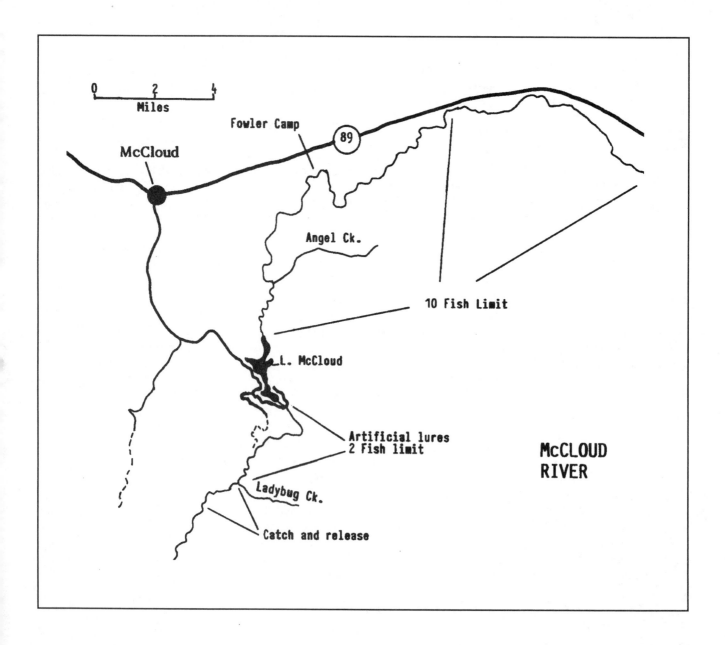

cess. McCloud Lake is traditionally very slow in the warmer months. For information contact the McCloud Ranger District, Drawer 1, McCloud CA 96057, (916) 964-2184.

Pit River

There are seven hydroelectric dams along a stretch of the Pit River from below Fall River Mills to about 30 miles upstream. Despite this, there is also a natural rainbow trout fishery of 12 to 15 inches, with some up to 4 pounds. Flow on the Pit is determined by release of water from the plants. So, if you choose to fish here, note that flows can drastically increase in a short period of time. Be cautious while wading or shore fishing. The key to fishing the Pit River is to be there when the water is down and to stay out of the slow water. Best fly waters are from Pit #3 to Pit #5, since the river is more open here. Adams and Cahills are good, as are Jug Bugs and Leeches. Bait anglers (using nightcrawlers, crickets and eggs) do well between Pit #1 and Pit #3. Lure tossers score all along the hydroelectric chain. This is a unique fishery and requires good knowledge. Contact either Vaughn's Sporting Goods in Burney, (916) 335-2381, or Intermountain Fly and Tackle in Fall River Mills, (916) 336-6600.

Lower Sacramento River

Here is some great fishing for large, native rainbows that is often overlooked. Salmon are taken from about September to December, but fat rainbows can be taken all year long. Salmon hooked out of season must be released. The Lower Sac is fished primarily with drift boats working from Redding to Red Bluff.

Locals report that some of the best 'bow fishing can actually be found in and around the city of Redding and all the way up to Keswick Dam.

Drift fishermen dragging lures consistently take some of the best stringers of rainbows on the Lower Sacramento. Preferred lures include the #50 or #30 Hot Shot plug and Storm's Wiggle and Wee Wart crankbaits in silver or gold with black backs. The #F-4 and #F-5 Flatfish are also regional favorites which are drifted behind a sliding sinker to fish in 30 to 35 foot depths. Most drifters use spinning or baitcasting outfits with light 6 to 8 pound test monofilament. Bait fishermen "mooch" offerings drifted along the river bottom. Nightcrawlers, salmon roe, or a large single salmon egg rigged on a dropper line with 3-way swivel and pencil lead will be the ticket.

From late April through mid-September, the Lower Sac offers some exciting fly fishing opportunities, especially on 10 to 22 inch 'bows. Dry fly patterns—sometimes all the way up to a size #10—which are effective include Adams, Goddard Caddis, Henryville and Elk Hair Caddis. Many rainbows along this run will be taken by fishing flies "wet." Because of the swift currents, consider using extra weighted patterns. Nymphs, such as the Bird's Nest, Cricket, Prince and Hare's Ear, will work. A strike indicator is recommended. For information contact the Shasta Cascade Wonderland Association, 1250 Parkview Ave., Redding, CA 96001, (916) 243-2643.

Upper Sacramento River

As you travel the 45 miles from Box Canyon Dam at the base of Siskiyou Lake all the way down to Lakehead at the upper end of Lake Shasta on I-5, you will be paralleling one of California's premier stretches of trophy trout water. There are lots of 10 to 14 inch fish, some wild trout, rainbows, browns, an occasional brookie and some trophy-sized fish too. Along I-5 there are numerous roadside accesses at wilderness hamlets such as Delta, La Moine, Gibson, Sims, Flume Creek, Costell and Dunsmuir. The season usually begins the last Saturday in April and lasts through November 15.

There are many deep pools along the Upper Sac and bait offerings will work for spin fishermen. Crickets, 'hoppers, 'crawlers and salmon eggs will take their share of fish. Lures such as the black and gold Panther Martin and brown Rooster Tail spinners should be tried in the deeper pools, pockets and tailout areas. Similarly, spoons like the Kastmaster and Li'l Cleo should work. The major interest in this water, however, is for its outstanding fly fishing. There has traditionally been a great hatch from late July to early October. Start by fishing "wet" in the early morning hours. Popular local patterns include the following: Cro Fly, Brown or Black Spent Wing, Yellow Jacket, Peacock and other black or brown nymphs. Dry fly activity is best in the late evenings on the Upper Sacramento. Fish the Humpy, Adams, Red Quill, Burlap Wrap, Mosquito, Gray Hackle or Yellow or Light Cahill patterns. Definitely consider doing a little "dapping" in these deeper pockets along this run of the Sacramento. For information contact the Shasta Cascade Wonderland Association, 1250 Parkview Ave., Redding, CA 96001, (916) 243-2643.

Lake Shasta and Keswick Reservoir

Lake Shasta encompasses over 30,000 surface acres. It has one of the finest trout populations in the state with rainbows and browns and even Kamloop trout featured. Shasta provides troutin' on a 12-month basis. It excels in the early spring when greater surface and subsurface feeding activity occurs. Top-line trolling is one of the best techniques at this time. A Ford Fender or Dave Davis lake troll with a nightcrawler trailer is a good setup to try. Popular places to troll on this large lake include Big Backbone Creek Inlet, Waters Gulch, Elmore Bay, and between the Pit River Bridge and Shasta Dam.

As water temperatures warm, the trout become more actively oriented to the schools of threadfin shad. Storm Thin Fin plugs and Rebel and Rapala minnows will fish well under these conditions here, again primarily on the troll. Be on the alert for boils of trout pushing the shad to the surface. Make long casts past the thrashing fish and retrieve assorted hardware just under the water. Spoons such as the nickel Kastmaster and silver Z-Ray will definitely work. The Triple Teazer and the regionally favorite Speedy Shiner can also be dragged near the schools of bait.

By midsummer both the trout and the bait fish will sound into deeper water, sometimes all the way to 100 feet. Use a graph or L.C.R. to monitor thermoclines and these deeper strike zones. Switch to lead core or Pink Lady diving planes using any of the popular lures. Bait fishermen demonstrate their prowess with the famous "Shasta Fly," a marshmallow and salmon egg combo. Nightcrawlers, crawdads, Power Baits, and red worms will also produce, fished 15 to 100 feet. More ambitious anglers will net their own threadfin shad and fish them with either a float or a single split-shot.

Most fly fishing enthusiasts stay with streamer models at Shasta. Muddler Minnows, Wooly Worms and White Marabous will produce on traditional fly gear and sinking lines. For information contact the Shasta-Cascade Wonderland Association, 1250 Parkview Ave., Redding, CA 96001, (916) 243-2643.

Keswick Reservoir is the afterbay for Lake Shasta. It's small—only 630 acres—but filled with cold water from Shasta and with lunker rainbow. Operated by Shasta County, it's a local secret. Troll Humdingers and Z-Ray Spoons for rainbows in the dam area. It's open to all types of boating and has a launch ramp and picnic area. For information contact Shasta County, 1855 Placer St., Redding, CA 96001, (916) 246-5661 or Shasta Lake Information Center, (916) 275-1589.

Siskiyou and Shastina Lakes

Lake Siskiyou and Lake Shastina are both within view of magnificient, snowcapped, 14,162 foot Mount Shasta. And they're both magnificent in their own right. They have fine fishing, boat launching, a marina, a fully developed campground and a beautiful setting with crisp mountain air and sparkling blue water.

Lake Siskiyou, the smaller of the two lakes, is located about 2 miles from Mt. Shasta City, off I-5. It is at 3,200 feet elevation, has 440 surface acres of water and its shoreline is just over 5 miles long. There is a swimming beach and boat speed limit of 10 mph. Trout fishing is very good at Siskiyou. Trout action is usually best in the Sacramento River Arm. Sliding sinker rigs with bait work good at inlets, early and late in the day. Trolling is also good in the Sacramento Arm. Most rainbows and browns range from 10 inches to 3 pounds, but brood stock from the nearby Mt. Shasta are sometimes "put out to pasture" in Siskiyou, so be prepared. Contact Lake Siskiyou at P.O. Box 276, Mt. Shasta, CA 96067, (916) 926-2618.

Lake Shastina, about 5 times larger than Siskiyou, is located about 7 miles northeast of Weed, off I-5. It has 2,700 surface acres of water and even boasts a water slide for the kids and some rental homes for lake visitors. Lake Shastina is well known for its outstanding trout fishery. In fact, big rainbows from 8-10 pounds have come out of the lake. Trout fishing is good at the inlets and at the dam. Troll over the old river channel in summer. Shastina Creek between I-5 and Lake Shastina produces many brown trout in the 7-10 inch range but also has some up to 3 pounds. Use small spinners, dark-patterned wet flies or red worms. Access is in Englewood. Contact Lake Shastina at 6006 Lake Shastina Dr., Weed, CA 96064, (916) 938-4385, and Lake Siskiyou, (916) 926-2618.

Susan River

Here is a little-known trout stream that combines good rainbow and brown trout fishing with history, scenery and easy hiking. Trout here go for #12 Royal Coachman, Captain, Western Bee, hardware and bait (especially when the water is up). The Susan runs from west to east towards Susanville. Paralleling this gentle stream for most of its way is the Buzz Johnson Trail, a reclaimed railroad bed. The 25 miles of trail are used mostly be hikers and mountain bikers, but anglers are finding it a great way to find trout in the Susan River Canyon. Main access points are Goumaz, Devil's Corral and one upstream from Hobo Camp. Fishing pressure is heavy only in the spring at the lower end of the trail near Susanville. For a map, contact the Bureau of Land Management, Eagle Lake Resource Area, 2545 Riverside Dr., Susanville, CA 96130, (961) 257-5381. For more information contact Lassen County Chamber of Commerce, 75 N. Weatherlow St., P.O. Box 338, Susanville, CA 96130, (916) 257-4323.

Thousand Lakes Wilderness and Caribou Wilderness

There are two wilderness areas, both in Lassen National Forest, that offer good back country trouting. One nice feature of these two areas is that, for the most part, the trails are relatively short and gentle. Beginning backpackers, or families with smaller children, do well here.

Thousand Lakes Wilderness is small (about 16,000 acres) as wilderness areas go, and doesn't have 1,000 lakes. It's terrain is varied, including rugged rocky areas, pine forests and alpine peaks. Elevations range from 5,000 to 9,000 feet. Although there are many lakes, only about 8 offer good fishing. Eiler Lake is the largest lake and is noted for the largest fish in the area. It is also the most accessible. At about 7,200 feet, Magee Lake and Everett Lake are most difficult to reach, but are rewarding to the determined angler. Other fishing lakes include Barret, Durbin and Hutford. Bait, lures and flies all work at Thousand Lakes. Forest Service Road off Hwy. 89, between Burney and Lassen Volcanic National Park, provide access.

Caribou Wilderness is on the east side of the National Park, off Hwy. 44. Trail heads are at Silver Lake. Caribou is much like Thousand Lakes in terrain and size, but fishing is not rated as good. Caribou has 20 major lakes. Fish are caught in both areas throughout the access season (late May through fall).

Northern Sierra Trout

The Northern Sierra offers some of the most consistently good troutin' to be found in California, with limited angling pressure. Too many Southern Californians make the mistake of hammering it out with the crowds on lower eastern Sierra waters. Taking the time to drive a little further north is well worth the effort.

The magnificent Feather River area with Lakes Almanor and Oroville has extensive facilities for the weekender. The Plumas-Eureka sector with the Gold Lakes Basin, Davis, Frenchman and Bucks Lakes is a virtual smorgasbord of diverse troutin' waters. Gold Lakes Basin and Jackson Meadows feature clusters of smaller trout lakes. And finally, the Truckee River and its satellite waters, Donner, Prosser, Stampede and Boca, can generate fine trout fishing on an all-year basis!

Lake Almanor, Butt Valley Reservoir and Upper Feather North Fork

Trophy-sized German browns, rainbows and king salmon await the eager trouter at Almanor. There is a full range of popular areas to fish for trout on this lake.

These include the shoreline near the A-Frame, the east side of the dam, Recreation Area #1, Recreation Area #2, Old Crawford's, the Hamilton Branch, Big Springs Cove, Bailey Springs and the Powerhouse area.

Still-fishing with 'crawlers, salmon eggs or marshmallows is popular with both bank and boat fishermen. A slide-float with native minnows fished 20 to 30 feet deep is also effective. Drifting or "mooching" a live nightcrawler, particularly around the deeper, cooler underwater springs can result in some stellar catches. Fly fishermen should try a menu of Wooly Buggers, Caddis and Birdsnest nymphs.

But day in and day out, the major take will be on artificials. Trolling accounts for a lot of fish. Try either a jointed or CD-7 Rapala on a fast top-line troll. A fluorescent orange Flatfish can be equally potent when trolled by itself, or try the locals' favorite—a silver or gold Speedy Shiner.

With increases in water temperature, shift gears and use either lead core or downriggers. Flasher blades teamed with lead core is a really hot combo. Drag these with a Needlefish, Super Duper or a nightcrawler trailer.

Occasionally there will be some highly visible surface-feeding action evident. A popular tactic is to work the strangely designed Z-Ray spoon through these trout boils.

Finally, take a shot fishing a small white crappie jig under a bobber or on the drift. Often, large subsurface cruising rainbows bushwhack these tiny lures mistaking them for pond smelt or shad. There is also the chance of nailing one of Almanor's legendary smallmouth bass on this same crappie lure while fishing for trout!

The North Fork of the Feather drains into Almanor at Chester. Starting right in town, the North Fork and its streams (Rice Creek, Warner Creek, Hot Springs Creek, Willow Creek, Brenner Creek, Last Chance Creek) have good access, relatively low fishing pressure and native trout. The North Fork itself is a fairly large stream, even in autumn. Most of the streams are spring fed and run clear and cold throughout the summer. Several types of fishing are offered. Willow Creek is very brushy and is best for bait angling. Some others, like Rice Creek, are good fly casting waters. There are a number of campgrounds along the creeks providing access and overnighting.

On the northeast shore of Lake Almanor, the Hamilton Branch flows into the lake. It offers good fishing in a series of big pools, separated by white water riffles flowing through a scenic canyon. The Feather River flows out of Lake Almanor at its south end. Senaca Road parallels the river for about 10 miles and leads to Senaca Resort. Lake Almanor dam provides a regulated flow of very cold water to this stretch of water. The best access is where Senaca Road crosses the North Fork. Fish away from this access, either upstream or downstream, for best results. Butt Valley Reservoir, a fine trout and smallmouth fishery, is also just south of Lake Almanor. This 1,000 acre gem offers big browns trout, rainbow trout and king salmon. Facilities are limited to a single lane launch ramp, two PG&E campgrounds and a picnic area, but

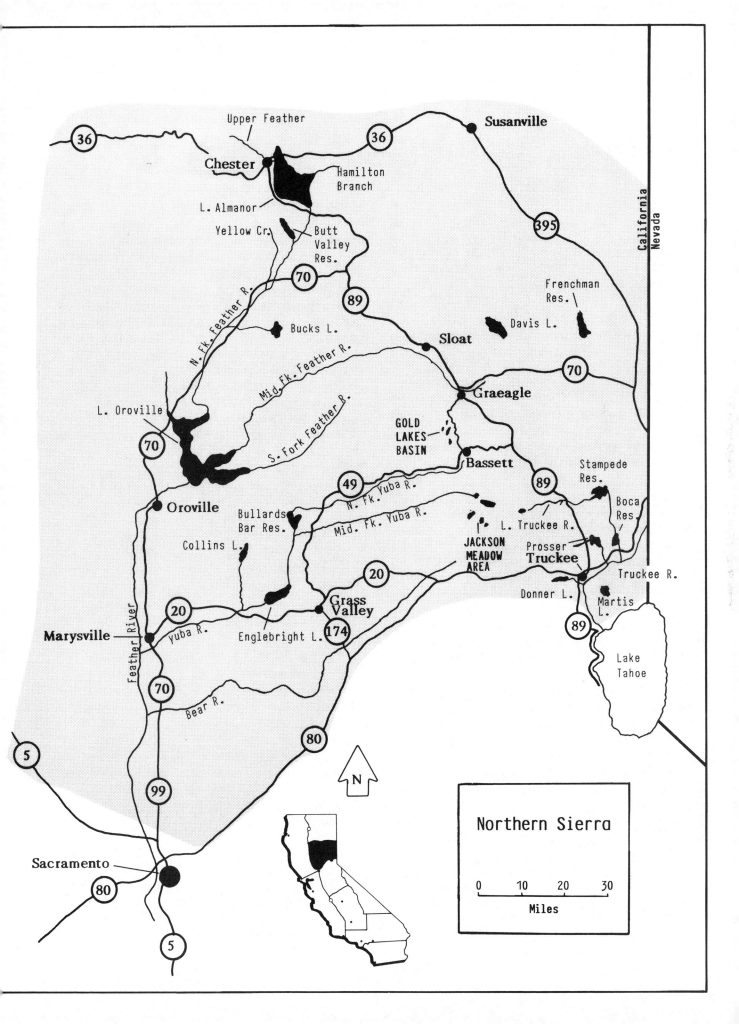

Northern Sierra

don't let this keep you from trying Butt Valley Lake when you're in the Almanor area. For information contact the Almanor Ranger District, Box 767, Chester, CA 96020, (916) 258-2141, and PG & E Regional Land Dept, (916) 529-6316.

Upper Yellow Creek, accessible from Humbug Road, off Rte. 89 along the west shore of Lake Almanor, is a fine mountain-meadow stream. There is a PG&E campground in the east end of Humbug Valley. The canyon below the valley is also good fishing with flies or bait. A section in the valley has the following regulations: 16-inch minimum size, two-fish daily, artificials only. Browns here in this restored native fishery are said to be the most beautiful of fish.

Boca, Prosser and Stampede Lakes

These three "gems" are only one-half hour from Lake Tahoe, but are often overlooked by all but the local trouter. Each lake has its own "personality," so to speak, with different ecologies and trout populations.

Boca, at just under 1,000 acres, is best known for its German browns and rainbow trout. Best areas to fish are from the Boca Rest Camp to the dam and from the point across the lake from the Rest Camp. Fast-troll Rebels and broken-back Rapalas in these locations. Augment this with trolling blades pulled ahead of small spoons for planter quality trout. The action is usually concentrated in 10 to 20 foot depths for browns and 'bows. Gold Kastmasters and Hopkins spoons in larger sizes with single hooks can be thrown and retrieved through deeper strike zones at Boca for bigger fish. The top baits are an inflated 'crawler, peeled crawdad tail, or "Shasta Fly" fished on a sliding sinker rig. Boca also has decent Kokanee action on lead-core line. Ford Fenders ahead of Kokanee King, Triple Teazer or Knobby Wobbler lures is the hot setup. Add a kernel of white corn for extra insurance. All types of boating is permitted and there is a developed campground.

Prosser is primarily a trolling lake for rainbows and browns. It has 750 surface acres of water and there is a 10 m.p.h. boat speed limit. The same offerings used at Boca pretty much produce at Prosser. Troll plugs on the Highway 89 arm of this lake. Trade off, and use blades fished deep in the warmer months. A Wooly Worm or a mylar streamer can also be effective at times on the slow-troll. The area near the mouth of Prosser Creek is a consistent producer. Late summer deep trolling is good near the dam. There is a good launch ramp, campsites and a picnic area. Prosser Creek, above the lake, is a very good trout

stream. The main stream is accessible off Hwy. 89. The north and south forks (near this junction is good fishing) are reached via a Forest Service Road. Prosser Creek flows cold and clear, even in late summer. Small lures and nymph patterns on a light leader are excellent choices.

Stampede, at 3,500 acres, is recognized for its larger browns. Troll deep with plugs in the summer using lead core or a downrigger. The steep banks across the lake from the ramp are prime territory. Baits identical to those outlined for Boca can also be productive at Stampede. There is also some decent action on kokes at Stampede. Lake regulars prefer lead-core line and the Wedding Ring spinners as one of their top lures. There are excellent camping and launching facilities at the south side of the lake. Prime spots include the Little Truckee inflow area and near the dam. Stream trout anglers often find the Little Truckee River to be a good producer. Access is via Rte. 89 and Jackson Meadows Road, which both parallel the stream. Small spinners, nightcrawlers and marshmallows are effective. The Little Truckee runs above and below Stampede Reservoir.

All three of these lakes should be considered strong candidates for some cold footin' action, since ice fishing often can be very good here. For information on the area north of Lake Tahoe, contact the Truckee Chamber of Commerce, Box 361, Truckee, CA 95734, (916) 587-2757, and the Truckee Ranger District, Box 399, Truckee, CA 95734, (916) 587-3558.

Bucks, Davis and Frenchman Lakes

These three decent-sized lakes offer outstanding troutin' just out of the Portola-Quincy area. Frenchman and Davis are to the east on the way to Reno, while Bucks is to the west, heading towards Oroville.

Bucks has a good stock of rainbows, some big browns, and an occasional brookie. Lead-core on downriggers are the preferred methods for consistent action. Work blades'n 'crawlers or jointed Rebels on these deep-water rigs. The areas around Haskin's Cove and the mouth of Mill Creek should hold some fish. Lead-core trolling using a Needlefish is the ticket for kokanee in the summer.

Frenchman has an incredible volume of 10 to 12 inch planter-sized rainbows. Blades matched with a few red worms for a trailer produce limits on a regular basis. Consider fan-casting small gold spoons such as the Phoebe or Kastmaster along with gold-bladed Panther Martin or Mepp's spinners. Bait chuckers at Frenchman will rack up their share of fish on Zeke's floating baits, presented with a sliding egg sinker and light 2 pound test leaders.

Ice fishing off the dam in the winter is another bait-dunking possibility here. Cheese, salmon eggs, mini 'crawlers, Power Baits, and red worms also get 'em!

Davis has been slowly garnering a reputation as a "sleeper" trophy fishery. There are substantial numbers of 2 to 4 pound rainbows in this lake augmented by a smaller amount of browns in double-digit weights. Davis excels in the early spring. By midsummer, extensive weed growth makes troutin' tough, though not impossible. During the height of the season, top-line trolling is unquestionably the key method. Pull lake trolls—especially those with prism-lite finishes such as the Les Davis Bolo series—around Camp #5, Lightning Tree and the island. Half a nightcrawler is the best all-around trailer. The Needlefish fished "clean," or with a chunk of 'crawler laced on, will produce with lead-core line behind a set of blades. Rapalas and Rebels in both the floating and sinking models will take Davis trout on the troll. Fly fishers prefer to drift or slow-troll with Wooly Worms or Wooly Buggers. Brown, black and olive-bodied versions have traditionally been very effective. For information contact Plumas County Visitors Bureau, 91 N. Church St., Quincy, CA 95971, (916) 283-6345, and Plumas National Forest, (916) 534-6500.

Donner Lake

This beautiful lake can be seen from I-80 as you motor 100 miles east of Sacramento. Donner lies about two miles west of Truckee. It's about 3 miles long and about 1 mile wide, with complete facilities. The lake really turns on in the springtime. The winter bite is possible through the nasty cold, and the summer activity requires some deep-water tactics. Donner, like Tahoe, has a resident population of giant mackinaw lake trout. Using downriggers, locals troll the main channel with magnum-sized J-plugs or live minnows behind a brilliant Dodger reflector.

Most trolling occurs at 100 to 200 feet, but consider working shallower after a trout plant. The mackinaws will go into a virtual "mac attack," feasting on planted rainbows or browns in the shallows right after a scheduled plant. Troll the east end and the boat ramp area and the Donner Tahoe Beach stretch for marauding macs. At this time, switch to either a rainbow or brown trout pattern minnow plug and troll 30 to 60 feet. The larger browns can be taken spot-casting larger gold Kastmasters and Hopkins spoons into deeper water. The Mepp's Luxsox spinner is exceptionally heavy and is often used for greater depth control. Standard Rapala and Rebel

plugs worked on top, or later in the year, deep, will produce on rainbows or browns as will blades'n worms.

Bait fishermen can score on some quality fish with 'crawlers, either inflated or drifted under a bobber. Or, try live crickets and grasshoppers tied on behind a cast-a-bubble. Salmon eggs and Velveeta will nail the smaller, stockier rainbows. Bait can produce near the outlet estuary in Donner Park, or the beach off the State Park. Spin fishermen using a fly and bubble will also be effective with various flies. Fish the Wooly Worm, Black Ant, Brown Bivisible, Dusty Miller and even the Li'l Rainbow Trout streamer fly with this rig. Donner also has a modestly thriving kokanee fishery. Troll deep at the drop-off near China Cove and near the west end inlet for kokanee action. The basic kokanee "menu" also works here: lead-core line with Wedding Rings, Needlefish, Kokanee King and Triple Teazer lures. For information contact the Truckee Chamber of Commerce, P.O. Box 2757, Truckee, CA 95734, (916) 587-2757, or (800) 548-8388.

Feather River—North and Middle Forks

Between Lake Almanor and Lake Oroville, the North Fork of the Feather River flows along Rte. 70 for much of its course through the Feather River Canyon. Where you can get down to it, the main river is good trout water. A good eight mile stretch is from Nelson Creek to Audie Bar. Perennial hot spots include the confluence of the North Fork and the East Branch of the North Fork, and the mouth of the Yellow Creek. These are both just above the town of Belden. The lower section of Yellow Creek, near the Feather, is fished heavily, but is still productive. Excellent fly fishing occurs from the Queen Lily to Ganser Bar Run. A variety of other offerings will produce including nightcrawlers, salmon eggs, grasshoppers and crickets. The Middle Fork of the Feather is accessible along Rte. 70/89 between Sloat to Portola. The Middle Fork in such spots as the area between Little Bear Campground and Nelson Point, around Graeagle and Sloat can be very good at times. There is a very prominent annual stonefly and caddisfly hatch along this stretch which translates into good fly fishing. Tributary creeks out of Portola such as Smith, Bear, Deer, Mohawk, Graeagle and Frazier generate some nice 'bows and browns in the early season. Area locals feel that the best spots for trophy fish along the Feather are Two Rivers, Carmac Mine and Camp Layman. The area from the town of Graeagle to Rio Bridge is popular for spin fishermen using bait. Nightcrawlers, salmon eggs, Power Baits, and redworms should work well. Spoons and scaled-down spinners such as the 1/16 to 1/8 ounce Mepps and Rooster Tail series are also good possibilities.

Both of these runs produce best in the early spring. By midsummer, water levels are sometimes drastically low which makes the troutin' very tough at best. For information contact the Plumas County Visitors Bureau, 91 N. Church St., Quincy, CA 95971, (916) 283-6345.

Gold Lake Basin

Upon first visit, the western trouter new to this area near Plumas-Eureka will feel like a "kid in a candy store." Here we have a cluster of lakes—each one a little different—and almost all affording some very decent troutin'. Between the Middle Fork of the Feather River and the North Fork of the Yuba River, the angler can choose from Gold, Long, Lower and Upper Sardine, Lower and Upper Salmon, Parker, Silver, Round and Squaw Lakes. Access is from Graeagle on Hwy. 70 to the north or from Bassett on Hwy. 49 to the south.

Lower Sardine is one of the top picks in this basin. It is excellent for planter-sized rainbows and a stray brookie or two. Almost any ultralight spoon, spinner or plug will produce along with assorted flies. Upper Sardine requires a short hike from its lower namesake. If you follow the inlet stream from Upper Sardine, hiking   a little further, you will run into Young America Lake, which has a community of small golden trout. Boat fishing is best on both Lower and Upper Sardine. These two lakes are also your best choices for modest fly fishing opportunities in the basin.

Gold is the "flagship" of the chain. It is by far the largest in size and holds the biggest trout. Interestingly there are big, bruiser-class mackinaw trout in Gold, with specimens topping the 20 pound mark. Veteran anglers troll for these Macs down to 100 feet during the summer months. There are some bank fishing spots at Gold open to bait dunkin'. You will have better chances with artificials for rainbows and browns, especially during a good windy period. Bait tossers would do best with inflated 'crawlers or pink, yellow and orange Power Bait. Flasher'n worm trolling combos take some fish, along with a fly'n bubble outfit.

Kastmasters, red and white Hot Shot spoons, and CD-5 or CD-7 countdown Rapalas should be casted from boats or from the shore.

Not-to-difficult hikes to a wealth of other basin lakes and streams open up even greater angling potential in a

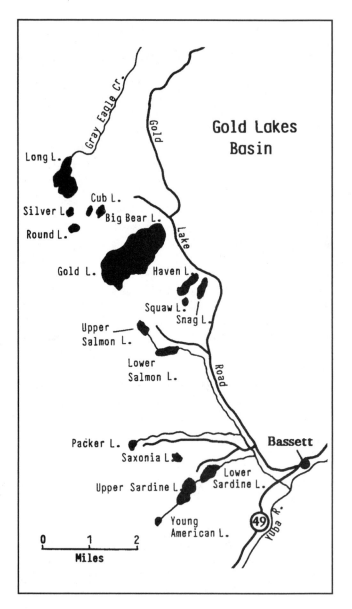

more solitary environment. Big Bear, Cub, Long, Silver, Round, Jamison, Grass, Rock, Wades or Eureka Lakes are all within a day's hike. A float tube can be dynamite on the brook trout populations on these higher elevation lakes. Assorted dry and wet patterns produce: Adams, California Mosquito, Black Gnat, Green Gnat and smaller light shaded Wooly Worms. There are several lodges and campgrounds in the Gold Lakes Basin. For information contact the Plumas National Forest, P.O. Box 7, Blairsden, CA 96013, (916) 836-2575; Plumas County Visitors Bureau, 91 N. Church St., Quincy, CA 95971, (916) 283-6345.

Jackson Meadows Area and Milton Lake

Here at the headwaters of the Middle Fork of the Yuba River, some road access can be nearly impossible at times. Boat launching can thus be problematic, governed a lot by snow and storms. But if you can get into Jackson Meadows, look for heavy action on 8 to 12 inch rainbows with an occasional quality brown or bigger 'bow thrown in for good measure.

There are several good fishing opportunities in the Jackson Meadow Area. Jackson Meadow Reservoir, it- self, is a full-service recreation lake with 150 campsites, group camping, boat ramp, picnic area, etc. This 1 1/2 square mile lake with 11 miles of shoreline has good brown and rainbow trout fishing and is on a paved road.

Trolling is a good approach. The CD and floating Rapalas in rainbow trout finish have historically worked on these trout. The blades'n worm combo should also be tried on a top-line troll. Change over to deep-trolling methods in the summer with lead-core line as the first choice. Bait fishermen can drift nightcrawlers or salmon eggs under a bobber. The dam area is a good bet or the

points on the east side. This lake is a good place to stay alert for surface-feeding swirls. A gold Kastmaster on the end of a long cast is a solid option for subsurface action. But a variety of flies presented with either traditional gear or a spin bubble might even be better. Proven patterns are the Female Adams, Joe's Hopper, Black Ant, Rio Grande King and the brown or olive Zug Bug.

The 1.5 mile stretch of the Middle Yuba, below Jackson Meadows, as well as Milton Lake, is a special regulation trophy trout fishery. Only artificial lures with single, barbless hooks may be used and the limit is two fish, both smaller than 12 inches. Other good trout lakes in the area include Bowman (brown trout), Lake of the Woods (brook trout), Webber Lake (browns) and Weaver Lake. Bowman has very steep banks necessitating a boat for good fishing. Lake of the Woods is a gorgeous little lake that also is best fished by boat. In the Canyon Creek drainage, there is good fishing in Canyon Creek (several miles of good bait fishing waters), Faucherie Lake (good shore fishing) and Sawmill Lake (launch near the dam or shore fish in selected spots).

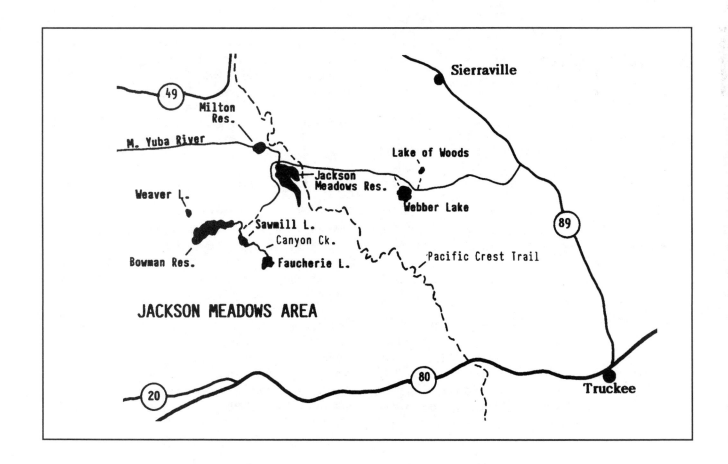

Milton Lake (or Reservoir) is a little gem of a trout lake. Cal Trout and DFG have turned this into a haven for a wild, self-sustaining population of brown trout. Rainbow are also taken. Anglers may take two fish, maximum 12 inches in size, per day, on artificials only. Tubes, prams and canoes are recommended. Spring and summer are good. Shore fishing is good where the Middle Yuba pours in. The Yuba below Milton is also good. For information on the Jackson Meadows Area contact the Sierraville Ranger Station, Box 95, Sierraville, CA 96216, (916) 994-3401.

Lake Oroville

This large, 15,000 acre lake lies in the western foothills of the Northern Sierra. It is open all year long and can provide some excellent action for the California trouter. Rainbows, browns, kokanees and even coho salmon are possibilities at Oroville. There are full facilities at several locations on the lake.

There are a lot of pond smelt and shad minnows in this lake. These indigenous bait fish account for some trophy-sized catches, particularly on larger brown trout. They can be fly-lined or drifted with a bobber setup. A conventional snap-on bobber or a slide float will work with these minnows if you are fishing from the bank. The face of the dam is an especially popular place to try these techniques. Bank fishing is also worth trying at the Bloomer Area, the Spillway and Lime Saddle. Smaller plants will readily take salmon eggs and redworms.

Trollers should stay with floating and countdown Rapalas, Rebels, Storm Thin Fins and Flatfish lures when it comes to plugs. Top-lining with Rooster Tails and silver Kastmasters will also produce. Flashers in small- to medium-sized blades with nightcrawler trailers are very effective. As the trout sound deeper, switch to either lead-core line or downriggers. When fishing deep to 60 feet, try Rebels and Rapalas, and the ever-popular Needlefish lures. For information contact Limesaddle Marina, (916) 534-6950; Bidwell Canyon Marina, (916) 589-3165; Lake Oroville State Recreation Area, (916) 534-2324.

Truckee River and Martis Lake

The Truckee River originates at Lake Tahoe and tumbles along beside Hwy. 89 towards the town of Truckee and then northeast along I-80 to the Nevada border. The DF&G stock the water from Tahoe to Truckee with pan-sized rainbows, but these waters also contain large native brown trout. Baits such as live crawdads, nightcrawlers, and worms will account for some lunker browns on the Truckee. Red salmon eggs are always good for a share of smaller 'bows. Also, consider trying some other larger live insect offerings, most notably 'hoppers and crickets.

Bigger browns and 'bows can be stalked in a one-mile section below the Truckee lumber mill and between Hirshdale and Floriston. There is also a restricted zone from the east side of Truckee to the Glenshire Bridge. Here only single barbless hooks may be used.

The Truckee is recognized as one of the state's finest fly fishing waters. The Adams, Yellow Humpy, Blue Dun, Grizzly Wolf, small Bucktail Caddis, Black Fur Ant and Royal Coachman are established patterns. For really large fish, the stretch of fast flowing water that parallels the traffic along I-80 northeast of Truckee, really produces. This is a special regulation area with 15 inches being the minimum size.

Martis Lake (700 surface acres) was the first designated by the California DF&G as a wild trout lake. The idea was to support a population of rare Lahontan cutthroat trout. It worked for a while, but more aggressive rainbow and browns have become dominant. This is not all bad. Trout to eleven pounds have been landed. Martis is a catch-and-release, artificial lures and flies only lake. May, June and to mid-July are prime. October can also be good. No motors are allowed. The lake is located just off Hwy. 267, south of Truckee. There is a campground and wildlife area. For information contact the Truckee Chamber of Commerce, P.O. Box 2757, Truckee, CA 95734, (916) 587-2757.

Yuba River Region—Collins, Bullards Bar and Englebright Lakes

Here is a cluster of three reservoirs (less than 20 miles separate them) in the lower reaches of the Yuba drainage that provide fine trout fishing and a wide range of boating and camping activities. They're all between Marysville and Grass Valley, off Hwy. 20. Collins is a 1,000 acre lake that has an extensive trout planting program from February to May, including some lunkers. Bullards Bar, the largest of the three, at 4,000 surface acres, is the least developed. Watch out for floating debris in the spring at this top kokanee lake. Englebright, more like a long, wide canyon river than a lake, specializes in campsites that can only be reached by boat.

Collins is an underrated lake, especially based on past performances in the early spring period. The recreational angler will find ample numbers of 'bows and browns to keep him interested at this lake located out of Marysville. In the early part of the season, fish the creek entering into the lake near Oregon House, the camp area near the dam, and the swimming beach. Bait fishing with worms, eggs and marshmallows should do the trick. From April to May, troll shallow, top-lined gold Kastmasters and Phoebe spoons, Mepp's and Rooster Tail spinners, and CD-7 Rapalas. As the water temperature warms at Collins, employ a deeper trolling technique. Drag flashers'n 'crawlers from the swim beach to the dam. Use a Pink Lady, or a Deep Six diving plane to get the blades down to 35 feet. In the early morning and in the late afternoon, try drifting a black or brown Wooly Worm.

Bullards Bar, equally a sleeper of sorts, is loaded with rainbows and kokanee salmon. This lake is about 90 minutes from Sacramento. Trolling is the "choice of champions" here. Top-line, starting in early February, with almost any popular spoon, spinner or plug. But definitely give some time to the kokanee at Bullards Bar. Lead core is one preferred tactic, running at least four colors. The kokes will be found anywhere from 40 to 140 feet. The Wedding Ring spinner is a regional mainstay. Other koke killers include the Knobby Wobbler, Lucky Knight and Needlefish. A local variety of lake troll popular here is the Teeny Troll blade teamed with a bead-like fly called the Teeny Dancer, or the companion kokanee spinner, the Teeny Nymph Plus.

Englebright Lake is similarly dominated by serious trollers. Top-line tactics will be in order for the early spring. Here, as with Bullards Bar, shift to deep-water methods by June. Rainbows and browns will hit the standard menu of spoons, plugs and spinners on a top-line presentations (Mepps, Rooster Tails, Phoebes, Kastmasters and Rapalas). But again, the kokanee bite can be the real thriller! Let out as many as 12 colors by summer and hold on! Most patented kokanee favorites are viable choices here. Bait fishing at Englebright is possible near the inlets and on the river area. Salmon eggs and nightcrawlers—either still-fished or drifted—are the two best baits. For information contact Collins Lake, (916) 692-1600; Bullards Bar, (916) 228-3231; Englebright, (916) 639-2343.

Central Sierra Trout

This region of the state offers some sensational troutin' with minimal pressure. The lakes in the Carson Pass area, the Crystal Basin, along with larger impoundments such as Camanche, Don Pedro, Amador, New Melones and the "twins," McClure and McSwain, have a variety of trout adventures awaiting the California trout angler.

Backpacking trouters can have an absolute field day selecting from the scores of lakes in this region of the Sierras. For example, wilderness areas offer an extensive selection of waters to consider. Some of these more remote waters experience only a handful of visiting hikers each season and are virtually "pregnant" with catchable rainbows, browns and brookies!

Amador Lake

This little lake, about 400 acres, situated 40 miles northeast of Stockton, receives phenomenal plants of catchable rainbows each season. Some of these trout hold over through the fall months and five-pound-class fish are not that unusual. Late winter and early spring are the best times to plan a troutin' safari to Amador.

Trolling is the "hot ticket." Start with top-lining down the center of the lake, along Jackson Creek, Rock Creek and Carson Creek. Rapalas and Rebel floaters would be a good choice. Ford Fenders with a 'crawler trailed behind are also solid producers. But try to top-line troll other lures including the Mepps, Rooster Tail, Triple Teazer, Needlefish and Kastmaster. By April or May shift gears and begin to troll deeper. Downriggers or lead-core lines are in order to get the lures down to 40 to 50 feet.

Bait dunkers working the shorelines near the spillway and the dam may tie into some nice 1 to 3 pound rainbows on the "Shasta Fly" (a salmon egg/marshmallow treat). There is also some good potential for night fishing with a lantern. Night troutin' is best near the dam and off the docks. For information contact Lake Amador Resort, 7500 Lake Amador Dr., Ione, CA 95640, (209) 274-4739. There are complete boating and camping facilities at this dedicated angler's lake.

Camanche Lake

Camanche is a motherlode lake, located just south of Amador. It's 30 miles east and a little north of Stockton. This is a sizeable lake with 7,600 acres of water. There are complete facilities on both the north and south shores.

Put simply, trolling is the name of the game if you want to catch trout consistently at Camanche. The old river channel that runs down the center of the lake is a primary trolling stretch. Rabbit Creek, the dam area and spillway, south shore coves and main channel are also key trolling runs.

Lead core and downriggers are essential during the summer months. Consider going to 6 to 12 colors or use the downrigger to reach 40 to 60 feet. Rainbows, king salmon and some kokanee lurk at these depths. Troll Needlefish and Rainbow Runners with or without flashers. Standard flasher and 'crawler combos or kokanee spoons and spinners are popular. There can be some good shore fishing along the areas mentioned above. Still-fish nightcrawlers, Power Bait, salmon eggs or a marshmallow and nightcrawler "package." Another ploy that works at Camanche is to drift nightcrawlers down the center of the coves either weightless or with a pinch of shot. For information contact (209) 763-5178 or (209) 763-5151.

Carson Pass

Carson Pass, bisected by Rte. 88, is about 35 miles south of Lake Tahoe's South Shore and is best known as home of Kirkwood Ski Resort. But trout fishing, hiking, camping and drinking-in the alpine scenery reigns in the summertime. The pass is at 8,573 feet elevation, so the summer season is short. Many visitors come in July and August. But fishing is best in early summer and early fall.

There is a wide variety of trout angling opportunities. The most accessible is the planted waters of the Carson River as it flows alongside Rte. 88. Several small lakes are also easily reached from the highway, including Red Lake, Round-Top Lake, Frog Lake and Winnemucca Lake. Blue Lake Road, off Rte. 88, leads through Faith

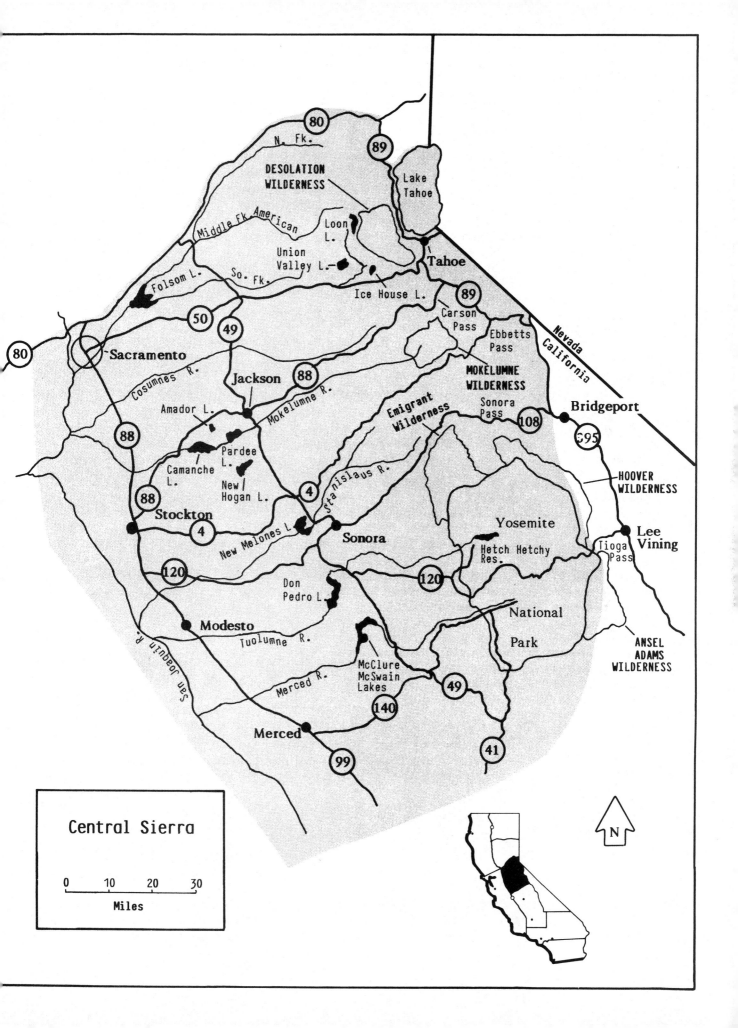

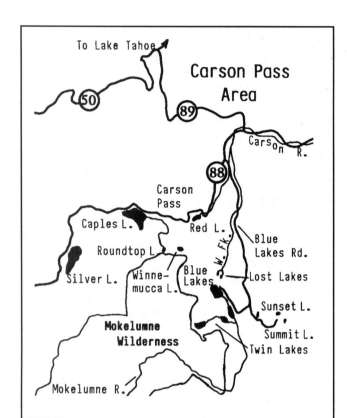

Valley to a marvelous collection of small lakes and campgrounds. There are Upper and Lower Blue Lake, Lost Lake, and Twin Lake, among others. Blue Creek tumbling down to the Mokelumne from Blue Lake is a rugged but productive stream. And Lost Lake (actually 2 lakes) harbors some large brook trout.

Blue Lakes, and especially Lower Blue, have some hungry cutts and 'bows eager to snap at a blades'n crawler combo. Drag a silver or gold #F-3 or #F-4 Flatfish behind the flashers as a variation on this theme. Shore fishing is also good at these lakes as is ice fishing in the winter. Caples Lake similarly has great ice fishing for the cold footer with a snowmobile. Rainbows and German browns are the primary quarry here. An occasional big mackinaw might also jump on a #T-50 or #U-20 silver or pearl Flatfish behind blades. Troll near the spillway. Also, Caples and Woods Creek are often good for small brookies.

Lost Lake is the real "sleeper" of the Carson Pass region. It has a few real trophy-sized brookies up to 20 inches. Work nymphs that mimic small freshwater shrimp. The Carson River as well as Devil's Corral and Summit

City Creeks are also worth investigating. Water levels get dramatically low in the summer, so key in on the early season bite. Drifting baits such as 'crawlers, red worms and 'hoppers through the deeper holes can be very productive. Rainbows and an occasional cutthroat are found in these creeks. There are several good camping facilities in the Carson Pass area. Contact the Eldorado National Forest Office, 100 Forni Rd., Placerville, CA 95677, (916) 622-5061.

Lake Don Pedro

Take your pick of rainbows, Eagle Lake strain rainbow, silver and king salmon or an occasional brown trout when sampling Don Pedro. This is another extensive, sinuous lake where trolling will be your best chance to find fish in any volume. Start by pulling lures in the main bay in front of the marina heading towards the dam. Troll the face of the dam and then circle back to Ramos Creek. Or, try another variation and drag the shorelines of the north and south bays. In the summer, cooler water can be found in the Tuolumne River Arm. The center channel that traverses the lake is also another prime choice for sustained trolling action.

Speedy Shiners, blue/silver Kastmasters, silver Z-Rays, Triple Teazers, Phoebes, and blades'n 'crawlers are standard fare. Locals prefer to use smaller flashers with nightcrawlers in the summer months. Fish this rig at 40 to 60 foot depths. Lead-core aficionados using Dave Davis or Ford Fender lake trolls can also score high marks with the popular Needlefish lure. The rainbow trout, bikini and silver finishes are favored Needlefish patterns. It is very important to monitor the schools of shad at Don Pedro. The trout and salmon will follow these migrating bait fish around the lake. Visual spottings of surface-feeding boils will help, but proper usage of electronic fish-finders will give more accurate results. This is especially true when the bait is schooled deep.

If the fish come up to the surface, cut your engine and make long casts to the commotion. Kastmaster and Super Duper spoons will work. Or, throw a small white Mini-Jig on light line for these top-water trout. There is a modest still-fishing bite at Don Pedro. Fish the shoreline across from the south marina with eggs, Power Baits, nightcrawlers and marshmallows. Give night fishing a shot, soaking some bait primarily at the marina. Don Pedro is located in the Sierra foothills east of Modesto. There are fully developed camping and boating facilities at the lake. For information contact Lake Don Pedro, Star Route Box 81, La Grange, CA 95329, (209) 852-2396.

Emigrant Wilderness Area

There is a wealth of lakes spread out among the 100,000 acres of this pristine wilderness. The Department of Fish and Game estimates that 42 lakes in this basin have rainbows, 28 have brookies, 6 have goldens, 2 have rainbows and brookies and 1 has rainbows and brown trout. Emigrant Wilderness, located south of Hwy. 108, the Sonora Pass, is about 30 miles out of the town of Sonora. Terrain varies from rolling hills to ridges and granite domes, with many lakes surrounded by stands of lodgepole pine.

There is a variety of trailheads the angler can use as departure points. Kibbie Ridge, Kennedy Meadows, Crabtree and Bell Meadow are the most frequented. The best troutin' is in the more remote lakes, many located in the southwestern portion of the area. Pingree, Black Hawk, Shallow Hyatt, Rosasco, Lost, Cow Meadow, Yellow Hammer, Big and Deer Lakes are just a few of the more productive waters. Native brown trout can be found in Summit, Lily and Horsemeadow Creeks.

Fly fishing will be overwhelmingly your best strategy on these alpine takes. A few of the regionally popular patterns fished dry are the California Mosquito, Light Cahill, Black Gnat, Elk Hair Caddis and Joe's Hopper. Flies can range from #12 to #18 depending on the size of the indigenous trout. Natural baits, including pine grubs, hellgrammites, 'hoppers, crickets and nightcrawlers, are super choices. Salmon eggs will also work to a limited degree.

Hikers with strong backs should also consider packing in a small inflatable boat. A #10 Dave Davis or Model-T Ford Fender with a 'crawler behind it can produce astonishing results on these unpressured fish! Ultralight Krocadiles, Rooster Tails, Mepps and Panther Martins can also be trolled or fan-casted from the bank on almost any of the Emigrant Wilderness Lakes. A word of caution is in order. You must arm yourself with a good topographical map and a compass to find some of these high country lakes. Many are not on marked trails and some rock scrambling may be necessary. Be sure to file a trip itinerary with the local ranger's office and obtain necessary permits before heading out into this remote wilderness.

Folsom Lake

Long recognized as one of the state's premier bass lakes, Folsom also kicks out its share of quality rainbows and even land-locked king salmon. Still-fishing from the bank will definitely be a strong option on this suburban lake. Locals recommend using a minnow hooked below the dorsal fin suspended 5 to 6 feet below a bobber. Salmon eggs, marshmallows and 'crawlers also account for some nice fish. Work the banks near Dike #8, Beal's Point, Doton's Point, the dam area, Brown's Ravine and the south end of New York Creek Cove.

Folsom can be an excellent location for trollers dragging blades'n 'crawlers for early season trout. By late June, bring out the lead-core gear. Try to get the 'crawler down to 30 to 35 feet. Use the lead line with and without attractor blades. Working 6 colors, lead-core fans will also find the Speedy Shiner to be productive. The Needlefish is equally favored in grasshopper, silver, brass, rainbow trout, shad, bikini and flame with pearl finishes. Triple Teazers, Super Dupers and Kastmasters have also proven effective at Folsom. The dam and the mouth of the South Fork are popular trolling runs. By midsummer, the trout will be holding at 50 foot depths. Other than bait fished deep, diving planes or downriggers will be the primary way to reach these fish. However, some lake regulars will pull up to 15 colors of lead-core line to reach the deeper summer thermocline.

This nearly 12,000 acre lake just out of Sacramento can become very crowded in the summer with extensive traffic. There is virtually no angler or boater pressure during the winter months. Folsom is a fully developed lake, offering several campgrounds, a full-service marina, etc. For information contact Folsom Park Headquarters, (916) 988-0205.

Lakes McClure and McSwain

McClure and McSwain are adjoining reservoirs on the Merced River that are perfect opposites. McClure is a warmer water lake, is very large (82 miles of shoreline), has numerous coves and inlets, and allows all types of boating (including houseboating and waterskiing). McSwain, on the other hand, is a cold-water lake (trout only), is narrow and relatively small, and has no houseboats or waterskiing. What these lakes have in common is fine fishing and outstanding and complete recreational facilities. McClure and McSwain are located in the Sierra foothills east of Modesto (42 miles away) and Merced (27 miles away).

At McClure, fish deep in the Horseshoe Bend and Hunter's Point regions. In the spring troll the river channel from Barrett Cove to the dam or up the river from the dam toward Bagby. An unusual trolling tip is to drag a shad minnow behind flasher blades using a downrigger. Locals try to get the shad to spin slowly to generate the strikes. Still-fishing can be good around the Big Island with 'crawlers, Power Baits, salmon eggs, marshmallows, Velveeta and live minnows drifted under a bobber. Night fishing with shad is also productive at McClure. Be sure to watch for diving birds feeding on schools of threadfin shad. Be prepared to run onto a school of 'bows in a feeding frenzy and fly-line a live shad on the surface. Kastmasters, Z-Rays, Speedy Shiners, hammered gold Triple Teazers, and trout-colored Needlefish are all effective. McClure's rainbows will also chase minnow-style plugs such as Rapalas, Rebels and Cordell Spots.

At McSwain, try trolling from McSwain Dam to Exchequer Dam. There are some outstanding bank fishing possibilities from the marina to the dam. Live crickets and grasshoppers are local favorites, along with 'crawlers, Power Baits and the "Shasta Fly." Don't be surprised if you hang a "dog" at McSwain. Rainbows up to 10 pounds have been taken from this impoundment. For information contact the Lake Administrative Headquarters, (209) 378-2520.

Mokelumne and Merced River

Here are two rivers that offer some good stream trouting opportunities in their lower reaches.

Merced

This popular river really gets hammered by the summer throngs visiting the Yosemite basin. However, from early spring through May there can be some superb opportunities with limited angling pressure. The stretch from below Crocker-Hoffman Dam down to Merced Falls usually has a solid population of planter-sized 'bows. Locals say that the best run is from Redbud to the South Fork. Both dry and wet fly fishing will work, especially if you are wading. Red salmon eggs, crickets and 'hoppers are preferred baits. The Merced can get very clear

and hot in the summer. Better possibilities await the fisherman deeper inside Yosemite Park during this time of year.

Mokelumne

There are a few prime runs along this river that are worth trying. The stretch from Camanche Dam to Clements is good. Below the Elektra Powerhouse, the Middle Bar Bridge at the top of Pardee Lake and the North Fork at West Point are also choice locations. You can wade this river or, better yet, drift the Mokelumne with a boat when the water is high. Bait fishing excels here. Bank cast, wade or drift live crickets, red salmon eggs or nightcrawlers. Dry fly fishing can also be outstanding in late spring to early summer. Although there are a lot of catchable-sized rainbows planted along the Mokelumne each season, large 16-inch-class fish are possible working the quiet, less accessible deep pools.

New Melones Lake

New Melones Lake is a newer reservoir (completed in 1980) that offers excellent fishing. However, shore facilities, such as camping, are still under development. This is a large lake (about 8 miles across) that extends up the Stanislaus River Canyon over 10 miles. Campsites are available at Glory Hole Recreation Area, and picnic facilities are available at Tuttletown. Night fishing is permitted, as are waterskiing and swimming. New Melones is located South of Angels Camp, off Hwy. 49, in the Motherlode. For information call (209) 984-5248.

Northern California anglers have been relatively quiet about the phenomenal troutin' that is possible at New Melones. Quality rainbows and browns abound in this lake as well as the Eagle Lake rainbow strain. If you had to pick one surefire method to connect with these New Melones trout, trolling would be the choice. Lead-core and downrigger outfits are particularly effective. Look for schools of shad and the trout will be stratified with them.

In the colder months, try top-lining near the dam, Bear Creek, the spillway and Angel's Cove. The Countdown Rapala #7 in gold, silver or rainbow trout finish is tops. Continue to use 'crawlers and blades with both top-line and lead-core or downrigger approaches. A 1/2 chunk of nightcrawler laced together with a mealworm is a local hot tip. Trolling shad minnows behind the flashing blades is also effective as are Speedy Shiner lures. Key in on the mouths of the tributaries for spring trolling action. Bait fishing success will be possible using another local se-cret—a nightcrawler and a salmon egg threaded onto the same long-shank hook. Cap this unusual combo with a marshmallow to float it off the bottom.

Pardee Lake

Pardee is best known for excellent trout. Trout in the 3-4 pound class are not uncommon. It is a dedicated fishing lake. No waterskiing is allowed. The waters of Pardee are clean and clear. It was built in the 1920s as an East Bay Municipal Utility District reservoir. Facilities include campground, restaurant, store, launch ramp and two swimming pools. Pardee has about 37 miles of shoreline. It is located in the Motherlode about 40 miles east of Stockton. For information call (209) 772-1472.

Pardee is a good choice for early season troutin' without the High Sierra crowds common on other lakes. There are rainbows, browns and kokes in this lake. Top-line trolling is the way to go in the early season. Ford Fenders, Half Fasts and Dave Davis flashers are preferred by the locals. An interesting secret tactic is to inflate the 'crawler that is used as a trailer with the blades. Needle-fish lures worked behind the lake trolls are another staple. The popular colors are bikini, red/pearl and fire/pearl. For the kokanee salmon, stick with the Lucky Knight, Knobby Wobbler and Triple Teazer lures. Troll straight out from the marina, along the face of the dam, and by the buoy line near the narrows at the beginning of the season in February and March. Later in the year switch to lead core (5 to 8 colors) or even downriggers. Look for the kokanee in the Mokelumne River Arm or at the south end of the lake.

There is some fairly decent bank fishing at Pardee. Salmon eggs and nightcrawlers teamed with a miniature marshmallow are favored. Inflated 'crawlers are also widely used. Asia Beach, the north spillway and the marina area are popular bait dunkin' haunts. Another technique is to gently drift red salmon eggs in the current near the log jam. Fan-casting hardware from the shore or from boats can also be productive in the early season. Choose from Kastmaster, Vibrax or Rooster Tail lures.

Lake Tahoe

This magnificent crystalline body of water is home to gigantic mackinaw trout. Submersible research vessels have observed schools of this species in the 40 to 50 pound range! These denizens of the deep are typically found from 150 to 600 foot depths. The trolling methods for macs range from monel wire line to intricate downrigger setups. Deep-water jigging with large jigs loaded with indigenous minnows is also used at times. This aspect of Tahoe's "trout picture" requires much study and perseverance to connect on these deep-water dwellers. The novice angler would be wise to invest in a professional guide who specializes in mackinaw fishing, to at least become initially introduced to these unusual techniques.

There are, however, considerable numbers of rain-bows, kokes and the occasional brown trout to keep the more traditional trouter occupied at Tahoe. Top-line trolling, especially in the fall months, would be a prin-ciple method to try. Troll from Emerald Bay to Sugar Pine Point, around Al Tahoe Buoy and Tahoe Key for rain-bows and browns. A variety of plugs are preferred by local guides including a Bomber Long-A minnow in rainbow trout finish, the Rebel Crawdad plug, assorted Rapalas and Flatfish and copper or black spoons. Be-cause the water is so clear at Tahoe, the pros recommend trolling **fast** to give the 'bows and browns less opportu-nity to study the lure.

Tossing bait from the bank has limited possibilities. However, your chances are heightened right after a big wind when the surface water is churned up with a lot of forage bait and other food sources. Boaters can still-fish at the mouth of Emerald Bay and at Logan Shoals. Air-injected nightcrawlers and minnows are favored baits. Sometimes a live grasshopper slowly drifted on a lead-core outfit will also produce on rainbows or browns holding deep on this super clear lake.

Try the south end near Taylor Creek and Richardson Bay for sustained kokanee action. The kokes can be taken on 10 colors with the Super Duper, Wedding Ring spin-ner and Red Magic lures. Put a kernel of white corn or some fluorescent spinner and yarn to tip-off the hooks on these kokanee lures. Fly fishermen have sporadic success drifting or trolling the Li'l Rainbow Trout streamer fly.

Fallen Leaf Lake, a small lake just south of Tahoe, has mackinaws, rainbows and browns. Top-line troll Rapalas for the latter two and drift minnows down to 120 feet for the big macs. The Forestry Pier at the north end is a popular spot for bait dunkers using inflated nightcrawlers. For information contact the Lake Tahoe Visitors Authority (South Shore), (916) 544-5050, or Lake Tahoe Visitors Bureau (North Shore), (800) 824-6348.

Union Valley, Ice House and Loon Lakes

The Crystal Basin Recreation Area of the Eldorado National Forest is the home of three deep, clear and cold lakes that offer excellent fishing for rainbows and browns as well as kokanee salmon. Just over 20 miles east of Placerville on Hwy. 50 is the town of Riverton. From here Forest Service Road takes you into the recreation area and all three lakes. Each lake has campgrounds and launch ramps. These aren't small lakes either; Union Valley is 2,800 acres, and the smallest, Ice House, is almost 900 surface acres. All types of boating are allowed, but some say the water is too cold for waterskiing. But it's just right for the trout at elevations ranging from 5,000 to 6,500 feet. There are over 400 campsites at these three lakes that are surrounded by pine and fir forests.

Union Valley reservoir is one of the most consistent producers of kokanee in the Sierras. They range in size from 8 to 11 inches and are firm and delicious. Spoons such as the Knobby Wobbler, Kokanee Killer and 1/8 ounce Kastmaster are winners for Union Valley kokanee. Nightcrawlers, both still-fished and trolled, are a local favorite for rainbows and browns, at all three lakes.

Yosemite National Park

Trout fishing at Yosemite means getting out of the Valley and up into the high country. The most popular access is along Hwy. 120 in the Tuolumne Meadows area. Here, above Hetch Hetchy Reservoir, the Tuolumne and its branches—the Dana Fork and the Lyell Fork—provide abundant brook, brown and rainbow trout in the 6-18 inch range. The fishing season is short at this 8,600 foot elevation. The waters are still high in June. Fishing is usually good in July, peaking in August.

The Tuolumne is easily fished in the Meadows itself as it runs along Hwy. 120. A mile or so downstream of the Meadows, the Tuolumne quickens its pace as it falls over granite structure. Fish here, and about a mile's walk up from the Meadows in Dana Fork, are larger than those caught right in the Meadows. A short drive east on Hwy. 120 from the Meadows provides access at several points to more of the Dana Fork. Follow the John Muir Trail south from the Meadows to fish the Lyell Fork. This beautiful trout stream meanders through the Upper Tuolumne Meadows and offers good brook trout fishing in the mornings and evenings. Expect about a 4 hour walk. Hike another day to Ireland Lake (10,725 elevation) for some more fine trouting. At Yosemite, especially, it pays to put yourself as far away as you can from parking lots and campgrounds.

The trailhead at Hetch Hetchy Dam provides a less-used launching point for some more Yosemite trouting. Two good rainbow lakes about 15 miles out are Edith Lake and Wilmer Lake. If you're out this far, take another day and hit Tilden Lake (20 miles from the trailhead). It offers both rainbows and goldens. A caution: there are over 300 major lakes in Yosemite high country, but only about 1/3 of them offer good fishing. Yosemite Park and Curry Co., retail office at Yosemite National Park, CA 95389, offers a booklet, "Yosemite Trout Fishing" for $1.50, that rates the lakes. Phone (209) 372-1227 for more information.

Artificial lures and especially the bubble'n fly combo are dynamite in Yosemite. Scale down to light 2 pound mono and #14 to #16 dry flies. Brown, gray and white shades are a must for dry fly patterns. Also, give small drab-colored nymphs and wet flies a shot. Hardware slingers should opt for chrome or gold Super Dupers, Mepp's Lightning spinners in yellow or orange, gold Kastmasters and Panther Martins in gold and black. Here, too, stay with small, ultralight sizes.

Southern Sierra Trout

Troutin' can range from spectacular to just plain tough in some of the waters of the southern Sierra. Lakes like Shaver and Huntington can be "standouts" in the early season.

Other lakes such as Isabella, Pine Flat, Buena Vista and Success are recognized primarily for their warmwater fisheries but also support a planted population of trout awaiting the crafty angler. Sometimes it will be necessary to fish both early in the year and deep to trick trout living in these lower elevation lakes.

The Kings River, the Kern River and the Bear Creek drainage area offer some remarkably good fishin' for the stream trekker. Again, keep in mind that the more remote the areas you venture into, the better the troutin' will be!

Bear Creek, Mono Creek, Edison and Florence Lakes

Situated in a remote basin in the Sierra National Forest, 100 miles east of Fresno, the Bear Creek drainage is a trouter's dream come true! There are over 50 lakes and 25 miles of streams from which to choose. You can catch rainbows, brookies, browns and goldens in the same day here in the John Muir Wilderness. As a matter of fact, Bear Creek itself supports all four species.

Bear Creek runs 18 miles and dumps into the South Fork of the San Joaquin River near Mono Hot Springs. It has everything the California trouter could ask for: deep pools, sustained runs, riffles and rocky bottoms. Within hiking distance, ranging from less than a mile to over five miles, are a wealth of lakes to sample, many holding prized goldens. These include Seven Gables, Beverly, Sandpiper, Three Island, Rose, Apollo, Lou Beverly, Orchid and Vee, to name a few. Look for small goldens, particularly in the upper stretches of Bear Creek, the East, West, and South Forks and along the Hilgard and Orchard Creek tributaries.

Bait tossers will do best with natural offerings: pine grubs, hellgrammites, crickets, red worms or grasshoppers. Salmon eggs and yellow and pink Power Bait will also take their share of fish. Fly fishermen can have a "picnic" along these waters. You can be fairly creative with regard to pattern selection. However, your staples would have to include the Renegade, Jug Bug, Adams, Humpy, Mosquito and Black Gnat. And don't forget Joe's Hopper.

Nothing fancy is required in the way of hardware choices—just keep it scaled down to the ultralight sizes. Rooster Tails, Mepps, Panther Martins, Super Dupers, Kastmasters and Daredevles are sure bets. To reach the Bear Creek area drive about 100 miles along Hwy. 168 out of Fresno. Trail heads are at Bear Dam or Edison Lake.

Besides the Bear Creek drainage, there are several other fine trouting opportunities in the surrounding area. Edison Lake and Florence Lake are twin reservoirs that surround the Bear Creek area. They both offer good trouting, launch ramps and Forest Service campgrounds. A ferry service for backpackers heading into the John Muir Wilderness is available at each lake. One fine back country locale is the Mono Creek drainage. Mono Creek is the stream that Edison Dam was constructed on. Mono Creek drainage, above Edison Lake, has 31 lakes, ranging in size from less than one acre to over 70 acres, that provide super high country trouting. The streams connecting these lakes are all fine trout waters. Golden trout are a prime quarry in these lakes and creeks. For information on the entire area contact the U.S. Forest Service, Shaver Lake, (209) 841-3311.

Buena Vista Lakes

Buena Vista Lakes combine great winter-spring trout fishing with a modern, complete 1,600 acre recreational facility. Lake Evans, the smaller (86 acres) of the two Buena Vista Lakes, is dedicated to angling. Its main attraction is the trout plant (nothing less than 3/4 pounds) that runs from November to early April. Lake Webb is much larger (873 acres) and provides excellent warmwater fishing, as well as sailing and water-skiing. Buena Vista Lakes is located 23 miles southwest of Bakersfield. Most of the rainbows in these are basic, stocker-size fish. Still, occasional "hawgs" topping the 7 pound mark are recorded from time to time.

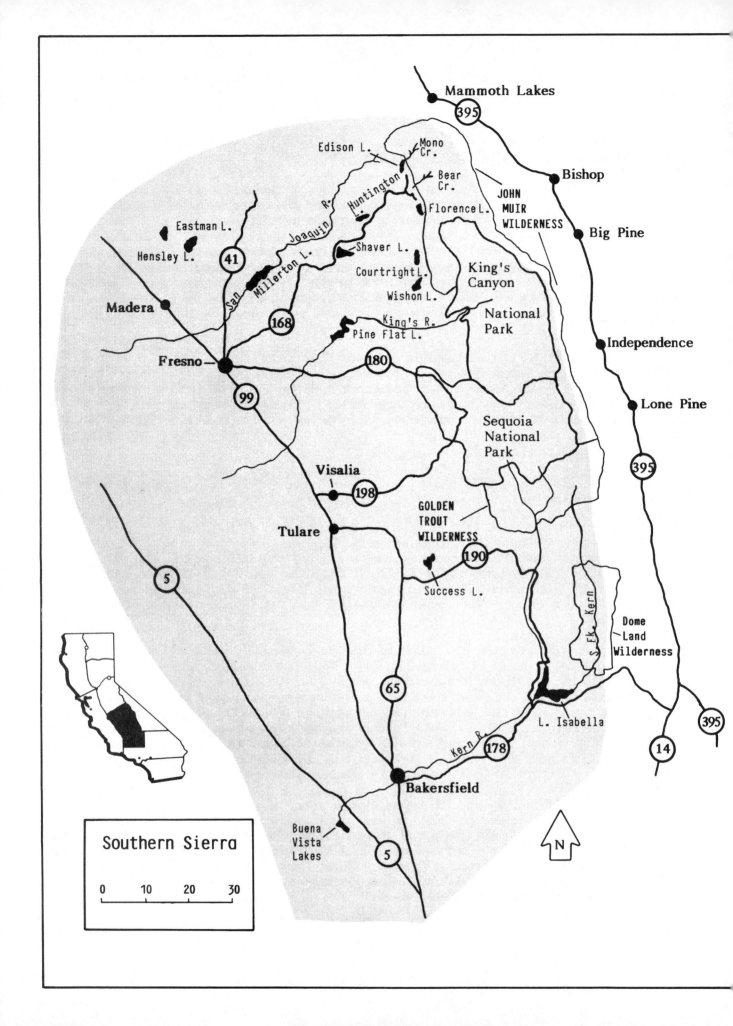

Mammoth Lakes
395
Bishop
Big Pine
Independence
Lone Pine
395

Edison L.
Mono Cr.
Bear Cr.
Florence L.
JOHN MUIR WILDERNESS
Eastman L.
Joaquin R.
Huntington L.
Hensley L.
41
San
Millerton L.
Shaver L.
King's Canyon
Madera
168
Courtright L.
Wishon L.
Fresno
King's R.
Pine Flat L.
180
National Park
99
Sequoia National Park
Visalia
198
GOLDEN TROUT WILDERNESS
Tulare
190
Success L.
S. Fk. Kern
Dome Land Wilderness
65
L. Isabella
395
Kern R.
178
14
Bakersfield
Buena Vista Lakes
5

N

Southern Sierra

0   10   20   30

Bait fishermen can keep it simple: salmon eggs, Velveeta, nightcrawler and marshmallow combos, and inflated 'crawlers. Surprisingly, there can also be a good snap on hardware. The yellow/black patterns in either the Rooster Tail or Panther Martin spinners seem to be particularly effective. For information contact the Kern County Parks, 1110 Golden State, Bakersfield, CA 93301, (805) 861-2345.

Courtright and Wishon Reservoirs

These two little lakes are situated out of the town of Dinkey Creek via Hwy. 168 and Dinkey Creek Road, out of Fresno. Wishon sits at an elevation of 6,500 feet while up the road a little further is Courtright at 8,200 feet.

Courtright is at the gateway to the southern entrance of the John Muir Wilderness area. Good early season troutin' is on tap with a lot of small planter 'bows available. A modest amount of larger trout hold over from the previous year. Live crickets, Wob-L-Rite and Phoebe spoons, and scaled-down wet flies like the Wooly Worm will take their share of Courtright's rainbow population. Top-line trolling with smaller flashers and 'crawler trailers are equally effective.

Wishon is perfect for car-top boaters and bank fishermen. Salmon eggs and a variety of floating cheese concoctions produce. Small lures such as the Super Duper, Phoebe, Mepps, Rooster Tail, and Panther Martin should be tried at Wishon with light lines. As with Courtright, small blade'n 'crawler combos are also effective along with the fly'n bubble rig. For information contact the Wishon Village, (209) 865-5361.

Huntington Lake

Here is another fine trout lake along Hwy. 168, out of Fresno. Often depicted as the "clone" of Shaver Lake, Huntington has its own unique topography and trout ecology. Rainbows, browns, kokanees and a few wayward brookies abound in this lake. There is some really good boat and shore activity on 12- to 16-inch-class trout at Huntington. There are usually some larger hold-over fish that survive the previous season. The angler working the lake has 14 miles of shoreline to explore.

Early May can be an outstanding time to fish Huntington. By summer, the lake experiences a lot of recreational pressure from power boaters, windsurfers and sailboaters, in addition to fishermen. So, if you can make it to the lake between early spring and June, start with a trolling program. Troll in front of the Boy Scout Camp on the south side and between Will-O-The-Wisp and Cedar Crest Resort. Cowbells, Ford Fenders and Dave Davis flashers with a crawler chunk trailer are favored. The Needlefish or Triple Teazer matched with a set of blades also produces steady action. By mid-August, be prepared to pull 5 to 10 colors of lead-core line to reach rainbows holding deep.

Bank fishermen should try the Lakeshore Marina area. Inflated nightcrawlers, salmon eggs, or either one combined with a marshmallow as a "floating cap" are effective. Many locals also prefer to fish a fat, juicy nightcrawler from the bank suspended under a red and white bobber. This is a proven killer for Huntington's larger brown trout. There are Forest Service campgrounds and private resorts at Huntington. For information contact the Pineridge Ranger District, P.O. Box 300, Shaver Lake, CA 93664, (209) 841-3311.

Lake Isabella

Located at the base of the southern Sierras, Isabella is heralded as a premier largemouth trophy fishery. This 11,400 acre lake is tucked up in the foothills about 45 miles northeast of Bakersfield. It has complete facilities with eight campgrounds around the lake. Troutin' can be a tough proposition at Isabella, but not an impossible one. Fishing in spring and late fall will maximize your chances for some sustained trout action. You will have to fish deep in the summer as the water warms and the trout sound.

Plan on making two primary trolling runs: from the main dam right down the South Fork channel, and from the main dam traversing the center channel of the North Fork. Floating and Countdown Rapalas, Floating Rebels, Kastmasters, Needlefish, Bangtail spinners, Cripplures, Krocadiles, #F-5 and #F-6 Flatfish, and Wob-L-Rite spoons can be top-lined. Pull these on lead core or downriggers in the warmer months.

The dam is a prime trout spot for still fishing. Use marshmallows, Velveeta cheese or salmon eggs. Many lake regulars prefer inflated nightcrawlers as their number one choice for bait dunkin'! For information contact the U.S. Forest Service, (619) 379-5646, or Lake Isabella Chamber of Commerce, (619) 379-5236.

Kern River (above Lake Isabella)

The main body of the Kern River runs northward above Isabella, starting at Kernville. For 16 miles this stretch of water is planted regularly all the way up to the Johnsondale Bridge. Access is by a road paralleling the river. This southern Sierra river is one of the most popular fishin' holes in the state. There are usually a lot of smaller, stocker rainbows to be had in the early season. But the more cunning trouter may also encounter a lunker brown or jumbo 'bow by using artificials. A simple maxim to follow is "The higher up the river you travel, the better chance you have of tying into a 'hawg.'"

Quantities of the smaller rainbows will fall victim to red salmon eggs. Gold and silver Panther Martins, gold blade Blue Fox spinners, and yellow, white, brown or black Rooster Tail spinners will take planters plus some larger specimens. Veteran fly fishermen may score the highest successes during the season on trophy fish. "Flips Bug," a regional favorite fished wet, is a black and white nymph with black legs that has been "hot" on the Kern. Try the Montana Girdle Bug in similar black, dark brown or mottled green patterns. Other worthwhile patterns are the Mosquito, Black Ant, Black Gnat, Stonefly, Nymph and Elk Hair Caddis. For information contact the U.S. Forest Service, P.O. Box 6, Kernville, CA 93238, (619) 376-3781.

Farther north the main Kern flows through the Golden Trout Wilderness. Also in the Golden Trout Wilderness is the headwaters of the South Fork of the Kern. Here, of course, the anglers either backpack or use horses. Most come in from trailheads along Hwy. 395 along the eastern slope of the southern Sierras. There is one other wilderness fishing opportunity in the Kern system. It's where the South Fork runs through the Dome Land Wilderness. The Kern here is a pristine trout stream flowing approximately 20 miles through a deep, rugged, rock stream gorge. This area is probably too rugged for novice backpackers, but for the experienced, it's a great adventure.

Pine Flat Lake and Kings River

Pine Flat is located in the Sierra foothills about 30 miles east of Fresno in the Kings River Canyon. There is a full-service marina and camping facilities. This 21-mile-long, snake-like body of water has a respectable population of rainbows and browns, but you will have to work for them. Top-line troll from Windy Gap to Big Creek. Needlefish lures in nickel, frog, red dot, rainbow trout and bikini finishes are staples for this approach. So are Ford Fenders and Dave Davis flashers. Trail these with 'crawlers or the Needlefish or Triple Teazers with a 'crawler combo. Consider shifting to lead core (6 to 10 colors) or downriggers for the deeper summer bite.

Shore fishing is sometimes good in Big Creek Cove. Still-fish smaller nightcrawlers and Power Baits. Big browns make their haunts in the Kirch Flat region. Bait fishermen will fare well by drifting either minnows or nightcrawlers. For information contact Pine Flat Lake, P.O. Box 171, Piedra, CA 93649, (209) 787-2589.

The lower Kings River running below Pine Flat Lake can be a dynamite spot for the trouter! You will find many catchable planter rainbows that can be taken using a variety of methods. Fish from below the dam to Alta Weir for about 5 miles. Salmon eggs, nightcrawlers, live crickets and red worms will get 'em. Popular spinners such as the Panther Martin, Rooster Tail and Mepps models have traditionally worked along the Lower Kings. The cold water that filters down from the deep pocket of the Pine Flat Dam also helps to sustain some pretty good fly fishing. The Blue Wing Olive, Black Midge and Kings River Cabin Fly are regionally favored patterns.

The Upper Kings River above Pine Flat is a great wild trout river. Work this run from April through May for the hot bite. The river is best from Garnet Dike upstream, keying in on the inlets around Garnet Dike and above Bailey Bridge. Only flies and artificial lures with single barbless hooks are permitted on the Upper Kings. Fly fishers prefer the regionally tied Kings River Caddis, the Deer Hair Caddis, Elk Hair Caddis, Hare's Ear, Stonefly Nymph and Long Tail March Brown. For information contact the U.S. Forest Service, Kern River Ranger District, Sangor, CA 93657, (209) 855-8321.

Shaver Lake

At 5,500 feet and surrounded by forests, Shaver is a high mountain delight for trouters. It's quite large at 2,000 acres and has complete camping, boating and recreation facilities. This lake is one of the real gems of the southern Sierras. It receives high marks for early season fishing, particularly before Memorial Day when the crowds increase. Trolling is the way to go at Shaver. In the spring, try top-lining with either Cowbells or Half Fast flashers. Take your pick as to what to trail behind the blades.

Some locals prefer flashers with a chunk of nightcrawler. Others use a Needlefish either by itself or with a piece of worm laced on the single hook. Popular Needlefish colors are frog, red dot or pearl. The Triple

Teazer will also work behind the lake trolls. Kastmaster, Floating Rebels and Rapalas in gold or rainbow trout finishes are also preferred for top-lining. An alternate approach used at Shaver is to drag a #F-4 or #F-5 Flatfish in silver or frog patterns.

There are rainbows, big browns and kokanee salmon in this lake. The trolling strategy will cover the most territory when fishing for any of these species. Work trolling paths near the dam, around Camp Edison, and in a circular route in the midsoutheast section of the lake. As the summer heat approaches, stick with the Needlefish in a rainbow trout pattern, pulled on lead-core line, 3 to 8 colors deep.

There are some excellent shore fishing possibilities at Shaver. Standard baits such as red worms, inflated night-crawlers, salmon eggs, Power Baits, live crickets, the "Shasta Fly" and salmon roe are favored. Still-fishing at night can be productive with a good chance at tying into one of Shaver's trophy brown trout. Fish the rocky area around the Tunnel Creek entrance or tie off to the 5 m.p.h. buoys located 100 yards off the shore on the west side.

Fly fishing is also worth the effort at Shaver. The commonly used patterns include the Mosquito, Adams and a locally tied fly known as the Strawberry Roam. Nearby Tunnel, Stevenson and Rock Creeks are also conducive to both fly and bait fishing tactics. For information contact the U.S. Forest Service, (209) 841-3311; So. California Edison Campgrounds, (209) 841-3444; Sierra Marina, (209) 841-3324.

Success Lake

Like Pine Flat, the troutin' at Success can be tough at times since this is primarily a warm-water fishery. The key to finding trout in warmer lakes like this is to look for flowing water or even subtle currents of some kind. At Success, fish where the fresh water comes into the lake down from the golf course, in the North Fork of the Tule River arm. This will be the cooler more oxygenated water necessary to sustain a limited trout community.

Early spring will be the best time to fish trout at Success with the rainbows moving shallow to spawn. Limited summer action is possible using lead-core line. Bait fishermen have historically scored well with Velveeta

at Success. Hardware chuckers should give the Mepps and Kastmaster lures a try.

Success Lake is located about midway between Fresno and Bakersfield, near Portersville, on the Tule River. It holds 2,400 surface acres of water, with 30 miles of shoreline. There are both developed and primitive campsites and a full-service marina. For information contact Success Lake, Box 1072, Portersville, CA 93258, (209) 784-0215.

Other Southern Sierra Trouting

There are three conveniently located southern Sierra lakes that are worth trying in the cooler months, when they are planted regularly. They are all located in the Sierra foothills north and east of the Fresno-Madera area.

Millerton Lake

Here is a large lake (about 5,000 surface acres) that can produce some nice stringers of planted rainbow during the winter and early spring. Shallow trolling, bait below a bobber, and casting hardware all work. Concentrate on the launch ramp areas, the stream inlets, and up the main river arm. The dam area and old river channel can also produce. There are full facilities at Millerton. For information call (209) 822-2225.

Hensley Lake and Eastman Lake

Here are two lakes that are as close to being twins as just about any two lakes in California. Each is in the 1,700 surface acre size range, each is administered by the Corp. of Engineers, and they are less than 15 miles apart as the crow flies. Hensley Lake is 17 miles northeast of Madera on the Fresno River. There are campsites but no store. Good trout locales include the launch ramp, shallow coves and the river inlet.

Eastman Lake is about 25 miles east of Chowchilla. It also has camping and paved launching, but no store. The best trout action is in the late fall, winter and spring, using hardware fished near the surface. Shore anglers find almost as much success as boaters. For information contact Hensley Lake, (209) 673-5151; Eastman Lake, (209) 689-3255.

Eastern Sierra Trout

This sector of the Golden State exhibits greater angling pressure than any other area during the height of the season. No wonder this is the case, for the Eastern Sierra has not only magnificent scenery, but magnificent troutin' as well.

Two of California's most majestic rivers, the Walker and the Owens, tumble through this region. Both are world renowned as trophy waters for lunker browns. Similarly, Bridgeport and Twin Lakes are heralded as "home" to world-record brown trout exceeding 30 pounds! Many professional "hawg hunters" spend long hours at these lakes in quest of that elusive world-record fish.

To top it off, there is perhaps nothing in the Western troutin' world that comes close to the gala tradition of the Lake Crowley Opener. This does not just signal the start of the Sierra trout season. Rather, it has become almost a celebration among anglers from all over the state who converge once a year in fishing's version of the Rites of Spring. Plus there are dozens of other fine trout lakes and streams in this Inyo and Mono County Trout Heaven.

Note: For clarity, the waters in this section are arranged from south to north.

Lone Pine, Independence, Big Pine Area

Here are the first of a series of fine mountain trout fishing locales along Hwy. 395. Each of these small towns has a stream (same name as town name) that runs west from Hwy. 395 up into the eastern Sierras. The roads along these creeks take the angler to good stream fishing, campgrounds and trailheads, for backpacking or pack-in adventures. Lone Pine, Independence and Big Pine Creeks are stocked weekly with catchable size rainbows. Typical fish are 8-12 inches. This maintains a high catch-per-angler ratio throughout the summer months.

The high country in this area offers marvelous fishing opportunities. There are pack services available at each, or anglers can backpack. At Lone Pine, Cottonwood Creek, Cottonwood Lake and the Golden Trout Wilderness are the destinations of choice. Out of Independence there is Pothole Lake and Heart Lake. At Big Pine, there are about seven fine trout lakes (numbered 1 through 7) on the trail that leads out. They range in size from 4-5

acres to over 25 acres, at altitudes of about 10,000 to over 11,000 feet. These lakes are inhabited by both rainbow and eastern brook trout. Of course the lakes (and streams) that are more remote receive less fishing pressure. Because of the altitude, this is a trip best taken after the ice melts. Suggested months are June through September.

Fishing is best generally in the early morning or late evening. That's when trout eat. Artificial flies are especially effective at these times. At midday, lures and bait are the best bet.

Here are some very general approaches that will work for most of the waters in this area. To begin with, definitely employ the fly'n bubble setup to maximize distance when fly fishing here. Commonly used dry flies include the Mosquito, California Mosquito, Adams, Royal Coachman and Black Gnat. You usually won't go wrong with any of these proven patterns. Smaller spinners and especially those with gold blades are patented producers. The simple Colorado, along with the Panther Martin, Mepps and Rooster Tail models should do the trick, but scale down in size somewhat.

Similarly, the entire spectrum of prepared commercial baits will work, but natural offerings will generate even more strikes. Grubs, beetles ants, grasshoppers, crickets, hellgrammites and, of course, red worms and medium-sized nightcrawlers can be very "hot" on these lakes. Sometimes a sliding cast-a-bubble or a slip float will work best for fishing bait suspended or slowly dropped into deeper water some distance off the bank.

Bishop Area

The town of Bishop is one of the centers for eastern Sierra trouting. Elevation varies in the Bishop area from 7,000 ft. to 9,000 ft. Lower elevation fishing is usually more popular in the cooler months. Streams and lakes at higher elevations are more popular in the warmer months since air and water temperatures are cooler and most of the higher elevation waters are closed to fishing in the winter months. Some of the major fishing waters in the Bishop area (like Crowley Lake, Owens River and Pleasant Valley Reservoir) are featured following this section.

Bishop Creek and the lake at its headwaters offer a good variety of trouting. All are planted regularly. The creek is 10-20 feet wide and several feet deep, but there are deeper holes. There is South, Sabrina and North Lake on the Bishop Creek Road, all accessible by car. Boats can be rented at South and Sabrina Lakes. And at the head of Rock Creek is Rock Creek Lake, which also has boat rentals. The same holds for Pine Creek. The headwaters of Bishop, Pine and Rock Creeks are all possible jumping-off points for wilderness pack-in trouting.

Lower Rock Creek, which runs from Tom's Place parallel to Rte. 395 to Pleasant Valley Reservoir, is a very special trout stream. This stream holds both wild and planted fish including some very large browns and rainbows. The upper reaches of the stream, accessible by a good trail, is a small clear water area that harbors many wild brown trout. The last mile of Lower Rock Creek, before it empties into Pleasant Valley Reservoir, has an entirely different character. At the Los Angeles DWP power plant, Lower Rock Creek is joined by waters from Pine Creek and the Owens River Aqueduct system, to produce a large river. Here trophy-sized browns and rainbows are caught. Nightcrawlers, Rapalas and Mepps and Rooster Tail spinners are the top producers.

Maps of the region are available by writing Inyo National Forest, 798 Main St., Bishop, CA 93514, (619) 873-4207. The John Muir Wilderness Map is $1.00.

It has topographical information. The Bishop Chamber of Commerce can be reached at (619) 873-8405. Fishing information is available at Culver's Sporting Goods, (619) 872-8361 and Brock's Sporting Goods, (619) 872-3581.

Pleasant Valley Reservoir

Pleasant Valley Reservoir has to be one of the most underrated trophy trout fisheries in California. There is a super healthy population of medium-sized rainbows to be found at Pleasant Valley, but the real secret is the giant browns that are known tackle-busters! There are definitely 20-pound-class fish in this impoundment and some experts feel 35-pound world-record browns are a reality!

Be prepared to do some serious rock-hopping in order to get around the rugged shoreline. There are no boats allowed so all the "hot spots" will have to be approached by walking the bank. The fish ramp and Mickey Mouse Rock off the north shore and the area where the Owens River empties into the lake are primary fish-holding locations. Early and late in the season will be the best

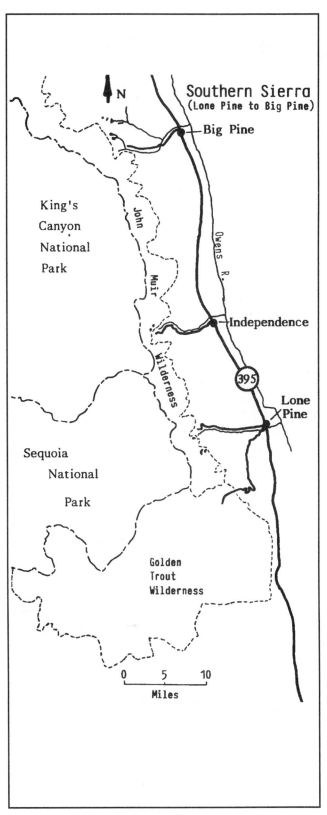

For continuation, see next page

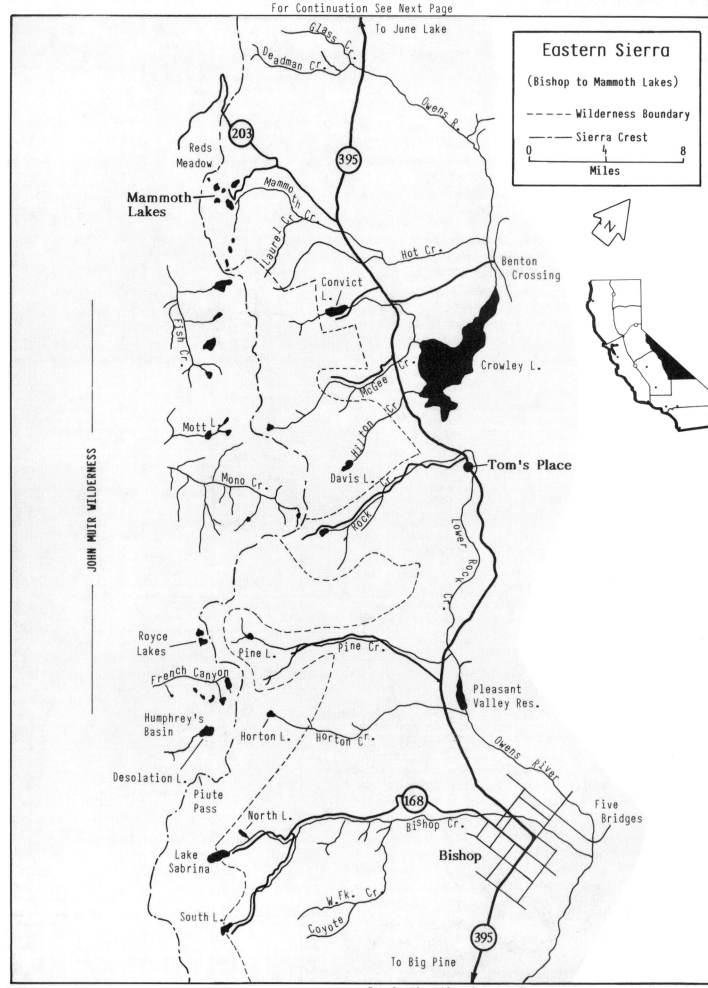

To June Lake

Eastern Sierra

(Bishop to Mammoth Lakes)

- - - - Wilderness Boundary

— · — · Sierra Crest

0   4   8

Miles

N

Glass Cr.

Deadman Cr.

Owens R.

203

395

Reds Meadow

Mammoth Cr.

Mammoth Lakes

Hot Cr.

Benton Crossing

Laurel Cr.

Convict L.

Fish Cr.

Crowley L.

McGee Cr.

Mott L.

Hilton Cr.

Davis L.

Tom's Place

Mono Cr.

Rock Cr.

Lower Rock Cr.

JOHN MUIR WILDERNESS

Royce Lakes

Pine L.

Pine Cr.

French Canyon

Pleasant Valley Res.

Humphrey's Basin

Horton L.

Horton Cr.

Desolation L.

Owens River

Piute Pass

North L.

168

Bishop Cr.

Five Bridges

Lake Sabrina

Bishop

W. Fk. Cr.

South L.

Coyote

395

To Big Pine

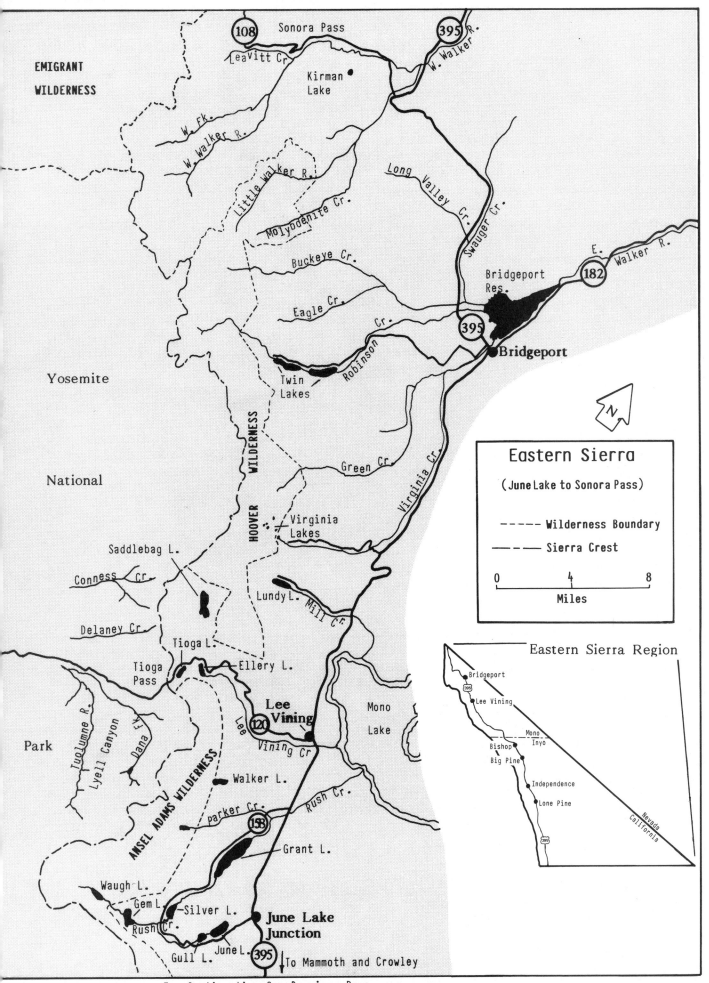

EMIGRANT
WILDERNESS

(108) Sonora Pass

Leavitt Cr.

Kirman Lake

(395) W. Walker R.

W. Fk.

W. Walker R.

Long Valley Cr.

Little Walker R.

Swauger Cr.

Molybdenite Cr.

E. Walker R.

(182)

Buckeye Cr.

Bridgeport Res.

Eagle Cr.

(395)

Cr.

Bridgeport

Robinson

Yosemite

Twin Lakes

National

Green Cr.

Virginia Cr.

HOOVER   WILDERNESS

Virginia Lakes

Saddlebag L.

Conness Cr.

Lundy L.

Mill Cr.

Delaney Cr.

Tioga L.

Tioga Pass

Ellery L.

Mono Lake

Lee Vining

(120)

Lee

Vining Cr.

Park

Tuolumne R.

Lyell Canyon

Dana Fk.

Walker L.

ANSEL ADAMS WILDERNESS

Parker Cr.

Rush Cr.

(158)

Grant L.

Waugh L.

Gem L.

Silver L.

Rush Cr.

June Lake Junction

Gull L.

June L.

(395)

To Mammoth and Crowley

Eastern Sierra

(June Lake to Sonora Pass)

- - - - - Wilderness Boundary

— - — Sierra Crest

0   4   8
          Miles

Eastern Sierra Region

Bridgeport

(395)

Lee Vining

Mono

Inyo

Bishop

Big Pine

Independence

Lone Pine

(395)

Nevada

California

For Continuation See Previous Page

times to challenge Pleasant Valley. A variety of baits are effective at this reservoir. The rainbows will readily strike at Berkley Power Baits, Zeke's floating cheese, inflated 'crawlers, marshmallows and salmon eggs.

It's another story when it comes to the giant browns. Too often the recreational angler fishing Pleasant Valley makes the mistake of using tackle that is too light. Scale up in line weight, use a stiffer, beefier rod, and a reel that permits long casting. Bigger versions of contemporary trout spinners and spoons are recommended in order to make far away casts to marauding browns. Kastmasters, Krocadiles, Z-Rays, Mepp's Syclops, Phoebes and larger Rooster Tails are good choices. Magnum-sized minnow-shaped plugs from Rapala and Rebel in rainbow trout finish are, as expected, very popular among Pleasant Valley's "hawg huntin'" fraternity. Also, try the rainbow trout patterns in both the A.C. Plug and A.A.'s Super Shad.

One local tip is to try surface plugs on big browns in the late twilight hours. Stick baits such as the Heddon Zara Spook, Storm Chug Bug or Rebel Pop-R are interesting alternatives to throw on these bruiser browns. Another tactic is to crank one of those miniature Rebel plugs shaped precisely like a natural crayfish. Big browns and 'bows forage on these little crustaceans and this crankbait comes closest to matching the real McCoy. For information, contact the sources listed at the end of the Bishop Area section. For information contact Inyo County Parks, (619) 878-2411.

Crowley Lake

There is probably no greater fishing spectacle than the traditional Opening Day extravaganza at Lake Crowley which inaugurates trout season in the Sierras. Anglers from all over the Golden State converge on this modest-size lake to celebrate the start of the California Sierra trout season. This pilgrimage to Crowley has become a ritual practiced by generation after generation of California fishermen. Lake Crowley was formed by a dam at the end of a long valley and is a key link in the City of Los Angeles' water system. It is planted with hundreds of thousands of small rainbow trout each summer. By the next opening day, these fish average almost one pound each.

The best opportunities for larger rainbows or browns will be to troll in the early season. Rainbow trout colored Rebels and Rapalas work well on top, as do Needlefish and Z-Ray spoons. The Les Davis Bolo series of flashers, teamed with a nightcrawler trailer, is also frequently

dragged this time of year, either on top, or a few colors deep with lead-core line. The Triple Teazer spoon is an alternative to the 'crawler. Fan-casting from either the bank or a boat produces in the early spring. Heavier sinking Rapalas (#CD-7 or #CD-9), the Rapala Shad Rap and Kastmaster spoons are recommended. Mepps, Rooster Tail and Panther Martin spinners will also take a good tally of rainbow from the shore.

The areas around McGee Bay, Hilton Point, Leighton Springs to the Chalk Cliffs on the east side and the upper north, and where the Owens River dumps into the lake are all good locations to fish. A favorite trolling run is from the Chalk Cliffs to McGee Bay. Zeke's floating cheese in yellow garlic, corn and original flavors, salmon eggs and inflated nightcrawlers produce for bait fishermen at Crowley.

From August 1st to October 31st, a second season goes into effect geared to the trophy rainbows and browns that spawn in the fall. Only artificial lures with one barbless hook are permitted. You can only keep two trout per day and they must be 18 inches or longer. At this time of year, a legion of dedicated float tubers visit the lake in quest of these larger trout. They will work the weed beds using flies that closely replicate small Sacramento perch, a dominant forage food for the bigger 'bows and browns. The Marabou Muddler, Doc's Twin Lake Special, Brown Wooly Worm and the legendary Olive Matuka streamers are potent patterns during Crowley's second season. For information see the Bishop Area sources listed earlier and contact the Crowley Lake Fish Camp at (619) 935-4301.

The Owens River

The Owens River is a highly prolific stretch of water capable of kicking out many trophy-sized trout. The two runs of the Upper Owens from Benton Crossing and Big Springs are primo spots. The Owens Gorge below Lake Crowley similarly has a reputation for quality fish. From April 25th to June 30th, there is a two-fish, artificials-only restriction on the Upper Owens. Only single, barbless hooks are allowed and the trout must be a minimum of 18 inches long. From July through September the restrictions are removed and even bait fishing is permitted. Then, in October, the restrictions are placed in effect once again.

The Upper Owens River feeds Lake Crowley. It is a meadow stream with open banks. It's a good fly fishing stream. Concentrate on the undercut banks in late evening. Several-pound browns hold in these areas. Access to the

Upper Owens River is at Benton Crossing. Go north from Rte. 395 at Witmore Hot Springs for about 6 miles. You can fish upstream or downstream from Benton Crossing. Going downstream early in the season might catch you some rainbows that come up from Lake Crowley to spawn. Locals use streamers and nymphs. Rooster Tails, Mepps and Panther Martin spinners in black/yellow blends are hot on the Upper Owens. Super Duper and Phoebe spoons can be equally productive. But the most excitement is generated by some spectacular fly fishing. Purists note the Black or Brown Marabou, Muddler, Hornbug and Matuka streamers are tops. Both the March Brown and Captain Nymphs are also favored. Both No. 7 and No. 9 floating Rapalas or countdown models in silver foil finish are early morning killers here on the river.

The Lower Owens is a less restrictive, year-round fishery. There is, however, a 10-mile run from below the Pleasant Valley Dam to Five Bridges that is a dedicated wild trout stretch of river. Browns are primarily the only trout populating this trophy water, and standard wild trout restrictions apply. Regionally popular fly patterns for the Lower Owens are the Captain, Renegade, March Brown, Dark Hendrickson, Joe's Hopper, Green Giant, Olive Nymph, Black Gnat and Light Cahill. The ultra-tiny #22-#24 Griffith Gant is another area favorite for Owen's wild trout. A fly'n bubble combo is very effective on the Lower Owens. So is dapping in the little pockets and white water.

Convict Lake

Convict Lake is just up Rte. 395 a short way past Crowley Lake. Many consider it one of the most beautiful spots in the eastern Sierra, with rugged peaks surrounding clear, cold waters. Launch ramp, cabins, boat rental, grocery, restaurant, etc., support anglers in pursuit of rainbow and brown trout. Fishing is best in late spring and early fall, but also holds up well in the summer months. From this base camp, it's possible to hike to about 6 small mountain lakes and numerous streams to enjoy fine fishing and spectacular scenery. Convict Lake itself is about 1 mile long by 1/2 mile wide. It is at an elevation of 7, 600 feet so summer daytime temperatures are in the mid 70s.

Convict is a great early season lake for some quality rainbows. However, there are some "toad" browns that live here, too! Locals prefer either the early part of the spring or later in September or October to stalk the bigger browns at Convict. Troll gold Kastmasters, Super Dupers, frog Needlefish, silver Quickfish and Flatfish, and smaller Rapalas on top for the standard rainbow bite.

Dave Davis lake trolls with 'crawler trailers work too, as does lead core down to 6 to 12 colors.

Shore fishermen can limit out with worms, inflated nightcrawlers, Velveeta cheese and salmon eggs. A highly effective way to target Convict's trophy rainbows and browns when they suspend during warmer months is to dangle a live nightcrawler under a slip-float, in 15-35 foot depths. A variety of colors also produce here using Berkley Power Bait. The bank near the boat launch and the picnic area at the rear end of the lake are good spots to try. Think "BIG" for the lunker browns that lurk at Convict. Slow-troll larger Rebel and Rapala lures in rainbow trout finish along the drop-offs. For information contact Convict Lake Resort, (619) 934-3800.

Mammoth Lakes

Long recognized as the mecca for Southern Californian snow skiers, the Mammoth Lakes basin also excels as a super trout fishery in the warmer months. The Mammoth Lakes Area is only a short way (about 12 miles) up Rte. 395 from Crowley Lake. The town of Mammoth Lakes serves as a launching point for a wide variety of trout fishing experiences, including lake fishing, stream fishing, day-hike fishing and pack-in fishing. There is an immense assortment of twisting creeks and secluded mountain lakes. Lodging, camping facilities and other amenities are plentiful in the Mammoth Lakes area.

One of the most popular destinations here is Twin Lakes. They are just out of town on Hwy. 230. They offer complete facilities and good fishing. Twin Lakes is actually three lakes joined by a small stream. They are weedy and range in depth to about 40 or 50 feet. Brook trout, browns and rainbow are all available. Most trout are pan-sized, but some range up to 5 to 6 pounds. Also accessible by car are four more lakes located right near Twin Lakes. Lake Mary, Lake Mamie, Horseshoe Lake and Lake George all offer housekeeping cottages and/or camping facilities and good trouting. Lake Mary is the largest of the four, with depths of up to 60 feet, and is a favorite for trolling. The other three are productive, using a variety of techniques. After the ice clears, they are planted regularly during the summer.

It is probably best to start fishing a little later in the year, around May, due to Mammoth's higher elevation and possible iced-over conditions. After the thaw, attack the various lakes with bait and smaller lures.

Twin Lakes is a good choice for brookies and rainbows. You can rent a boat, but no motors are allowed. Velveeta, red worms, salmon eggs and dry flies are all effective at Twin.

LOCATOR—Eastern Sierra Trout Waters

Including Trout Plant Information

(All Waters Listed Are Planted by the DFG)

Injo County

BAKER CREEK: Take Highway 395 to the north end of Big Pine. Turn west on the County Campground road just north of the ball field in Big Pine and travel 1 1/2 miles to the campground. Fish are planted in the campground area.

BIG PINE CREEK: Turn west off of 395 at the Chevron station located in the center of Big Pine and continue to the top of the grade. The creek is planted from Sage Flat Campgrounds to Glacier Lodge.

BISHOP CREEK, LOWER: Take Highway 395 to the town of Bishop. Turn west on West Line Street and continue to Bulpitt and Isaac Walton parks. Plants are made upstream from Bulpitt Park to the Powerline Road.

BISHOP CREEK, MIDDLE: Turn west on West Line Street in Bishop and continue 15 miles to Intake 11. Trout are planted from Intake 11 to Lotte and from Lake Sabrina downstream to the North Lake turnoff.

BISHOP CREEK, SOUTH FORK: From Bishop, turn west on West Line Street and continue to the South Lake turnoff just below Intake 11, turn left at the fork. The creek is planted at access points from Habegger's to the US. Forest Service Campgrounds and from Parcher's Resort to Weir Lake.

COTTONWOOD CREEK: From Highway 395, turn south at the Cottonwood Power House turnoff located about 10 miles south of Lone Pine. Keep to the left as you cross the Los Angeles Aqueduct. The creek is planted from the campgrounds at the power house intake to the end of the road.

DIAZ LAKE: Located on the west side of Highway 395, three miles south of Lone Pine.

GEORGES CREEK: Approximately 7 miles south of Independence on Highway 395 turn south on the small road located one-quarter mile northwest of the Los Angeles Aqueduct crossing. The fish are planted at the sand trap.

INDEPENDENCE CREEK: Turn west off Highway 395 on the road just north of the Post Office in Independence. The trout are planted from Independence Campground located one-half mile west of Independence to where the main road the creek above Seven Pines village, a distance of about 7 miles.

LONE PINE CREEK, UPPER: Travel Hwy. 395 to Lone Pine. Turn west at the traffic signal located in center of Lone Pine, (Whitney Portal Road) and continue up the grade for 13 miles. The fish are planted at the campgrounds along the creek from this point to the pond at Whitney Portal store.

LONE PINE CREEK, LOWER: From Highway 395 turn west at the traffic signal located in the center of Lone Pine. The creek is planted at access points from the Los Angeles Aqueduct to Lonc Pine Campgrounds.

NORTH LAKE: From Highway 395, turn west on West Line Street in Bishopand continue up the grade for approximately 18 miles. Turn right at North Lake sign.

OWENS RIVER, SECTION II: In the Bishop area, turn east off Highway 395 on East Line Street, Hwy. 6, Warm Springs Road or Collins Road. The trout are planted from Laws Bridge on Hwy. 6 to Collins Road. In the Big Pine area, travel east fiom Highway 395 on Westgard Pass Road or on Stewart Lane. The river is planted at these sites.

PINE CREEK: Travel Highway 395 to approximately 15 miles north of Bishop. Turn off on Pine Creek Road and drive west to where the road crosses the creek. Creek is planted at this point up to where the road crosses the creek at the Union Carbide storage area.

ROCK CREEK, STATION III: From Highway 395, turn west at Tom's Place located 30 miles north of Bishop (Rock Creek Road). Turn right when the road ends at Rock Creek Lake. The creek is planted from the first point where the road crosses the creek to the end of the road.

LOCATOR (*continued*)

ROCK CREEK LAKE: From Highway 395, turn west at Tom's Place located 30 miles north of Bishop (Rock Creek Road), and follow the road to the lake.

SABRINA LAKE: Drive to Bishop on Highway 395 and turn west on West Line Street. Follow the signs to the lake which is located approximately 20 miles southwest of Bishop.

SHEPHERDS CREEK: Turn east at the road with a cattle guard located approximately 5 miles south of Independence on Highway 395. Follow this road until it ends at the Los Angeles Aqueduct. Turn right and continue to the creek. The trout are planted at the sand trap where the road meets the creek.

SOUTH LAKE: Travel to Bishop via Highway 395 and turn west on West Line Street (Highway 168). Continue to approximately 15 miles to the South lake Road turnoff. Turn left and drive for another 6 miles to the lake.

SYMMES CREEK: Turn west off Highway 395 on the road just north of the Post Office in Independence. Continue to Foothill Road and turn left. Follow the road to Symmes Creek Campground. The creek is stocked at the campground.

TABOOSE CREEK: Travel Highway 395 to 14 miles south ot Independence and turn west at the Taboose Creek Campgrounds sign. Turn left at the first road past Old Highway 395 and continue to the stream. The creek is stocked in the campgrounds from Old Highway 395 to 1 mile upstream.

TINNEMEHA CREEK: Drive to approximately 8 miles south of Big Pine and turn west off Highway 395 at the South Fish Springs Hatchery road sign. Turn left on the Tinnemeha Creek Road and continue on this road to Inyo County Campgrounds. The creek is planted at the campgrounds.

TUTTLE CREEK: Travel Highway 395 to Lone Pine and turn west at the traffic signal in the center of town. Continue up the road (Whitney Portal Road) for 3 miles to Horseshoe Meadow Road and turn left. Drive for about 2 miles to the Tuttle Creek Campgrounds. The creek is planted at access points in the campgrounds.

Mono County

BRIDGEPORT RESERVOIR: Turn north off Highway 395 at Highway 182 at the south city limits of Bridgeport and continue for approximately 3 miles to the lake.

BUCKEYE CREEK: Travel Highway 395 to the west end of Bridgeport and turn south at Twin Lakes Road. Continue for approximately 8 miles and turn north on Buckeye Creek Road located at Doc and Al's Pack Station. Proceed for another 4 miles to where the road crosses the creek. The trout are planted from this location upstream and in Buckeye Campground.

CONVICT CREEK: Travel Highway 395 to 10 miles south of Mammoth and turn west on Convict Lake Road. The creek is planted from Highway 395 to the campgrounds at the east end of Convict Lake.

CONVICT LAKE: Travel Highway 395 to 10 miles south of Mammoth Lakes and turn west on Convict Lake Road. Continue for approximately 2 miles to the lake.

CROWLEY LAKE: The most popular eastern Sierras fishing lake, Crowley, is located 35 miles north of Bishop just off Highway 395. Turn east at the Crowley Lake sign to enter at the south end of the lake. Drive farther north on Highway 395 to Benton Crossing Road. Turn east and follow road to north lake entrance.

DEADMAN CREEK: Travel Highway 395 to 9 miles north of Mammoth Lakes Junction. Turn west on White Wing Camp Road and drive 6 miles to Deadman Campground. The creek is planted in the campground area.

ELLERY LAKE: Drive Highway 395 to one-quarter mile south of the town of Lee Vining and turn west on Highway 120, the Tioga Pass Road. The lake is located approximately 12 miles distance on the south side of the road.

GEORGE LAKE: Travel Highway 395 to approximately 12 miles north of Crowley Lake and turn west on Mammoth Lakes Road. Drive past Twin Lakes and bear left at the fork in the road to Lake Mary and follow the Forest Service signs to Lake George.

LOCATOR (*continued*)

GLASS CREEK: Drive 10 miles north of Mammoth Lakes on Highway 395 and turn west on the road located across from Crestview Maintenance Station. Continue for one-half mile to the creek crossing. The stream is planted in the campground area north of the road.

GRANT LAKE: Turn west off Hwy. 395 onto the June Lake Loop Road, north. Continue to the lake.

GULL LAKE: Turn west off Highway 395 onto the June Lake Loop Road, south. Continue through June Lake Village to Gull Lake.

HILTON CREEK: From Highway 395, turn west on Crowley Lake Drive located just south of Crowley Lake and continue to Long Valley Drive (Old Hwy. 395). Turn north on Long Valley Drive and continue for one-quarter mile. The stream is planted at various points in the area along Hilton Lane, Juniper Drive and Pinion Drive.

JUNE LAKE: Turn west off Highway 395 onto June Lake Loop Road, south. June Lake is approximately 1 1/2 miles from the turnoff.

MARY LAKE: Travel Highway 395 to approximately 12 miles north of Crowley Lake and turn west on Mammoth Lakes Road. Continue past Twin Lakes and bear left at the fork in the road to Lake Mary.

LEE VINING CREEK: Drive one-quarter mile south of the town of Lee Vining on Highway 395 and turn west on Highway 120. Continue for approximately 3 miles to Azusa Camp Road. The creek is planted along the road that parallels the creek from Azusa Camp Road, and for 5 miles to the bridge where the road crosses the creek.

LEE VINING CREEK, SOUTH FORK: Travel to one-quarter mile south of Lee Vining on Highway 395 and turn west on Hwy. 120. Continue on Highway 120 for 15 miles to just past Ellery Lake. The creek is planted from the west end of Ellery Lake to Toiga Lake, located 1 mile south of Ellery Lake.

LUNDY LAKE: Turn west off Highway 395 at Lundy Lake Road, located 6 miles north of the town of Lee Vining. Continue west on Lundy Lake Road to the lake located at the end of the road.

MAMIE LAKE: Turn west off Highway 395 to Mammoth Lakes Road located approximately 10 miles north of Crowley Lake. Continue on Mammoth Road past Twin Lakes to Mamie Lake.

MAMMOTH CREEK: Drive on Highway 395 to Highway 203, the road to Mammoth Lakes, and turn west. Drive to Mammoth Lakes and turn left on Old Mammoth Road. Continue to a road that is located just before the bridge and turn left. The creek is planted at access points from the bridge downstream to Old Highway 395.

MCGEE CREEK: Drive 28 miles north of Bishop on 395 and turn west on McGee Road located just past the McGee Lodge. Continue one-quarter mile south on Old Highway 395 to McGee Pack Station Road. The creek is planted off access roads from Old Hwy. 395 to Upper Campground.

MILL CREEK: Turn west off Highway 395 at Lundy Lake Road located 6 miles north of Lee Vining. The creek is stocked at access points along the road from Highway 395 to the lake.

OWENS RIVER, SECTION III: Drive 35 miles north of Bishop on Highway 395 and turn east on Benton Crossing Road. Continue on Benton Crossing Road to the bridge. The trout are planted at access points one-half mile upstream and 2 miles downstream of bridge.

OWENS RIVER, SECTION IV: Drive Highway 395 to approximately 8 miles north of Highway 203, the Mammoth Lakes turnoff, and turn east on Big Springs Road. Continue for 5 miles and then turn north at the Big Springs Campground turnoff. The river is planted at the campgrounds.

REVERSE CREEK: Drive north on Highway 393 to the June Lake Loop Road and turn west. Continue past June and Gull to the point where the road crosses the creek. The stream is planted from access roads from this point, just east of Carson Park Inn, to Dream Mountains Resort, located just off the June Lake Loop Road across from Whispering Pines Resort.

ROBINSON CREEK: Travel Highway 395 to Twin Lakes Road at the north end of Bridgeport and turn south. The creek is planted at the bridge at Doc and Al's Resort on the road that goes to Buckeye Creek, and at campground access points along Twin Lakes Road from Doc and Al's to Lower Twin Lakes.

LOCATOR (*continued*)

ROCK CREEK, SECTION I: Travel Highway 395 toTom's Place, approximately 20 miles north of Bishop. The creek is planted in Tuff Campground across the highway from Tom's Place. Continue south from this point on Highway 395 approximately 1 mile to Old Hwy. 395 and turn south. The creek is planted along the Old Highway from Highway 395 to Paradise Lodge.

ROCK CREEK, SECTION II: Turn west off Highway 395 at Tom's Place, located approximately 20 miles north of Bishop. Continue to Iris Meadow Campground. The creek is planted from Iris Meadow Campground to Rock Creek Lake Lodge.

RUSH CREEK: Drive on Highway 395 to the June Lake Loop Road and turn west. Continue to Silver Lake. The creek is planted at access points from the Southern California Edison power plant bridge, north to the lake and in Silver Lake Campgrounds located north of the lake, and for approximately one-quarter mile north of the campgrounds.

SADDLEBAG LAKE: Drive Highway 395 to one-quarter mile south of the town of Lee Vining and turn west on Highway 120. Continue for approximately 16 miles to the Saddlebag Lake turnoff and drive to the lake at the end of the road.

SHERWIN CREEK: From Highway 395, turn west on Mammoth Road turnoff, approximately 10 miles north of Crowley Lake. Continue to east end of Mammoth Lakes and turn south on Old Mammoth Road. Drive 3 miles to Sherwin Creek Campground. The creek is planted from access roads on both sides of Sherwin Creek Road at Sherwin Creek Campground.

SILVER LAKE: Turn west off Highway 395 at the June Lake Loop Road and continue past June Lake, June Lake Village, and Gull Lake to Silver Lake.

SWAUGER CREEK: Drive to the dirt road located 9 miles north of Bridgeport and turn east. The creek parallels Highway 395 and is planted for one-quarter mile above and below the bridge located in the campground area.

TIOGA LAKE: Travel Highway 395 to one-quarter mile south of the town of Lee Vining to Highway 120, the Tioga Pass Road. Turn west and continue for 18 miles to the lake, located just outside the entrance to Yosemite Park.

TOPAZ LAKE: Lake is located on the California-Nevada border just off Highway 395.

TRUMBULL LAKE: Drive Highway 395 to the top of Conway Summit, 17 miles north of the town of Lee Vining, and turn west on Virginia Road. The lake is on the right side of the road near Virginia Lakes Resort area.

TWIN LAKES BRIDGEPORT, UPPER AND LOWER: Turn south off Highway 395 onto Twin Lakes Road located at the north end of the town of Bridgeport and continue to the lakes.

TWIN LAKES MAMMOTH, UPPER AND LOWER: Drive Highway 395 to Mammoth Lakes Road, 10 miles north of Crowley Lake, and turn west. Twin Lakes are the first lakes on the right that you come to, approximately 7 miles up the road.

VIRGINIA CREEK, LOWER: The creek is located along the west side of Highway 395, 7 miles south of the town of Bridgeport. It is planted from Creekhouse Resort to approximately 2 miles upstream.

VIRGINIA CREEK, UPPER: Drive Highway 395 to the top of Conway Summit, 17 miles north of the town of Lee Vining, and turn west on Virginia Road. Continue to Creek Road, which veers to the left off Virginia Lakes Road. The stream is planted at access points and in the campgrounds along Creek Road until it once again joins Virginia Lakes Road at the Pack Station located at the end of Lower Virginia Lake.

VIRGINIA LAKES, UPPER AND LOWER: Travel Highway 395 to the top of Conway Summit, 17 miles north of the town of Lee Vining, and turn west on Virginia Lakes Road. The lakes are at the end of the road.

LITTLE WALKER LAKE: Travel Highway 395 to 2 miles north of the north junction of June Lake Loop Road, and turn west on the dirt road. Turn left at a fork in the road just before you reach a locked gate. Continue to the first road on the right and turn right. Drive a short distance to the Walker Lake Trailhead and park your car. Follow the footpath for a short distance to the lake.

Shift to trolling the Needlefish lure at Lake Mary. Smaller Rebels and Rapalas will also produce as well as flies.

Lakes Mamie, Horseshoe and George are tinier lakes where standard commercial baits and smaller spoons and spinners are in order. After ice out, consider hiking into Barney, Skeleton or Arrowhead Lakes. Spin fishers armed with float tubes and fly'n bubble combinations will find most of the Mammoth Lakes to their liking particularly for mid-season dry-fly action. A solid gold, 1/8-1/4 oz. Kastmaster spoon remains a solid favorite.

Some of the favorite day-hike fishing lakes in the Mammoth Lakes area are Arrowhead, Skeleton, Wood and Barney Lakes. These lakes are generally not reachable early in the trout season because of snow on the trails. But they are all along the same trail. It begins near the Lake Mary campground. If you're interested in other day-hike and pack-in fishing excursions in the Mammoth Lakes area, the Mammoth Ranger District of the Inyo National Forest offers (for about $1.00) a Mammoth Trails Booklet. It provides complete information on about 15 different hikes of varying length and degree of difficulty. The Mammoth Ranger Station is at Box 148, Mammoth Lakes, CA 93546. Fly anglers new to the area should check with Mammoth tackle outlets to determine which offering is working best. A good source is Mammoth Sporting Goods, (619) 934-8474. Mammoth Visitors Center can be reached at (800) 367-6572. The Mammoth Lakes Chamber of Commerce is at (619) 934-3068.

The June Lake Loop

Outside of Lake Crowley, there is no other area of the eastern Sierra that is synonymous with gala opening day troutin'! The June Lake Loop, comprised of June, Gull, Silver and Grant Lakes, generates some sensational early season catches. As a general rule, the bigger fish come from Gull and June, with the best bank fishing at Silver, and a better volume of browns at Grant. Each of the four lakes has its own unique "personality." They are all reached by taking Hwy. 158 out of June Lake Junction. The first lake you'll hit, just about 2 miles out of town, is June Lake (160 acres). Next, in order, comes Gull Lake (64 acres), Silver Lake (80 acres) and finally Grant Lake (1,100 acres). These lakes are at an elevation of about 7,000 feet and offer spectacular eastern Sierra mountain scenery. All these lakes have developed facilities including campgrounds, boat rentals, etc. Lodging is available at some lakes as well as in the town of June Lake.

June Lake

Shore fishing can be good along the rocks parallel to the June Loop Road. The north and southeast shoreline are also very productive. Velveeta, Zeke's floating cheeses, yellow, pink and orange Power Bait, red eggs, marshmallows and live grasshoppers account for some hefty stringers by bank walkers. Also, use a cast-a-bubble or slip float to dangle baits or tiny 1/32 to 1/64 ounce mini jigs along the steep drop-offs at June. Trollers should drag lures from Big Rock Marina, 40 feet off the shore, to the "Icy Road" sign along the highway. Rapalas, Krocadiles, silver Phoebes and Kastmasters can be top-lined. The Dave Davis flashers with nightcrawlers or Needlefish trailers also produce at June. For information contact one of the following: Grant Lake Marina, (619) 648-7964; Silver Lake Resort, (619) 648-7525; Gull Lake Boat Landing, (619) 648-7539; June Lake Marina, (619) 648-7726.

Gull Lake

Of the four lakes, Gull is probably the best bet for the accomplished bait dunker. Both rainbows and brookies are fair game here. Still-fishing with Zeke's pink garlic cheese or miniature marshmallows produce north of the boat launch area and off of Fisherman's Trail. Trollers working three colors with lead-core line will stick their share. The brass-colored Triple Teazer, Phoebe, Needlefish and Rooster Tail are preferred lures at Gull. Similarly, the #CD-5 or #CD-7 Rapalas in gold finish are excellent flat-lining picks. Two other trolling options include the widely used Dave Davis flasher'n nightcrawler combo, or the Hornburg streamer fly-pulled on straight mono. For information contact one of the following: Grant Lake Marina, (619) 648-7964; Silver Lake Resort, (619) 648-7525; Gull Lake Boat Landing, (619) 648-7539; June Lake Marina, (619) 648-7726.

Silver Lake

Still-fishing, trolling, fly casting and lure tossin' are all viable approaches at Silver. Soak bait along the beach near the cabin resort area. Troll flashers 2 to 3 colors deep with lead core. Fly fishing aficionados prefer either a Black Gnat or white nymph. If you can catch them, live, mountain grasshoppers are also deadly split-shotted on light 2 to 6 pound line at Silver. Some of your bigger brown trout will be scored on 'hoppers. For information contact one of the following: Grant Lake Marina, (619) 648-7964; Silver Lake Resort, (619) 648-7525; Gull Lake Boat Landing, (619) 648-7539; June Lake Marina, (619) 648-7726.

Grant Lake

The most exposed lake of the loop offers solid action on rainbows and browns. Start by trolling Privy Point on the west side. Use Rapalas and Rebel plugs or silver Kastmaster spoons. The versatile flasher'n crawler combo should also be tried. This same area is excellent for bait fishing or chuckin' a lure from the bank. The Grant Lake marina, the dam and the inlet to Rush Creek are equally good spots to fish. Bubble'n fly rigs work super on this large, windy lake. Regional favorites include the California Mosquito, Humpy, Royal Coachman and Black Gnat —all fished "dry." Some bonus Kamloop action is also possible at Grant. Gold Phoebes, Kastmasters, Super Dupers, Panther Martins and Rooster Tails will nail these fish. Grant may occasionally kick out a double-digit brown or rainbow. Don't hesitate to cast or troll Rapala #13 or #18 series floating minnows, A.C. Plugs, or A.A. Super Shads in, of course, baby rainbow trout patterns.

Information on the June Lake Loop Area is readily available. For general and accommodation information call the Chamber of Commerce at (619) 648-7584. Camping information is available from the U.S. Forest Service in the town of Lee Vining at (619) 647-6525. A good source of fishing information is Ernie's Tackle in June Lake at (619) 648-7756. You can also contact one of the following: Grant Lake Marina, (619) 648-7964; Silver Lake Resort, (619) 648-7525; Gull Lake Boat Landing, (619) 648-7539; June Lake Marina, (619) 648-7726.

Rush Creek

One of the most frequented spots in all the Sierras is Rush Creek, located in the June Lake Loop Area. The popular sections are where the creek flows into Silver Lake, out of Silver into Grant Lake, and then all the way into Mono Lake. Many locals feel the hottest stretch is just above Silver Lake.

There is usually an ample supply of plant-sized rainbows in Rush Creek following weekly stockings. Don't be fooled, however, by this unassuming little creek. There are some "big boys" that call Rush Creek "home." Rainbows and browns over 5 pounds are a real possibility for the stealthy angler. Trophy fish are usually taken as Rush meanders between Silver and Grant Lakes.

Grasshoppers, red worms and salmon eggs are great for the stocker bows, while nightcrawlers are dynamite on the trophy browns. Smaller spinners such as the simple Colorado, Rooster Tail or Panther Martin series are deadly on the smaller trout in Rush Creek. Spoon fishermen prefer ultralight to medium-sized Kastmasters and Super Dupers. Better quality trout can also be taken on two other presentations: Rapalas or flies. Dry-fly specialists use the Adams, Royal Coachman, Royal Wolff, Renegade, Humpy, and, of course, California Mosquito, along this creek. The Matuka streamer is a traditional winner for fishing a larger wet fly.

Tioga Pass

Motoring northbound on Hwy. 395 beyond the June Lake Loop and the town of Lee Vining, the angler can venture west onto the Tioga Pass. This eastern gateway to Yosemite National Park offers some sensational troutin' for the weekender.

Ellery and Saddlebag Lakes are the primary stops with roadside access. Rainbows are the principle species at Ellery and almost all standard bait offerings produce. Saddlebag has rainbows, brookies and a smattering of Kamloops. Trolling is perhaps your overall best tactic here, along with bait.

There is also an interesting service available at Saddlebag. Instead of hiking over land roughly five miles to get to the other end of the lake, a "water taxi" shortens the trip. The taxi leaves in the early morning, ferrying fishermen to the other side. It then makes intermittent back-and-forth runs throughout the day.

The Twenty Lakes Basin, mostly within a one-day hike from the Saddlebag Area, offers some excellent high elevation fishing. Rainbows, eastern brook, some goldens and even cutthroats at Greenstone Lake await the hiker. Shamrocks, Odell, Lower Twin and Potter are particularly good waters for golden action. Leave your prepared baits at home when fishing these back country lakes. Natural offerings such as nightcrawlers, red worms, crickets, grasshoppers, pine grubs and hellgrammites are far superior.

Bridgeport Reservoir

Bridgeport Reservoir is considered to be one of the most prolific waters for trophy brown trout in the Golden State. Both rainbows and browns are caught here, and they are good-sized (1-4 pounds). Planted fish grow fast here because of the abundance of food. The reservoir is about 5 1/2 miles long and covers almost 4,500 acres. But Bridgeport is not deep, so the water warms up in the summer months. This contributes to moss and algae growth which affects fishing techniques and hot spots. There are complete boating facilities at the lake. And the town of Bridgeport and surrounding area provide a full range of resort and camping services.

For trophy browns, early in the season, start right off with trolling big plugs like trout-colored Rapalas all the way up to size 18! Larger jointed and unjointed Rebel minnows are also viable options. Fan-casting bigger spinners and spoons from the shore or from boat will also account for some lunker browns early in the season or late in the fall. Krocadile spoons along with the Vibrax, Rooster Tail, and Mepps spinners have historically been effective. Again, to emphasize, use larger than normal sizes. On that note, troll both the A.C. Plug and A.A. Super Shad in rainbow trout patterns, too!

There are also a lot of rainbows available to the early season angler at Bridgeport. Troll in front of the marina and along Rainbow Point. Both flat-line and lead-core (3 to 4 colors) approaches work. Use the Needlefish in frog, rainbow trout, or bikini patterns, along with the Flatfish and smaller Rapala in silver, gold or rainbow trout.

Bank fishermen have a chance working either lures or bait near the dam, along Sandy Point, Rainbow Point and the inlets of Robinson or Buckeye Creeks. Bait fishing can be a super alternative to trolling later in the summer when the weed growth at Bridgeport fouls blades and lures. Use inflated 'crawlers, salmon eggs, Velveeta and floating cheese spreads, and fresh roe.

Trail and camping information in the Bridgeport area is available from the U.S. Forest Service, Bridgeport Ranger District, Box 595, Bridgeport, CA 93517, (619) 932-7070. Fishing information is available at Ken's Alpine Shop and Sporting Goods in Bridgeport at (619) 932-7707 and Falling Rock Marina at Bridgeport Lake, (619) 932-7001.

Twin Lakes

Like Bridgeport, these modest-sized lakes are a world-class brown trout factory for specimens up to 25 pounds. However, reliable reports indicate world-record browns over 40 pounds inhabit this rich, bait-laden water! Many of the same strategies that work at Bridgeport Reservoir will also produce at Twin Lakes. Twin Lakes are located about 12 miles southwest of Bridgeport at an elevation of about 7,000 feet. There is camping and a full-service marina at the lakes.

Locals say the first and last months of the season are best for huntin' monster browns at Twin. At the start of the season, big fish are making up for the long winter hibernation. Later in the fall, the lunkers move into the shallows to spawn. It is estimated there is a greater volume of fish in Upper Twin, with the bigger trout coming from Lower Twin. Trollin' the big minnow plugs,

as mentioned previously, is the patented "inside secret" for browns of gargantuan proportions. Pulling other assorted lures also produces terrific results for those fishing the rainbow population at Twin. Panther Martin, Mepps, Needlefish, Wob-L-Rite and Phoebe lures will stick a good share of smaller rainbows. So will Dave Davis blades'n crawler combos.

Bait dunkers should toss garlic marshmallows, yellow and chartreuse Power Bait, red salmon eggs and night-crawlers from the bank. Twin also has a budding stock of feisty kokanee salmon. The Dave Davis rig works for the kokes from June to August. An Olive Leech streamer is equally effective at times. Lake regulars have their own secret tactic for these smaller rainbows and kokes : use a small #000 Luhr-Jensen Dodger with about an 18-inch leader and a nightcrawler trailer. This is an interesting alternative to the traditional flasher'n crawler rig. For information contact the Bridgeport Chamber of Commerce, (619) 932-7500, or Bridgeport Ranger District, (619) 932-7070.

Bridgeport Area Streams

There is a wealth of streams awaiting the roadside angler in the Bridgeport region. Here's a brief rundown on some of the more popular waters.

Lower Robinson Creek

Look for lots of 8 to 12 inch stocked rainbows here. Cheese baits, red or white salmon eggs, and red worms will fool them. So will a silver-bladed Panther Martin, Rooster Tail and Mepps spinner. Hot Shot and Phoebe spoons are also worth trying. Fly fishers should stick with the Wooly Worm, Zug Bug, Gold Ribbed Hare's Ear, Yellow or Olive Humpy, Caddis, Royal Wolff or California Mosquito.

Upper Robinson Creek

This creek will require some hiking but the walk may be worth some quality 10 to 14 inch brookies or rainbows. Scale down with smaller Rooster Tails, Mepps or Panther Martin spinners. The Mosquito and Black Ant are regionally favored dry fly patterns on the Upper Robinson.

Upper Buckeye Creek

Native 6 to 10 inch brook trout are found on the Upper Buckeye. Assorted flies such as the Yellow Humpy, Joe's Hopper and Black Ant in smaller sizes are effective. So are spinners in yellow finishes.

In addition to Robinson and Buckeye Creeks there are literally scores of other small, productive Bridgeport trout streams. Some of the best known are Eagle, Swauger, Leavitt, Sardine, Wolf, Silver and Molydenite. Many smaller streams are lightly fished. But it's important to remember to fish these waters slowly and carefully. Walk quietly. Crawl up to pools in meadows. Keep your shadow off the water. Move upstream so you stay behind the fish. Trout fishing in small streams is akin to stalking in a hunt.

Walker River (East and West)

Flowing out of Bridgeport Reservoir toward Nevada is the East Walker River. When lunker browns are mentioned among seasoned Sierra trouters, the East Walker River quickly comes to mind. Trout in the 14 to 18 inch range are commonplace. A "hawg" over 5 pounds is not that rare. There is a two-fish, 14-inch minimum size limit along this length of the Walker, and only single, barbless hooks on artificial lures are permitted. Anglers work this river in chest waders. Submerged roots and overhanging branches add to the character of the East Walker. Trouters use spinning or fly casting gear.

Consider using somewhat heavier "gear" in fishing the East Walker, more so than perhaps any other stream or river in the state. Veteran fly fishermen think nothing of casting a #8 to #10 fly rod, #4 to #1/0 size streamer flies, a minimum of a 4 pound tippet for fishing dry, and up to 15 pound leader for wet. Similarly, spin fishers will use anywhere from 6 to 20 pound test mono for working lures for these jumbo brown trout. It is clearly possible to tie into a 20 pound class German brown while fishing the East Walker! For spinning, toss Rebel and Rapala floating minnows in gold and rainbow trout colors. You can cast anything from a short #7 all the way to the lengthier #13 Countdown series in the sinking Rapalas. Be sure to remove all treble hooks and replace them with a single #1/0 Siwash hook.

Fly fishers have a variety of flies to select from their war-chests. Time-proven patterns in the East Walker include: Caddis, Mayfly, Joe's Hopper and Mosquito fished dry. The Caddis Nymph, Emerger and Wooly Worm are popular for a "wet" presentation. But "hawg hunters" armed with a fly rod prefer streamers as their best option for a trophy. The Black/White, Black/Yellow, or Brown Marabous, Yellow or Black Muddlers, Spudler, Sculpin, Baby Rainbow Trout and, of course, the Hornburg, are key streamer patterns.

The West Walker originates near Sonora Pass in the Leavitt and Pickel Meadows Area. Then it flows steeply toward the Walker Canyon where it parallels Hwy. 395 for about 16 miles. It grows in flow as more streams drain in. This stretch is heavily planted in campgrounds and other access points. Moving away from these plant spots improves your chances for hold-over rainbow and native browns.

The West Walker opens up an entirely different avenue of river troutin'. Rainbows, brookies and browns fall prey to bait fishermen. Nightcrawlers, salmon eggs, red worms, 'hoppers and crickets are a solid menu for these fish.

Rapala and Rebel lures, Mepps, green Rooster Tails and silver-bladed Panther Martin spinners are preferred by spin fishermen. West Walker trout will also snap up a well-presented fly. Try the California Mosquito, Black Ant, Black Gnat, Coachman, Royal Coachman, Caddis, Olive and Yellow Humpy, Royal Wolff and Joe's Hopper, "dry"; or the Zug Bug, Sinking Ant, Wooly Worm and Beetle, "wet."

Other Eastern Sierra Trouting

It's hard to believe, but here are even more great fishing opportunities in the eastern Sierras. Try these on for size!

Heenan Lake

How about fishing in a trout hatchery? That's what you can legally do at Heenan Lake, the broodstock holding area for Lahontan cutthroat trout. Fish here average 17 inches in length and 2 1/2 pounds. There is a short open season in the fall, angling permitted on Fridays, Saturdays and Sundays. A modest fee is collected at the gate. You can tube or boat, but shore fishing and wading also work. Small lures are dynamite, and streamers and Wooly Worms also do the job. Black is a great color. Late September and early October are prime. Heenan Lake is between Bridgeport and Markeeville on Hwy. 89, about 10 miles south of Markeeville. For information contact the Department of Fish & Game, (916) 355-7090.

Kirman Lake (a.k.a., Carmen Lake)

Here's your chance to catch 3 to 5 pound brook trout. All it requires is a three-mile hike from Sonora Bridge Campground on Hwy. 108, just past Hwy. 395 going up the Sonora Pass. There is a two-fish limit. The brookies, all stocked, thrive on shrimp-like scuds. Pack-in a float tube. Best angling is just after ice-out and again in October. The preferred offering is olive-colored streamers, using fly gear or a casting bubble on spinning gear.

They say the flesh of Kirman brookies is deep orange and very tasty. For information contact the Kirman Summit Ranger District, (209) 965-3434.

Lundy Lake

Just north of Mono Lake, about 4 or 5 miles west of Hwy. 395 on Mill Road, is Lundy Lake. It is a picturesque gem of a small lake full of rainbows and browns. Plus, there are brookies in the beaver ponds up above the lake, and good brown trout angling in Mill Creek below Lundy Lake Dam. Lake fishing is good from shore or boat in the regularly stocked water. Try a casting bobber, a long, light leader (about 6 feet) and a Mosquito fly. Black Gnats also work. Bait anglers score with salmon eggs and nightcrawlers. Floating nightcrawlers down Mill Creek is probably best due to the heavy brush. Lundy Lake Resort (camping, cabins, boat rental) is at the top end of the lake, P.O. Box 265, Lee Vining, CA 93541. Mono County Parks, (619) 932-7911, operates a campground along Mill Creek.

Virginia Lakes

Just 5 miles up from Lundy Lake along Hwy. 395 is Virginia Lakes Road. Go west about 6 miles to 10 wonderful little fishing lakes amidst tall pines at 9,700 feet. There is a lodge, pack station for forays into the Hoover Wilderness, and a Forest Service campground. Big Virginia and Little Virginia Lakes are the best known and the most accessible. Some hiking is required to get to the other lakes and miles of small streams. Cheese, salmon eggs and flies-and-bubbles all produce. The locally tied Virginia Lake Mosquito and generic mosquitoes both work. Angling pressure is light here and also at Lundy Lake, compared to some of the better known eastern Sierra waters. For information contact the Bridgeport Ranger District, (619) 932-7070.

Wilderness Trouting

The eastern Sierras are a mecca for pack trips and backpack hikes into the several high elevation wilderness areas west of Hwy. 395. We've already mentioned trailheads at Lone Pine, Independence, Big Pine, Mammoth Lakes and Virginia Lakes, and these are but a few. That's because there are so many desirable wilderness areas within easy reach including The Hoover Wilderness, The John Muir Wilderness, The Ansel Adams Wilderness and The Golden Trout Wilderness. There are numerous pack stations and each offers a wide variety of trip options.

Northern Coast Trout

Some of the most overlooked troutin' terrain in the Golden State is found in the northern coast. Trinity, Lewiston and Whiskeytown Lakes are superb trout fisheries for the recreational angler. A variety of techniques will produce at these lakes and there is the chance of tying into some really nice trophy fish.

For the back country angler, the Trinity Alps and the Trinity Divide offer extensive excursions into some remote lakes teeming with hungry trout. The backpacking enthusiast who prefers even greater solitude can consider the wealth of creeks and lakes in the Marble Mountain Wilderness. Scrappy brookies, 'bows and browns await the stealthy hiker.

Farther south, three lakes are really standouts for quality troutin': Berryessa, Indian Valley and Ruth. All three of these impoundments offer consistently good fishing on an all-year basis. The quality of the fish—primarily rainbows—also exceeds that of most of the other lakes in the state in terms of size. Trollers, still-fishermen and lure tossers will all find the northern coast to their liking with stops at Berryessa, Indian Valley and Ruth Lakes!

Finally, the north coast is the home of most of the headwaters and main flows of the great steelhead and salmon streams of California. These waters offer trout fishing also, with special restrictions to protect the juvenile migratory fisheries.

Lake Berryessa and Putah Creek

The adventurous angler should plan on spending some time on Berryessa to really learn this incredible impoundment. It is over 25 miles long and up to 3 miles wide. There is no telling what trout species you may tie into at Berryessa. It could be an average(!) 14 inch rainbow, a bigger "toad" brown, or a feisty Eagle Lake strain trout. Troutin' at this lake really swings into high gear from November to May. Lake Berryessa is one of California's premier recreation areas, combining fine fishing with resorts, camping, water- and jet-skiing and sailing. And it's right near Napa Valley's wine country.

Minnow plugs that replicate threadfin shad are hard to beat for both native and smaller hatchery 'bows. Troll or cast these plugs as well as gold or red-tipped Kastmaster spoons, Speedy Shiners, Z-Rays, gold hammered Triple Teazers, Abalone Demons and Needlefish lures. Work 1/2 mile up from the dam, the Spanish Flat Wall from the marina entrance north, the narrows, down the creek channel from Putah Creek, around Markley Cove, and along the entrances to Big and Little Portuguese Creeks. Slow-troll indigenous minnows for some solid action. Use a pinch of lead shot about 5 feet above the bait. These minnows can be purchased directly at the lake concessions.

Some other trolling programs are worth considering. Lake locals like to use herring dodgers or Al's Big Flash in lieu of traditional flashers. Red worms or minnows serve as trailers. Or shift to downriggers and drag either 6 to 7 inch Rebels or 4 inch Rapala in rainbow trout finishes. The bigger browns in particular will really chomp on that broken back Rebel. Boaters should also try drifting live minnows under a bobber. This technique recurrently produces nice stringers of rainbows each season. Still-fish the mouths of Pope and Putah Creeks with the "Shasta Fly" for additional action with bait.

If you are in this area of the state in the early part of the year, mosey down below Lake Berryessa and fly fish Putah Creek. The expansive area below Monticello Dam can be a fantastic spot at times for bigger German browns and lots of rainbows. Float tubers armed with traditional fly fishing gear score high marks along this stretch of Putah Creek. There are numerous sources of fishing information and bait and tackle shops at Lake Berryessa. Many of the resorts and marinas, as well as several sporting goods stores, are anxious to provide information and supplies. For information contact the Chamber of Commerce, P.O. Box 164, Spanish Flat Station, Napa, CA 94558. Lake visitor information: (707) 966-2111.

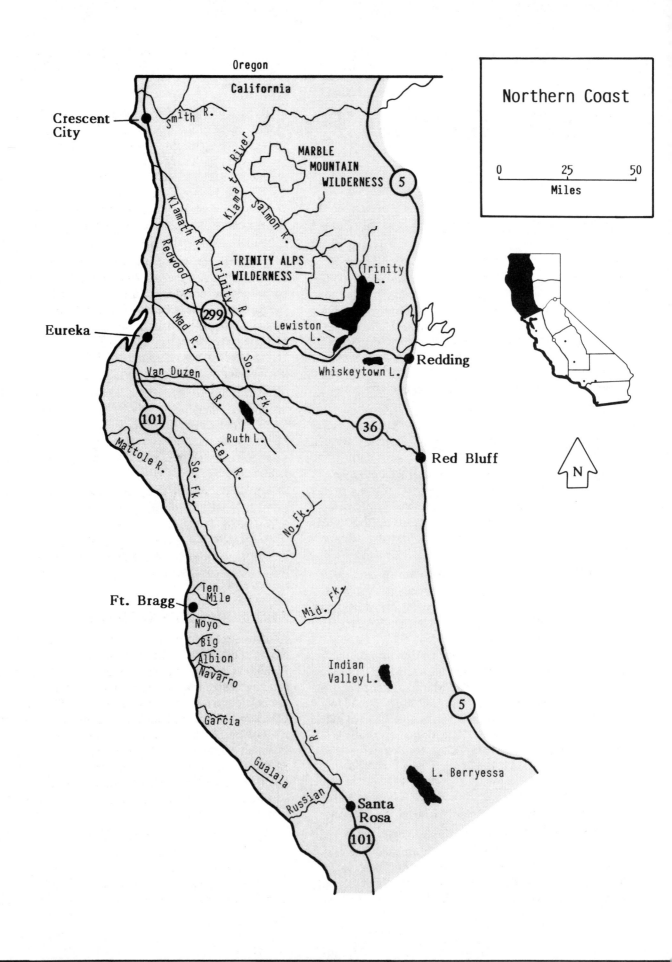

Northern Coast

Indian Valley Reservoir

Indian Valley Reservoir is more remote than many other Northern California fishing hot spots. Getting to the lake requires a long drive down an unpaved road. This means that the fishing pressure is lighter than most other lakes. And none of the brush and trees in the lake canyons and valleys were cleared before fishing began in 1974; therefore, this is an excellent fish habitat. Indian Valley has about 40 miles of cove-studded shoreline. It is about 35 miles west of Williams. Located at 1,475 feet elevation, most of the lake is about 120 feet deep, and up to 200 feet at the dam. At the south end there is a launch ramp, store, boat rental and 30 campsites. Look for some outstanding troutin' on this remote 4,000 acre lake! This is truly a year-round fishery. Early spring and early fall are peak for trout. They can put on some surface fireworks this time of year.

Start by trolling from the dam in the south and head toward the north shore, keeping to the center of the lake. Dave Davis and Ford Fender lake trolls dragged ahead of a nightcrawler will perform well at Indian Valley near the surface. Or use a basic flat-line approach with Flatfish, Triple Teazer, Needlefish, silver Kastmaster, black/silver and black/white Rooster Tails, bucktail Mepps or red/black and yellow/red Z-Ray lures. Also, fan-cast these baits from the shore or from boats. Rapalas and Rebels can score some tallies on the larger rainbows with a top-line troll. Drop down to 4 to 8 colors of lead core with a Triple Teazer for late season action.

Still-fish nightcrawlers by the dam during the summer. Be prepared to fish as deep as 80 feet down—the trout will be there. An unusual ploy used by lake locals is to toss small white Marabou streamers or 1/64 to 1/16 Marabou jigs on Indian Valley's rainbow population. Believe the lake regulars when they tell you these trout will eagerly bushwhack a small Marabou fished on light line! Figure on driving 8 to 10 miles of gravel road to get to Indian Valley Lake. When you arrive, be sure not to exceed the 10 m.p.h. speed limit for all boats. For information contact the Indian Valley Store (at the lake's south end), (916) 662-9697.

Lewiston Lake

This may very well be the "flagship" lake of the northeast part of the state. Lewiston is a rather unusual lake as it is in some sense just the afterbay of Trinity Lake, located below the dam. Colder water flowing from below Trinity Dam into Lewiston means that this lake can be a remarkable choice for summer troutin'. Troll shallow between Cooper Gulch Campground and Mary Smith Campground. Then try below the dam and in the flat near Pine Cove Resort. Blades'n nightcrawlers, smaller Mepps spinners, as well as gold Li'l Cleo and Fjord spoons are good for this tactic. Consider also trolling flies. Nymphs fished with light, long tippets in the summer due to high water clarity can be fantastic. Wooly Worms, Marabou Streamers and assorted dry flies can also be slow-trolled.

Drifting at Lewiston is a new "twist" to conventional bait fishing. Use either a bobber or a light shot to keep the baits—either 'crawlers or a small crawdad—just a few feet above the moss beds. Traditional still-fishing with bait can be fairly consistent at the north end of the lake near the public launch ramp and off of Lakeview Terrace. Nightcrawlers are the long-time first choice of lake regulars for bait fishin'!

Don't underestimate this little 600 acre lake. There are lots of rainbows in the 12 to 18 inch class for the taking. But Lewiston has also kicked out browns topping the 24 pound mark. Plus, if you deep-troll during the later summer period, look forward to some excellent kokanee action.

There is a strictly enforced 10 m.p.h. speed limit on Lewiston. Small inflatables, float tubes and prams are perfectly suited for this lake. Lewiston has a launch ramp, campgrounds and several resorts. For information contact the U.S. Forest Service Ranger Station, Weaverville, CA 96093, (916) 623-2121.

Marble Mountain Wilderness

Recreational trout fishermen who also like to backpack should consider the Marble Mountain Wilderness in Siskiyou County. There are 89 lakes in this remote area ranging in size from 1/2 to 67 acres. Most of these lakes are nestled in mountainous terrain at 5,000 to 7,000 foot elevations. They will ice-out later in the year and are perhaps best fished from late summer all the way through October. Numerous creeks in the area sustain small-sized rainbows and brookies. Canyon, Elk, Shackleford, Ukonom and Wooley Creeks along with the North and Little Fork of the Salmon River are examples of such waters.

Plan on spending anywhere from 1 to 2 hours, up to over a day, to reach many of the lakes. Three of the most popular are: Campbell Lake, which evidences good fly fishing for brooks, browns and 'bows; Clear Lake, which also has all three species and perhaps the largest fish on tap; and Cliff Lake, again, with all three species and depths over 175 feet. You don't need a lot of tricks up your sleeve to fish the Marble Mountain lakes and creeks. Keep your leaders very light, stay with tiny U.L. spinners and spoons. Natural baits are excellent, and definitely work dry flies behind a cast-a-bubble in the evening.

The Marble Mountain Wilderness (242,000 acres) is within the boundaries of the Klamath National Forest in Siskiyou County. The area where the Marble Mountains now exist was once part of the flat bottom of an ancient, shallow ocean. Millions of years ago, violent volcanic upheaving and the erosive cutting action of rivers and glaciers combined to form the present day landscape. Almost all of the lakes of the Marble Mountain Wilderness were formed by ancient relentless glacial activity. The colors of this wilderness area, from the majestic white of Marble Mountain, to the lush green of Morehouse Meadow, to the deep blue of Cliff Lake, interspersed with various hues of sheer rock cliffs and densely timbered mountainsides, provide a spectacle not soon to be forgotten. These mountains are relatively low—scarcely a peak among them exceeds 7,000 feet—but they have an alpine flavor. There are a number of pack guides in the area. Wildlife in the wilderness includes black bear, deer and osprey. The extensive trail system is served by nine trailheads, five of which are open to pack animals. Maps of the wilderness area and of the surrounding national forest are available from the Klamath National Forest, 1312 Fairlane Rd., Yreka, CA 96087, (916) 842-6131.

North Coast Mountain Trout Streams

The fact that migratory fish like salmon and steelhead trout share the flowing waters of the northeast with rainbows and browns makes fishing regulations designed to protect juvenile ocean-bound fish somewhat complicated! There are waters open to fishing all year with a limit of three trout or salmon, but no more than two salmon. Then there are a few streams open during the normal trout season (last Saturday in April through November 15) with a 10-trout limit. There are waters that are closed to fishing completely. And, finally, there is an "all other streams" category regulation that runs from the Saturday preceding Memorial Day to November 15 with a limit of five trout. This last category is usually referred to as the north coast stream trout season.

The "Saturday preceding Memorial Day" opener allows trout anglers to explore literally hundreds of miles of smaller, mountain tributary streams that are the permanent homes of resident wild trout. Many of the mountain stream fish are in the 6 to 8 inch range, but 10-12 inchers are caught. U.S. Forest Service Maps and topographical maps are recommended.

Ruth Lake

There is only one problem with Ruth Lake. It's the drive along Hwy. 36, either east from Hwy. 101 (south of Eureka) or west from Red Bluff. But if you decide to make the trip, you won't be sorry. Ruth, a 1,200 acre reservoir on the Upper Mad River, is just southwest of the town of Mad River. There is a full-service marina, launching, campgrounds and a large resort at the lake. Ruth Lake has to be considered one of the true "sleepers" of the northern coast! Both spring and winter troutin' can be terrific here. From the end of November to April, anglers can encounter some of the best trout fishing in the state for rainbows. There will also be a smattering of steelhead and kokanee salmon available for good measure.

Fish the south end of Ruth where the Mad River enters the lake. There is accessible shoreline along the east and west banks of the south end of the lake. Still-fishing is good at Ruth Recreation Area Campground. Top-line troll Super Dupers, Rooster Tails and Kastmasters. Use lead-core line later in the season. Bait dunkers will have good results with either salmon eggs, Power Baits and marshmallow combos or nightcrawlers. For information contact the Ruth Lake Recreation Area, (707) 574-6251.

The Trinity Alps Wilderness and Trinity Divide

There are over 100 serene little lakes to pick from in the alpine mountains north and west of Trinity Lake. Some areas are primarily accessible by auto, and not just four-wheel drive. Other waters require not much more than a two-mile walk. But some require a multi-day pack-in.

The Trinity Alps Wilderness has about 55 fishable lakes within its 283,000 acres. Lakes vary from 1 to 40 acres and most are found between 5,000 to 7,000 feet. This wilderness area, the second largest in the state, is a land of rugged granite mountains, alpine basins and lush meadows. Two convenient access points are Stuart Fork near Trinity Alps Resort (Hwy, 3) and Big Flat (end of Coffee Creek Rd). The following are trip suggestions in the alps or the divide.

Alps

Take Union Creek Trail to Landers Lake for medium-sized rainbows, or Swift Creek Trail to Ward and Horseshoe Lakes for hot brookie action. For additional rainbow and brookie activity, take the Boulder Lakes Trail to the lakes of the same name.

The Trinity Divide is west of I-5, north of Lake Shasta. The town of Dunsmuir is central to the divide. There is minimal snowpack in this forest playground with most lakes in the 6,000 to 8,000 foot elevation.

Divide

"Hoof" it a little with short-day hikes into Deadfall Lakes for brookies and browns. It's about a 90-minute walk. Or, take the jeep road from the South Fork of the Sacramento River to Cedar Terrace, Lower, Middle and Upper Cliff Lakes. Brookies, rainbows and German browns are possible. For the more adventuresome who like to "four-wheel-it," motor out of Castella on Hwy-5 to Tamarack and Twin Lakes for rainbow and brookie fishin'. Baits like red worms, crickets, grubs and salmon eggs will produce throughout the Alps and Divide waters. However, don't forget to pack in some fly'n bubble rigs. You can cover a lot more territory on these mountain lakes with this setup. The Black Ant, Joe's Hopper, Light Cahill, Coachman, Mosquito, Adams and California Mosquito are winning dry fly patterns in this region.

Maps of the wilderness area and of the surrounding national forest are available from Shasta-Trinity National Forest, 2400 Washington Ave., Redding, CA 96001, (916) 246-5222. Also contact the Shasta-Cascade Wonderland Association, 1250 Parkview Ave., Redding, CA 96001, (916) 243-2643.

Trinity Lake

Trinity is a beautiful, alpine-type lake located on the southern fringe of the Trinity Alps. It has complete resort, boating and camping facilities and is located about 45 miles west of Redding. Way up in this rugged section of the state, Trinity Lake offers some terrific troutin'. This large, 17,000 acre lake, rests at only 2,400 feet elevation. It receives heavy plants of 9 to 13 inch rainbows but quite a few 20 inch class fish hold over each year. There is a similar, but smaller, hold-over population of quality German browns.

An orchestrated trolling program will definitely produce results at Trinity. Troll from the dam to the western arms of the lake in the spring. The dam area is also a good trolling spot later in the year with its cooler, deeper water. Blades'n crawlers, assorted Needlefish, chrome Kastmasters, Z-Rays, Phoebes, Triple Teazers and Deep Wee-R plugs are trolling favorites. Remember, you may have to go to lead core or downriggers by mid-August to drag the lures at 40 foot depths.

Still-fishing in the west coves, the mouths of the feeder streams, Stuart's Fork, the North Fork of the Trinity River and the Swift Creek area are popular bank fishin' places. You can't go wrong with salmon eggs, assorted cheese baits, red worms or live nightcrawlers. Dry fly fishermen can demonstrate much prowess on Trinity's trout by fishing the locally preferred Adams or March Brown patterns.

Beside the standard lake troutin', try two other things while visiting Trinity. There are substantial numbers of kokanee salmon here. Use a downrigger with trolled Kokanee Killers. Another option is to give the feeder streams themselves a try later in the year. Coffee Creek, Stuart's Fork, Swift Creek and the Upper Trinity River are all worth exploring. For information contact the Trinity Country Chamber of Commerce, Box 517, Weaverville, CA 96093, (916) 623-6101.

Bay Area and Central Coast Trout

Quite often anglers living in a major metropolitan complex simply do not have the time to take extensive outings to more remote trout lakes and streams. Fortunately, in the Bay Area there are a wealth of smaller urban lakes that offer surprisingly good troutin'. Some are small, 35 acre lakes like Parkway out of San Jose. Others are larger such as Del Valle Lake near Castro Valley, approaching 1,100 surface acres.

Most of these lakes undergo very prominent "infusions" of weekly planted trout during the colder months. Plus, there are special commercial plants occurring that augment the standard 8 to 12 inch rainbows. You can stick real "dogs" on some of these lakes, upwards to 13 pounds! So don't just assume you are visiting a "put'n take" fishery when exploring the different Bay Area waters. Stay with light lines and subtle offerings. Be very selective, particularly with the baits you decide to use. Plan on moving around these small lakes to cover as much ground as possible, looking for concentrations of trout.

Of all the geographical sectors in the Golden State, the Central Coast, from Santa Barbara to Monterey, is conspicuously sparse in terms of major trout fisheries.

The weekender motoring into this territory will probably find the most consistent troutin' at either Lake Cachuma or Lopez Lake. Both of these medium-sized impoundments undergo extensive stocking programs of planter and larger rainbow trout. Although some of these fish will hold over from season to season, the best action will usually be from midwinter through midspring.

Lake Cachuma

Lake Cachuma is a good trout lake in a beautiful setting. The lake itself is about 7 miles long, one mile wide and covers about 3,200 surface acres. There is no swimming or water-skiing at Cachuma, so life is a little more pleasant for the summertime angler. Adding to this tranquil, oak-covered hills setting is the abundance of wildlife, including deer, bobcat and quail. Lake Cachuma is located 25 miles north of Santa Barbara and has more than 400 campsites. They are close to the lake, and some have hookups.

Year after year, Cachuma consistently kicks out a number of 1 to 2 pound rainbows for the weekend angler. Occasionally, a 5 to 6 pound "lunker" will also show up at the dock.

The lake is planted from October through March. Trollers will definitely have an advantage in the cooler months. Troll Cachuma, Johnson and Santa Cruz Bays. Then work the backside of Arrowhead Island with the trolling gear, or the south shore. Two other favorite trolling runs favored by lake locals are from the mouth of Cachuma Bay to the dam, and from the east side by the Chalk cliffs to Santa Cruz Point. Needlefish lures are far and away the stellar trolling baits. They can be either toplined or trolled behind lead-core line. The silver and bikini patterns are recommended. Kastmasters, silver Phoebes, Super Dupers and Rooster Tail spinners similarly produce with this tactic.

Bait fishermen use nightcrawlers (straight or inflated), marshmallows, salmon eggs, and Zeke's floating cheese. Be prepared to fish as deep as 40 feet when the weather starts to warm in late spring. For information contact Cachuma Lake, Star Route, Santa Barbara, CA 93105, (805) 688-4658.

Chabot Lake

Lake Chabot rates among the best Northern California urban lakes. This 315 acre lake is in the almost 5,000 acre Anthony Chabot Regional Park. Located just east of San Leandro, Chabot boasts a solid and steady supply of stocked rainbow trout. This lake has good stretches of shore fishing access, lots of large fish and a year-round schedule. Private boats are not allowed. Rowboats, canoes and electric powered boats are available for rent. The park has horse rentals, hiking, camping, a motorcycle hill area, picnicking and fishing piers. To get to Chabot, take Lake Chabot Road from Castro Valley or Fairmont Drive east from San Leandro.

Most of the rainbows caught in this heavily stocked lake are nice, 14 to 16 inch specimens. This is a very healthy average for a small impoundment. There are also some "toad" 'bows, however, surpassing the 8 pound mark at Chabot.

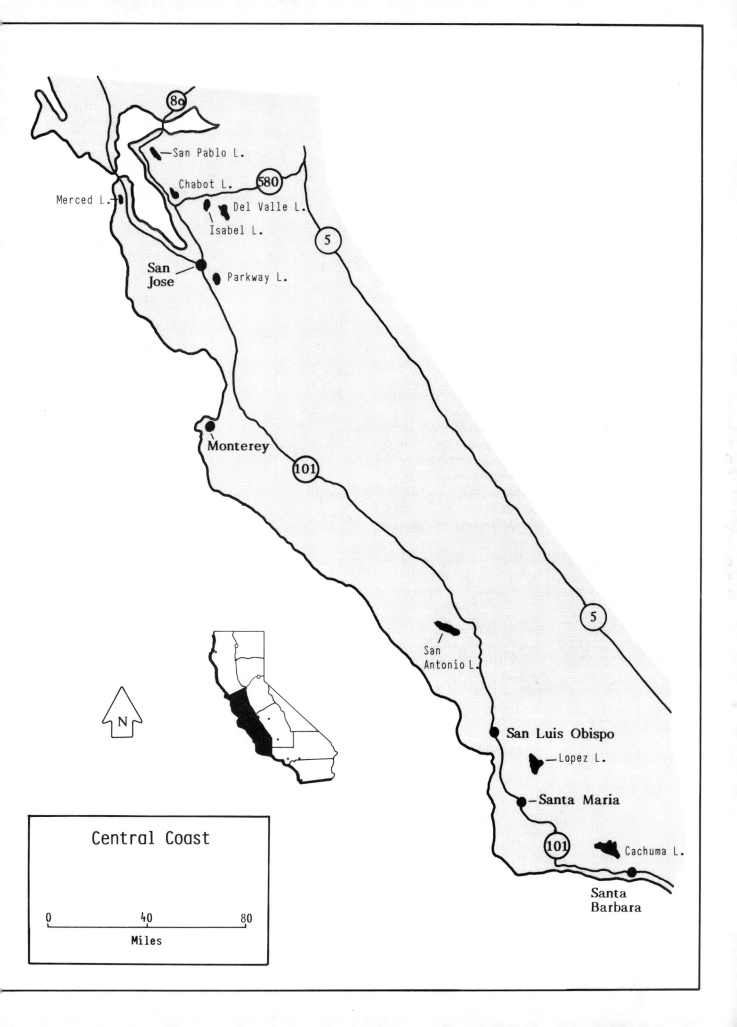

San Pablo L.

Chabot L.

580

Del Valle L.

Isabel L.

Merced L.

5

San Jose

Parkway L.

Monterey

101

San Antonio L.

5

San Luis Obispo

Lopez L.

Santa Maria

101

Cachuma L.

Santa Barbara

N

Central Coast

0   40   80

Miles

Boat anglers fill their stringers using both bait and lures. Over 90% of the shoreline is accessible by foot, so bank fishermen have an equal shot at Chabot's 'bows. The nine fishing piers are especially good for still-fishing with bait. Trollers can also get in on the action with blades'n 'crawlers, Rooster Tails, Kastmasters, Rapalas and Panther Martins on a flat-line presentation. Other areas to try from either the shore or from a boat are Alder Point, Raccoon Point, the Burner Area, the western bank and the second stairway on the east shoreline. Marshmallow and nightcrawler combos, the "Shasta Fly," chartreuse Power Bait, red eggs and Velveeta cheese are staple baits. Kastmaster and Super Duper spoons are preferred by hardware chuckers. For information contact the East Bay Regional Park District, (510) 881-1833.

Del Valle Lake

Lake Del Valle is located in Del Valle Regional Park in Livermore. This park offers year-round camping, fishing and day use. It has 1,000 surface acres of water and 16 miles of shoreline. Del Valle attracts large crowds in the summer, but October through May provides plenty of open space for trout fishing. Facilities include developed campsites, snack bar, day use areas, complete bait and tackle sales, boat rentals and a six-lane boat launching ramp. Swimming is allowed and a 10 m.p.h. speed limit is enforced on the lake. Just out of Castro Valley, Bay Area anglers can find some fantastic action is just a short drive. Del Valle is another prominently stocked lake in this metropolitan basin.

The southeast shoreline is a super section of the lake to fish with either bait or lures. In warmer months, lake regulars huddle near Swallow Rock in the cove near the dam for some deep-water bait soakin'. The narrows is another spot to try. Del Valle trout are not overly sophisticated and keep their tastes pretty simple: red salmon eggs, Velveeta cheese, chartreuse and yellow Power Bait, marshmallows and inflated nightcrawlers. Kastmasters, Panther Martins, Rooster Tails and Rapalas are the major types of hardware used on Del Valle's rainbows. They can be tossed from the bank or trolled from a boat. For information contact Del Valle Park, 6999 Del Valle Rd., Livermore, CA 94550, (510) 373-0332.

Lake Isabel

If you live in the Bay Area near Livermore, then sharpen your hooks, get out your bait dunkin' rigs and head to Isabel! This little lake gets a 1,000 to 3,000 pound plant of solid stocker rainbows each week during the cold weather months. But don't be shocked if you hang a 5 to 10 pound "lunker" 'bow that was thrown in to spice up the action. You can fish Isabel from shore or boat, but no private boats are permitted. Rental boats with electric trolling motors are available.

Equip yourself with a "grocery list" of baits including red worms, nightcrawlers, salmon eggs, marshmallows and mealworms. Lake regulars like to use marshmallow'n 'crawler or worm'n marshmallow combos. Sometimes, the mealworms work best in conjunction with other baits as a "topping." Fan-casters can get into the excitement with 3/8 ounce gold Kastmasters, assorted Rooster Tails and small Rebels and Rapalas. For information contact Lake Isabel, 1421 Isabel Ave., Livermore, CA 94550, (415) 462-1281.

Lopez Lake

Lopez Lake, located between San Luis Obispo and Santa Maria, off Hwy. 101, provides excellent angling for trout. Known by some as an outstanding sailboarding spot, it's also a fine boating, camping and fishing locale. The lake is in a beautiful hilly setting, surrounded by oak trees. Lopez is open all year and has campsites, bait and tackle, grocery store, picnic areas and hiking trails.

There are lots of pan-sized rainbow trout at this lake during the early part of the season. It is estimated that from 70,000 to 100,000 catchable trout are planted each year at Lopez! There are over 22 miles of shoreline on this modestly sized 950 acre lake and much of it is accessible for shoreline fishing.

Still-fishing from either bank or boat is the most popular technique. A variety of areas around the lake seem to produce. The main gate sector, the gas dock, Lopez Arm, the horse corral in the Wittenburg Arm, Cottonwood Cove, the Arroyo Grande Arm and along the dam are all good spots to try. Bait offerings should include Velveeta, inflated 'crawlers, salmon eggs, and the "Shasta Fly" (salmon egg/marshmallow combo).

Trolling should also be contemplated at Lopez. In the colder months, top-line with gold Super Dupers or silver Kastmasters. Use these and similar lures on lead-core line, working down to 40 feet during the late spring. For information contact Lopez Lake, Rte. 2, Box 850, Arroyo Grande, CA 93420, (805) 489-2095.

Merced Lake

Both lakes at Merced provide very good trout fishing year-round. No need to travel hundreds of miles when this fine fishery is located in San Francisco, in the heart of the Bay Area. Trout fishing tends to be best in the spring and fall but the coastal weather keeps water conditions good throughout the summer. Because of limited run-off, the water remains clear in the winter providing good fishing conditions. Rainbow trout are king, with fish ranging from 6 inches to 10 pounds. Two pound trout from the North Lake are very common. Sometimes the bite is "hot" on the North Lake, other times it seems to center around the South Lake. One thing is for certain, though, definitely work off the tule banks on these lakes, especially with bait. The trout will home in on cheese spreads, nightcrawlers, salmon eggs, miniature marshmallows, assorted Power Baits, and Zeke's garlic cheese floating baits.

Shore fishing is possible all around the lakes. Bank walkers geared up with 4 to 6 pound monofilament and spinning combos can cover a lot of territory and string some of Merced's stocker bows. It is essential to keep moving, and use light leaders in about 2 to 3 pound test. Mepps, Rooster Tails, Panther Martins and Z-Rays will nail these planters while casted from the bank. These same offerings will also produce on a top-line trolling pattern, or switch to small flasher blades and a night-crawler trailer. For information contact the Lake Merced Boating and Fishing Co., 1 Harding Rd., San Francisco, CA 94132, (415) 753-1101.

Parkway Lake

Parkway Lake is a very good, urban trophy trout fishery that is located only about a 30 minute drive for most anglers in the South Bay. Head south on Hwy. 101 in San Jose, take Bernal Road to Monterey Road (Rte. 82) south to Metcaff Road and into Parkway Lake. With the expres-

sion, "good things come in small packages" in mind, consider little 35 acre Parkway Lake for some "red hot" troutin'. This tiny, private lake is well-stocked with rainbows from September to May. Most of these are chunky 1 to 1 1/2 pound class fish, but there have been brooders caught over 13 pounds!

The best areas to try are at the northwest corner and the south end of the lake. Both lures and bait will be effective with the edge going to bait soakers. Garlic-flavored miniature marshmallows, chartreuse Power Bait, red salmon eggs, inflated nightcrawlers and regular white marshmallows are recommended. A local tip is to use a small marshmallow with a mealworm laced together.

Gold Kastmasters, Panther Martins, the Mepps Lightning series of spinners, and Rooster Tails in assorted colors are standard choices for lure slingers at Parkway. Definitely try spot-casting the south shoreline with any of these popular trout lures. For information contact Parkway Lakes, (408) 463-0711.

San Pablo Lake

Excellent fishing is available at this day-use reservoir located just east of the San Francisco Bay near Berkeley. San Pablo Reservoir is a narrow lake about 4 miles long. The San Pablo record rainbow is 9 1/4 pounds, and many are caught in the 3-6 pound range. Trout plants, done weekly, average about 1 pound per fish. Anglers at San Pablo frequently average 2-3 trout per rod, from both boat and shore. This lake offers many good shore fishing locations for trout. For boaters, a topographical map showing the holes for fish is for sale at the lake for less than $1.00. San Pablo is closed from mid-November to mid-February.

Trout shore fishing at San Pablo is best using a sliding sinker rig and salmon eggs, yellow and chartreuse Power Bait, marshmallows, nightcrawlers and cheese. Inflating nightcrawlers or using marshmallows to float up the eggs, nightcrawlers or cheese are effective. Casting spinners and spoons also works from shore. Boat anglers troll nightcrawlers, Rooster Tails, Triple Teazers, Needlefish, Kastmasters and Panther Martins. For information contact That Dam Company, 7301 San Pablo Dr., El Sobrante, CA 94803, (510) 223-1661.

Mid South Trout

It is no understatement that trout fishing near this major urban center of the Golden State can be very challenging. The key to success is timing. The water warms quickly in these lower elevation lakes. So the best times for some serious troutin' is typically late winter through early spring. Most trout caught in these waters are planted rainbows in the 8 to 12 and pan-sized class. But, don't underestimate some of the lakes. Commercially subsidized stocking programs augment the fish the state provides, with larger, magnum-sized specimens up to 10 pounds! So always make sure your tackle is in proper order.

Two real treats in this zone are the West Fork of the San Gabriel River and Upper Sespe Creek. They are bonafide wild trout rivers offering some of the most spectacular troutin' in the state. These are protected stretches of stream where all trout caught must be immediately released. True sportsmen will appreciate the fighting qualities of the West Fork and Sespes' wild rainbows!

There are three standout trout lakes in the San Bernardino area that offer an alpine setting a few hours from downtown Los Angeles. In order of performance these are Big Bear Lake, Lake Gregory and Lake Silverwood. All are popular escapes for the weekend urbanite. Boaters, shore fishermen, trollers, hardware chuckers, bait dunkers—the whole spectrum of trouters—will find these three lakes to their liking.

Fly fishing purists should consider exploring the three major streams of the San Bernardino Mountains: the Santa Ana River, Bear Creek and Deep Creek. Each has its own unique brand of troutin' on tap and all three are excellent getaways for the angler seeking more isolated waters in Southern California.

Big Bear Lake

Long considered the "Jewel" of Southern California trout lakes, Big Bear is the largest lake in the San Bernardino Mountains. Full, four-season opportunities await the serious angler here, including ice fishing in the winter. The best troutin', however, is later spring through fall. It is 7 1/2 miles long and up to 1 1/2 miles wide, with about 22 miles of shoreline. Maximum depth is about 70 feet. Big Bear is located about 90 miles east of Los Angeles in the San Bernardino National Forest. A wide variety of facilities are available, including marinas, campgrounds, restaurants and motels at this popular resort area.

After the first major warm spell, look to the east end of the lake near the Stanfield cut-off for early season action. This is the shallowest section of the lake and is where the water will warm up first in the spring. Standard bait offerings will work at this time. Floating baits such as Zeke's in yellow garlic, corn or salmon egg flavors are particularly good since they suspend above the weedy bottom. Inflated 'crawlers are similarly effective. Spoons tossed from the bank such as gold Phoebes and Kastmasters will produce in the deeper waters moving west on the lake.

As temperatures increase, try some of the sheltered bays such as Boulder and Metcalf, the fishing dock at Gray's Landing, or the dam area at the far west end. Salmon eggs—particularly a larger single red egg—will often be the "hot ticket" still-fished in this deep water. "Christmas tree" combinations of either Velveeta cheese and red salmon eggs, or white marshmallow and red eggs on a treble hook are long-time favorites at Big Bear as is orange, chartreuse or pink Power Bait. Light 2 to 3 pound leaders and sliding sinkers are best. Gobs of red worms sometimes work right on the bottom.

Trollers will do well during the height of the season moving back and forth in front of the observatory or down mid-lake. Both flat-line and lead-core strategies are viable options. Assorted lake trolls such as the Dave Davis and Ford Fender with a 'crawler trailer are effective as are various plugs such as the chrome Pope Fishback or gold or rainbow trout CD-7 Rapala. Spoons like the gold Phoebe, frog- or bikini-colored Needlefish or Z-Ray are also good trolling choices. A tiny Scrounger lure in chartreuse, silver or smoke sparkle is also a Big Bear secret, especially on the slow-troll.

Fly fishing can also be remarkably spectacular at Big Bear during the warmer months. Shore casting or fly-trolling with traditional fly fishing gear will work. Bubble and fly rigs will give bank fishermen and waders an excellent opportunity to take some quality 1 to 3 pound 'bows. Preferred patterns include the Royal Coachman, Renegade, Adams, California Mosquito, White Miller, Black Gnat and Ginger Quill. Again, light leader material

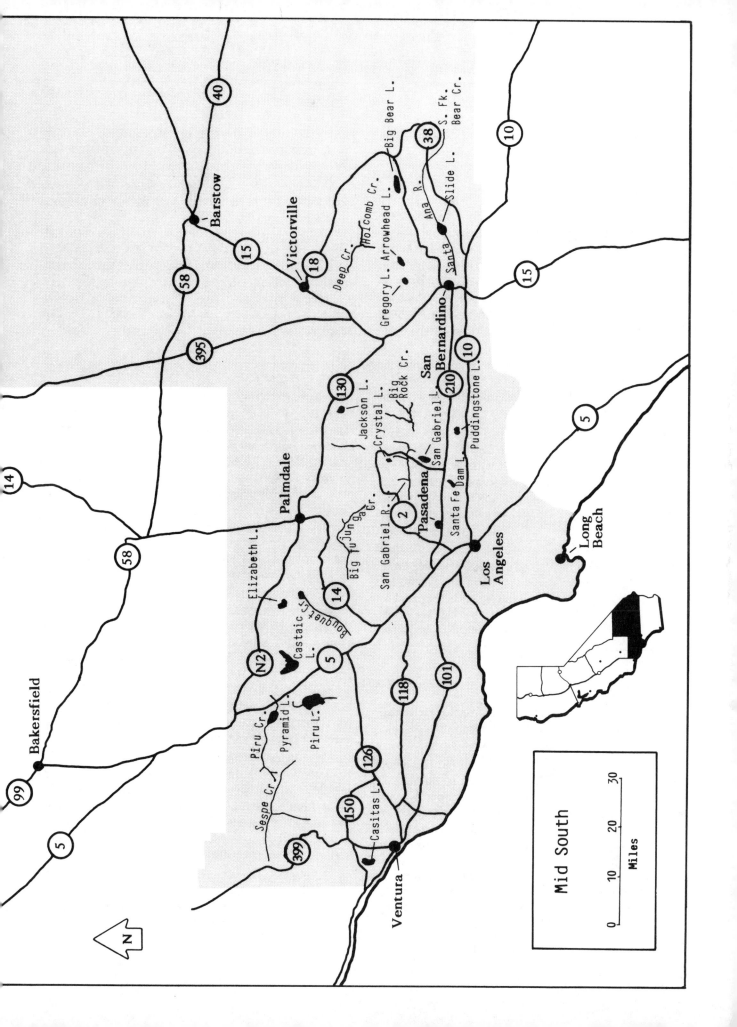

is a must. For information contact the Big Bear Chamber of Commerce, (909) 866-4607.

Lake Casitas

Often considered one of the most highly visited lakes in the entire state, Casitas does offer some substantial troutin' for recreational fishermen. Rainbow trout are stocked in Casitas from October to May. The lake has 32 miles of shoreline around its 2,700 acres of water. Facilities at Casitas are complete. There are 480 developed camp-sites. No bodily contact with the water is allowed. Lake Casitas is located 78 miles from Los Angeles; 12 miles north of Ventura.

The Wadleigh Arm is no doubt the top spot to try in the late winter through early spring. Other locations that are frequented by boaters are the dam, the coves west of the main island, and the buoy line.

Nightcrawlers are "Numero Uno" as far as trout baits are concerned. The rainbows at Casitas inhale these magnum-sized worms, especially in the Wadleigh Arm. Velveeta cheese, Power Baits, and salmon eggs would be strong second and third choices. Interestingly, trollers seem to stick the larger fish, while bait dunkers rack up the volume.

As the weather and water warms, bring out the lead-core outfits and pull lures 6 to 10 colors. The deep water by the dam is perfect for this approach. The Needlefish spoon in frog, grasshopper or bikini patterns are your best trolling bets. For information contact the Casitas Recreation Area, 11311 Santa Ana Rd., Ventura, CA 93001, (805) 649-2233.

Castaic Lake

Being so close to the downtown Los Angeles metropolitan area means a lot of weekend pressure for this lake. Trout fishing ranges from poor to excellent.

Timing is critical in planning your trips. The colder months are the best for sustained troutin' on Castaic. Both the main lake and the afterbay hold trout. Keep in mind, however, that no power boats with large motors are allowed on the afterbay. Only boats with electric trolling motors are permitted. The Afterbay is 180 acres, while the lake itself is about 2,500 acres. Castaic is located in a recreation area of over 9,000 acres, but there are no public camping facilities. Picnicking, a snack bar, marina, bait and tackle facilities and camping are nearby. Take the Hughes Exit off I-5. Castaic can be a good trout fishery because of Dept. of Fish and Game plantings nearly nine months of the year. The largest rainbow is over 10 pounds.

Time after time, the best trout action will be found along the face of the main dam. Bank fishing, trolling and still-fishing from boats are popular along this stretch. Trollers also will drag trout up from the ski arm with lead-core outfits. Bait dunkers use Velveeta, salmon eggs, marshmallows, eggs'n 'mallow combos and inflated night-crawlers. Trollers, either flat-lining or using lead core, will rack up some scores with Kastmasters and Needle-fish lures. For information contact Castaic Lake, Box 397, Castaic, CA 91310, (805) 257-4050.

Lake Gregory

Located out of Crestline in the San Bernardino Mountains, Lake Gregory offers year-round troutin' with less than a two-hour drive from Los Angeles. The lake rests at an altitude of 4,500 feet. Bank fishing is permitted all year, while rental boats are available only from the last Saturday in April to the third Sunday in October. Sailboats are the only private boats allowed on Gregory. Lake Gregory has 41 miles of shoreline (most of it providing fine shore fishing) and 120 surface acres of water. There is no charge for shore fishing. Bank anglers can fish from one hour before sunrise to one hour after sunset. There is no camping at the lake. Swimming and picnic facilities are provided June through August.

It is possible to catch trout on a variety of methods at this little alpine lake. Bait dunkers traditionally take their share of 1 to 2 pound fish with standard fare. Marshmallows, cheese, floating baits, salmon eggs and nightcrawlers, fished separately or in combination, will generate strikes. Still-fishing is very popular near the dam area, across from the bait house, and near the south parking lot. Bait offerings do particularly well in the summer months when the trout move to deeper water by midday.

Top-line trolling and lake trolls are also productive. Regionally popular lures such as the Rooster Tail, Panther Martin and Mepps spinners are favorite top-line picks. Similarly spoons such as the Super Duper, Needle-fish and Kastmaster will also be effective on the troll. Dave Davis combos with a nightcrawler trailer are solid choices for added trolling possibilities.

During the warmer months the dry fly action can be outstanding at Gregory. The bubble and fly setup is popular with spin fishermen. The bobber and Finger Jig combo can be equally deadly. Conventional fly fishers can fly-troll or cast from the shore. No wading or float tubing is permitted. Stay with basic dry fly patterns such as the California Mosquito, Renegade or Black Gnat. Larger streamer flies like the Muddler, Carey Special, Hornbeck or Matuka will produce, fished deeper or on the fly-troll. For information contact Lake Gregory Regional Park, Box 656, Crestline, CA 92325, (909) 338-2233.

Lake Piru

This lake provides considerable troutin' activity from December to March. Although water levels can fluctuate at this lake from season to season, the trout fishing appears to be unaffected. Lake Piru is a fine, all-around outdoor recreational complex that is about 50 miles north of Los Angeles. Camping and other facilities are very nice, and all water sports (including water-skiing and swimming) are permitted. At capacity, Piru covers 1,200 surface acres. There are about 250 campsites, a five-lane concrete launch ramp, a tackle shop, snack bar and boat rental. Rainbow trout are planted in the winter months; this is the best angling time, especially for shore anglers along the west shore. But trollers who can get down will catch fish in the summer.

There are some prime locations at Piru that seem to hold trout year after year. Bait fishers should try the north end, especially if the creek water is running into this portion of the lake. Cow Cove, San Felicia Cove and the dam are also viable spots. Nightcrawlers, Velveeta, yellow and pink Power Bait, Zeke's garlic cheese, marshmallows and salmon eggs are reliable baits for Piru's rainbows.

Lead-core enthusiasts also seem to consistently drag up limits at Piru. Work 8 to 10 colors, particularly in the dam area and down the center of the lake. Without question, the #3 Needlefish lure is the "prime" trolling lure for this lake. Bikini, gold, pearl, frog and silver all produce. Occasionally, bank walkers will get into a hot bite tossing gold Kastmasters from the shore. For information contact Lake Piru, Box 202, Piru, CA 93040, (805) 521-1500.

Puddingstone Lake

Puddingstone Lake, at an elevation of 940 feet, is located in the 2,000 acre Bonelli Regional Park, administered by the Los Angeles County Department of Parks and Recreation. This is a complete recreational facility and the 250 surface acre lake has full marine services and is open to all boating.

Puddingstone warms too much in the summer to foster any trout life, making hold-overs virtually non-existent at this metropolitan lake. But with bolstered stocking programs during the late winter and spring, it is often possible to tie into a 10 pound brood stock rainbow at Puddingstone. Bank fishing is very popular at this lake. Velveeta cheese, chartreuse and yellow Power Bait, and nightcrawlers produce well. Most of the shore angling is done at the west and east ends. Shore fishermen should also walk around the bank and fan-cast with gold Super Dupers, Kastmasters, Mepps Syclops or Phoebe spoons. Later in the spring, try using lead-core line along the cliffs in deeper water. All of the above-mentioned lures will pull nicely on the end of a lead-core rig. For information contact Bonelli Park, 120 E. Via Verde, San Dimas, CA 91773, (909) 599-8411.

San Bernardino Area Streams

There are three rather interesting streams in the San Bernardino Mountains that are typically overlooked by the average trouter. The Santa Ana River, Bear Creek and Deep Creek each have different ecological complexions and support some modestly good fisheries.

The Santa Ana River

There are basically four distinct stretches of this river. The "Lower Canyon" runs from the Edison Plant on Greenspot Road upstream to where Bear Creek converges. The "Gorge" is upstream from Bear Creek and tumbles four miles to where the paved Seven Oaks Road intersects with the stream. The "Seven Oaks" stretch itself meanders upstream from this intersection to where the South Fork joins it. Finally, the "Headwaters" are comprised of the South Fork and Fish Creek tributaries that filter out from the wilderness area.

The Lower Canyon can have a decent rainbow community in high water years. Look to find better concentrations of fish where the feeder creeks enter into the main river. The Gorge is renowned among fly fishers for its solid brown trout fishing. Many 12 to 15 inch class browns are caught in the Gorge each season. Be ready to do some hiking into this rugged terrain and watch out for rattlesnakes! The Seven Oaks stretch is occasionally planted with hatchery rainbows but typically sustains a population of smaller wild trout. The Headwaters has some spectacular colored brown trout, but here again, most specimens are 6 to 7 inch fish.

Bear Creek

Entry into this secluded stream is reached by Hwy. 38 from the road or from Hwy. 18 for trail access. Most anglers prefer to take Forest Service roads IN10 or IN09. The upper canyon of this creek is considered best. As with other creeks, the higher up you hike into this remote canyon, the more isolated, less-pressured fishing spots you will encounter.

Deep Creek

This is a true, designated wild Trout Stream dictating a strict catch'n release policy. There are both browns and rainbows inhabiting this water, many pushing the 16 inch mark. Only barbless single-hook artificial lures or flies are allowed. Take Hwy. 18 north from San Bernardino to Cedar Glen, then follow the Hook Creek Road down to Spinter's Cabin, which will be your departure point.

A word of caution: secure a good topographical map of the San Bernardino Forest Area when venturing into this region. All three of these streams should be considered wilderness territory despite their proximity to urban centers. Also, during warmer months, always be on the look out for rattlesnakes that inhabit the banks of these streams.

Novice hikers could get disoriented or lost without the use of topographical maps.

As for fishing these waters in the unrestricted areas, natural baits such as hellgrammites, stonefly nymphs, beetles, ants, caddisfly larvae, 'hoppers or crickets are superb. Leave your commercial baits at home. Fly fishermen should scale down with smaller dry or wet flies and use light tippets. Popular dry fly patterns in this region include the Royal Coachman, Adams, Renegade, Black Gnat and Elk Hair Caddis. Smaller wet offerings like the Hare's Ear, Ram Caddis and Wooly Worm similarly produce. For information contact the San Bernardino National Forest, 144 N. Mt. View Ave., San Bernardino, CA 92408, (909) 383-5588.

San Gabriel River

The word "amazing" would be appropriate to describe this little river, located 90 minutes from downtown L.A. Once given up on as a lost proposition, the West Fork of the San Gabriel has been revived into one of the finest

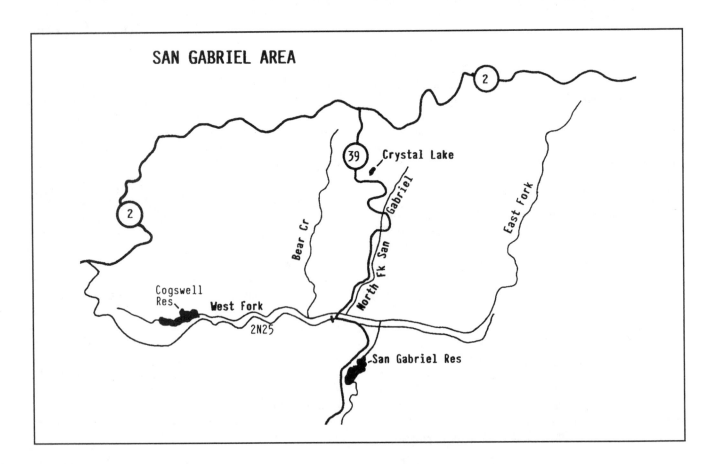

wild trout waters in the West! A concerted effort among environmentalists, dedicated fly fishermen and Department of Fish and Game authorities has made this possible.

Start out past the Rincon Ranger Station and go by foot, or by bike. The section from the second bridge where Bear Creek converges with the West Fork on downstream is unrestricted. Small nightcrawlers, salmon eggs, and red worms are commonly used by spin fishermen. Ultralight Colorado spinners and, occasionally, dry flies, will also produce on this stretch.

The water upstream from the second bridge to the base of Cogswell Dam is a strict catch'n release run. Only artificial lures with single, barbless hooks can be fished here. This amounts to almost 5 1/2 miles of wild trout water—the uppermost reaches providing the best action. These are mostly 8 to 12 inch wild rainbows; however, 15 inch fish have been caught and released.

Spring and fall are the best seasons on the West Fork for fly fishing buffs. Wet flies such as the Hare's Ear, Zug Bug, or Renegade are winners. So are assorted dry flies, but be prepared to scale down all the way to a tiny size 26 for super clear, shallow areas. A virtual cavalcade of popular dry fly patterns have historically produced along this protected segment of the San Gabriel River. Some of these are the Mosquito, Adams, Red Ant, Royal Coachman, Griffith's Gnat, Light Cahill, Humpy, Blue Wing Olive, Elk Hair Caddis and the Gray Parachute. Be extra careful to protect this delicate fishery. It is an absolute treasure hidden in the hills above L.A.!

The San Gabriel Mountains have more to offer anglers, beside the West Fork. There is also the North Fork and the East Fork of the San Gabriel River, Bear Creek, San Gabriel Reservoir and Crystal Lake.

The North and West Forks are right in the vicinity of the wild trout waters, as is Bear Creek. The North Fork is accessible from Rte. 39 along its entire length, whereas the East Fork requires use of a hiking trail that parallels it. These waters are heavily planted and heavily fished. Most anglers use salmon eggs and nightcrawlers, but flies are also popular.

Bear Creek runs north off of the West Fork right into the San Gabriel Wilderness. Fishing can be quite good, but the terrain is difficult. A backpacking permit is required.

Crystal Lake is a tiny (7 acre) trout water, off Rte. 39, along the North Fork. Since you can drive right up to it, it is heavily fished.

San Gabriel Reservoir is also conveniently located right near Rte. 39. But you can't drive to it. And, in fact, its banks are so steep that hiking along it is no easy task. But the rewards to determined anglers are many. Many of the trout that are planted upstream in the San Gabriel River end up in San Gabriel Reservoir. And because of the difficult terrain, this lake is lightly fished. So the trout are larger (14 inches or more) and less leery. Bait, spinners and spoons are suggested here.

There are a number of campgrounds in the San Gabriel River Area. For information contact the Angeles National Forest, Pasadena, CA, (818) 557-0500.

Santa Fe Dam Lake

This metropolitan reservoir near the city of Glendora is a real "rising star" among Southern California's troutin' fraternity! It is not a very large lake, but it undergoes substantial planting of healthy-sized rainbows in the cooler months.

Bank fishermen will love Santa Fe—you can walk and fish practically all around the perimeter. Coots Point, the island, the swimming beach, the pier, and the overflow area are all prime spots. Nightcrawlers, red eggs, meal worms (plain and with marshmallows), Zeke's floating cheese, Velveeta, red worms and marshmallows round out the smorgasbord of baits that produce at Santa Fe. Most offerings are fished off the bottom, but occasionally use a red'n white float to lazily drift worms, 'crawlers or eggs.

Recurrently there will be some larger brood stock rainbows taken here, many over the 5 pound mark. It would be wise to have an arsenal of lures ready which seem to score best with Santa Fe's lunkers. The Mepps Aglia and Black Fury spinners are excellent along with metallic green Rooster Tails. Other hardware to consider are assorted Panther Martin spinners and the gold fluorescent Kastmaster spoons. Lake locals have also found that small, green crappie jigs work effectively on Santa Fe's rainbow population along with bobbers and Crappie John Finger Jig combinations. For information contact Santa Fe Dam Park, 15501 E. Arrow Hwy., Irwindale, CA, (818) 334-1065.

Upper Sespe Creek

In 1986, twenty-six miles of this little wilderness creek out of Ojai were designated part of California's Wild Trout Program. The major starting point to fishing this creek is at the Lions Campground where the Forest Service Road dead ends. The wild trout section of the Sespe begins here. There is a dirt road that parallels the creek. Anglers walk this road, hiking into various access points. Most of the wild rainbows on the Sespe are 7 to 9 inch fish. A real "bruiser" would be 15 inches. But these little "firecrackers" put on some real acrobatics for the accomplished fly fishermen.

Veteran anglers cite numerous dry flies that are perennial winners on the Sespe. The Adams, Elk Hair Caddis and Gray Mayfly are solid picks. The Gold Ribbed Hare's Ear is recognized as the best overall wet fly choice.

The Upper Sespe is perfect for dapping and a "snoop and poke" approach for the stealthy stream walker.

Lake Silverwood

This alpine reservoir can provide some remarkable trout fishing just a short drive from the Los Angeles basin. Most of Silverwood's trout are rainbows, although there are still some magnum-sized browns remaining in the lake. Silverwood has a surface area of just under 1,000 acres and a shoreline of 13 miles.

It is located 85 miles east of Los Angeles and about 30 miles north of San Bernardino, on the edge of the high Mojave Desert. Silverwood Lake offers full recreational facilities. There are 135 developed campsites, launching ramps, boat rentals, hiking trails, etc. Water-skiing is permitted.

The Cleghorn and Miller's Canyon sectors have historically produced well for both boaters and shore fishermen, especially near the creek inlets. Velveeta, Zeke's, pink and yellow Power Bait, red eggs and nightcrawlers are all effective. Boaters should also try near the dam and spillway area. Drifting nightcrawlers can often be the "secret bait." Lead-core line and downriggers will drag up Silverwood's 'bows later in the season. Use rainbow trout colored Needlefish, silver Kastmasters, silver Phoebes and assorted Rooster Tail spinners.

Always be prepared for strong, gusty winds, rough water and drops in temperature when boating at Silverwood. Weather changes occur very rapidly in this canyon. For information contact Silverwood Lake, Star Route, Box 7A, Hesperia, CA 92345, (619) 389-2303.

Far South Trout

It would be hard to dispute the fact that more trophy-class rainbows are taken from Orange County waters than anywhere in California! Irvine and the Santa Ana River Lakes have an astonishing track record in this regard. Due to a concerted effort by lake concessionaires to purchase magnum-sized commercially raised rainbows, these three lakes offer the urbanite the chance to nail a lunker a few minutes from home. However, don't take these lakes for granted. It will take some cunning and skill to consistently take limits from these waters, especially for the larger specimens. Quality tackle, precise bait selections and fine diameter leaders are in order.

There are not that many takes in Riverside County that support a trout fishery, but those that do, offer some pretty good action. Lake Skinner has to be the hallmark of trout lakes in this region. Although not known for quality rainbows, Skinner kicks out quantities of 1 to 2 pound class fish for over 9 months a year. Corona Lake specializes in magnum-sized trout. It is always possible to tie into a rainbow in double-digit weight during the height of Corona's season. Lakes Perris and Cahuilla don't seem to get the respect from trouters they justly deserve. Both lakes have solid stocking programs during the cooler months with not that much angling pressure.

Southern Californians should consider visiting more of San Diego County's prominent trout waters during the winter and early spring. Most of these lakes are not trophy fisheries in the sense of kicking out 5 to 6 pound lunkers each season. But the volume of fish on lakes like Poway, Jennings and Cuyamaca is simply outstanding and limits are common!

Lake Cahuilla

It may be hard to fathom, but there is troutin' in the desert. Just head out to Lake Cahuilla during the winter and early spring. Lake Cahuilla, in Riverside County, is located about six miles southwest of Indio. This 135 surface acre lake and surrounding park (camping, swimming, etc.) are operated by Riverside County. You can launch small, non-gas powered boats from the bank at the beach area. Electric motors are permitted. The trout at Cahuilla are standard, pan-size rainbows, but don't be surprised to see a 5 to 8 pounder on a stringer from time to time.

The best shore fishing is at the beach area to the left of the station and around the inlet to the right of the station. Bait fishermen run up the best tallies at Cahuilla. Stay with the standard "menu" of eggs, 'crawlers, Velveeta, marshmallows, chartreuse and yellow Power Bait, and Zeke's. Light, 1 to 2 pound test leaders will result in more bites. On that note, give 1/32 to 1/64 ounce mini-jigs a try here suspended underneath a bobber or two pound test mono. Stay with smoke sparkle and chartreuse colors with the minis. For information contact Riverside County Parks, Box 3507, Rubidoux, CA 92519, (909) 787-2551.

Corona Lake

This little "patch" of water is only 86 acres at its fullest and yet it kicks out 15 pound class rainbows! There again, smart lake concessionaires take that extra effort to purchase some real "hawgs" from special hatcheries to keep angler interest at a high pitch. Corona Lake can be reached by taking Hwy. 91 (Riverside Freeway) to Corona. At Corona take I-15 south nine miles to the Indian Truck Trail off-ramp. Pass under the freeway and drive one block to Temescal Canyon Rd. Go right 1/4 mile to the lake entrance.

Bait fishermen working the bank will be pleased with the potential for nailing a lunker close to the shore. Velveeta, Zeke's, inflated 'crawlers, and marshmallows (either separately or in conjunction with a mealworm, nightcrawler or salmon eggs) consistently fill out stringers. Berkley chartreuse, orange and yellow Power Bait is also effective. Light 1 to 2 pound test leaders are mandatory for sustained action. Trollers working primarily the deeper waters by the dam and the northwest end often record the heaviest daily limits. The Mepps Lightning, Rooster Tail, Super Duper, Kastmaster and Phoebe lures are certified winners. Also, drag CD-5 or CD-7 Countdown Rapalas in gold foil or rainbow trout patterns. Keep your drags in good shape when fishing Corona—there is always the chance of tying into a real brute! For information call (909) 277-3321.

Lake Cuyamaca

San Diego County residents have kept Cuyamaca a secret for many years. Even now, with more reports filed on this lake, its remote location out of Julian still keeps it

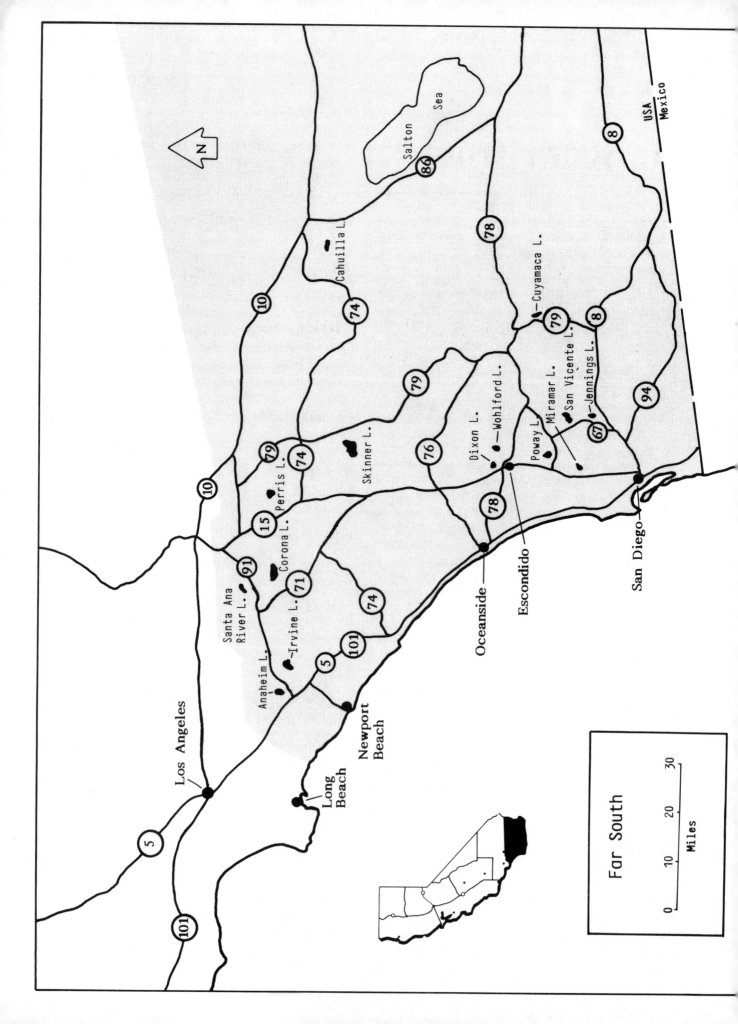

Far South

Miles

0   10   20   30

relatively unpressured. Cuyamaca is stocked with rainbows all year long. The span from November through March is the best for consistent troutin'. You can tackle the lake from either the bank or from a boat. Be forewarned that Cuyamaca can be very cold with snow during the winter. Cuyamaca is in an oak and pine cedar forest at an elevation of 4,600 feet. There is camping, horseback riding and hiking in the surrounding Cuyamaca State Park.

There's nothing magical about what these rainbows like to eat: Zeke's, Velveeta, orange Power Bait, red salmon eggs, marshmallows and inflated nightcrawlers. The log boom and the west shore areas are popular with still-fishermen. But boat anglers should not overlook the excellent trolling possibilities. Flat-line yellow or metallic green Vibrax Rooster Tails, gold Phoebes, orange Mepps Lightnings, Panther Martins, and brown, green or white standard Rooster Tails. Also try small CD-5 and CD-7 Rapala plugs, primarily in fluorescent orange, fire tiger and rainbow trout patterns. Lead core is another option during the late spring through early fall. Work a tiny Scrounger lure in either solid silver or smoke sparkle trolled 3-5 colors on the lead core line. Set up your trolling patterns along the north shore by Chamber's Park, working down the center of the lake. Cuyamaca has already produced rainbows over 8 1/2 pounds. This is no surprise to locals who fish this obscure little lake! For information contact Cuyamaca Rancho State Park, Julian, CA 92036, (619) 765-0755 or Cuyamaca Lake, (619) 765-0515.

Dixon Lake

Dixon is periodically stocked with heavy numbers of pan-sized rainbows during the cooler months (November through May). Trout in the 10 pound range are also a real possibility. Included in the standard plants, they add some "spice" to the fishery. There are no private boats allowed at Dixon. It's a 70 acre lake with 2 miles of shoreline. Boats are available with electric motors. On that note, trolling is just so-so at this lake, using small scale spinners—typically green, brown or yellow Rooster Tails and Sonic Rooster Tails. You are better off moving along fan-casting with Kastmasters, Phoebes and Mepps Syclops spoons. The buoy line by the dam, Catfish and Trout Coves are popular resting spots for still-fishermen in boats. Bank walkers like the boat dock area and Whisker Bay. Soak some Zeke's floating baits, Berkley Power Baits, Velveeta cheese, or nightcrawlers in any of the areas mentioned above. An interesting local innovation is to toss Crappie John Finger Jigs on ultralight lines for additional rainbow action.

Located just out of Escondido, Dixon is open every day and has a fairly decent warm-water program during the summer season. Dixon Lake Recreation Area, operated by the City of Escondido, is a 527 acre park with excellent camping. For information contact Dixon Lake Ranger Station, (619) 741-4680.

Irvine Lake

This little reservoir tucked away in the Orange County foothills is often heralded as the premier trophy trout fishery in the entire United States! Statistics would seem to back this claim. Irvine has taken the "put'n take" concept of commercial stocking programs one step further into the world of genetic engineering. This widely visited lake receives seasonal plants of the "triploid" strain of rainbow trout. These are special commercially raised rainbows that reach lunker-class weights in just a short time. The proprietors of this privately owned lake purchase these triploids (in addition to smaller normal hatchery rainbows) to really add to the excitement.

The trout season at Irvine begins in the late fall and lasts through late spring. The lake operators stage two major gala "openings." One signals the beginning of the fall planting program, the other coincides with the start of the Sierra trout season. The lake is really loaded with many big trout for these events. Anglers from throughout the state come to fish these openers, hoping to tie into a wallhanger. Numerous trout over the 5 pound mark are landed, with specimens the short side of 15 pounds also a possibility! It is estimated that more trophy-class fish over 5 pounds are caught at Irvine's spring opener than in all the High Sierra combined!

Numerous spinners account for some hefty stringers. The Mepps Lightning, Rooster Tail and Panther Martin are preferred. Fish these spinners in yellow, orange, black, brown and frog combinations. The water is characteristically stained here, so either dark or brightly colored lures are recommended. Try "fly-lining" a nightcrawler while drifting across the lake in a boat. Use 2 to 6 pound monofilament with no leader, and tie in a #8 to #10 baitholder hook directly to your main line. Allow these big trout to run with the bait before setting the hook. Berkley Power Baits combined with an ultrafine 2 pound test leader is another killer combo at Irvine.

Trolling or spot-casting with shad-colored plugs also can be dynamite at times. The Rapala #5, #7, #9 and #11 floating minnows, Rapala Shad Raps, and #5 Rapala Fat Rap, in particular, account for some nice Irvine 'bows. Also try some shad-colored mini-jigs on these trophy rainbow trout. Irvine's budding brown trout population is partial to silver Kastmasters and nightcrawlers. The south and west ends of Irvine have been historically the overall best spots for both boater and shoreline activity. Keep in mind, lake pros who regularly score at Irvine almost always use no more than 2-3 pound test leaders when soakin' baits. Stay "light 'n polite," as they say, to target trophy trout here. For information contact Irvine Lake, 4621 Santiago Canyon Rd., Silverado, CA 92676, (714) 649-9111.

Lake Jennings

Often overshadowed by other more prominent San Diego Lakes, little 85 acre Lake Jennings offers some of the best trout fishing in the Southland. The lake is regularly stocked in the winter through early spring. It is only opened three days per week and closes in June. It reopens in the winter. Most trout are in the 1 to 1 1/2 pound class but 6 to 8 pounders also appear each year. It's located east of El Cajon, off Hwy. 8, and there is year-round camping at the lake.

Bank fishing is truly exceptional at Jennings. The east bank is especially good. Boaters like to still-fish the deeper water by the dam. Nightcrawlers, Zeke's, Velveeta, pink, yellow and orange Power Bait, and marshmallow/mealworm cocktails are preferred baits. 'Crawlers are also good fly-lined and drifted down the center of the lake and down by the dam. Black, gray or yellow Rooster Tail spinners are popular among locals used for either top-line trolling or spot casting along the bank. For information contact San Diego County Parks, 5201 Ruffin Rd., San Diego, CA 92123, (619) 565-3600.

Lake Miramar

Miramar excels in the late winter and early spring. It is not known as a big trout lake per se, but there are a lot of 1 to 1 1/2 pounders to keep anglers happy following scheduled weekly plants. Trollers should try a flat-line approach in the early part of the season. Assorted lures including Kastmasters, CD-7 Rapalas, Mepps, Rooster Tails and Phoebes produce. All of these lures will also work for bank walkers, making long casts from the shore.

Commercial baits account for a wealth of Miramar's rainbows. Nothing fancy required: red eggs, assorted Power Bait combinations, Zeke's, Velveeta, marshmallows and nightcrawlers. The south shore is best for bait dunkers fishing from the bank. The buoy line is a favorite for boat fishermen who like to soak baits.

Lake Miramar is one of two San Diego City lakes to offer trout fishing. The other is San Vicente. Miramar is in the rolling hills below Poway. It has 162 surface acres of water, 4 miles of shoreline and is a day-use facility. For information call (619) 668-2060.

Lake Perris

Perris Lake is a fully developed, recreational area run by the California Department of Parks and Recreation. It is a good-sized lake (2,400 surface acres) that is located 70 miles east of Los Angeles and 80 miles north of San Diego. This is a great place for a family or group outing. There are three 100-foot fishing piers and three launch ramps, as well as 450 campsites, picnicking, boat rental, stores, bait and tackle.

The rainbow trout at Perris orient to the dominant threadfin shad forage. During the winter months, fish will follow the schools of bait all the way down to 80 feet. More enterprising lake regulars net their own live shad and fish them deep on split-shot rigs by the dam in 50 to 80 foot depths. Use a minnow/dropper loop rig with either CD-7 or #7-F silver foil Rapala plug.

Because this lake has the necessary depth, there are some 3 to 4 pound hold-over 'bows that survive each summer. Deep trolling with lead core or downriggers around Alessandro Island, along the dam, and Perris beach will often take one of these larger fish. Small flashers'n 'crawler combos, Mepps, Rooster Tails and Kastmasters can be pulled deep or top-lined in the colder months. Use your electronics to monitor both the trout and the threadfin shad.

Shore fishermen relegated to the marina area of the swim beaches use salmon eggs, marshmallows, chartreuse, yellow and pink Power Bait, Velveeta and Zeke's. For information contact Lake Perris, 17801 Lake Perris Drive, Perris, CA 92370, (909) 657-0676.

Lake Poway

In recent years Poway has really come into its own and is now recognized as a stellar trout lake for this portion of the state! From November through May, Poway is virtually loaded with fat, chunky rainbows. Most of the fish are nice 1 to 2 pounders, but larger 5 to 6 pounders are also intermittently recorded.

Poway is a bank fisherman's delight. The south shore, Boulder Bay, the boat dock area, the rocks at Jump Off Point and the fishing dock between the boat dock and Half Moon Bay are popular bank fishing hangouts. Inflated 'crawlers, assorted flavors of Zeke's, orange and yellow Power Bait, Velveeta, eggs and marshmallow and nightcrawler combos fished with light 2 pound leaders are the "tickets." Keep in mind that there is a lot of weed growth on the bottom so it may be necessary to "float" your bait offerings as much as possible.

Trollers work down the center of the lake starting at the log boom. Trolling is particularly good later in the year with Hot Shot spoons, Panther Martins, Triple Teazers, gold Kastmasters and either rainbow or gold CD-5 or CD-7 Rapala minnows. A variation to the trolling program pioneered by Poway's regulars, consists of drifting a 1/2 chunk of nightcrawler along the north and west side of the lake. Pinch on a small BB-sized lead shot to keep the 'crawler drifting just below the surface. Lake Poway, run by the City of Poway, is a little lake (just 60 acres) with big fishing opportunities. It is located 3 miles east of I-15 and northeast of the city of Poway. Private boats are not allowed, but boats (both row and electrically powered) are available for rent. Poway is stocked regularly with both pan-sized and larger rainbow trout. For information contact Lake Poway, Box 785, Poway, CA 92064, (619) 679-4386.

San Vicente Lake

"San Van" is a deep, often clear lake that will definitely have hold-over trout from season to season. Most of the fish are 1 to 1 1/2 pound stocker 'bows, but larger 2 to 5 pound trophies are annually included in the plants.

Trolling is the best strategy for fishing San Van's rainbows. Troll from the dam down the center of the Toll Road Arm and from the dam to North Point on the west side of Lowell Island. Lead core and downriggers will get the lures down deep to where the rainbows stratify. Rainbow trout and gold-colored sinking Rapalas, Kastmaster spoons and smaller lake trolls with 'crawler trailers should be tried. Spoons such as Hot Shot Wobblers, Kastmasters and Mepps Syclops can be fan-casted, particularly anywhere that flowing water enters into the lake. Baits such as Zeke's, red eggs, Velveeta, assorted Power

Baits and inflated nightcrawlers will account for a share of planted bows.

San Vicente Lake is one of the six lakes in the San Diego area that is owned by the City of San Diego and operated as a fishing lake as well as a reservoir. San Vicente (about 1,100 surface acres) and the much smaller Lake Miramar (about 160 acres) are the two that function primarily as trout fisheries. San Vicente Lake is open for fishing from the end of September through July 4th, Thursdays through Sundays. San Vicente is about 25 miles northeast of downtown San Diego. Facilities include boat launching, picnic area, boat rental and a store. For information contact San Vicente Lake, Lakeside, CA 92040, (619) 688-2060.

Santa Ana River Lakes

There are actually three lakes in this urban complex: Trout Lake, Catfish Lake and Chris's Pond. It is the first lake that receives the greatest fanfare with its explosive troutin'. During the early winter through spring, Trout Lake is heavily planted with "tanker class" specially bred rainbows. There are 14 pound giants in this tiny lake and larger trophies will no doubt be caught in the future.

For the city dweller, the Santa Ana River Lakes are easily reached and you can park and fish all around the lakes. Some of the traditional "hot spots" on Trout Lake are Archie's Point, La Palma Point, the Pumphouse, Rainbow Spillway and Cliff Shore. You can troll around the entire lake.

Bait dunkers consistently put the "whammy" on boaters, although trollers often score better on lunker fish. Red worms, chartreuse Power Bait, Velveeta, Zeke's floating spreads, red eggs, inflated 'crawlers, marshmallows, 'crawler or mealworm combos and single mealworms all perform quite well. The key is to keep that leader very light, preferably 2 pound test. Mepps Lightning spinners in yellow or orange, Rooster Tails in yellow or frog, and gold Kastmasters comprise the favored picks of lure tossers at the Santa Ana River Lakes. Santa Ana Lakes are located in the City of Anaheim, just north of Hwy. 91 (Riverside Fwy). Take Tustin Avenue north to La Palma. Rental boats are available and private boats can be launched in Trout Lake. For information: call (714) 632-7851.

Lake Skinner

Although this small 1,000 acre lake doesn't usually kick out any magnum-sized trout, what it lacks in quality it makes up with quantity. From late fall through mid-spring, Skinner gets planted with larger, weekly stocks of 10 to 14 inch rainbows. Far and away, the prime spot to catch trout at this lake is near the spillway at the west, but watch out. If the water in this aqueduct is flowing, get ready for some hot'n furious action! This flow creates a lot of whirlpool and turbulent currents that churn up the bait and stimulate the bite. Sheltered coves in the east and south ends of the lake and long rocky points are also good trout-holding spots at Skinner.

The southeast sector of the lake is the only area open for shore fishing and is frequented primarily by bait tossers. Salmon eggs strung in clusters on a single baitholder hook are a good bet. A marshmallow/mealworm combo is also a secret bait among lake locals. A third choice for larger fish is a 'crawler either inflated or fished on the bottom. Smaller spinners and spoons are most effective at Skinner when presented by top-line trolling. Assorted Mepps, Rooster Tails, Panther Martin spinners, and Kastmasters, Phoebe and Syclops spoons are bonafide winners. Small- to medium-sized lake trolls will also work at Skinner. These seem to perform best with half a nightcrawler used as a trailer.

As summer approaches and the remaining trout head for cooler, deeper water, definitely give lead-core trolling a try. The frog or bikini colored Needlefish is overwhelmingly the best lure to use with lead core. Bigger hold-over fish will also strike nightcrawlers still-fished in the deeper parts of the lake near the dam. Interestingly, fly fishing is noticeably absent at this lake, perhaps due to limited insect activity. However, there is a solid threadfin shad population at Skinner that the trout feed on. White Marabou streamers and small Scrounger jigs in white, clear, silver and yellow will definitely work as shad imitations for these planted rainbows. Drifting or very slow-trolling with 1/32 to 1/64 ounce mini-jigs has also caught on with Skinner's trouters. Use smoke sparkle, chartreuse or motor oil colors with these minuscule lures.

Don't overlook split-shotting live shad minnows at 30-60 foot depths—if you can catch these bait fish.

Lake Skinner, and the surrounding 6,000 acre park, is located about 90 miles southeast of Los Angeles and about 70 miles northeast of San Diego. It's 9 miles from Rancho California, east of I-15 in Riverside County. The lake is owned by the Metropolitan Water District and leased to the Riverside Parks Department. This is a dedicated fishing lake with no bodily contact with the water and a 10 m.p.h. speed limit on the water. For information contact the Parks Department, P.O. Box 3507, Rubidoux, CA 92519, (909) 926-1541.

Lake Wohlford

Just out of Escondido, Lake Wohlford has been a weekend playground for San Diego trouters for many years. From early January through the end of May, action is steady on plant-sized 'bows. Once in a while, a 10 pound brooder sneaks in at the weigh-in dock.

Shore fishermen should try the boat docks and Oakdale and Willow Coves. Boaters like the buoy line by the dam and the cove across from the docks. The standard "California Cuisine" of troutin' baits perform day in and day out at Wohlford: salmon eggs, marshmallows, nightcrawlers, Zeke's, yellow and orange Power Bait, and Velveeta. Mix and match these in combinations as well as soaking them as separate offerings. Trollers work Rooster Tails and Super Dupers along the dock areas for modest action on pan-sized bows. Also try Rapala countdown minnows in the CD-5 and CD-7 models, in either gold or rainbow trout patterns.

The City of Escondido owns the reservoir and it is maintained in conjunction with the Escondido Mutual Water Company. This is a lake that is convenient to the urban area, yet still offers a get-away-from-it-all atmosphere. Lake Wohlford opens each year around January (call for exact date) and remains open for fishing through summer. There is an unpaved launch ramp and a boat speed limit of 5 m.p.h. But many anglers fish from shore here. For information contact (619) 738-4346.

LOCATOR—Mid South and Far South Trout Waters

Including Trout Plant Information

(Only DFG Planted Waters Are Listed; Parentheses Note Planting Seasons)

Los Angeles County

ARROYO SECO CREEK (*Spring*)—Drive north on Route 2 from Foothill Boulevard at La Canada to the Switzer Forest Station. Trout plants are scattered in the creek throughout the campground.

BIG ROCK CREEK (*Spring through Winter*)—On the north side of San Gabriel Mountains. Turn off Highway 138 at Pearblossom to Valyermo and go south five miles. Stocked from Anglers Forest boundary upstream about 2 miles.

BIG TUJUNGA CREEK LOWER SECTION (*Early Spring through early Summer*)—Drive to Sunland on Foothill Boulevard. Turn north on Sunland Boulevard to Mount Gleason Avenue and continue to creek. Stocked at public access points.

BIG TUJUNGA CREEK UPPER SECTION (*Spring and early Summer*)—From LA Canada, go north on Route 2, bear left at Clear Creek Station, then north on Angeles Forest Highway (which may also be reached via Foothill Boulevard at Sunland); just above Monte Cristo Station watch for sign on your right marking turnoff to Upper Big Tujunga Canyon Road, drive south to vicinity of old Wickiup Camp. The stream is stocked from about 1/2 mile above old campground to 1 mile above Alder Creek. You can also reach the area by driving east on Route 2 then north on county road 3NI9 through Upper Big Tujunga Canyon.

BOUQUET CANYON CREEK (*Late Spring through Summer*)—Northeast of Saugus Road, parallels stream. Stocked from below Bouquet Reservoir downstream about 9 miles to Texas Canyon.

CASTAIC LAKE AND DOWNSTREAM POOL (*All year*)—14.5 miles northwest of San Fernando on Interstate Highway 5. Take Hughes Road to Castaic Lake entrance.

CRYSTAL LAKE (*Spring through Fall*)—In San Gabriel Mountains 26 miles north of Azusa via San Gabriel Canyon Road (Highway 39).

EL DORADO PARK LAKE (*Early Spring through late Fall*)—Between Willow Street and Spring Street west of 605 Freeway. Three lakes on the north side of Willow are stocked.

ELIZABETH LAKE (*Spring and Fall*)—From Los Angeles take Interstate 5 north to Castaic, turn right on Lake Hughes Road and follow it to Elizabeth Lake Road.Turn right past Lake Hughes and Munz Lake about 3 miles to Elizabeth Lake.

JACKSON LAKE (*Spring and Summer*)—In Big Pines Recreation Area west of Wrightwood on north side of San Gabriel Mountains. The location is off Interstate 15, northwest of Highway 138 to Highway 2.

LEGG LAKES (*All but Summer months*)—Between El Monte and Whittier, at intersection of Pomona Freeway and Rosemead Boulevard.

LITTLE ROCK CREEK (*Spring and carly Summer*)—Above Little Rock Reservoir in the Antelope Valley. Stocked from upper end of Little Rock Reservoir for 5 miles.

LITTLE ROCK RESERVOIR (*Spring and Summer*)—Southeast of Palmdale on desert side of San Gabriel Mountains. Turn off Highway 138 about 4 miles west of Little Rock and go south on Chesboro Road to the Reservoir.

MALIBU CREEK (*Spring*)—Travel on Highway 1 to one mile west of Malibu. Turn north on Las Virgenes Road (state highway N-1) at Pepperdine University and continue for approximately 6 miles to Malibu State Park turnoff. Turn left on the park road and proceed to parking lot; or, drive Highway 101 north to the Las Virgenes Road turnoff, 2 miles west of Calabasas. Travel south on Las Virgenes Road for 3 miles to the park entrance located on the right. Walk to the stocking areas at first and second bridges.

PECK ROAD PARK LAKE (*Fall through Spring*)—From Los Angeles take Interstate 10 east to Peck Road off ramp. Go north about 2 1/2 miles to Peck Road Park. Park will be on left going north; watch carefully for signs.

LOCATOR (*continued*)

PIRU CREEK/FRENCHMAN'S FLAT (*Late Summer through Spring*)—From Interstate 5, take Templin Highway turnoff, about 7 1/2 miles north of Castaic. Follow old Highway 99 west and north, about 5 miles to Piru Creek at Frenchman's Flat.

PUDDINGSTONE LAKE (*Fall through Spring*)—Northwest of Pomona or south of San Dimas. Turn off San Bernardino Freeway (Interstate 10) at Ganesha Drive, go north 1 mile to Puddingstone Drive and turn left to lake.

PYRAMID LAKE (*All year*)—West of I-5, about 21 miles north of I-5 and Highway 126 Intersection at Castaic Junction. Follow signs near Hungry Valley turnoff.

SAN DIMAS RESERVOIR (*Winter and Spring*)—North of San Dimas. From Foothill Blvd. go north 3 miles on San Dimas Canyon Road.

SAN GABRIEL RESERVOIR (*Spring*)—Take Foothill Freeway (Interstate 210) to San Bernardino Freeway (Interstate 10) to Azusa Avenue off-ramp (Highway 39). Go north about 9 miles to the reservoir (about 3 miles above Morris Dam).

SAN GABRIEL RIVER EAST, NORTH, WEST FORKS (*All year except North Fork, early Spring*)—All reached via San Gabriel Canyon road north from Azusa. East Fork enters San Gabriel Reservoir about 10 miles north of Azusa and is stocked from near its mouth upstream 3 miles to Cattle Canyon Guard Station. West Fork is farther up main San Gabriel Canyon, half a mile past Rincon Guard Station. Park at mouth of West Fork and fish upstream. Planted upstream to second bridge. Wild trout fishing above that point for 4 1/2 miles up to Cogswell Reservoir. North Fork parallels main canyon road and is stocked for 3 miles above its conjunction with West Fork.

SANTA FE RESERVOIR (*Fall through Spring*)—Located in the Irwindale area. From Los Angeles drive east on Interstate 210, exit south on Irwindale Avenue, drive south to First Street, turn right on First then on Peckham Road and into the county park where the lake is located.

Orange County

LAGUNA NIGUEL LAKE (*Fall through Spring*)—Take Interstate 5 (San Diego Freeway) to La Paz Road. Go west on La Paz Road to entrance to Laguna Niguel Regional Park. La Paz Road turnoff is opposite the town of Mission Viejo.

SAN JUAN CREEK (*Spring*)—Take Interstate 5 to Highway 74. Stocked from lower San Juan Campground for about 5 miles to Forest Service boundary.

TRABUCO CREEK (*Spring*) - From Interstate 5 at El Toro take El Toro Road turnoff, go north 7 miles. Bear right on Live Oak Canyon Road, then left on Trabuco Canyon Road past O'Neill Park. Stocked 2 1/2 miles above O'Neill Park.

Riverside County

CAHUILLA LAKE (*Late Fall and Spring*)—Take Intersection 10 to Indio Boulevard to Jefferson Avenue to 58th Street to reservoir southwest of Indio.

DARK CANYON CREEK (*Late Spring*)—Take Interstate 10 to Banning-Idyllwild Road (Highway 243). Stocked in the vicinity of Dark Canyon Camp.

EVANS LAKE (*Fall through Spring*)—Off Highway 60 in Fairmount Park on the northern edge of the city of Riverside.

FULLER-MILL CREEK (*Spring*)—Off Interstate 10 on Banning-Idyllwild Road (Highway 243). Stocked in vicinity of Fuller-Mill Campground where creek crosses Banning-Idyllwild Road.

FULMOR LAKE (*Spring through late Fall*)—Off Highway 243 between Banning and Idyllwild. Watch for sign on highway.

HEMET LAKE (*All year*)—On west side of Highway 74 about 4 miles south of Mountain Center. Free fishing from U S. Forest land on north side of lake.

PERRIS LAKE (*Fall through Spring*) From Highway 395 between Riverside and Perris go east on Ramona Expressway toward Lakeview about 3 miles, watch for sign.

SKINNER LAKE (*Fall, Winter, Spring*)—From the northwest on I-15 (Higwhay 394) take Temecula off-ramp, go northeast over freeway overpass, take Rancho California Road, follow signs to lake.

LOCATOR (*continued*)

STRAWBERRY CREEK (*Early Spring*)—Take Interstate 10 to Highway 243 (Banning-Idyllwild Road) through town of Idyllwild. Stream crosses under highway just south of town.

San Bernardino County

ARROWBEAR LAKE (*Late Spring*)—Off Interstate 10 east of San Bernardino, take Highway 30 to Highway 330 (City Creek Road), continue to Highway 18, right on 18 for 2 miles, lake on right side of road, watch for sign.

BIG BEAR LAKE (*Spring through late Fall*)—On Highway 10 (Rim of the World Highway) in San Bernardino Mountains. Same directions as Arrowbear only continue on to lake.

COLORADO RIVER-HAVASU (*November-December*)—From Riverside, drive north on Highway I-5 to Barstow and then travel east on Highway 40 to Needles. Turn south on Highway 95 and continue for approximately 22 miles to Havasu Lake Road. The lake is about 16 miles east of Highway 95. Turn left at the town of Havasu Lake and continue north on the highway for approximately one mile. Trout plants are at a marina in nearby waterfront housing tract.

COLORADO RIVER/NEEDLES (*Late Fall through Spring*)—Take Interstate 40 to Needles. Stocked upstream from Topock Bridge below Needles.

CUCAMONGA CREEK (*Spring*)—Northeast of Upland. From Upland go north on Euclid Avenue, turn east on Base Line Road for 1 1/2 miles, then north on Sapphire Avenue for two miles to its end. Go west one-eighth mile to get around private property, then north on paved road to dirt road then up canyon to creek crossing.

CUCAMONGA-GUASTI PARK LAKE (*late Fall through early Spring*)—One-quarter mile north of Interstate 10 on east side of Archibald Avenue.

GLEN HELEN COUNTY PARK LAKE (*Early Spring through late Fall*)—Eight miles northeast of the City of San Bernardino off Interstate 15. Take Devore off-ramp off Interstate 10.

GREEN VALLEY LAKE (*Spring through late Fall*)—Between Arrowhead and Big Bear Lake, turn north off Highway 18, which is 3 miles above Running Springs. Same directions as Arrowbear.

GREGORY LAKE (*Spring through late Fall*)—Off Highway 18 east of Crestline. Free fishing from unfenced portion of northeast shore. See directions to Arrowbear.

HOLCOMB CREEK (*Mid-Spring*)—Tributary to Deep Creek northwest of Big Bear Lake. From Fawnskin go north past Hanna Flat Campground 1 1/2 miles to Holcomb Creek crossing on Forest Road 3N14. Stocked in beaver pond areas and Crab Creek Crossing at 3N16. Same area can be reached from big Pine Flat Campground by going southwest on Road 3N16 for 5 miles to Holcomb, crossing and fishing upstream.

JENKS LAKE (*Spring and Summer*)—East from Redlands via Highway 38 to Barton Flats. Watch for sign on highway.

LYTLE CREEK, MIDDLE FORK (*Spring and Fall*)—North from Fontana via Sierra Avenue to Lytle Creek cabin area. Turn west on first dirt road past Camp Bonita Road. Stocked for 1 to 2 miles upstream.

LYTLE CREEK, NORTH FORK (*Spring and Fall*)—Same directions as Middle Fork, creek runs along Lytle Creek Road. Planted in Applewhite campground area and below middle fork junction.

MILL CREEK (*Late Spring through early Summer*)—East of Redlands on Mill Creek Road (Highway 38). Planted in immediate areas of Forest Home and Fallsvale.

MOJAVE NARROWS PARK LAKE (*Fall through early Summer*)—Off Interstate I-5, about 4 miles south of Victorville city limit. Take Bear Valley cutoff road 4 miles east; after crossing over railroad, watch for sign on left.

PRADO REGIONAL PARK (*Early Spring through late Fall*)—Take Highway 91 to Highway 71 turnoff. Travel north on 71 for 4 miles to Highway 83 and continue north on 83 for about 1 mile to the park.

LOCATOR (continued)

SANTA ANA RIVER (*Spring through mid-Winter*)—Take Highway 38 past Camp Angeles left on Seven Oaks Road to river. Stocked from Seven Oaks upstream about 7 miles to South Fork Bridge on Highway 38.

SANTA ANA RIVER SOUTH FORK (*Spring through early Fall*)—From junction with main Santa Ana River, stocked upstream from South Fork highway bridge to one mile through cabin area.

SILVERWOOD LAKE (*All year*)—Located north of San Bernardino. Take Interstate I-5 northwest of San Bernardino 17 miles to State Highway 138. East 11 miles on 138, watch for sign to lake entrance.

YUCAIPA PARK LAKE (*Fall through Spring*)—Drive Highway 10 east through Redlands to Yucaipa Boulevard turnoff. Drive northeast on Yucaipa Boulevard to Oak Glen Road, turn left.

San Diego County

CUYAMACA LAKE (*Spring through Fall*)—On Highway 79 between Julian and Descanso, 15 miles from Interstate 8.

DOANE POND (*Spring through late Fall*)—Small lake in Palomar Mountain State Park, east of Highway 395 (Interstate 15) on Highway 74, left on S6.

SAN LUIS REY RIVER (*Early Spring through late Fall*)—Flows out of Lake Henshaw. Stocked below Henshaw Dam downstream 3 miles to public campground. The stream flows along Highway 75. Same as Doane Pond except take S7.

SWEETWATER RIVER (*Spring*)—Stocked in Green Valley Camp area of Cuyamaca State Park and above highway and Green Valley area on Highway 79 between Descanso and Julian.

Santa Barbara County

CACHUMA LAKE (*Early Spring through late Fall*)—Lake is in county recreation area on Highway 154 about 20 miles northwest of Santa Barbara.

DAVY BROWN CREEK (*Early Spring*)—Take U.S. 101, right on Hwy. 154, continue to town of Los Olivos, turn north on Figueroa Mountain Rd. and go about 24 miles to Davy Brown Campground. Plants are scattered from campground to Manzana Canyon.

MANZANA CREEK (*Early Spring*)—Continue 1 1/2 miles beyond Davy Brown Campground to Manzana Creek. Plants are scattered to the end of the road.

SANTA YNEZ RIVER (*Early Spring through early Summer*)—From Highway 101 at west end of Santa Barbara turn north on Hwy. 154 (San Marcos Pass Road) for about 12 miles, then go east on Paradise Rd. to Los Prietos Ranger Station. Stocked upstream from ranger station to Red Rock Camp. (Paradise Road is often closed due to high water.) Call ahead to Los Prietos Ranger Station, (805) 967-3481.

Ventura County

CASITAS LAKE (*Early Spring through early Summer*)—Twelve miles north of Ventura via Highways 33 and 150.

MATILIJA CREEK (*Spring*)—From Highway 33 about four miles north of Mainers Oaks, turn west on Matilija Lake Road. Stream stocked from gate downstream for one-quarter mile.

PIRU LAKE (*Early Spring through Fall*)—North on I-5 to Highway 25, west on Main Street, Piru, to lake. Free fishing access if you park at dam or along road and walk down to the lake. Nominal fee if you drive in and use facilities.

REYES CREEK (*Spring, early Summer*)—North from Ojai on Highway 33 for 38 miles to Ozena Guard Station, then east on Lockwood Valley road 3 1/2 miles, then south to Reyes Creek Public Camp. Fish upstream from campground.

ROSE VALLEY LAKES (*Spring, early Summer*)—Take Highway 33 north from Ojai for about 6 miles past Wheeler Gorge Camp, then east to Rose Valley Helitac Base and lakes.

SANTA PAVLA CREEK (*Spring*)—Take Hwy. 126 to Hwy. 150 about 3 miles north of Santa Paula; fish from Steckel Park upstream to Ferndale Ranch.

SESPE CREEK, UPPER SECTION (*Spring*)—Take Highway 33 north from Ojai to about 6 miles past Wheeler Gorge Camp, turn east on Forest Road for 6 miles to Lion Campground. Also stocked along Highway 33 from Beaver Campground to Sespe Gorge Campground.

VENTURA RIVER NORTH FORK (*Spring*)—From I-101 take Hwy. 33 north from Ventum approximately 20 miles to Matilija Canyon Road. Fish are planted to Wheeler Gorge campgrounds.